Women, Branch Stories, and Religious Rhetoric in a Tamil Buddhist Text

FOREIGN AND COMPARATIVE STUDIES/SOUTH ASIAN SERIES 12

WOMEN, BRANCH STORIES, AND RELIGIOUS RHETORIC IN A TAMIL BUDDHIST TEXT

PAULA RICHMAN

MAXWELL SCHOOL OF CITIZENSHIP AND PUBLIC AFFAIRS,
SYRACUSE UNIVERSITY

Printed in the United States of America.

This publication has been supported by the National Endowment for the Humanities, a federal agency that supports the study of such fields as history, philosophy, literature, and languages.

This book has been printed on acid-free paper.
Bindings were selected for stability and longevity.

∞

The following publishers have generously given their permission to reprint their copyrighted materials in this volume: Eugene Watson Burlingame, *Buddhist Legends Translated from the Original Pali Text of the Dhammapada Commentary*, Part 2, Harvard Oriental Series, vol. 29 (Cambridge: Harvard University Press, 1921), pp. 257-60. Reprinted by permission; George L. Hart, III, trans., *Poets of the Tamil Anthologies*, p. 208. Copyright 1979 by Princeton University Press. By permission; Karen Lang, "Lord Death's Snare: Gender-Related Imagery in the Theragāthā and the Therīgāthā," *Journal of Feminist Studies in Religion* 1 (Fall 1986): 74-75. By permission; A. K. Ramanujan, *The Interior Landscape: Love Poems from a Classical Tamil Anthology* (Bloomington: Indiana University Press, 1967), p. 111. By permission; A. K. Ramanujan, *Poems of Love and War*, pp. 60 and 191. Copyright 1984 by Columbia University Press. By permission; Mrs. (Caroline) Rhys Davids, trans., *Psalms of the Early Buddhists*, vol. 1 of *Psalms of the Sisters* (1909; Luzac and Co. for the Pali Text Society, 1964), pp. 106-10. By permission; and Andrée Sjoberg, ed., *Symposium on Dravidian Civilization*, Asian Series of the Center for Asian Studies, University of Texas at Austin, no. 1 (Austin: Jenkins Publishing, 1971), pp. 80-81, figs. 3 and 4. By permission.

Richman, Paula.
Women, branch stories, and religious rhetoric in a Tamil Buddhist text/
Paula Richman.
p. cm. -- (Foreign and comparative studies. South Asian series ; no. 12)
Bibliography: p.
Includes index.
ISBN 0-915984-90-3
1. Cāttaṉār. Maṇimēkalai. I. Title II. Series.
PL4758.9.C3M337 1987
894'.81111--dc19 87-31551
CIP

For Mike

CONTENTS

ACKNOWLEDGMENTS xi
INTRODUCTION 1
The Text 1
Methodological Assumptions 4

1 A TEXT WITHOUT A COMMUNITY 7
The Literary and Linguistic Community 7
Religious Communities outside of Tamilnadu 12
The Academic Community 14
Conclusions 16

2 FEMALE RENUNCIATION IN THE MAIN STORY 19
The Structure of *Maṇimēkalai*'s Main Story 19
Monastic Procedures and Rules for Buddhist Nuns 23
Portrayal of the Heroine's Renunciation 26
Combating Criticism of Female Renunciation 31
Conclusions 33

3 THE PORTRAYAL OF PERSUASION 37
The Main Story and Branch Stories 37
Translation: "Cātuvan̲ and the Nākas" 39
Negotiations between the Preacher and the Cannibals 42
The Dramatized Audience as a Rhetorical Strategy 46
Conclusions 50

4 TAMIL LITERARY CONVENTIONS AND LIFE'S IMPERMANENCE 53
Translation: "The Story of the Cosmic Place" 54
Classical Tamil Poetry and the Transience of Life 58
The Desert Landscape in Classical Tamil Tradition 62
The Desert and Cāttan̲ār's Cremation Ground 65
Moving Beyond the Classical Tamil View of Love 69
Meditation on Life's Impermanence 71
Conclusions 77

5 COSMOLOGY AS RHETORIC 79
Cāttaṉār and "The Mustard Seed Story" 79
Standard Cosmological Features from Buddhist Tradition 82
Cāttaṉār's Way of Presenting Buddhist Cosmology 92
Cosmos as Cremation Ground 96
Conclusions 100

6 RELATIONSHIPS BETWEEN LAYPEOPLE AND RENOUNCERS 101
Translation: "Maṇimēkalai Is Put under Protection" 102
The Duties of a Layperson 107
Royal Responsibility to Protect Female Renouncers 112
Likening Female Renouncers to Chaste Wives 117
Conclusions 119

7 THE COMPARISON STORY 123
Criticism of Competing Religious Viewpoints 123
Translation: "The Story of Āputtiraṉ's Begging Bowl" 126
Enlisting the Reader's Admiration for Āputtiraṉ 130
Disparaging Brahmanical Religiosity 133
Discrediting Vedic Deities 135
Indra as Āputtiraṉ's Opponent 140
Conclusions 141

CONCLUSIONS 143
A Community Envisioned 144
Rhetoric in *Maṇimēkalai* and Other Buddhist Texts 147

APPENDICES
A: Authorship, Genre, Dating, and Sectarian Affiliation 157
B: Translations of Three Pali Versions of "The Mustard Seed Story" 167
C: The Design of Figure 2: Cartographic and Buddhological Considerations Informing Figure 2 175

NOTES 177
BIBLIOGRAPHY 243
INDEX 265
NOTE ON THE AUTHOR 273

List of Tables and Figures

Tables

1 *Maṇimēkalai*'s Main Story and Its Branch Stories 3

2 The Five Landscapes, Their Corresponding Phases of Love, and Selected Native Elements 29

3 An Analysis of the Negotiations between Cātuvaṉ and the Nākas 45

4 Elements of the *Pālai* Landscape Found in "The Story of the Cosmic Place" 66

5 Cāttaṉār's Description of the Cremation Ground 74-75

6 Cosmic Inhabitants Listed by Cāttaṉār 83

7 The Beings Who Dwell in the Cosmos and the Realms in Which They Dwell 86

Figures

1 *Pālai*'s Relationship to the Other Four Landscapes 72

2 The Components of the Cosmos 85

ACKNOWLEDGMENTS

I welcome the opportunity to acknowledge the many contributions other people have made to this project. Wendy Doniger O'Flaherty encouraged me at every stage of my research and writing, sharing her insights about Hindu mythology and giving me careful and instructive readings of chapter drafts. Drawing upon his extensive knowledge of Buddhism, Frank Reynolds helped me relate material in *Maṇimēkalai* to that in other Buddhist texts, especially with respect to cosmology. A. K. Ramanujan first introduced me to Tamil poetry, taught me new approaches to Indian texts, and proposed ways to make my translations more felicitous. K. Paramasivam led me through the syntactic and interpretational intricacies of *Caṅkam*, *kāppiyam*, and grammatical texts. Norman Cutler, Charles Hallisey, and Karen Lang gave me invaluable critiques — both stylistic and substantive. V. S. Rajam and David Buck thoughtfully commented on my translations. David Shulman and Indira Peterson provided penetrating readings of an earlier draft, and their responses encouraged me to pursue new avenues of interpretation. The suggestions of Peter Budeiri, Jan Cooper, Edward Dimock, Susan Huntington, W. Michael Kelsey, Sally Noble, Jean Sanborn, John Strong, Donald Swearer, and Susan Wadley were greatly appreciated. All of these people bear no responsibility for any unremedied weaknesses, but deserve considerable credit for many improvements.

I want to thank members of the staff at the following resource centers for helping me to locate relevant research materials: the Dr. U. V. Swaminathaiyer Library in Thiruvanmiyur, the Maraimalai Adigal Library in Madras, the Tamil University Library and Sarasvati Mahal Library in Tanjore, the Tamil Sangam Library and American College Library in Madurai, the India Office Library and British Museum Library in London, the South Asia Reference Department at the Regenstein Library of the University of Chicago, and the Suzzalo Library at the University of Washington. Special thanks also go to the members of the interlibrary loan staff at Western Washington University, Colby College, and Oberlin College for locating and procuring for me what must have sometimes seemed to be incredibly obscure volumes.

The financial support of several funding agencies and groups made my research possible. My initial field trip to South India was funded with a Haskell (Oberlin Alumni) Fellowship for Research Abroad. My subsequent fieldwork was financed by a Fulbright-Hays Doctoral Dissertation Abroad Fellowship. Funds for write-up were provided by the Bellingham, Washington, branch of the American Association of University Women. At the later stages of writing and revising, support was provided by a National Endowment for the Humanities Summer Stipend and a Colby College Mellon grant. In addition, I am grateful to Douglas Archibald (Colby College), Alfred MacKay and David Love (Oberlin College), and William Stoever (Western Washington University) both for their encouragement of my work and for providing institutional support at crucial times.

I am grateful to Karen Bourassa and Thelma Kime for cheerfully typing innumerable drafts of this manuscript. Jessica Bucciarelli, Susan Edwards, Amanda Udis-Kessler, and Mary Alice Weller proofread various versions with meticulous care. I thank Mary Beth Ritter and Joanna Giansanti for the enthusiasm and efficiency with which they have handled this manuscript in the stages on its way to publication. I appreciate Peter Knecht's kindness in allowing me to reprint, in slightly altered form, my article titled "Framed Narrative in a Tamil Buddhist Epic," *Asian Folklore Studies* 44 (April 1985): 81-103, as chapter three of this monograph. Also, I have analyzed some of the material in chapter two of this book from a different perspective in "The Portrayal of a Female Renouncer in a Tamil Buddhist Text," in *Gender and Religion: On the Complexity of Symbols*, ed. Caroline Bynum et al., pp. 145-55 (Boston: Beacon Press, 1986).

I would especially like to thank Michael H. Fisher, my toughest critic and greatest support. He read every single chapter in every single draft, never failing to make acute observations and insightful suggestions. Three other people have also given me special encouragement in my work over the years: Caroline Bynum, Frank Conlon, and Stevan Harrell. Finally, I would like to express my gratitude to my colleagues and students at two very special, small, liberal arts colleges — Oberlin and Colby — for their friendship, support, and interest in *Maṇimēkalai*.

INTRODUCTION

This book is about connections. It explores how the story of a courtesan's daughter intertwines with five other tales. The book demonstrates the links between a text and a series of communities. It analyzes how an author, Cīttalai Cāttaṉār, conveys to his audience the validity of a particular worldview. It surveys the ways in which Cāttaṉār acts as a mediator between that audience and other bodies of religious literature. Finally, it explains to the modern reader the rhetoric of religious discourse in a Tamil Buddhist text from the sixth century.

The Text

Maṇimēkalai is unique in both Buddhist and Tamil literary communities. Although it was one among several Tamil Buddhist texts written during the period when Buddhism flourished in South India, at present it is the only extant Buddhist text written in Tamil. Despite the fact that about 50 million people speak Tamil and nearly 250 million other people identify themselves as Buddhists, *Maṇimēkalai* is largely unknown today. Chapter one of this monograph explains how it came to be a text without a community.

Maṇimēkalai tells the story of a courtesan's daughter who embraces the life of a Buddhist nun. Beginning with the news of the tragic death of the heroine's father, Cāttaṉār gives an account of her spiritual progress in her search for true knowledge. Simultaneously, he portrays Maṇimēkalai's service to society through her ability to feed countless downtrodden and starving people with the inexhaustible supply of food springing from her miraculous begging bowl.

Unfortunately, Maṇimēkalai encounters and must overcome formidable obstacles during her quest. Most daunting is Prince Utayakumaraṉ, who refuses to accept the validity of her chosen religious path. He treats her as if she were still a dancing girl and follows her relentlessly, seeking her sexual favors. In cahoots with him we find the matriarch of the courtesan community, who wants to unite this granddaughter of hers with the prince as a way of forcing her to rejoin the community into which she was born.

To combat these two, Maṇimēkalai receives aid from a powerful goddess, after whom she was named. This deity bestows upon her both knowledge of her past births and miraculous powers. The former reveal to her past events that have shaped her present situation. The latter allow her to escape from the traps her enemies set for her. More crucial to her spiritual maturity, she also gains Aṟavaṇa Aṭikaḷ as her mentor. This Buddhist sage teaches her how to evaluate the validity of philosophical arguments and then instructs her in the key tenets of Buddhism.

The action of *Maṇimēkalai* intensifies twice in the course of the story. The climax of Prince Utayakumaraṉ's pursuit of Maṇimēkalai occurs one dark night when he follows her to a temple in order to rape her. There he is killed by a demigod hiding nearby. This event occurs approximately three quarters of the way through the text. The culmination of Maṇimēkalai's spiritual journey, however, occurs in the very last few chapters of the text, where our heroine acquires the knowledge that will enable her to cut off the bonds of rebirth.

Essentially, the story of Maṇimēkalai concerns, explains, and justifies female renunciation. This topic is not found in other Tamil texts of this period, but the courtesan-turned-nun motif appears in several Indian Buddhist texts.[1] Cāttaṉār deals with the motif in his own particular way, using the classical Tamil literary conventions to portray the life of his female renouncer. Chapter two of this monograph explains precisely how Cāttaṉār portrays the conflict between sexual desire and renunciation as well as what didactic use such a portrayal serves.

The tale of Maṇimēkalai, however, is only one of many stories contained in Cāttaṉār's text. Sprouting from this central story are sixteen "branch stories" — some very short and others quite lengthy. Although some scholars have used terms like "minor," "digressive," and "framed" to describe such stories, the term "branch story" (a translation of a Tamil term for such tales, *kiḷaikkatai*) seems most appropriate as a label for the many shorter stories supported by, but vital to, the development of the whole narrative. The design of Table 1 is based on this tree metaphor, with the main story as its trunk and the stories sprouting from its left and right as its branches.

Among the sixteen branch stories found in *Maṇimēkalai*, there are five that are much longer, more complex in structure, and more sophisticated in their use of religious rhetoric than any of the others.[2] Chapters three through seven of this monograph, therefore, focus upon these five branch stories. These chapters contain full and annotated translations of the stories under discussion.

Table 1: *Maṇimēkalai*'s Main Story and Its Branch Stories

Maṇimēkalai and Utayakumaraṉ	Incidents in the Main Story by Chapter	Maṇimēkalai and the Buddhist Path
	30. Culmination of Maṇimēkalai's efforts	
	29. Learning Buddhist logic	
	28. Visiting Kōvalaṉ's father	P. Building the *caitya*
	27. Hearing various religious specialists	
	26. Conversing with Kaṇṇaki	O. Kaṇṇaki and Kōvalaṉ are cursed — PL
	25. Āputtiraṉ on Maṇipallavam Island	
N. The curse on Pukār	24. Aṟavaṇa Aṭikaḷ's preaching	
	23. Maṇimēkalai and the queen	
*M. Vicākai and the prince		
*L. Maruti and the prince	22. The king learns of his son's death	
K. Utayakumaraṉ kills his cook — PL	21. Maṇimēkalai learns of her future	
	20. Utayakumaraṉ is murdered	
	19. Maṇimēkalai visits the king	
	18. Cittirāpati encourages Utayakumaraṉ	
J. Kāyacaṇṭikai gets "elephant hunger"	17. Ending Kāyacaṇṭikai's hunger	
	16. Accepting alms from Ātirai	*I. Cātuvaṉ and the Nākas
	15. Maṇimēkalai seeks alms	
	14. } 13. } The history of the begging bowl	*H. The origin of the bowl
	12. Visiting Aṟavaṇa Aṭikaḷ	G. Vīrai and Tārai die — PL
	11. Receiving the bowl	F. Circumambulating the hill — PL
	10. Receiving mantras	E. Feeding Catucakkaraṉ — PL
	9. Learning past births	
	8. Maṇimēkalai and the Dharma Seat	D. Buddha and the seat
	7. Travels of the goddess	
*C. The Story of the Cosmic Place	6. Girls sent to the Cosmic Place	
B. How Cutamati became a Buddhist	5. Arrival of the goddess	
	4. Utayakumaraṉ comes to the garden	
A. Cutamati's abduction	3. Maṇimēkalai goes to the garden	
	2. Mātavi's renunciation	
	1. Celebration of the Indra Festival	

KEY:
PL = story of one of the character's previous lives.
* = indicates this branch story is analyzed in one of the chapters that follows.

Each of these stories serves a particular function in setting out key Buddhist concepts and ideal behavior. The tale discussed in chapter three, about a shipwrecked merchant preaching to cannibalistic islanders, explores how people can modify their behavior in order to practice *ahiṃsā* [noninjury to sentient beings]. The story analyzed in chapters four and five, which depicts the death of a young boy in a cremation ground, becomes the vehicle for a graphic and terrifying discourse on life's impermanence (*anicca*), the unalterability of the consequences of action (karma), and the nature of Buddhist cosmology. Chapter six explores the relationship between two stories told together, by an ascetic to a king, concerning the links between female renouncers and devoted laywomen. In chapter seven, I show how a story about an iconoclastic protector of needy people presents a devastating attack on brahmanical tradition while promoting the virtues of generosity (*dāna*). The thread that ties these diverse tales together is their concern to present people acting in accordance with specific Buddhist ideals in particular situations.

Methodological Assumptions

Throughout this book, I demonstrate that Cāttaṉār employs a number of rhetorical strategies in order to persuade his audience that the Buddhist worldview is valid and satisfying. "Rhetorical strategies" are defined here as those techniques, devices, and designs used in the service of convincing one's audience of the reasonableness and attractiveness of certain beliefs, actions, and concepts of religious community. Rhetorical analysis is not just another way of analyzing *Maṇimēkalai*. It is one of the most appropriate ways; an analysis of Cāttaṉār's rhetorical strategies helps to reveal the nature, characteristics, and underlying structure of *Maṇimēkalai.*

In a text such as *Maṇimēkalai*, where we know practically nothing about its author or the circumstances of its composition (see Appendix A), any discussion of the text's development and the possibility that it contains interpolations will remain, at best, largely speculative. It is quite possible that sections, or even entire chapters, were added to an existing text at a later time, by authors other than Cāttaṉār. For example, chapter twenty-nine of *Maṇimēkalai*, which provides an extremely lengthy, elaborate, and highly technical exposition of valid and invalid forms of argumentation (concentrating particularly on defining and illustrating kinds of syllogisms and fallacies), could easily have been added later.[3] If one accepts certain kinds of methodological assumptions, one could even suggest that the text is composed of an *ur*-text, the story of Maṇimēkalai, around which a great many extraneous stories and didactic passages have "accreted."[4] The actual historical reconstruction of *Maṇimēkalai*, however, lies beyond the scope of this book.

Instead, eschewing this type of speculation, I turn to the form of the text at hand; it is the logic of this present form of *Maṇimēkalai* with which I am concerned. The "Cāttaṉār" to whom I attribute the rhetorical designs in the present text may himself be a construct rather than the actual person who composed each verse, but it is that authorial presence behind the entire text whom I seek.[5] Because I consider all parts of *Maṇimēkalai* to be integral to the didactic success of the text, I take the branch stories seriously, devote a large part of my analysis to them, and show ways in which they resonate with, and add depth to, the exploration of themes found in the main story.

Working with *Maṇimēkalai* as a literary whole, I take it to be a religious whole as well. That is, I assume that from beginning to end *Maṇimēkalai* is informed by a coherent Buddhist vision. As shown in the section titled "Sectarian Affiliation" in Appendix A, the Buddhism in *Maṇimēkalai* is not easily identifiable as belonging to a known form of Buddhist sectarianism. In interpreting the text, I have found the need to bring in concepts from different parts of the Buddhist spectrum. That approach, however, seems appropriate for the exegesis of Cāttaṉār's art since, as we will see, he is a master of bricolage, drawing upon a wide range of sources. The religious unity of the text is rooted in its popular and didactic nature. As with similar Buddhist texts, the emphasis is on attracting new converts and reaffirming the commitment of established followers through story-telling, rather than settling sectarian controversies about philosophical points. By building upon cosmology, legends, and ideals from different parts of the Buddhist spectrum, Cāttaṉār has the scope to persuade people in the most appropriate and convincing ways possible.

A survey of Pali and Sanskrit literary texts demonstrates that Indian Buddhist literature contains a vast array of local and folk materials effectively put to use in the promotion of Buddhist ideals. From the earliest periods onwards, Buddhist authors developed a tradition of using "popular" literary materials and genres for religious instruction.[6] Although the didactic tone and rhetorical strategies in Cāttaṉār's epic might be relatively unfamiliar in Tamil literature, they can be found not only in Buddhist works that are primarily devoted to the exposition of religious ideals but also in some of those that are cast in the mold of Sanskrit *kāvya* [ornate literary creations].[7] Thus, it will come as no surprise to students of Buddhist literature that *Maṇimēkalai* is filled with didactic tales.

Part of Cāttaṉār's achievement, however, lies in his ability to bring together both Buddhist and non-Buddhist materials. In texts such as *Maṇimēkalai*, the author acts as a mediator between the religious tradition and the audience. He interprets a huge set of religious thought and practice so that it becomes intelligible and convincing to a new audience. Cāttaṉār's stories effectively convey Buddhist ideas to his audience because they synthesize disparate materials from both Tamil and non-Tamil texts. Such sources include classical Tamil poetic tradition, Buddhist cosmological texts, and Hindu purāṇic mythology.

Through my analysis of *Maṇimēkalai*, I hope to make it accessible to a wider audience than it now possesses. Much of *Maṇimēkalai*'s language and rhetoric is rooted in Tamil literary tradition. Therefore, I explain the conventions of that tradition so that scholars of Buddhism can see the masterful way in which Cāttaṉār uses those conventions to express Buddhist ideas. Conversely, I explain key sections of Buddhist materials for Tamil scholars unfamiliar with the Buddhist tradition. My goal is to provide neither an overview of Buddhist philosophy nor a history of Tamil literary tradition. Rather, in providing such analysis, I seek to illuminate the intricacy and inner logic of Cāttaṉār's religious rhetoric in *Maṇimēkalai* for the modern reader.

In making *Maṇimēkalai* accessible to that reader, the role of the translations in this monograph is crucial. In earlier translations of the text, word-for-word literal accuracy has sometimes obscured the overall purpose of Cāttaṉār's language. In translating the branch stories here, my greatest concern has been to reproduce Cāttaṉār's rhetorical effects in English. The numbers in the right-hand margin next to the translations indicate the verse in the Tamil text. In my translations of the long stories, the headings and material in brackets, which do not occur in the original, have been added so that the reader can see the divisions in the story that are indicated syntactically, semantically, or grammatically in the Tamil by Cāttaṉār. As Cāttaṉār sought to translate Buddhist ideas in a way comprehensible to his sixth-century Tamil audience, so too I seek to translate parts of Cāttaṉār's text in a lucid way for my twentieth-century audience.

1

A Text without a Community

"How can one grasp the intricacy of the text about Maṇimēkalai?" queries the seventeenth-century Śaiva poet Civappirakācar,[1] and the question remains appropriate even today. *Maṇimēkalai*, a sixth-century Tamil Buddhist text, lacks a community able to grasp its true intricacy. Drawing upon the poetic resources available in Tamil literary tradition, the text's author, Cāttaṉār, wrote his work as part of the process of fostering a Buddhist community in Tamilnadu, South India. By the eleventh century, Buddhism began to disappear from the area, but *Maṇimēkalai* was preserved over the centuries although other Buddhist texts were not. Since U. Vē. Cāminātaiyar rediscovered it in the late 1800s, Tamilians have pointed to *Maṇimēkalai* with pride, as part of the ancient greatness of Tamil culture. But today no community — linguistic, religious, or academic — claims the text as particularly its own, nor has any scholar displayed its intricacy so that all may appreciate it fully.

The Literary and Linguistic Community

Within Tamil literary history, *Maṇimēkalai* falls into three groups of texts. It is one half of the "twin" *kāppiyam* (Sanskrit *kāvya*, ornate literary creations), the only extant text among the Tamil Buddhist works, and one of "the five great *kāppiyam*." Its modern fate, however, has depended not on its membership in one of these literary categories but upon its rediscovery in the last century.

Traditionally, *Cilappatikāram* and *Maṇimēkalai* are known as the "twin" *kāppiyam*. Since young Maṇimēkalai plays a small role at the end of *Cilappatikāram* and then becomes the heroine of *Maṇimēkalai*, the second text may be understood as a sequel to the first. Traditional commentators also call the two texts "twin" *kāppiyam* because they claim that *Cilappatikāram* focuses upon duty, wealth, and love, while *Maṇimēkalai* focuses primarily upon religious liberation. Together, then, they are said to cover the four aims of man (*puruṣārtha*) as conventionally enumerated in classical India. (See Appendix A.)

Although the author of *Cilappatikāram* focuses most of his attention upon Kōvalan̲ and Kōvalan̲'s wife, the events in their lives determine the fate of Maṇimēkalai and her mother. The tension in *Cilappatikāram* begins when Kōvalan̲ leaves his faithful wife, Kaṇṇaki, so that he can enjoy the charms of the dancing girl Mātavi, Maṇimēkalai's mother. Later, after exhausting the family fortune, he abandons Mātavi and she gives birth to Maṇimēkalai. When he returns home impoverished, Kōvalan̲'s loyal wife suggests that they sell her jeweled anklet in order to begin their married life anew. Therefore they set out for Maturai, where, unbeknownst to them, an unscrupulous goldsmith has stolen the queen's anklet. When Kōvalan̲ comes to town bearing the anklet that he wants to sell, the goldsmith seizes the opportunity to accuse Kōvalan̲ of the crime. That accusation leads the king to condemn Kōvalan̲ to death. After his execution, his wife, Kaṇṇaki, chastises the king for his unjust deed and, in her anger, burns down Maturai. In contrast, Mātavi (Kōvalan̲'s former mistress) reacts with resignation rather than vengeful anger: seeing Kōvalan̲'s death as evidence of life's transience, she decides to become a Buddhist. Her daughter by Kōvalan̲, the young Maṇimēkalai, then receives the tonsure preliminary to entry into the Buddhist order, at Mātavi's command. There *Cilappatikāram* ends. *Maṇimēkalai*, backtracking a bit, begins with Mātavi's decision to renounce her hereditary occupation in order to embrace Buddhism.

Thus, the two stories are linked, and tradition links their authors as well. Each text's preface (*patikam*) mentions the author of the other work. According to lines 95 through 99 of *Maṇimēkalai*'s preface, Cāttan̲ār first recited his composition for Prince Iḷaṅkō, the author of *Cilappatikāram*. According to the preface of *Cilappatikāram*, Cāttan̲ār also told Iḷaṅkō the story that became the basis of *Cilappatikāram*. But Cāttan̲ār urged him to write that story in literary form. Cāttan̲ār reasoned that the prince should write it because it concerned three kings, and Cāttan̲ār was a mere grain merchant: "As this story relates to all the three crowned monarchs, it is only proper . . . that you should write of it."[2] In response to the merchant's request, Iḷaṅkō is said to have composed *Cilappatikāram* and read it to him. Hence, at least according to tradition, the two authors were very much involved in each other's compositions.[3] (See Appendix A.)

Scholars feel that *Cilappatikāram* was recited, and it may be that the same is true of *Maṇimēkalai*. It is possible that all but the concluding chapters of *Maṇimēkalai* were originally recited. The ancient literary corpus of the centuries preceding *Maṇimēkalai* grew out of a long tradition of bardic recitation, as Kailasapathy has demonstrated.[4] *Cilappatikāram* is recited even today.[5] *Maṇimēkalai* uses a common type of meter and a pattern of rhyme called *etukai*, which would function well as an aid to the memory. In addition, the majority of the text contains subject matter appropriate for recitation; parts of the first three quarters of *Maṇimēkalai* portray men and women in situations that both hold one's interest as well as keep one's mind on Buddhism. One wonders, however, about the final section of the text, which is fairly technical in parts. In chapter twenty-nine, for example, there is a detailed exposition of syllogisms and fallacies according to the school of Buddhist logic. Similarly, most of chapter thirty comprises a densely packed "Buddhist manual," setting out key Buddhist formulations such as the four noble truths and the twelve preconditions of dependent co-arising (*nidānas*). Recent scholarship on South Asian oral epics suggests that texts need not always be recited in their entirety. Perhaps the later chapters of *Maṇimēkalai* were not included on the occasions when the rest of the text was recited.[6]

Despite the many characteristics that *Cilappatikāram* and *Maṇimēkalai* share, they did not have equal cultural influence. For the most part, *Cilappatikāram* eschews extensive religious preaching; it also lacks staunch sectarian commitment and does not denigrate the Jain, Buddhist, or Hindu characters it portrays. In contrast, *Maṇimēkalai* is definitely a Buddhist work. (See Appendix A.) Its Buddhist assumptions provide the text with its overall coherence and structure. By its conclusion, no doubt exists that its author considers Buddhism superior to any other religious system. For this reason, while appreciation for *Cilappatikāram* was not necessarily tied to the fate of any one particular religious group in South India, *Maṇimēkalai* was linked to the presence of a Buddhist community and a group of people who were potentially interested in joining that community.

What kind of people comprised *Maṇimēkalai*'s audience? We know very little about Buddhism in Tamilnadu (see Appendix A), but *Maṇimēkalai* itself provides some clues about Cāttaṉār's intended audience. The text includes a number of different types of discourse; thus, it seems likely that different parts of the text would have special appeal for different kinds of people. For example, chapter six tells a story that cannot be understood fully without some familiarity with Tamil conventions for love poetry. Thus, this particular story would appear to have been directed to an audience of literary connoisseurs, people schooled in classical Tamil poetic traditions. In a somewhat different vein, in chapter twenty-seven the heroine goes to speak with representatives of the major religious perspectives (*darśanas*) in order to determine the ways in which Buddhism is a superior system of thought. This particular chapter would make the most sense to those with some background in the philosophical schools of thought discussed in the chapter. On the other hand, most of *Maṇimēkalai*'s narrative would be understandable without extensive training either in Tamil literary tradition or in Indian philosophy. One assumption that seems reasonable is that some of the members of the audience for *Maṇimēkalai* would have been relatively ignorant of Buddhism. Cāttaṉār spends so much time explaining extremely basic concepts of Buddhism — increasing the complexity of his discussion only toward the end of the text — that it seems reasonable to make such an assumption.

Although *Maṇimēkalai* is the only extant Tamil Buddhist narrative, at least two other Buddhist narratives written in Tamil did once exist. Camaya Tivākara Vāmaṉa Muṉivar's commentary on *Nīlakēci* cites a few lines from *Pimpicārakatai*, a Tamil work concerning Bimbasāra, a king of Rājagṛha during the Buddha's time.[7] The story of another Tamil Buddhist text, *Kuṇṭalakēci*, has also been preserved in the commentary on verse 176 of *Nīlakēci*. It tells the story of a woman who becomes a Buddhist nun after killing her husband in self-defense.[8] Although these other Buddhist Tamil texts were lost, *Maṇimēkalai* continued to be preserved over the centuries, perhaps because it was linked to the non-Buddhist *Cilappatikāram*.

Maṇimēkalai also forms part of the traditionally grouped *aimperuṅkāppiyam*, "five great *kāppiyam*." Mayilainātar first mentions the five texts by this title in his fourteenth-century commentary on *Naṉṉūl*.[9] *Maṇimēkalai* literally means "jeweled" (*maṇi*) "belt" or "girdle" (*mēkalai*, from Sanskrit *mekhalā*), so a pun on the text's title is part of a traditional metaphor still learned by today's Tamil schoolchildren. In it, Tamil literature is personified as a mother adorned with five types of jeweled ornaments: the Tamil mother (*tāy*) wears *Cilappatikāram* as her anklet (*cilampu*), *Maṇimēkalai* as her belt (*mēkalai*), *Vaḷaiyāpati* as her bracelet (*vaḷaiyam*), *Kuṇṭalakēci* as her earring (*kuṇṭalam*), and *Civakacintāmaṇi* as the jewel around her neck.[10]

Despite its status as a "great *kāppiyam*," *Maṇimēkalai* lost its audience over the centuries. When Buddhism died out in Tamilnadu after the eleventh century and Hinduism gained dominance, there was less and less incentive to study the text. Since it did not have an extensive commentary, which helps the reader to construe complex verses, it was also less accessible to readers than other Tamil Hindu texts.

A sentiment that became increasingly prevalent in the mid-eighteenth century probably exacerbated *Maṇimēkalai*'s neglect: Śaivite spokesmen like Cuvāmināta Tēcikar argued that non-Hindu *kāppiyam* and *Caṅkam* texts were inferior to orthodox Śaivite works. For example, in his gloss of a verse in his book titled *Ilakkaṇakottu*, Cuvāmināta Tēcikar reiterated the orthodox view that the works attributed to Māṇikkavācakar were written by Lord Śiva himself. The strictly vegetarian Cuvāmināta Tēcikar then went on to make an analogy that indicated the folly of studying nonorthodox texts:

> When these [Śaivite] texts exist, men who desire those other texts are like fish born and living in the milk-ocean who do not want milk, desiring many other things instead.[11]

In this image, the pure milk is superior food, but the deluded fish eat instead only impure things, such as mud and smaller fish. The attitude indicated by this quote discouraged the teaching on non-Hindu texts at Śaivite monasteries, which functioned as educational institutions.[12] Although such non-Hindu texts were seldom studied, some manuscripts of them were preserved in the private collections of families of learned men as well as in a few monasteries.

The story of Cāminātaiyar's rediscovery of *Maṇimēkalai* in the late nineteenth century is instructive because it indicates the degree to which the text was unknown even to those versed in Tamil literature.[13] U. Vē. Cāminātaiyar studied with the renowned Śaivite teacher Mīṉāṭci Cuntaram Piḷḷai, poet laureate of the monastery at Tiruvāvaṭuturai.[14] As his disciple, Cāminātaiyar memorized and learned the meaning and grammar of the many texts considered appropriate for a Tamil scholar of that time. One day in October of 1880, he paid a call to Rāmacūvami Mutaliyār, who had just been transferred to Kumpakoṇam to serve as munsif [judicial officer]. Mutaliyār asked him to enumerate the texts he had mastered. In reply, Cāminātaiyar proudly listed the medieval books that he had studied: twenty *antātis*, twenty *kalampakams*, fifteen *kōvais*, thirty *piḷḷai tamiḻs*, twenty *ulās*, as well as many *tūtus*, *purāṇas*, philosophical texts, grammatical texts, and the entire *Kampa Rāmāyaṇam*. The munsif was not impressed. "Is that all? . . . Have you read any of the books that provided the inspiration for the books mentioned by you? . . . Have you read *Mani Mekalai*? Have you read *Silappadikaram*?" he asked. Cāminātaiyar notes, "I had not read any of the books he enumerated. Nor had my Master himself read them. As a matter of fact, I had not even set eyes on any of these."[15] After this meeting with the munsif (who wanted a scholar to read these texts and explain them to him), Cāminātaiyar began collecting ancient texts, annotating them, and arranging to have them published.

Since Cāminātaiyar knew little about Buddhism, the task of mastering *Maṇimēkalai* was not an easy one. Collecting editions of the manuscript was itself an enormous task. Munsif Mutaliyār provided the first copy of *Maṇimēkalai*, and Cāminātaiyar traveled by bullock cart to other places in Tamilnadu — both to Śaivite monasteries and to the houses of Tamil savants — seeking manuscripts. He even acquired a handwritten copy of the palm-leaf text in the Bibliothèque Nationale, sent to him by the French Indologist J. Vinson. Getting the manuscripts was just the first step; he had to teach himself about the history and characteristics of Buddhism. To do so, he eagerly read references to Buddhism in Tamil works such as *Vīracōḻiyam* (an old grammar) and the commentary to *Nīlakēci* (a philosophical work). He also called upon a friend to translate into Tamil the English works by Buddhologists such as Rhys Davids and Oldenberg, and he corresponded with Sumangala, a Buddhist elder in Colombo, Sri Lanka.[16] He even had to arrange for funding in order to get his edition of *Maṇimēkalai* published.

Cāminātaiyar's enthusiastic labor resulted in an edition with a comprehensive introduction, a set of word glosses, and an extensive set of indices. He based his 1898 edition on ten palm-leaf manuscripts that he collected in Tamilnadu and Sri Lanka. For his 1921 edition, he consulted two additional manuscripts.[17] This 1921 edition has been reprinted again and again, also serving as the foundation for commentaries by later scholars.[18]

As a result of Cāminātaiyar's pioneering work, at least the name *Maṇimēkalai* is now a familiar one in Tamilnadu. Secondary school curricula often include a selection from its early chapters. Popular, inexpensive versions of the text have been published,[19] along with several paraphrases and English translations.[20] There are even a few children's books based upon it.[21] The story has been the basis for presentation in other media as well. A film of *Maṇimēkalai* appeared some years back, and several dramas based upon incidents from the epic have been written.[22] In addition, the iconoclastic and celebrated poet Bharatidasan composed his own (very brief) version of *Maṇimēkalai.*[23]

However, this superficial familiarity with *Maṇimēkalai* cannot belie the basic neglect of the text as a whole in modern times. Schoolchildren learn the chapters with little Buddhist content, and very few people outside the academic community ever read the text from start to finish. The film has not been reissued, several of the English translations are out of print, and the dramas entailed large modifications of the original. Bharatidasan's interest in the text stemmed partly from its anti-brahmanical viewpoint, which meshed with his political concerns.[24] *Maṇimēkalai* today remains, in many ways, a text without a true linguistic community in Tamilnadu.

Religious Communities outside of Tamilnadu

At the time when Cāttaṉār wrote his Buddhist epic, trade between Tamilnadu and other nearby kingdoms was flourishing. *Maṇimēkalai* reflects the importance of such trade; several of its characters are merchants or passengers on trading vessels.[25] Apparently as a result of such commercial voyages, parts of *Maṇimēkalai* were carried to Sumatra. Winstedt comments that "A guild of Tamil traders in the same century [the eighth century] left scraps of their Buddhist story of Manimekalai in Sumatran folk-tales that have been re-told in the Malay peninsula and written down in modern times."[26] Although bits of the story remain, the text has not been a central part of Sumatran religious identity.

The goddess Maṇimekhalā, who is a major character in *Maṇimēkalai*, appears in many stories throughout South and Southeast Asia in the areas of Tamil maritime trade. In *Cilappatikāram*, we are told that Mātavi's daughter was named after the goddess Maṇimēkalai (the Tamil transliteration of Maṇimekhalā[27]) because that goddess had saved one of Kōvalaṉ's ancestors from drowning in a shipwreck. In *Maṇimēkalai*, the goddess takes her namesake to an island in the middle of the ocean to learn of her past births (chapters 8-11). Sylvain Lévi's extensive research on Maṇimekhalā in Southeast Asian tales leads him to conclude that Maṇimekhalā was originally a Tamil goddess. He says, "I have suggested that this deity belongs to Southern India and that her place of worship may have been Kāñcī [a city north of Madras] or Kāveripaṭṭana [a city east of Tanjore on the coast]."[28] In Pali *Jātaka* tales, the goddess Maṇimekhalā periodically arrives to rescue drowning people. For example, the *Saṃkha-Jātaka* tells the story of a generous brahmin who sets off for "The Gold Country" [usually identified with Burma and Siam] in order to bring back wealth and distribute it to the destitute. On his way to the seaport, he bestows his sandals and sunshade upon a needy person. This act of compassion comes to fruition when the ship springs a leak and sinks on the high seas. By eating sugar mixed with butter, oiling his body, and clinging to the mast, the brahmin survives for seven days after the ship goes down. Then the goddess Maṇimekhalā arrives, feeds him, and provides him with a miraculous jeweled ship, which she guides safely home.[29] The *Mahājanaka-Jātaka* also records Maṇimekhalā's miraculous rescue of a shipwrecked man.[30]

In some other Southeast Asian texts, however, the goddess Maṇimekhalā is not even connected with Buddhism. For example, in a Cambodian version of the *Rāmāyaṇa*, the goddess Maṇimekhalā leaves her house to attend a celestial gathering, carrying a luminous gem. The deity Rāmaparusa (Sanskrit Paraśurāma) covets that jewel and pursues her in order to obtain it, but when Varjun (Arjuna) sees her distress, he challenges her pursuer to a fight. After Rāmaparusa vanquishes his foe, Maṇimekhalā returns to the sea, where she continues to act as guardian.[31] A Siamese *Rāmāyaṇa*, composed during the reign of King Rama I (1783-1809), presents a similar version of this story, with Arjuna as Rāma's vanquished foe.[32]

From this survey, it appears likely that the motif of Maṇimekhalā as sea goddess does not necessarily indicate a familiarity with the Tamil text *Maṇimēkalai*. In fact, since the Pali *Jatākas* preceded *Maṇimēkalai*, the character Maṇimekhalā clearly does not appear for the first time in Cāttaṉār's epic. Rather than creating Maṇimēkalā, Cāttaṉār integrated an already existing deity into his narrative and gave her additional responsibilities. Thus, these texts do not indicate that *Maṇimēkalai* was important in these countries, despite the presence of the sea goddess in their texts.

Sri Lanka seems like the logical place to look for evidence of *Maṇimēkalai*'s role in a religious community.[33] And, in fact, evidence of the influence of *Cilappatikāram* and *Maṇimēkalai* does exist in a corpus of rituals still performed in Sri Lanka for the goddess Pattiṉi, another name for Kaṇṇaki. In *Cilappatikāram*, (as discussed earlier) when Kaṇṇiki's husband (Kōvalaṉ) is murdered on a trumped-up charge, she burns down

Maturai in her anger. In chapter twenty-six of the text's sequel, *Maṇimēkalai*, Cāttaṉār portrays Kaṇṇaki and her husband as Buddhist deities, whose images are venerated in a temple in Vañci. Sri Lankan Pattiṉi rituals, therefore, draw on stories from both *Cilappatikāram* and, to a lesser extent, *Maṇimēkalai*. Obeyesekere emphasizes the continuity between these incidents from the Tamil texts and the Sinhalese ritual texts:

> Though these texts [the Pattiṉi ritual texts] vary in style and content from the *Cilappatikāram* and *Maṇimēkalai*, they have an important feature in common — they are all rooted in the heterodox religions, with the Sinhala texts continuing the Buddhist elements of the *Cilappatikāram* and the *Maṇimēkalai*.[34]

In keeping with the familiar pattern found throughout South and Southeast Asia, the goddess Maṇimekhalā saves shipwrecked people in Sinhala ritual texts as well.[35] More unusual, however, is Cāttaṉār's appearance as a character in the ritual texts: the author of *Maṇimēkalai* appears in a song that describes the cowherd wives cooling the anger of Pattiṉi. There Cāttaṉār entreats the goddess to be gracious.[36] Even though the author of Maṇimēkalai and the sea goddess figure in Sinhalese ritual drama, the text's heroine does not.

Evidence from these far-flung materials throughout South and Southeast Asia does not suggest that *Maṇimēkalai* has played a major role in Buddhist communities outside of Tamilnadu. The ubiquitous motif, rescue by the goddess of the sea, appears to be a free-floating mythic incident not connected with *Maṇimēkalai*. Nor does Sinhalese ritual material linked with *Maṇimēkalai* indicate that the people participating in the Sri Lankan Pattiṉi cult are intimately involved with *Maṇimēkalai* as a text. Today no Buddhist community claims *Maṇimēkalai* as a work crucial to its own religious identity.

The Academic Community

In scholarly circles, *Maṇimēkalai* is anomalous.[37] As a text, it falls between two fields of study. On the one hand, those versed in ancient Tamil literary and grammatical texts usually lack intimate knowledge of Buddhist philosophical terminology and, hence, find sections of *Maṇimēkalai* extremely obscure. On the other hand, Buddhologists rarely know Tamil and, hence, *Maṇimēkalai* remains inaccessible to them except through translations. Although *Maṇimēkalai* has been translated several times, each translation has been incomplete in some way.[38]

Tamil and English histories of Tamil literature usually deal with *Maṇimēkalai* in a rather summary fashion, often focusing upon its didacticism.[39] For example, Jesudasan cites it as the text's major flaw:

"*Maṇimēhalai* looks like a pure mouthpiece of Buddhist propaganda."[40] In the same vein, Jakannātaṉ feels that *Maṇimēkalai*'s Buddhist didacticism is a step toward the writing of texts that become excessively polemical over the years:

> We see in *Maṇimēkalai* the tendency to extol the Buddhists and describe other religious adherents disparagingly. Since that attitude became excessive in later times, the beauty of the poetry and the *rasa* [the audience's relish] of the epic were lost. Religious quarreling and the composition of poems in which one reviled the other increased.[41]

Value judgments about the literary worth of teaching literature are at stake in such evaluations of *Maṇimēkalai*'s merits.[42]

Reverend G. U. Pope's work is an exception to this school of scholarship because he treats *Maṇimēkalai*'s didacticism as one of its major strengths. Pope analyzes *Maṇimēkalai* as a unified Buddhist argument, designed to convince its readers that they should adopt the Buddhist religion. He feels that Cāttaṉār's goals are clearly polemical, commenting that "the real object of the poem is to represent Buddhism as superior to every form of Hinduism, and especially to the Jain system. Its great interest in fact consists chiefly in this."[43] Pope interprets *Maṇimēkalai* as an exemplary account of religious conversion, seeing each of the incidents in the text as part of ten stages of religious progress.[44] Pope takes Maṇimēkalai's polemicism seriously and praises Cāttaṉār for his ability to be persuasive.

If most scholars of Tamil literature have provided overviews of the entire text, most Buddhologists have tended to focus upon very limited Buddhist components of *Maṇimēkalai*. For example, Lévi focused specifically on *Maṇimēkalai*'s depiction of the goddess Maṇimekhalā because he wanted to compare it with her portrayal in other South and Southeast Asian texts.[45] Similarly, several scholars of Buddhism have analyzed chapter twenty-nine of *Maṇimēkalai* in and of itself, because they want to determine its relationship to Dignāga's writings on logic.[46] Although this kind of research serves a purpose, enabling scholars to compare parts of *Maṇimēkalai* with sections of other texts, it does not illuminate the nature and characteristics of Cāttaṉār's epic except in extremely specific ways.

Kandaswamy's work on Buddhism in *Maṇimēkalai* is an exception to the pattern just cited. His *Buddhism as Expounded in Maṇimēkalai* provides a comprehensive summary of Buddhism in Cāttaṉār's text. He systematically assembles material from *Maṇimēkalai* and compares it with other relevant Buddhist texts in chapters on Buddhist theology, cosmology, logic, and philosophy.[47] In this endeavor, Kandaswamy deals with the text holistically.

Pope and Kandaswamy do not constitute an academic community for *Maṇimēkalai.* Although one finds a large group of (Indian and Western) scholars working on Tamil bhakti texts, no such group exists for *Maṇimēkalai.* Pope, a Christian missionary whose work on *Maṇimēkalai* was published in 1911, died long ago. Kandaswamy, a scholar at Annamalai University, has written the only other comprehensive and analytical monograph on Cāttaṉār's text that is currently available.

Conclusions

In order to understand *Maṇimēkalai*, didacticism must be taken seriously. Morally instructive texts play crucial roles in the transmission of culture. Too often historians of religion submit the rhetoric of philosophically-oriented religious texts to careful scrutiny but neglect story literature as mere "popular" entertainment. Its themes and motives may be catalogued, but its religious rhetoric often remains unexplored. If we seek to determine the ways in which bodies of religious material are conveyed to various audiences, we must pay more attention to the rhetoric of texts that attempt to teach and persuade. Religious rhetoric, therefore, is the focus of the rest of this book.

In order to appreciate *Maṇimēkalai*'s complexity, the relationship between its component parts must be understood. Ramanujan's comments about perceptions of Indian texts apply well to *Maṇimēkalai.* He says,

> Scholars have often discussed Indian texts . . . as if they were loose-leaf files, ragbag encyclopedias; taking the Indian word for text, "grantha" (derived from the knot that holds the palm leaves together), literally, scholars often posit only an accidental and physical unity. We need to attend to the context sensitive designs that embed a seeming variety of modes. . . . This way of constructing the text is in consonance with other designs in the culture. Not unity (in the Aristotelian sense) but coherence, seems to be the end.[48]

Ramanujan here argues against the view of Indian texts as a random collection of parts, urging the reader to be sensitive to the manner in which component parts contribute to the whole. Therefore, in the remainder of this monograph, the relationships between the main story and selected branch stories will be explored to determine how they contribute to the text's persuasiveness and overall coherence.

The chapters that follow explain why Civappirakācar praised the intricacy of *Maṇimēkalai.* Naturally, the text generates interest because of its status as the only Tamil Buddhist narrative now in existence. But it deserves attention for other reasons as well. Insofar as we know Cāttaṉār through reading his composition, he is resourceful, humorous, subtle, engaging, and persuasive in his attempt to present Buddhism as an attractive way of viewing the world. If *Maṇimēkalai* lacks a true linguistic and religious community at this point in its history, at least we can appreciate Cāttaṉār's achievement.

2

FEMALE RENUNCIATION IN THE MAIN STORY

Maṇimēkalai's main story tells of a woman torn between love and renunciation. In the final chapters of the epic, renunciation triumphs. Although Cāttaṉār portrays a nun's spiritual maturation over time, the text yields little information about the corporate or institutional aspects of female monastic life in ancient Tamilnadu. To seek such information would be to ignore the didactic pattern in the narrative: *Maṇimēkalai*'s main story is structured to teach about and justify female renunciation.

The Structure of *Maṇimēkalai*'s Main Story

Maṇimēkalai's interest in the Buddhist religion pulls her in one direction, but her attraction toward Prince Utayakumaraṉ — both the object of her affection and the obstacle in her path to renunciation — pulls her in the opposite direction. Maṇimēkalai can devote herself fully to her quest for religious liberation only after she has understood and rejected her attachment to the prince. *Maṇimēkalai*, which can be divided into four narrative sections,[1] depicts Maṇimēkalai's move away from sexual passion and toward Buddhism.

The first section of *Maṇimēkalai* described Prince Utayakumaraṉ's increasing fascination with Maṇimēkalai and her attraction to him (chapters 1-6). As the text opens, the courtesan Mātavi (Maṇimēkalai's mother) announces that she will not dance at the annual city festival in Pukār this year. The unjust death of her lover Kōvalaṉ (Maṇimēkalai's father) has convinced her to forsake the life of a dancing girl in order to follow the Buddhist path, and she intends that her daughter do the same. When Maṇimēkalai hears of her father's death and her mother's unhappiness, she begins to weep. Since her tears ruin the flower garland she was stringing when she heard the news, she sets off with her companion Cutamati to pick some fresh blossoms in the Uvavaṉam Garden on the other side of town.

Cāttaṉār introduces Prince Utayakumaraṉ into the narrative by having him subdue a rampaging, sexually-maddened elephant that had run loose through the city and terrified its inhabitants. After he catches the rutting beast, a citizen mentions to him that the beautiful Maṇimēkalai has just gone by. He immediately sets off to find her, but when he reaches the garden where she has gone, he finds only Cutamati, Maṇimēkalai's companion. To her he praises the beauty of Maṇimēkalai. Ignoring his pointed interest in her friend, Cutamati tells the prince of her own conversion to Buddhism, concluding her tale with a lecture on the impermanence of the human body's physical beauty.

Suddenly, the prince catches sight of Maṇimēkalai, who has locked herself in a glass pavilion in the grove in order to escape from him. Seeing that his pursuit is thus hopeless, Utayakumaraṉ departs in frustration. As he leaves, he vows that Maṇimēkalai's grandmother, the matriarch of the courtesan community, will arrange for him to enjoy union with her granddaughter. As soon as he departs, Maṇimēkalai confesses to Cutamati that, despite all her resolve, her heart has followed after the prince. She then expresses the fervent hope that she will be able to overcome her feelings of love for him.[2]

In this first section, Cāttaṉār sets out the dimensions of Maṇimēkalai's conflict; although she decides to renounce her hereditary role as a courtesan, that choice leads to unexpected problems. Prince Utayakumaraṉ cannot accept that this lovely young girl would give up the life of a dancer to become an ascetic. To complicate matters even further, Maṇimēkalai herself feels ambivalent about her decision because she is attracted to the prince.

In the second section of the narrative, Cāttaṉār shifts his focus away from the love story to chart the path of Maṇimēkalai's spiritual progress (chapters 7-15). After the prince's departure, the goddess Maṇimēkalā (after whom the girl was named) comes to carry the girl off to Maṇipallavam Island. There a dharma seat, where the Buddha once sat, discloses many events that transpired in her past lives.[3] The goddess then reveals that Maṇimēkalai feels drawn to Prince Utayakumaraṉ because he was her husband in a former birth. Nonetheless, she discourages the young girl from any further relations with him. After telling her what she must do in order to fully practice virtue, the deity prepares her for the tasks ahead by teaching her special mantras [sacred syllables] that will enable her to change her bodily form, fly, and rid herself of hunger.

Maṇimēkalai's visit to the island culminates with her acquisition of an extraordinary begging bowl. After the goddess departs, the guardian of the dharma seat leads Maṇimēkalai to a pond where an inexhaustible begging bowl appears each year on the anniversary of the Buddha's birth. The bowl awaits a person who desires to perform compassionate deeds. Since Maṇimēkalai is such a person, it enters her hands. The young girl vows to nourish hungry people with the bowl, which will never be empty after it is filled for the first time.

Returning to Pukār with her miraculous begging bowl, she seeks out her next spiritual guide, the Buddhist sage Aṟavaṇa Aṭikaḷ. He reveals to her more about the deeds of her past life and describes in detail how the whole world will prosper when the Buddha returns to preach on earth. Then the sage explains that more events must ensue before Maṇimēkalai can truly become his disciple. He ends by telling Maṇimēkalai the story of the miraculous begging bowl.[4]

This second section of the text portrays the beginnings of Maṇimēkalai's involvement with Buddhism. Her trip to Maṇipallavam Island removes her from the clutches of the prince and brings her to a holy place. This island gains its religious significance from the presence of both the dharma seat and the pond from which the begging bowl emerges on the Buddha's birthday. Through the gift of the bowl, Maṇimēkalai receives the ability to nourish countless suffering people, thus practicing the Buddhist ideals on compassion (*karuṇā*) and giving (*dāna*). She also learns that her present experiences have resulted from the deeds that occurred in her and Prince Utayakumaraṉ's past lives. In addition, she receives miraculous powers that will enable her to overcome obstacles she might encounter in her quest to cut off the bonds of birth. Finally, her meeting with Aṟavaṇa Aṭikaḷ acquaints her with her future mentor, indicates the shape of events to come, and explains how she came to possess the inexhaustible begging bowl. Unencumbered by Utayakumaraṉ's advances, Maṇimēkalai has been free to deepen her ties to Buddhism in this section of *Maṇimēkalai.*

In the third section of the narrative, Cāttaṉār again focuses on the relationship between Maṇimēkalai and Utayakumaraṉ (chapters 16-25). He begins by describing how Ātirai, who is known throughout the city as a chaste and virtuous housewife,[5] places the first alms in Maṇimēkalai's begging bowl. From this point onward, it never again becomes empty. Wandering through the streets of the city with her miraculous vessel, Maṇimēkalai distributes food to the needy. Cāttaṉār compares her generous acts to rains nourishing the land and to a cow nurturing its calf. Because of her dedication, she convinces the king to transform the city prison into a complex of religious buildings — including rooms where virtuous people can reside, and halls for cooking and dining.

In stark contrast with Maṇimēkalai's concern with the well-being of the populace, Utayakumaraṉ becomes increasingly possessed by his obsession to unite sexually with the young girl. So he seeks out Maṇimēkalai's grandmother Cittirāpati, who schemes with him to thwart the girl's vow of asceticism. Furious at the way that Maṇimēkalai's renunciation has brought criticism upon the courtesan community, she vows before an assembly of dancing girls to ensure that Utayakumaraṉ obtains his desire.

Meanwhile, Maṇimēkalai uses one of her mantras in order to take on another form — that of a woman named Kāyacaṇṭikai — so that she can avoid the prince's attentions. Unfortunately, the prince eventually recognizes her despite her transformation and follows her about relentlessly. At one point, while Maṇimēkalai is lecturing the prince on the transience of the human body, Kāyacaṇṭikai's husband appears. Upon seeing a woman whom he assumes to be his wife conversing intimately with another man, he burns with anger. Late that night the prince arrives at the temple where Maṇimēkalai dwells, determined to have his way with her. Kāyacaṇṭikai's husband lies in wait. Thinking that the prince seeks his wife, the jealous husband slices him to pieces with his sword.

Reactions to the murder of Utayakumaraṉ end this third section of *Maṇimēkalai.* His death serves as the occasion for religious instruction, whose focus shifts away from the specific circumstances of the prince's death to an explanation of the underlying nature of reality according to Buddhist philosophy. An ascetic first reveals the news of Prince Utayakumaraṉ's death to the king, using the occasion for a sermon on the evils of lust.[6] When, soon afterwards, the queen learns of her son's death, she furiously determines to wreak vengeance upon Maṇimēkalai, holding her to be the agent of his demise. Although the queen tries in succession to have Maṇimēkalai drugged, raped, and suffocated, Maṇimēkalai's mantras protect her from all harm. When the queen beholds all her efforts failing, she comes to understand that the young renouncer is an extraordinary woman and begs for forgiveness. Maṇimēkalai quickly takes the opportunity to instruct the queen about life's impermanence.

The events in the third section end Maṇimēkalai's conflict and provide a suitable occasion for Buddhist preaching. The "anti-love" story builds to a tragic climax, heightened by the forces arising from the schemes of Cittirāpati and a jealous husband's mistaken identification. Violent death abruptly ends the relationship between Maṇimēkalai and Utayakumaraṉ, and the grief that his death produces provides an appropriate starting point for preaching about life's transience.

In the last section of *Maṇimēkalai*, Cāttaṉār abandons the love theme altogether, concentrating on the heroine's attainment of ever-higher levels of religious understanding (chapters 26-30). To this end, Cāttaṉār portrays the stages through which Maṇimēkalai passes as part of her on-going training in Buddhist philosophy. These stages begin when Maṇimēkalai surveys current non-Buddhist philosophies of significance during a visit to the city of Vañci, and they continue during a period of study in Kāñci, a well-known center of South Indian Buddhism, with sage Aravaṇa Aṭikaḷ.

During Maṇimēkalai's sojourn in Vañci, she carefully evaluates the major non-Buddhist philosophies popular at the time. She goes, one by one, to each of the learned men who specialize in different viewpoints (*darśanas*).[7] In describing these religious systems, Cāttaṉār provides extremely brief, focused summaries of the different schools of thought. Maṇimēkalai hears discourse after discourse but finds none satisfactory. No Buddhist spokesman presents his view, but Maṇimēkalai's interspersed comments and criticisms indicate the perspective against which all other viewpoints are measured.

After her time in Vañci, Maṇimēkalai goes to Kāñci both to end its famine with her miraculous bowl and to study with the great Buddhist sage Aṟavaṇa Aṭikaḷ.[8] Now that she has learned and rejected other philosophical viewpoints, the sage deems her ready for comprehensive and detailed instruction concerning the valid and invalid forms of argument. Cāttaṉār devotes an entire lengthy chapter to reporting Aṟavaṇa Aṭikaḷ's exposition, outlining the various parts of syllogisms and the circumstances under which individual components of an argument may be judged fallacious or true. This session of teaching, which is directed solely to Maṇimēkalai, prepares her for the next stage of instruction — an exposition of major Buddhist tenets: Aṟavaṇa Aṭikaḷ first teaches the heroine what constitutes valid argument and then goes on to reveal the major arguments that comprise the Buddhist worldview.

These major arguments, about the nature of reality according to Buddhist tradition, culminate the text. Through his report of Aṟavaṇa Aṭikaḷ's lecture to Maṇimēkalai, Cāttaṉār provides what might be termed a "Buddhist manual,"[9] a chapter densely packed with explanations of key Buddhist tenets. He concentrates on explicating the principle of co-dependent origination (especially upon defining and explicating the twelve *nidānas*), the four noble truths, and the three flaws (desire, anger, and delusion). At the end of this chapter, Cāttaṉār describes Aṟavaṇa Aṭikaḷ's preaching as "free of any inconsistency," implicitly contrasting it with the words of the Vañci philosophers, whose religious systems contained flaws. After hearing this discourse composed of dharma, Maṇimēkalai dedicates herself to avoiding rebirth. In this way, Cāttaṉār's composition ends with the ripening of Maṇimēkalai's renunciation and her commitment to the Buddhist path.

Monastic Procedures and Rules for Buddhist Nuns

Despite the fact that Cāttaṉār calls Maṇimēkalai a nun, her behavior is highly unusual for a member of a Buddhist monastic order. Its members live in a highly institutionalized fashion according to the *Vinaya*, canonical verses setting out the rules for monastic discipline. Although it would be impossible to compare all the rules and procedures in these texts with Maṇimēkalai's actions, a look at a few representative ones indicates how inadequately such rules account for Maṇimēkalai's behavior.

The rules for female monastic life are found in Buddhist texts dealing with the *bhikkhuṇī-saṅgha.* *Saṅgha* literally means "assembly" and refers to the monastic order as a corporate entity. The Pali term *bhikkhuṇī* (Sanskrit *bhikṣuṇī*) literally means almswoman, although the more familiar term "nun" is often used in translation. *Bhikkhuṇīs* are to set out each day on their almsrounds, receiving food in their begging bowls from devoted laywomen. Practically speaking, because these nuns have renounced the life of the housewife, which involves the cooking and preparation of food, they need to beg for sustenance. The almsround also serves a spiritual purpose, enabling nuns to live lives characterized by detachment and poverty. In addition, the begging round provides laypeople with the opportunity to give generous gifts, thereby earning merit. Texts dealing with the *bhikkhuṇī-saṅgha* reveal a set of highly routinized patterns at the core of female monastic life.[10]

Over time, members of the monastic community formulated a set of procedures by which they admitted new members into the order. Novices went through a probationary period, normally lasting two years, culminating in *upasaṃpadā*, or ordination.[11] They usually spent their two years of noviceship in the *bhikkhuṇī-saṅgha,*[12] requesting an *upasaṃpadā* ceremony at the end of this period. In front of the entire order at the ceremony, the candidate answered a series of questions that determined her suitability for the monastic life. She proclaimed that she was free of medical problems (e.g., leprosy, consumption) and societal responsibilities (e.g., indebtedness), confirmed that she had reached at least twenty years of age and possessed her parents' permission to join the order, and testified that she possessed an almsbowl and a robe.[13]

Rather than this elaborate and highly routinized ceremony of admission to the order, a curious series of events appear to comprise Maṇimēkalai's "religious initiation." It remains unclear when — if ever — Maṇimēkalai receives ordination. The structural equivalent of an initiation into the life of an almswoman appears to occur on Maṇipallavam Island. However, Maṇimēkalai does not request a *upasaṃpadā* ceremony. Instead, as we have seen, a goddess carries her to a tiny island with a gem-studded throne, which reveals events that transpired in her past lives. Then she receives a miraculous begging bowl and supernatural powers that enable her to fly through the air or change form. Is this island sojourn an initiation? Perhaps not. Another possible initiation might be her instruction at the feet of Aṟavaṇa Aṭikaḷ, her mentor, at the end of *Maṇimēkalai.* In any case, neither event bears the slightest resemblance to the asking of the questions that forms the basis of the *upasaṃpadā* ceremony.

An elaborate set of regulations also exist concerning the style of living that members of the *saṅgha* must assume. The prescribed pattern entails wandering from place to place except during the rainy season. During the majority of the year, a nun travels about collecting alms. However for the three-month monsoon season, members of the order observe a rain retreat

(Pali *vassa*; Sanskrit *varṣa*), remaining in one place. At the end of the season, the community holds a termination ceremony (Pali *pavāraṇā*; Sanskrit *pravāraṇā*) in order to confess any misdeeds performed by its members during this period so that the purity of the assembly can be restored.[14]

While Maṇimēkalai certainly wanders about the countryside, the rain retreat and the *pavāraṇā* ceremony play no part in Cāttaṉār's text. Maṇimēkalai may be characterized as a wanderer *par excellence*, since her aerial travels take her to distant cities where she spreads Buddhist teachings and combats hunger. While monks and nuns settled for three months in one place because the seasonal rains interfered with their wanderings, the closest thing to excessive water disturbing one's freedom to move about in *Maṇimēkalai* is the tidal wave that destroys Pukār. There is no mention of Maṇimēkalai undergoing a rain retreat — let alone the purificatory ceremony that follows the retreat.

Moving from procedures to rules, again there is little correspondence between Maṇimēkalai's activities and prescribed behavior in the *Vinaya*. Most of the Eight Chief Rules, which determine the relationship between monks and nuns, seem irrelevant to Cāttaṉār's portrayal of Maṇimēkalai. The first rule states that "Any nun, no matter how long she has been in the order, must treat any monk, even the rudest novice, as if he were her senior." Maṇimēkalai does treat the few monks she meets (for example, Aṛavaṇa Aṭikaḷ and Kōvalaṉ's father) with great respect. However the remaining seven rules do not seem to apply to *Maṇimēkalai*. According to those prescriptions (2) nuns should not live during the rain retreat in a place where there are no monks, (3) monks must set the dates for biweekly assemblies (Pali *uposatha*; Sanskrit *poṣadha*), (4) nuns need to invite criticism of their behavior during the rainy season from monks as well as other nuns, (5) monks should share in determining and supervising penances for nuns who have transgressed the rules, (6) monks must share in the ordination of nuns, (7) nuns cannot criticize monks, and (8) nuns should never reprimand monks.[15] Cāttaṉār, however, portrays no rain retreats, no monastic assemblies, no prescribed penances for transgression of rules, no ordination, and few interactions with monks.

If Cāttaṉār does not gear his account of Maṇimēkalai's renunciation to the procedures and rules prescribed for the *bhikkhuṇī-saṅgha*, should we conclude that she did not really embrace the monastic life or that Cāttaṉār misunderstood the *vinaya* texts? Hardly. Such interpretations would be unnecessarily literal. Despite the discrepancies just noted between Buddhist regulatory texts and Cāttaṉār's text, the same principles that lie at the heart of monastic discipline have shaped Maṇimēkalai's life as well.

Most important, Cāttaṉār portrays Maṇimēkalai as a woman dedicated to renouncing sexual desire. Celibacy is one of the defining characteristics of Buddhist monastic life in ancient India. In *Maṇimēkalai*, Cāttaṉār carefully explains to a skeptical audience how a woman can renounce sexual desire and why such renunciation is crucial if one is to attain religious liberation. He makes his explanation through his use of Tamil literary conventions.

Portrayal of the Heroine's Renunciation

Cāttaṉār describes a new idea, female renunciation, by showing how it differs from an old and familiar idea, the union of a woman and her lover. In ancient Tamil literature, poets portrayed this union according to a highly schematized set of literary conventions. Cāttaṉār — always resourceful in the service of persuasion — uses these conventions and then twists them in order to define and advocate female renunciation.

None of the existing literary evidence prior to *Maṇimēkalai* suggests that the ancient Tamils are very familiar with the idea of renunciation. Even for males, a life of asceticism is rare. Ancient Tamil literature contains a few scattered descriptions of male ascetics, which allow one to assume some familiarity with the idea.[16] The concept of female renunciation, however, would have been a relatively unfamiliar one for the audience to whom Cāttaṉār addresses his text.

Whereas the classical texts (usually referred to as *Caṅkam* literature) do not mention renunciation for women, they are rife with descriptions of women as lovers. The classical corpus contains two types of poems — *akam* and *puṟam*. While *puṟam* (literally "outer") poems deal with the public sphere, *akam* (literally "inner") poetry concerns love in the private sphere. Tamil love poems — comprising more than half of the 2,380 and odd extant poems, many of which date from the first to third centuries A.D. — are composed according to a shared vision that manifested itself in a body of literary conventions. These conventions have as their core the correlation between five natural landscapes and five respective phases of love. In the afterward to his recent translation of a selection of these poems, Ramanujan describes the consensual nature of classical Tamil poetic vision and explains the logic behind the term "*Caṅkam*," the name of this body of literature:

> . . . the Tamil poets used a set of five landscapes and formalized the world into a symbolism. By a remarkable consensus, they all spoke this common language of symbols for some five or six generations. Each could make his own poem and by doing so allude to every other poem which had been, was being, or would be written in this symbolic language. Thus poem became relevant to poem, as if they were all written by a single hand. The spurious name *Caṅkam* ("Fraternity," "Community") for this poetry was justified not by history but by the poetic practice.[17]

This shared vision includes a highly stylized representation of female behavior within the five phases of love.

If the poets share a common language, so does their special audience. Both the *Cankam* poets and Cāttaṉār are able to take for granted their audience's familiarity with the motifs and conventions they incorporate into their poems. As Bryant says, commenting about the nature of poetic convention in South Asian literature,

> The first assumption is that a poem is a message, from a given poet to a given audience, whose proper transmission depends upon (among other things) poet and audience sharing a common language, and not only language in the ordinary sense, but also the more specialized language of poetic convention.[18]

Cāttaṉār's readers are schooled in this specialized language of poetic conventions, so he can take for granted his audience's knowledge of them.

In Tamil literary convention,[19] the phases of love correlate with specific landscapes. A brief overview of these settings will help us to understand what role they play in *Maṇimēkalai*. Love between a man and a woman entails five phases, encompassing both love in union and love in separation.[20] Each of the five is depicted against the backdrop of a particular landscape:

kuṟiñci [mountain]	clandestine lovers' union
mullai [forest]	patient waiting, domesticity
marutam [countryside]	man with courtesan, wife sulking
neytal [seashore]	anxious waiting
pālai [wasteland]	separation mixed with danger

The use of these landscapes provides the poet with a clearly categorized set of images to employ in depicting love in union or separation.

Each landscape possesses an extensive set of characteristic features called *karupporuḷ*, "native elements." For example, in poems set in the *kuṟiñci* landscape, appropriate native beasts such as monkeys and elephants, native birds such as peacocks and parrots, native flora such as *kuṟiñci* and *vēṅkai*, and the reigning deity Murukaṉ appear. Because the situations of love are correlated with the five landscapes, the poem's reader can easily identify the phase of love and landscape of a given poem merely by noting the presence of a particular native element:

> As a result of this theory of composition, Tamil poets were able to use concise descriptive passages to create poems with complex layers of meaning, since reference to even one element of a landscape evoked the full

> range of subjects and themes associated with the landscape.[21]

Cāttaṉār uses native elements from the landscape of clandestine union in chapter four of *Maṇimēkalai* in order to raise certain expectations in the minds of his readers.

Cāttaṉār describes the Uvavaṉam Garden, where Prince Utayakumaraṉ goes to see Maṇimēkalai, using elements native to the *kuṟiñci*, or mountain, setting (see Table 2). He specifically incorporates scampering monkeys and dancing peacocks into his description of the garden scene. Each of these native elements is customarily associated with the mountain landscape. In addition, Cāttaṉār portrays the garden as a dark and mysterious place because its high trees block out the sun. The dimly lit setting thus suggests night, the stipulated time for lovers to steal away and meet in the mountains. The deserted and remote location of the grove, as well as the wild calls of the animals who inhabit it, create a mood considered appropriate for a clandestine tryst. The deity Murukaṉ, whom Cāttaṉār mentions in the description of the grove, presides over the *kuṟiñci* landscape, according to the poetic tradition. Thus, for those versed in Tamil literary convention, the description of the garden and the grove within it evoke the landscape of secret lovers.

In a similar way, Cāttaṉār creates an expected scenario for Prince Utayakumaraṉ. The reader first encounters the dynamic young prince when he subdues a wild elephant in rut. In accordance with the ancient Tamil technique of suggestion,[22] the image of the rutting elephant suggests the intensity of Utayakumaraṉ's passion for Maṇimēkalai. His subjection of the rutting beast foreshadows the restraints placed upon his own passion for Maṇimēkalai. Obstacles to realization of his desire beset him as soon as he reaches the Uvavaṉam Garden and meets Cutamati, Maṇimēkalai's companion. He begins his wooing of the heroine by waxing eloquent about her lovely eyes, comparing them to carp, and her glistening teeth, likening them to pearls. These phrases formulaically express Utayakumaraṉ's appreciation for the beauty of the heroine and his intention to obtain her sexual favors. In numerous classical love poems, the hero begins his courtship with such phrases.

Cutamati, Maṇimēkalai's companion, appears to play a role well-developed in classical Tamil love poetry. In the portrayal of the phases of love, a girlfriend almost always acts as a confidant to the heroine and as a go-between for the two lovers. In the garden, Utayakumaraṉ approaches Cutamati and praises Maṇimēkalai because he — and Cāttaṉār's audience at this point — assumes that she will facilitate a lovers' tryst.

Table 2: The Five Landscapes, Their Corresponding Phases of Love, and Selected Native Elements

Landscape (*tiṇai*)	Phase of love (*uri*)	Native elements, i.e., birds/beasts, flora, and deities (*karupporuḷ*)
kuṟiñci mountain	clandestine lovers' union	peacock, monkey, *vēṅkai*, Murukaṉ
mullai forest	patient waiting, domesticity	forest hen, deer, *koṉṟai*, Māyōṉ
marutam countryside	lover with courtesan and wife sulking	heron, buffalo, mango, Indra
neytal seashore	anxious waiting	seagull, shark, *puṉṉai*, Varuna
pālai wasteland	separation mixed with danger	vulture, wild dog, *kaḷḷi*, Kālī

Sources: Nāṟkavirāca Nampi, *Akapporuḷ Viḷakkam* (Tinnevelly: SISS, 1979), p. 24A; A. K. Ramanujan, *The Interior Landscape* (Bloomington: Indiana University Press, 1975), p. 107; M. Shanmugan Pillai and David Ludden, *Kuṟuntokai: An Anthology of Classical Tamil Love Poetry* (Madurai: Koodal Publishers, 1976), p. 30; Kamil V. Zvelebil, *The Smile of Murugan* (Leiden: E. J. Brill, 1973), p. 100; and my own reading of classical Tamil poetry.

Maṇimēkalai's feelings of lovesickness, after the departure of the prince, provide yet another example of the presence of conventional elements in this account. The heroine traditionally suffers great longing after parting with her lover. Classical poems whose subject is love in separation are replete with descriptions of a woman pining for her paramour.

Up to this point, everything in Cāttaṉār's tableau accords with expectation. The site, the cast of characters, the formulaic language, and the sequence of events all suggest that a tryst will take place. There is, however, no actual interaction, no sexual union, and no need for a go-between. Nothing even remotely like a lover's meeting occurs. Instead, Cāttaṉār uses the occasion to demonstrate the meaning of female renunciation.[23]

The culmination of this whole scene of foiled union occurs when Utayakumaraṉ sees that Maṇimēkalai has locked herself inside of the glass pavilion in the garden. There she is enclosed and unattainable.[24] Her beautiful body is not available to be enjoyed by the prince. Utayakumaraṉ's lust, like that of the rutting elephant he subdued earlier that day, must be frustrated because union cannot take place. In fact, at the end of the scene, Maṇimēkalai devoutly wishes that her love for the prince cease.

Maṇimēkalai's enclosure within the pavilion stands in one's mind as an image of female renunciation. The essence of Cāttaṉār's portrayal is unfulfilled union: a nun simply does not fulfill the role of lover, which poets so stereotypically portray in classical Tamil poems. Instead, she separates herself from such relationships, just as Maṇimēkalai sets herself apart in the glass pavilion in order to be free of Utayakumaraṉ. Cāttaṉār's assembly of the elements in this scene sets female renunciation in high relief. Whereas the portrayal of love in Tamil poetry dwells upon inner feelings, intimate personal relations, and the sexual realm, Cāttaṉār's portrayal of Maṇimēkalai's renunciation emphasizes the way in which bonds to this inner, sexual sphere must be cut.

Analysis of this one scene from *Maṇimēkalai* reveals the larger pattern of the work. Both the use of Tamil literary conventions and the theme of love versus renunciation remain crucial to the unfolding of *Maṇimēkalai*'s main story. Tamil literary conventions appear in several other sections of *Maṇimēkalai*'s main story, helping to advance Cāttaṉār's overall goals in significant ways.[25] Similarly, the love versus renunciation theme structures the portrayal of the heroine during the first three quarters of the text. The structure of *Maṇimēkalai*'s main story, thus, allows Cāttaṉār to explore in greater depth the lesson set out in the Uvavaṉam Garden — that a woman becomes a renouncer by forsaking sexual love in order to mature spiritually.

Combating Criticism of Female Renunciation

At the beginning of chapter three of *Maṇimēkalai*, Cāttaṉār depicts Pukār's citizens accusing a female who renounces marriage to practice religious discipline of wasting her beauty and giving up her womanhood. In this same chapter, as we have seen, Maṇimēkalai and her companion are walking to the Uvavaṉam Garden to pick fresh flowers for a garland. While describing their progress toward the garden, Cāttaṉār discusses occurrences on the street, including a drunkard's irreverent mockery of an ascetic. This mockery foreshadows the criticism of Maṇimēkalai's asceticism, which appears a few lines later in the text. There Cāttaṉār reports the comments of members of the crowd that has gathered to gawk at the sight of a female renouncer. After praising the gait and gracefulness of Maṇimēkalai, they comment that any mother who would encourage such a daughter to undertake extreme asceticism must be cruel and unsuitable for motherhood (3:150).

Line 146 of chapter three compares Maṇimēkalai to Arjuna when he took on the disguise of a hermaphrodite. This comparison refers to the section of the *Mahābhārata* where the five Pāṇḍavas must go into exile for twelve years and then conceal themselves for a thirteenth, as a result of Yudhiṣṭhira's losses in an ill-fated dice game. During the thirteenth year in the Matsya kingdom of Virāṭa, each of the five brothers takes on a different identity. Arjuna, for his part, assumes the guise of an "effeminate eunuch,"[26] working as a dancing teacher for the king's daughters. Vaiśaṃpāyana describes Arjuna this way:

> Then one more man appeared, a large man who bore
> The adornment of woman and beauty supreme,
> Wearing earrings the size of ramparts and walls
> And long bright conch shells set into gold.

Arjuna tells the Virāṭa king,

> The reason I have this form — what profit
> Is there in recounting it but great pain?
> Bṛhannaḍā, sire, is my name, deserted
> By father and mother as son and daughter.[27]

Neither completely son nor daughter, Arjuna plays the role of a person whose sexuality is unclear. The use of the Arjuna illusion at this point in Cāttaṉār's narrative implies that Maṇimēkalai might be considered abnormal. By renouncing her courtesan profession and embracing the celebate life, she too has, the allusion implies, embraced an anomalous and unproductive form of sexuality.

As a way of refuting such criticism, Cāttaṉār takes great care in his narrative to portray Maṇimēkalai as a beautiful heroine of the type depicted in classical Tamil love poetry, rather than a female equivalent of

Arjuna as eunuch. The manner in which Cāttaṉār depicts Maṇimēkalai differs greatly from the portrayal of Maṇimēkalai in (the earlier) *Cilappatikāram*. Maṇimēkalai plays only a small role in that text. The main action centers on her father, Kōvalaṉ, and to a lesser extent her mother, Mātavi. In fact, Maṇimēkalai gains prominence only in the final chapter of *Cilappatikāram*, where her tonsure and admission into the Buddhist monastic order are described.

In *Cilappatikāram*'s account of Maṇimēkalai's tonsure (chapter 30), its author, Iḷaṅkō, depicts a girl who has recently become sexually alluring. During her tonsure, she is deprived of one of the most visible signs of that allurement — her thick black tresses. An abbreviated version of the account of her tonsure in *Cilappatikāram* is reproduced below.

> . . . her [Maṇimēkalai's] dark tresses had grown in luxuriance so as to be divided into (the usual) five plaits, and her cool eyes delightfully red in the corners had acquired a new charm of which she was unconscious . . . her lovely breasts had developed, her bosom had broadened; her slender waist became narrower and her pretty *alkul* [mound-of-venus] had widened; her two thighs were rounded; her shapely tender feet, unable even to bear (the weight) [*sic*] of ornaments became glossy to the view. Yet men of noble families did not recognize her as a professional dancer because the dancing master had not initiated her into that art.
>
> At that time Mātavi's good mother [Cittirāpati] asked her daughter: "What is your intention? What am I to do?" Then Mātavi called Maṇimēkalai to her saying: "Come here, my dear modest daughter," and removed her locks with the flower-wreaths thereon, thus making the bodiless god fling to the bare ground his flower dart and his bow of sugarcane.[28]

This account stresses that Maṇimēkalai has blossomed into a woman: it contains conventional descriptions used in Tamil poetry to indicate the sexual ripening of a young woman. Because Maṇimēkalai has come of age, her grandmother (the matriarch of the courtesan community) desires that she quickly be initiated into the profession.

In this *Cilappatikāram* account, however, Maṇimēkalai's mother has an entirely different course of action in mind. Precisely because Maṇimēkalai has come of age, her mother determines that her daughter should receive tonsure at once. Therefore, she removes both the girl's long tresses and the flower garlands that adorn them. Lest the reader miss the significance of these acts, *Cilappatikāram*'s author, Iḷaṅkō, explains their meaning. He says that her tonsure made "the bodiless god fling to the bare ground his flower dart and his bow of sugarcane," referring to Kāma, the Indian god of love whose arrows create desire in the hearts of those whom he shoots. Here, however, Kāma lays down his bow and arrow, realizing it is inappropriate to attack Maṇimēkalai because she has become a member of the Buddhist monastic order.

Since Iḷaṅkō so carefully describes Maṇimēkalai's tonsure, a rite of passage into a life of renunciation, it is curious that Cāttaṉār never mentions this ritual in *Maṇimēkalai*, a text whose whose main purpose is to portray the renunciation of the eponymous heroine. Not only does Cāttaṉār avoid mentioning Maṇimēkalai's tonsure, but the text contains explicit references to Maṇimēkalai's beautiful tresses: Cāttaṉār describes her long, curling hair adorned with flower garlands (8:35-37, 26:62, and passim).

In fact, Cāttaṉār consistently presents the young nun as beautiful and attractively adorned, rather than as a desexed ascetic. References to Maṇimēkalai's lovely jewelry, especially her bangles, appear in all sections of the text (for instance, see 10:89 and 13:2). Cāttaṉār regularly describes his heroine as wearing a flower garland composed of different kinds of colorful blossoms (for instance, see 12:56 or 21:61). Specific images, usually found in an erotic context in Tamil literature, are used to describe Maṇimēkalai's alluring physical features: her shapely mound-of-venus like a green cobra's hood (28:220), her shoulders like bamboo (21:110), and her creeper-like body (22:7). The difference between these descriptions and the account of Maṇimēkalai's tonsure in *Cilappatikāram* is striking: Cāttaṉār describes his protagonist as an attractive young heroine.

Indeed, instead of presenting Maṇimēkalai as one who has wasted her womanhood, Cāttaṉār depicts her as a mother *par excellence*. Her inexhaustible begging bowl enables her to provide thousands of hungry people with nourishment. Because she can feed so many people with her bowl, Cāttaṉār uses the image of a mother suckling her young to describe the girl's actions: in lines 114-15 of chapter eleven, Maṇimēkalai compares herself to a cow who feels compassionate when she sees the face of a newborn calf.[29] In this image, her inexhaustible begging bowl represents the cow's udder that pours forth sweet milk to nourish her calf. By employing such language, Cāttaṉār suggests that criticism of Maṇimēkalai's renunciation is misguided.

Conclusions

Maṇimēkalai's main story centers upon a personal conflict between love and renunciation; the four sections of the main story describe the heroine's ever-growing commitment to Buddhist monastic life. Despite the subject matter, however, one cannot use the narrative as a source for study of the nature of female monastic life in the same way that scholars have used *vinaya* texts. Instead, *Maṇimēkalai*'s main story must be seen as a tale in the service of an argument. Tamil literary conventions, rather than monastic rules, provide the structure for that argument. Through those conventions, Cāttaṉār defines and advocates female renunciation. And by consistently presenting the nun as attractive, he refutes claims that nuns renounce womanliness. By portraying Maṇimēkalai as a universal nuturer, Cāttaṉār combats criticism of the nun's celibacy.

In his presentation of Maṇimēkalai as a great mother (without any biological children), Cāttaṉār employs a type of rhetorical strategy found elsewhere in Buddhist texts. This technique entails presenting an aspect of Buddhism as fostering in a superior way the practice of a particular virtue valued by the society at large. In this case, Cāttaṉār presents a nun, a type of person criticized for denying her femaleness, as a mother *par excellence*.

The same kind of rhetorical strategy occurs, for example, in early Chinese Buddhist apologetic writings about monastic life. In China, where Confucians designated filial piety as the supreme virtue, authors of anti-Buddhist memorials had criticized monasticism as an institution because monks no longer performed specific filial duties after they entered the monastery. Chinese Buddhists, however, countered such criticisms by arguing that Buddhist monks could practice *greater* filial piety than laypeople. Ch'en explains the logic behind this seemingly audacious claim in the following way:

> The Chinese Buddhists pursued this line of argument still further by contending that the Buddhist monk aims not merely at salvation for his parents, but at salvation for all living creatures. In this role, he would be fulfilling what the Chinese Buddhists call the *ta-hsiao*, or great filial piety. This great filial piety is considered to be far superior to the Confucian piety, which is confined to one family and limited to serving only one's parents, whereas the Buddhist piety is universal and all-inclusive, and embraces all living creatures, some of whom might well be our ancestors in different forms.[30]

This line of argument depends upon the premise that people undergo many rebirths. Thus if one desires to venerate all one's ancestors, it is best to work for the salvation of all creatures, something that monastic discipline helped one to do. The Buddhist apologists claimed, thus, that monks practice superior filiality. Both Cāttaṉār and Chinese apologists for Buddhism have developed a strategy that might be called "beating them at their own game by changing the definition of a key move." The Chinese Buddhists universalize the notion of filial piety. Cāttaṉār redefines "mothering" so that it encompasses the nurturance of any hungry person, rather than just one's offspring.

The presence of the inexhaustible begging bowl indicates another way in which Maṇimēkalai is more than a "mere" nun. Traditionally, the relationship between monastics and laypeople is conceived as a reciprocal one: a monk or nun provides religious instruction and receives alms, while a layperson gives alms and receives religious instruction.[31] Although Maṇimēkalai renounces sexual union as a nun should, she also gives food as a devoted laywoman would. In doing so, she joins the ranks of pious women such as Sujāta, who fed the Buddha milk before his enlightenment under the Bodhi Tree,[32] and Visākhā, the "foremost of the female lay disciples who delight in almsgiving" who ministered to monks by giving them — among other gifts — food;[33] Maṇimēkalai gives rice from her begging bowl instead of collecting rice in that bowl. Because she rejects sexual union (with Prince Utayakumaraṉ) and embraces a life of celibacy, she is an exemplar of female renunciation. At the same time, because she gives food, she can be seen as a model for the devoted laywoman. The reversal of the begging bowl's normal function indicates the conflation of the two female roles in Cāttaṉār's portrayal of Maṇimēkalai.

3

THE PORTRAYAL OF PERSUASION

The story of "Cātuvan̲ and the Nākas" shows a shipwrecked merchant persuading a tribe of naked cannibals to change the way they live. In the tale, Cāttan̲ār depicts a dazzling orator engaged in moral bargaining with the unsophisticated tribesmen. His story portrays both a preacher and the response to his preaching. That portrayal helps to shape and control the reader's own response to the story's message. By depicting the speaker's persuasive skills and their effect upon the dramatized audience, Cāttan̲ār demonstrates the response he has in mind for his actual audience. Branch stories like "Cātuvan̲ and the Nākas" function in an extremely compact way, allowing an author to include self-contained moral preaching while at the same time providing the text with narrative diversity.

The Main Story and Branch Stories

Until recently, scholars of South Asian texts have tended to overlook the contribution that branch stories can make to the overall goals of the text. Several well-known Indologists have described the inclusion of such stories in ways that disclose an assumption that such stories are superfluous. For example, in his classic history of Sanskrit literature, MacDonell describes the South Asian epic *Mahābhārata* as

> . . . a congeries of parts, the only unity about which is the connectedness of the epic cycle with which they deal; its epic kernel, moreover, which forms only about one-fifth of the whole work, has become so overgrown with didactic matter, that in its final shape it is not an epic at all, but an encyclopedia of moral teaching.[1]

Hopkins describes the same epic as "a heterogeneous collection of strings wound about a nucleus almost lost sight of."[2] Gowen, following a similar line of argument, says that the *Mahābhārata* "could with great advantage, be reduced, excluding the 'episodes.'" He characterizes these episodes as material that "interferes with the sequence of the narrative."[3]

A few scholars have turned their attention to the characteristics of the branch story in Tamil literature. Ceṉpakam divides epic stories into three types: *maiyakkatai*, "the central story," *iṇaikkataikaḷ*, "joined" or "connected stories," and *paḻaṅkataikaḷ*, "ancient" or "traditional stories."[4] Turaicāmi Piḷḷai discusses the branch stories in *Maṇimēkalai*, noting that they are smoothly, rather than abruptly, integrated into the whole:

> In this epic, the flow of the branch stories which join with the [main] plot brings to mind the image of a river: Beginning in the mountains, it swells with the addition of small rivers, here and there, which flow into it.[5]

This image of the river and its tributaries is a traditional Tamil way of talking about literary coherence. Balusamy claims that Cāttaṉār put branch stories in *Maṇimēkalai* for the sake of the dissatisfied reader. He claims that female asceticism is such a dull subject that the author could relieve his audience's boredom only by inserting branch stories:

> Every character who meets the heroine gives a part of his or her story. . . . Thus the narrative becomes interesting, for it arouses our suspense, invested as it is with a dramatic element. . . . Thus the story of Maṇimēkalai is endowed with a glitter which it otherwise lacks, for the story element is rather weak when we consider the main narrative dealing with Maṇimēkalai. Her story, to say the least is prosaic and uninteresting, but it forms the core, so to say, which is beautified with the romantic and interesting episodes throwing a halo around it.[6]

Clearly, the relationship between branch stories and the overall goals of the author in *Maṇimēkalai* deserves a more sensitive analysis than that of Balusamy.

Within the Buddhist tradition, a great deal of attention has been paid to the means by which people might be encouraged to enter upon the

Buddhist path. In his *Skilful Means*, Michael Pye notes that Buddhist teaching is pragmatically oriented, commenting that the key Buddhist concept of *upāya* (usually translated as "skilful means" or "skill in means") is "about the way in which the goal, the intention, or the meaning of Buddhism is correlated with the unenlightened condition of living beings."[7] According to the traditional Mahayana understanding of the term, the Buddha himself is said to have used "countless devices" to teach human beings what they need to know in order to become enlightened.[8] Because branch stories play a great role in presenting Buddhism as a persuasive explanation of reality in *Maṇimēkalai*, they may be seen as an illustration of the Buddhist practice of skill in means, *upāya*.[9]

Maṇimēkalai is neither a "ragbag encyclopedia" nor a story ruined by interspersed "interpolations." In addition to whatever part its branch stories play in their particular textual location, they also contribute to the general persuasive thrust of the entire text. From beginning to end, *Maṇimēkalai* is informed by a Buddhist vision of the universe. The vision may appear to be a mere sketch at first, but its finer details and subtle shadings have been painted in by the time the text concludes. Branch stories help to delineate parts of Cāttaṉār's Buddhist vision.

Despite the explicitly didactic role branch stories play, they are always related in some specific way to the main story in *Maṇimēkalai* — they are never mere digressions. Some branch stories explain what occurred during the previous lives of important characters in *Maṇimēkalai*. Others describe the history of a holy place or miraculous object that plays a significant role in the main story, and still others describe the deeds performed in the past by exemplary characters. Each story bears a particular and noninterchangeable relationship to the framing narrative, the main story. "Cātuvaṉ and the Nākas" explains why Maṇimēkalai went to Cātuvaṉ's wife, Ātirai, to collect alms after receiving the inexhaustible begging bowl on Maṇipallavam Island. In order to make manifest the bowl's miraculous powers to feed innumerable starving people, Maṇimēkalai had to fill it for the first time with alms provided by a chaste woman. Ātirai was so chaste that even the most virtuous women in the land admired her, as the story of "Cātuvaṉ and the Nākas" explains.

The story does more than explain the character of the bowl's first donor; it teaches the Buddhist principle of *ahiṃsā*, noninjury to living beings. It also informs the reader that the Buddhist path can be appropriate for all kinds of people, as the translation and analysis below reveals.

Translation: "Cātuvaṉ and the Nākas"

Hear, O woman with beautiful jewels, about Ātirai's husband Cātuvaṉ, who lost his good character. Leaving his beautifully adorned wife, he spent his time with a courtesan who fed him tainted food. He lost such large sums of money at dice and other forms of gambling that soon all of his funds were exhausted. Even the courtesan, who had taken him in, pointed out to him the excellence of other men. Then, with a wave of her hand, she dismissed him because he had no money. 16:05

After that, Cātuvaṉ gave into his uncontrollable desire to set out to sea with a group of merchants. In the vast and teeming ocean, the wind overturned their vessel. Tossed about by the rolling waves, Cātuvaṉ grabbed onto a length of the mast and eventually drifted to the shore of the mountainous land where the naked wanderers called Nākas (Sanskrit Nāga) lived. There he fell into their hands.

Some other passengers also survived just as Cātuvaṉ had escaped by holding onto a piece of the sturdy mast from the wrecked ship. After reaching home, they reported that Cātuvaṉ had perished in the dark middle watch of the night, along with the others who had drowned in the dashing waves of the great ocean.

When that good woman, Ātirai, heard the news, she cried, "Townspeople, build me a funeral pyre and set a bright fire to it." They dug a pit in the cremation ground and set fire to the brittle stiff wood. Then she entered the fire, declaring, "I will go where my excellent husband has gone, driven by the fruits of his deeds." But the bright fire touched neither the clothes she wore nor her resting place in the pyre. The garlands that adorned her blowing hair and the sandalpaste she had spread on her body did not even change color. Sitting there sweetly like the incomparable Fair One of Fortune on her fragrant lotus flower [the goddess Lakṣmī] she thought, "I have done such evil deeds that even the fire will not kill me. What will I do?" And she wept.

At that moment a voice came from the sky. It said, "Hear me, Ātirai: The rolling waves seized your precious husband and brought him to the mountainous shore where the naked wanderers called Nākas live. He will not stay there long. Soon he shall return in the merchant Cantiratattaṉ's boat. Cease your grieving." So that woman, whose eyes were adorned with collyrium and highlighted with beautiful red lines [a sign of beauty], stopped mourning. She entered the house, dismissing all grief from her mind like a woman who emerges from a pond after bathing. Then she proclaimed, "May he who is like the jewel of my eye[10] return quickly."

Subsequently, Ātirai did so many meritorious deeds that she was admired and worshiped lovingly even by those rare chaste women who, according to tradition, have the ability to bring pouring rain.[11]

Meanwhile, the pain that her husband had experienced in the cloud-covered ocean grew worse. Due to that pain, he fell into a deep sleep in the shade of a tree on the steep, mountainous, wave-washed shore. Then the naked wanderers, people without love who lived in that fearful mountain, appeared. As soon as they reached the spot where Cātuvaṉ slept, they said, "Poor man, he came here all by himself. He has suffered greatly. Nonetheless, the flesh of his body will be food for us." And so they woke him up.

Now Cātuvaṉ had learned the language of these people perfectly. So when he spoke, these people of cruel work, who had encircled him, backed off. After showing reverence to him, they conversed among themselves, and a few said to him, "You who have a rare strength, listen: Our guru is nearby. Be gracious enough to go to him."

When Cātuvaṉ reached the guru's dwelling, he saw pots for cooking toddy and dried white bones scattered about. The overwhelming stench of raw meat pervaded everything. Cātuvaṉ saw how the guru sat with his woman like a bear with his mate. Going into the cool shade of a lofty tree, he won them over with his spellbinding mastery of their language.

The guru asked why Cātuvaṉ had come. As soon as Cātuvaṉ told him of his experiences in the rolling sea, the guru proclaimed, "He suffered great hunger in the tossing ocean, poor man. Come, my people, give this distinguished man what he must desire — a young girl, intoxicating toddy, and meat."

Cātuvaṉ grew faint as he listened to that command and said, "I heard those vile words. I don't want those things!"

The guru grew angry and asked, "What is there for people to live for besides women, eating, and drinking? If there is something else, show it to us. Say what it is and let us see it."

Cātuvaṉ said, "People who are free of all confusion do not take lives and drink toddy, which deludes the mind. Listen. The truth is that the death of those who are born and the birth of those who die are like sleeping and waking. Resolute people avoid killing and drinking because they realize that those who are virtuous (*nallaṟam*) attain good worlds [after death] but those who are not virtuous (*allaṟam*) go to terrible hells [after death]. Understand this."

The Nāka guru laughed derisively and questioned Cātuvaṉ, saying, "You just told us that the life-breath runs away from the body, takes on another form, and enters a different place [in its next birth]. Tell us clearly how that life-breath can go and enter another place the way you just said it does."

Cātuvaṉ replied, "Listen to what I have to say and refrain from anger: While the life-breath resides in the body, the body knows what is happening. But, when the life-breath leaves, that very same body doesn't realize what is happening to it — even if it is cut apart and set on fire. If this is the case, you must realize an entity exists that can leave the body.

"It is not just me — everyone knows that whatever leaves must end up somewhere. You see, even when one dreams, the life-breath leaves the body behind and travels a long distance. You need to understand clearly how the life-breath travels in a similar fashion [after death] and then assumes the kind of body appropriate to its deeds."

As soon as Cātuvan̲ finished speaking, the fiery-eyed Nāka fell at the feet of the good merchant who knew virtue, saying, "If I give up toddy and meat, I cannot sustain the life-breath, which dwells in this body. Choose and explain to us which of the determined virtuous paths is appropriate for us to follow until we die."

Cātuvan̲ answered, "Your request is admirable. You will follow a good path. I'll tell you the path of virtue possible for you: If people escape shipwrecks and come ashore here, do not kill them. Instead, save their lives, which are precious. And give up the evil practice of eating the flesh of all beings except those animals that die of old age."

The low one said, "We will follow this virtuous path that is appropriate for us here, and you take these precious things that are appropriate for you there. Often in the past we have eaten shipwrecked people. We got all these valuable things from them. Take these fragrant woods, soft clothes, piles of treasure, and other things."

Bringing them along with him, Cātuvan̲ boarded the boat of the merchant Cantiratattan̲, which had arrived at that island. He returned to this city and lived here with Ātirai, giving many generous gifts.

Negotiations between the Preacher and the Cannibals

When this story concludes, Cātuvan̲ has convinced the cannibals never again to kill human beings and to eat only animals that die of old age. In Buddhism, the practice of *ahiṃsā* [noninjury to living beings] is enjoined for laypeople and monks alike. *Ahiṃsā* is a state of mind leading to the rejection of certain kinds of actions that entail harming living beings.[12] Noninjury, in its broadest sense, comprises an attitude of gentleness that grows out of a recognition that all living beings participate in *saṃsāra*, the cycle of rebirth. For example, a human being may be born as an animal in another birth or an animal might have been one's relative in a previous birth. Compassion, thus, must be extended not only to humans but to all living beings. In this story, then, Cāttan̲ār portrays the shipwrecked merchant persuading the tribesmen to practice *ahiṃsā*, one of the crucial practices of Buddhism.

Cāttaṉār's portrayal of Cātuvaṉ, the Nākas, and *ahiṃsā* suggests a preaching situation with three extremely unusual elements. Strangely enough, the preacher — though marooned upon a wild and hostile island — uses the obscure native language so well that he sweeps his listeners off their feet. And the members of his audience are cannibals likely to eat shipwrecked people such as Cātuvaṉ. And finally, the preacher's decision about the proper kind of behavior for the Nākas is based upon an unusual set of negotiations centering upon what actions can and cannot possibly be abandoned in order to be virtuous.

Cātuvaṉ's startling effectiveness as a preacher clearly arises from his mastery of a foreign language. His extraordinary linguistic abilities help him both to save himself from Nāka cannibalism and to convince the tribesmen to reform their lives. Cātuvaṉ must have studied the islanders' native tongue, since lines 60-61 state that he "had flawlessly learned the language of these people." This skill dissuades the Nākas from consuming him. Although they contemplate his body with hungry longing, as soon as they hear his discourse they tell him he has a "rare strength" and request that he visit their guru. When he preaches to the guru and his tribesmen, he literally "binds them with his language" (*pāṭaiyil piṇittu*) and wins them over (line 70).

Cātuvaṉ's impact upon the Nākas can be gauged from their leader's response to his preaching. Since the text refers explicitly to this leader as the guru, a spiritual preceptor, one can infer that until Cātuvaṉ's arrival, the islanders viewed him as their ultimate source of knowledge. At first the guru reacts with anger at Cātuvaṉ's new explanation of life's goals, but gradually he becomes convinced of their validity. Both Cātuvaṉ's wider range of knowledge and his convincing interpretive framework for analyzing experience persuade the guru to change his mind. As a gesture of submission to his superior spiritual mentor, the Nāka guru then falls at the merchant's feet.

Cātuvaṉ's flawless linguistic facility and grasp of the ethical implications of various actions contrast vividly with the parochialism and lack of sophistication of his audience. The language Cāttaṉār uses to describe the Nākas throughout the story indicates that they should be perceived as "savage" because of their lack of the standard accoutrements of society, their impure food habits, and their profound moral ignorance.[13] Wandering naked over the island, they remorselessly hunt and eat animals as well as shipwrecked human beings.

Even the most respected Nāka, the guru, lives in a squalid dwelling permeated by the stench from rotting carcasses. The text's graphic description of the toddy and bones lying about implies that such things should be considered repulsive. Because the guru consumes impure food, Cāttaṉār labels him "low," in the sense of low or impure status. He also describes the Nākas as "people without love" and "people of cruel work."

The guru's inability to conceive of goals in life other than the pleasures of sex, food, and drink is considered an indication of his stunted moral development. For this reason, Cāttaṉār compares the Nāka leader and his woman to a bear and his mate (lines 68-69).

Since the Nākas are so ignorant, Cāttaṉār uses simple arguments based upon their own limited experience in order to persuade them to give up their cruel ways. His basic line of reasoning focuses upon the inevitability of retribution for evil deeds in the next life. When the Nāka guru expresses doubt about the postulated existence of rebirth, Cātuvaṉ explains it in greater detail. He eschews technical language, phrasing his discourse entirely in terms understandable to the Nākas and in comparisons readily familiar to them (such as waking and sleeping, cutting up a dead body, and dreaming).

Cātuvaṉ's specific preaching about the nature of the body and karmic retribution, however, comprises only one section of a larger rhetorical pattern within the branch story. This larger rhetorical strategy consists of initially setting up uncompromising injunctions, but eventually specifying more realistic behavioral laws to set moral goals for the particular audience he addresses. In a sense, the interaction between Cātuvaṉ and the Nākas takes the form of a series of negotiations about how much "virtue" the tribesmen can actually accomplish.

Initially, Cātuvaṉ's condemnation focuses upon eating flesh, drinking liquor, and indulging in sexual pleasure. The guru's behavior horrifies Cātuvaṉ because he sees the great leader intoxicated with these pleasures. When offered meat, toddy, and a woman, the merchant grows faint with revulsion. The guru, however, claims that life is not worth living without them.

Cātuvaṉ then narrows the focus of his censure to drinking liquor and eating flesh. He warns the guru that unconfused people shy away from consuming toddy and meat. The guru again protests, claiming that without even these two, he could not go on living. Then he entreats Cātuvaṉ to propose a realistic set of moral injunctions that will be possible for them to follow.

Cātuvaṉ finally realizes the implications of the limited sources of food available on the island and modifies his original program greatly. He declares that abstaining from all meat, except that obtained from animals who died of old age, will suffice to guarantee that the Nākas are living virtuously.[14] Cātuvaṉ's ever-shrinking set of expectations for moral rectitude are set out in Table 3.

Table 3: An Analysis of the Negotiations between Cātuvaṉ and the Nākas

Lines	Incidents	Sexual Enjoyment	Toddy Drinking	Meat Eating
68-69	Guru disparaged for practicing:	X	X	X
76-77	Guru offers to Cātuvaṉ:	X	X	X
80-81	Guru asserts as aims in life:	X	X	X
84-85	Cātuvaṉ argues that unconfused people reject:		X	X
108-9	Guru counters that he could not live without:		X	X
114-15	Cātuvaṉ determines the path appropriate for the Nākas, which prohibits only:			X, if killing is involved

In this story, Cātuvaṉ effectively preaches noninjury (*ahiṃsā*) to a group of people who were performing the most extreme form of injury (*hiṃsā*) possible. These islanders have practiced cannibalism, freely murdering and consuming the human beings who washed ashore after shipwreck. But eventually they come to agree upon a more demanding moral code. The Nākas agree to eat only the meat of animals that they do not kill. This compromise — to refrain from killing living beings — does not include all the major proscriptions listed in Buddhist texts, but it does eliminate the most shocking way in which the Nākas were transgressing those moral laws, by killing and eating human beings and by intentionally killing animals.

The Dramatized Audience as a Rhetorical Strategy

The story of "Cātuvaṉ and the Nākas" conveys a broader message as well — that Buddhism is a suitable religious option for *Maṇimēkalai*'s readers. Through his portrayal of Cātuvaṉ's preaching, Cāttaṉār implies that Buddhism is accessible to all because its preachers provide moral codes appropriate for the lives of their listeners. Cāttaṉār makes this point through his use of a dramatized audience.

The response of a dramatized audience in a branch story to a particular idea shows the text's readers what their own reactions to a particular Buddhist idea should be. The branch story explores the implications of an idea, allowing its listeners to see how individuals in particular circumstances actually embrace that idea. Branch stories in *Maṇimēkalai* provide small-scale "preaching events," which explore the practical implications of doctrines *in situ*. A dramatized audience gives the readers cues about how to understand what the preacher in the story relates. In the story of Cātuvaṉ and the Nākas translated above, the response of the Nākas to Cātuvaṉ's preaching demonstrates how one should react to the story. Cāttaṉār's integration of biographical details, mythical material, and syntactical devices encourages his reader to identify with the audiences portrayed within the text.

The Preacher

Just as Cāttaṉār's intended audience (like any audience of people not yet converted to Buddhism) exists in a state of attachment to worldly desires, the preacher Cātuvaṉ, too, was ruled by such attachments earlier in his life. In fact, the short and selected biography of Cātuvaṉ provided in the text (lines 3-12) emphasizes his earlier decline into immorality. Although married to a virtuous woman, he neglects her in order to spend time with a courtesan. When even the sources of his wealth are depleted, his mistress loses all interest in him. According to tradition, a courtesan should abandon an impoverished client.[15] This Cātuvaṉ's mistress does, throwing his poverty in his face.

The specific theme of a man who bankrupts his family through attraction to a prostitute appears throughout Indian literature, in instances too numerous to mention. Of particular relevance, however, is its presence in *Cilappatikāram*, the text closest to *Maṇimēkalai* in date and genre. There Kōvalaṉ (Maṇimēkalai's father) abandons his wife for a dancing girl (Maṇimēkalai's mother), loses all his money, and must leave home in an attempt to regain his fortune.

Besides being a common Tamil theme, the "dissipation of a good man" motif in the story of a religious saint or preacher serves a rhetorical purpose. In structure, the saint's formerly dissolute state contrasts vividly with his later commitment to preaching. In religious biography, the "scoundrel then saint" pattern[16] serves to emphasize the magnitude of the transformation involved.

This pattern occurs in many South Indian religious biographies. For example, Ramanujan points out a pattern of stages found in the biographies of many of the saints he has studied. The stages include a life of pleasure followed by abasement, loss, and awakening. After a religious conversion or initiation, the saint then goes on to convert or defeat in debate men committed to other religions.[17] Although *Maṇimēkalai* does not mention Cātuvaṉ's own conversion per se, he does end a life of pleasure and become a preacher to the Nākas. The profligacy of his past life testifies to the strength of his present religious commitment. It adds authority to his preaching about what constitutes good and evil behavior since he has disdained moral action in the past and now is committed to the path of goodness.

The Audience

Cāttaṉār's choice of the term "Nāka" to describe Cātuvaṉ's audience indicates a great deal about what kind of audience it was. In many South and Southeast Asian texts, the term "Nāka" (Sanskrit Nāga) is strongly associated with societies that lack sophistication and knowledge. A quick survey of mythological texts roughly contemporary with *Maṇimēkalai* reveals that the word "Nāga" often denotes half-snake/half-human beings or snakes whose social order bears strong resemblances to human society. For example, in the *Mahābhārata*, the events that lead to Janamejaya's snake sacrifice describe how the Nāgas possess an ophidian social order, complete with kinship ties and status hierarchy.[18] Other texts go further, assuming an entire Nāga *loka*, or "world." For instance, the *Bhūridatta Jātaka* portrays such a world, complete with kings, messengers, palaces, and kinship relations modeled upon human ones.[19] Nāgas, in this first set of representative examples, are lower than human beings but they possess certain human characteristics.

In a second set of texts, Nāgas are humans beyond the pale of Indian civilization and thus considered very low, close to animals.[20] This second set of associations for Nāgas, which receives some of its mythological momentum from the first set, predominates in certain Southeast Asian origin stories.[21] An example of such a conception of Nāgas, specifically as those without the benefit of Indian culture, exists in a myth referred to in various documents dealing with the origins of Funan, a Southeast Asian kingdom. A Sanskrit inscription referring to the myth identified the queen of Funan as a daughter of the king of the Nāgas. It further describes Kauṇḍinya, the foreigner who conquers her, as an Indian brahmin.[22] By piecing together fragments from Chinese sources, we learn how Kauṇḍinya arrives from a foreign land and is immediately attacked by the Funan queen. After he subdues her, she becomes his wife.[23] But her new husband makes certain changes in her dress. According to Coedès, ". . . unhappy to see her naked, he folded a piece of material to make a garment through which he had to pass her head."[24] In the Cātuvaṉ story, Nākas are also held in contempt for their nakedness.

Cāttaṉār's use of the term "Nāka," as the name for the tribesmen to whom Cātuvaṉ preaches, reinforces the impression — given to his audience and evident in the branch story itself — that these naked wanderers are animal-like and "uncivilized." In both of the contexts identified above, the term Nāga connotes a being whose nature lies somewhere between human and serpentine.[25] The snake Nāgas have animal (or half-animal) bodies but still participate in some kind of rudimentary society organized along human lines. The Cambodian Nāgas lack clothing and sophistication, as do beasts, yet they possess human shapes. Thus, because Cāttaṉār chose to portray Nākas as the recipient of Cātuvaṉ's message, Cāttaṉār's historical audience can perceive a suggestion that civilized behavior is defined, at least partially, by the practice of Buddhist ideals such as *ahiṃsā.*

The Message

Cāttaṉār structures Cātuvaṉ's preaching on the subject of actions and their fruits — which lies at the heart of the story — so as to point out to the reader the most important formulations, junctures, and emphases of his preaching. The structure of his speech and the choice of words suggests that Cāttaṉār employed particular rhetorical devices designed to lead his audience carefully through the arguments being made. There mechanisms serve to hold the audience's attention, make explicit the connections among steps in complex arguments, and highlight the implications of the argument along the way. Although such devices form part of any Tamil author's tools of the trade, the presence of so many of them within the space of a twenty-five line passage is unusual.

Cāttaṉār's use of repetition indicates the direction of his argument in his lengthy discourse. For example, in lines 80-83, the guru begins by asking Cātuvaṉ, ". . . what is there (*uṇṭu*) for people to live for beside women and refreshment? If there is (*uṇṭu*) . . . say (*col*) what it is. . . ." In the next line Cāttaṉār repeats the verbs *uṇṭu* [to be] and *col* [to say], indicating that the discourse to follow will ultimately answer the guru's question about what one ought and ought not to do. Since the speaker necessarily explores many other issues first in order to answer the question, the repetition of these words helps the hearer perceive the overall direction of the discussion to come.

The Nāka leader often acts as a mediator between Cātuvaṉ and his two audiences — the Nāka listeners as well as the historical audience reading *Maṇimēkalai*. For example, in lines 92-95, the guru interrupts Cātuvaṉ, sums up his perception of what was said, and then asks for further clarification. The guru says, "You just told us that the life-breath runs away from the body, takes on another form, and enters a different place. Tell us clearly how. . . ."

Use of an emphatic marker also helps the hearer follow the preacher's logical progression. Lines 96-97 provide an example of this device: "While the life-breath resides in the body, the body knows what is happening. But when the life-breath leaves, that very same body (*uṭampē—uṭampu*, "body," plus emphatic *ē*) doesn't realize what is happening to it. . . ." Such emphatic repetition clarifies the argument as well as stresses it.

Cāttaṉār achieves a similar effect through the use of demonstrative prefixes. In Tamil, an "a" prefixed to a noun "x" makes it "that x"; an "i" so affixed makes it "this x." One finds an example of the "a" demonstrative in line 94: "Tell us clearly how that life-breath (*a[vv]uyir*) can go and enter another place that way (*a[v]vakai*)." This usage serves to summarize as well as stress what has just been said and to urge the merchant to explain more about the topic. Several other examples of these "a" or "i" demonstratives used to stress points and direct one's attention can be found within Cātuvaṉ's short discourse (lines 104-105, 118).

Cāttaṉār's use of another rhetorical device, antithetical parallel construction, ensures that his audience will comprehend two possible and mutually exclusive options. A literal translation of lines 88-89 indicates the parallelism of the lines:

nallaṟam	*ceyvōr*	*nalla*	*ulaku*	*aṭaital*
good virtue	those who do,	good	worlds	attaining
allaṟam	*ceyvōr*	*aṟu*	*naraku*	*aṭaital*
nonvirtue	those who do,	terrible	hells	attaining

The Tamil and English here indicate the almost exact semantic and syntactic symmetry used to describe the results of good acts and those of bad acts. The same technique is found in lines 86-87. Such symmetry serves to emphasize the rigidly dichotomous nature of the system of moral retribution under discussion.

Finally, the passage contains numerous commands that draw the reader's attention to particular points: "Listen" (line 85), "Understand this" (91), "Listen" (94), "Realize this" (99), and "Understand clearly" (105). These commands punctuate the text, marking the culminating point of each argument within the discourse.

The significance of these small-scale rhetorical techniques lies in the frequency of occurrence. Although each might be of little consequence in and of itself, the presence of carefully structured repetition, emphatic markers, demonstratives, antithetical parallel construction, and "guiding" imperatives within a very short passage indicates the care with which Cāttaṉār constructed this short discourse. These rhetorical devices help to make Cātuvaṉ's preaching readily understandable not only to the Nākas but to *Maṇimēkalai*'s audience as well.[26]

Conclusions

Although folklorists deal with framed or branching narrative in much of their research, not enough has been written about the actual manner in which a branch story functions. Folklorists refer to branch stories as "framed stories." One of the few explicit definitions of framed stories available, given by Maria Leach, describes them in this way:

> a story forming a frame in which stories are told; a narrative permitting the introduction of several (often many) other stories, unrelated to and having no effect on the frame story itself. The technique is to give a group of unrelated tales an overall unity and dramatic meaning by making them part of a common situation.[27]

This definition assumes that the distinguishing function of a frame story is to relate a series of stories to the main story. According to such a definition, framing is a technique that draws a group of stories together. Such stories are not related to and have no effect upon the frame story itself, according to the definition quoted above. A good example of this type of frame story is *Arabian Nights*. The text contains a framing narrative and a series of framed narratives. The framed stories do not necessarily relate to each other nor do they bear a special relationship to the exact point at which they are introduced in the framing narrative. For example, Scheherazade could have as easily told Story Y first and X second as the other way around. The order of the framed stories can, thus, be altered without much effect upon the overall text. Additional stories could have been included or included stories could have been omitted, again without much effect upon the overall text. In such a text, framing can be labeled "a technique for inclusion."

In a text such as *Maṇimēkalai*, however, frame stories play a much greater role in advancing the overall goals of the text than Leach's definition implies. Ramanujan suggests that we stop treating Indian texts like "ragbag encyclopedias" and start attending to their overall coherence. Ramanujan's suggestion moves away from the definition of frame stories provided by Leach and toward an implied definition of frame and framing narrative used recently by certain literary critics of English texts who have turned their attention to analyzing the variety of literary, hortatory, and rhetorical uses to which framed and framing stories have been put.[28]

Humma, in his analysis of Scott's *Old Morality*, rejects the claim that the framing structure introduces superfluous material. After a careful examination, he concludes,

> But what is important in these matters is that our attention to them leads us to the overdue recognition that the prolegomena and conclusion [the framing structure] of *Old Morality* are not, as is frequently charged, extraneous and distracting but that instead they stand in essential relation to the novel as a whole.[29]

"Cātuvaṉ and the Nākas" also stands in essential relation to the text as a whole. The story contributes directly to *Maṇimēkalai* by providing the background of two of its most generous donors, Cātuvaṉ and his wife. In addition, the story shows how a specific Buddhist virtue, *ahiṃsā*, came to be practiced. The story, thus, provides a chance to witness commitment to Buddhist ideals.

Glancy has explored Dickens's fascination with frame stories and his attempts to use them as a vehicle for moral exhortation. Dickens's early enchantment with *Arabian Nights* developed into a strong interest in a form that created a special relationship between the story and its teller.[30] Over time Dickens experimented with several different frame stories, exploring their potential as a means for moral exposition:

> He [Dickens] never ceased to hanker after frame tales, to see them as vital imaginative and moral expressions made possible through the relationship of narrator and listener, writer and reader.[31]

Cātuvaṉ's preaching explains the nature of rebirth, the workings of karma, and the fate of sinners after death. The story, thus, provides the reader with an opportunity to hear moral exposition, explaining the nature of action and its consequences.

In his examination of *The Turn of the Screw,* Goetz interprets the frame as a narrative that instructs the reader about how to understand the tale that follows.

> I would like to propose a different use for the 'frame,' and consider it not so much as an informative background to the principal narrative but as an exemplary scene by means of which James tells us how to read his tale. In this light, these opening pages of the text can be regarded as establishing a protocol for reading.[32]

Frame stories establish "a protocol for reading" in a number of different ways. Because Cāttaṉār's narrative includes a dramatized audience, the portrayal of that audience can give the reader cues about how to interpret the story. The reader is guided in his interpretation by particular rhetorical devices that Cāttaṉār employs. He uses the guru as a mediator who summarizes or clarifies certain points and then voices the objections that might logically come to mind so that Cātuvaṉ can refute them. In addition, the very syntactic and semantic choices Cāttaṉār makes in Cātuvaṉ's preaching to the Nākas establishes a protocol for reading, guiding the reader through the religious discourse and emphasizing key points.

4

Tamil Literary Conventions and Life's Impermanence

Of all the branch stories in *Maṇimēkalai*, "The Story of the Cosmic Place" best demonstrates Cāttaṉār's rhetorical skills. In it, Cāttaṉār introduces new ideas to his audience but phrases them in familiar language. By doing so, he simultaneously demonstrates the literary potential of classical Tamil poetic conventions and mounts a scathing attack on classical Tamil attitudes toward war and love.

Maṇimēkalai hears "The Story of the Cosmic Place" at a time when she is particularly receptive to its message. Because she has narrowly escaped being abducted by the prince, she fears to walk home late at night. Then, the goddess Maṇimēkalā arrives to suggest that the two girls spend the night at a nearby cremation ground, where great ascetics do penance. The name "Cosmic Place" (*Cakkaravāḷakkōṭṭam*) arouses the girls' curiosity. Then the goddess tells the story of the name's origin, a story emphasizing the absurdity of sexual love in light of life's impermanence. Since Maṇimēkalai feels troubled about her attraction toward the prince and desires to embrace a life of renunciation, the message of the story addresses her present concerns. In fact, when the goddess completes her account, Cāttaṉār remarks that Maṇimēkalai now understands the [impermanent] nature of living creatures, indicating the effect of the story on her thinking.

"The Story of the Cosmic Place" has three sections. It begins with an extensive, precise, and detailed description of a cremation ground. Next follows an account of a young boy's death and its aftermath. Cāttaṉār ends the story by explaining the composition of the cosmos, enumerating both the inhabitants and the geographical features of the universe. Each of these three sections (the last of which is analyzed in the next chapter of this monograph) has its place in the overall argument of the story translated below.[1]

Translation: "The Story of the Cosmic Place"

Introduction

"Beautiful, fair-skinned, and gentle goddess! All the people who live in this vast city call that place 'The Cremation Ground.' Only you and the cunning demigod Mārutavēkaṉ[2] call it 'The Cosmic Place,'[3] a name whose meaning I do not understand. Pre-eminent one, why do you call it by that name?" asked Cutamati.

The goddess with jewelry appropriate to her answered, "I will explain the reason so you will know. You and Maṇimēkalai listen, even if it takes until midnight":

The Description of the Cremation Ground

The cremation ground, with its pyres, lies next to this garden. It has existed since the time this awesome city arose. Through one of its splendidly flagged gates, the gods enter. On that gate is painted a celestial chariot. Another gate, resplendent and beautifully painted, depicts rice, sugarcane, water, and gardens. On another gate stands a tower covered with shining white lime, but nothing is painted on it. On the last gate looms an angry terra-cotta image with clenched lips, holding a trident and a noose.[4]

Within that unique cremation ground, haunted by demons and surrounded by a guarded fortress wall divided with these four clearly marked, towering gates, are the huge grounds of the goddess who dwells in uninhabited land [Kālī]. In its courtyard rises a pedestal on which great offerings are placed. Surrounding the grounds are tall trees, bent with the weight of heads of warriors who bravely discharged their debts with the payment of their lives.

Throughout the cremation ground, death memorials of burnt clay rise like high and low hills. The good people who built these memorials placed them in different sections according to the divisions of the four *varṇas,* which categorize even extreme ascetics, kings, and women who died along with their husbands.

There are also faultlessly constructed offering posts of powerful gods; raised stone platforms; circles where many paths intersect; huts where guards eat, sleep, and dwell while keeping their sticks and eating bowls near them; flags of smoke; festoons of flame; and sheds sheltering the pyres.[5]

These sights spread in all directions.

Here and there, some people burn corpses; others just abandon them. Some dig graves; others inter bodies in caverns or cover them with wide-mouthed urns.

Day and night the tumult of these people entering and leaving continues, but their disgust ensures that none remain long. The noise of the funeral drum, which makes the heart tremble, proclaims to those who are left, "There will be a pyre for you as well."[6] The death of ascetics calls forth the sound of worship, but the other dead receive only the wails of mourning. The long-faced jackal howls evilly, while the cry of the horned owl summons people to their death. The flesh-eating hoot owl screeches, and the man's-head bird, who seizes and devours heads of corpses, sounds his cry.[7] These noises continue ceaselessly, like the harsh roar of high ocean waters.

Tāṉṟi, oṭuvai, and *uḻiñcil* trees grow tall. *Kāṉṟi, cūrai,* and *kaḷḷi* bushes spread densely over the ground. Hosts of cruel ravenous ghouls gather beneath the *vākai* tree, on whose wide branches clouds settle. Birds rest beneath the *veḷḷil* tree, giddily consuming pallid fat and flesh. Those who vow to live in the cremation ground cook, unperturbed, beneath the *vaṉṉi* tree. Those with vows to mortify their bodies collect broken skulls and join them into long garlands beneath the *iratti* trees.[8] Out in the open, people who dine on corpses serve their guests from pots reeking with human fat.

Fire pots, funeral bowls, unadorned biers, cloth bundles with ritual implements, discarded garlands, smashed earthenware pots, unhusked rice, puffed rice, and small riceball offerings are scattered about.[9]

These desolate sights spread in all directions.

Heedless whether they be ascetics or wealthy people, women with newborn infants or children unable to bear sorrow, old people or young people, The Cruel Worker [Yama, the god of death] goes about killing and heaping up corpses. Even though they see the cremation ground consuming pyres with its fiery mouth, some people are still intoxicated with immense wealth and pleasure. Of all the people who exist, are any more ignorant than those who live thus, without desiring to perform most excellent *aṟam*?[10]

A boy named Cārṅkalaṉ went inside the Cosmic Place (*cakkaravāḷam*) all alone, thinking it was a well-fortified city. Instead he met with sounds proclaiming to people who love the body that it is only flesh, blood, and bones: there was the ceaseless, exultant howl of a jackal clutching in his jaws a corpse's foot decorated with red cosmetic cream, a lump of wormy decaying flesh. Then he heard the drawn-out shriek of a vulture piercing and consuming a naked mound-of-venus, the unrestrained howl of an evil dog who had snatched and torn apart a severed arm stacked with bangles, and the crunch of the hungry kite seizing and eating beautiful, erect, young breasts adorned with sandal paste.

These sounds served as the beats of a *muḻavam* drum played on a stage created out of white ashes from once-lovely bodies. A female ghoul gleefully mounted onto that stage and grabbed a charred head.

She did not ask herself, "What are these: clouds or woman's tresses? Carp or eyes? Is this a *kumiḻ* flower or a nose? Are these lips or *kavir* flowers? Teeth or pearls?" She did not show any mercy. [Instead], dancing with joy on her cloven feet, she gouged out the eyes of that head and ate them with insatiable glee.

Cāṅkalaṉ's Death and Its Aftermath

When Cāṅkalaṉ saw her, he was seized with fear. In great anguish he ran away screaming. Falling before his mother he cried, "Look mother, I gave my life to a cruel old ghoul in the cremation ground!" and laid his body down.[11]

"Was it a demoness or a ghoul[12] who ate the dear life of my son without even considering that he was the only son of a hapless woman, the lonely blind wife of a blind brahmin?" the mother asked herself.

That woman, whose name was Kōtamai, went to the gate just outside the fortress wall of the cremation ground and proclaimed her cruel suffering. Holding the body of her son to her breast, she said, "Campāpati, you protect the waterfront, gathering places, strong old trees, residences, and grounds. But you did not protect my son, did you? Are you incompetent?"

Campāpati, shining like gold, appeared and asked, "You called me here at midnight because you suffered cruelly at the gate that ghouls haunt. Tell me, what happened to you?"

Kōtamai answered, "My only child, an innocent boy, came to this cremation ground. Was it a demoness or a ghoul who ate his dear life? Look, he lies here as if he were only sleeping."

The goddess replied, "Neither a demoness nor a ghoul eats precious lives. Ripened deeds, buttressed by ignorance, ate the life of your son across whose chest lie the entwined threads.[13] Stop your terrible grieving."

Kōtamai asked, "Gracious deity, if you take my life and give him back his life, he can protect and support my blind husband. So, give back his life and take mine."

When she heard that, venerable Campāpati felt pity and replied, "If the precious life-breath leaves the body, it will obtain another birth on a path appropriate to the deeds it did. There is no doubt about that, is there? You want me to bring your son back to life to end your extreme distress, but I cannot do that. Do not grieve.

"As for my taking your life, I cannot. People who perform cruel works say that killing is doing *aṟam,*[14] but that is a sad and deceitful statement, ignorant woman.

"And, as for exchanging lives, are there not always people who would give their lives for the kings of the land? And yet, in this cremation ground, memorials have been erected by the thousands for such kings. So, stop speaking words that lead to hell."

Kōtamai continued, "You are a very great deity, and the Four Vedas, the good books of the brahmins, all say that divine beings give boons. If you will not favor me with this boon, I do not want to live."

The goddess informed her, "If the Primordial Lord were to give back your son's life, or those who wander inside the urn of the sphere[15] would give back his life, I would too, ignorant woman! So let my powers show you that right now."

The Cosmological Account

Then out of the entire cosmos — which contains the four traditional types of formless *brahmas,* the sixteen types of *brahmas* with form, the two types of luminaries [sun and moon], the six types of gods who have attained great beauty, demons of many kinds, the eight types of denizens of hell who suffer great misery, the assembly of stars that move through the vast sky, asterisms, and planets — the goddess Campāpati made those capable of giving boons come and stand before her.

"This woman has suffered greatly," she said. "End her grief." But Kōtamai heard those gods from all parts of the cosmos answer in the very same way that Campāpati had. So she abandoned her wretched sorrow, put her son on a pyre in the cremation ground, and left.

Then you see, the great Mayaṉ[16] created this "Cosmic Place" in the spot where the divine beings from all parts of the cosmos had gathered to demonstrate Campāpati's power. Following the prescriptive texts, he fashioned from beautiful terra cotta the creatures who live there and the places where they live. In order to inform people properly, this "Cosmic Place" shows each [of the following] in its proper place: Mount Meru standing at the center of the Cakkara Mountains, surrounded by the seven types of mountain ranges that rise around it, the encircling oceans, the four islands described by tradition, two thousand islands, and other features.[17]

Conclusion and Explanation

"Since the Cosmic Place is just outside the fortress wall of the ground where corpses are placed, people just call it the 'Cremation Ground.' This is the history of it," said the great goddess.

In the deep darkness of the middle watch of the night Maṇimēkalai, sorrowful and drained, commented on the nature of those who are born.

Classical Tamil Poetry and the Transience of Life

Throughout *Maṇimēkalai,* Cāttaṉār incorporates elements from Tamil classical (*Caṅkam*) tradition when they help to advance his overall didactic goals. Chapter two of this monograph demonstrates how Cāttaṉār manipulates the classical *akam* scenario for lovers' union in order to explain and advocate female renunciation. In "The Story of the Cosmic Place," Cāttaṉār incorporates elements of both *akam* and *puṟam* poetry in order to explain life's impermanence. *Akam* poems deal with the inner, intimate world of lovers' union and separation. In contrast, *puṟam* poems concern the outer or public realm, especially war, life at the king's court, judgment of men's actions, and praise. Use of classical *akam* and *puṟam* elements enables Cāttaṉār to present Buddhist ideas to his audience in ways that are both familiar and convincing.

In "The Story of the Cosmic Place," the material resembling that contained in classical *kāñci* poetry would have been most familiar to members of Cāttaṉār's sixth-century audience. *Kāñci* is a theme found in collections of *puṟam* poetry. Because certain types of *kāñci* poems concern the transience of life, some sentiments expressed in them closely resemble the message that Cāttaṉār seeks to convey in "The Story of the Cosmic Place."

Only certains kinds of *kāñci* poems deal with the themes explored in Cāttaṉār's "The Story of the Cosmic Place." As part of their analysis of *puṟam* literature, traditional Tamil commentators formulated a list of the major topics treated in *kāñci* poetry. These topics fall into two categories: those dealing with the human struggle to excel and those concerning the transience of human life. Since Cāttaṉār seeks to explain the Buddhist doctrine of *anicca* [impermanence], "The Story of the Cosmic Place" has affinities with *Caṅkam* poems concerning the transience of human life. A selected list of themes from those classical Tamil poems indicates their range of subject matter:

1. the great saying that Kūṟṟam [Yama], god of death, cannot be dissuaded from his tasks

2. pity for a man who died in battle and a description of his virtues

3. the piteous sight of wives who weep to exhaustion at the death of their husbands

4. the bitter weeping of the lonely wife who lost her husband in the desert

5. the great sorrow of friends and relatives of the dead

6. praise of the cremation ground, where the nature of the wide world is clearly illustrated by the many who have died while the cremation ground survives them all[18]

The theme most relevant to Cāttaṉār's story is the last one: praise of the cremation ground. In Cāttaṉār's story as well, the cremation ground bears witness to the impermanence of life.

Both certain *kāñci* poems and Cāttaṉār's story proclaim the inevitability of death. Consider, for example, the similarities in the theme between "The Story of the Cosmic Place" and the following *kāñci* poem by Kataiyaṅkaṇṇaṉār, categorized by commentators as "praise of the cremation ground":

The jungle spreads.
Cactuses grow.
Owls hoot even by day.
And haunted by she-demons
gaping in the light of crematory fires,
this ancient smoking cremation ground
looks fearful.
Lovers' tears
wept from the heart
quench the burning white
ash and bones.

This ground,
it is the end
of everyone in the world,
looks upon the backs of all men,
and hasn't seen anyone yet
who will look upon *its* back.[19]

This poem about the impermanence of human life argues that, ultimately, no one can escape the fearful cremation ground. It conquers all men — even the greatest warriors. In ancient battles, a brave Tamil fighter always meets his opponents head-on. "To look upon someone's back" means to see someone flee from a fight because he lacks courage. The poem, however, proclaims that all men lack courage in the face of death. Its last line notes that no man has seen the cremation ground's back, indicating that human beings can never send death fleeing. Cāttaṉār's "The Story of the Cosmic Place" echoes the theme expressed in this *kāñci* poem.

The careful reader also notices that Cāttaṉār and the author of this *kāñci* poem, Kataiyaṅkaṇṇaṉār, have included the same descriptive elements in their writing: hooting owls, female ghouls, crematory smoke and fire, bones, and ashes from cremated bodies. Several other notable *kāñci* poems from *Puṟanāṉūṟu* are built out of the sights of the cremation ground. *Puṟ.* 359 features owls, corpse-eating jackals, female ghouls, the stink of fatty flesh, and the light of the funeral pyres. Similarly, *Puṟ.* 360 and 363 describe funeral biers and mention the *kaḷḷi* plant. *Puṟ.* 238 also presents stereotyped sights of the cremation ground in its opening lines.[20] Cāttaṉār's account of the burning ground shares all of these elements.

Cāttaṉār and Kataiyaṅkaṇṇaṉār both use a particular kind of rhetorical strategy, as well as the same theme and crematory sights. Each author first describes a tableau to help the reader envision the horrible cremation grounds in graphic detail and then proceeds to take that vision as evidence that the reader must accept some religious truth or adopt some specified type of behavior. Kataiyaṅkaṇṇaṉār confronts his readers with a catalogue of fearful sights: the female demons, the consuming flames, the owl's terrifying cry, and the thorny forbidding cactus plant. Since those sights bear witness that no human being can ever defeat the cremation ground, the poet's rhetorical strategy leads the reader from a specific sight to a moral truth.

Another *kāñci* poem, by Antuvaṅkīraṉai Kāviṭṭaṉār, demonstrates this pattern of "tableau, then moral teaching" even more clearly than the previous poem. A glance at that poem (see below) reveals this pattern. Line 12 marks the transition between tableau and moral advice. Antuvaṅkīraṉai Kāviṭṭaṉār's catalogue of the inhabitants and sounds of the cremation grounds provides the reader with a graphic re-creation of that site of bodily decomposition and horror (lines 1-12). The ghastly vision then becomes the impetus for the poet's exhortation about generosity (lines 13-end).[21]

Cruel-mouthed owls,
sounding their different cries,
sit among the thorns
in that ruined exhausted land.

Low-slung jackals eat corpses,
their teeth glistening with fat.

Female ghouls,
who stink from eating pallid flesh,
clasp dead bodies.
Dancing on the brackish soil,
they flee the light
of funeral pyres.

Even men who conquer kingdoms
go to these cremation grounds.
The coming of that day
will be the same for you.

Blame endures.
Honor endures also.

So banish blame,
seek honor,
and speak dispassionately
to your suppliants.

If you tell them freely,
        "Take my towering chariots,
        dazzling with ornaments
        and my caparisoned horses.
        Take my herds of elephants
        with tusks like the crescent moon!"
then, even after you go there,
the fame you earned here
will shine a long time.[22]

Cāttaṉār's description in "The Story of the Cosmic Place" possesses this same "tableau, then moral teaching" structure. He begins by mapping the physical layout and setting out the inanimate objects we see upon entering the death grounds (lines 39-67). He adds an auditory dimension to our vision by relating the forbidding sounds heard within the four walls (68-79). He then landscapes the space before us by enumerating its trees and shrubs, specifying the ghastly events that occur beneath them (80-91). His description culminates with a catalogue of items used in funeral processions and cremations (92-95).

Cāttaṉār leads us from this tableau of desolation to moral advice. The lines immediately after this description make explicit the lesson that must be learned from the sights of the cremation ground:

> Heedless whether they be ascetics or wealthy people, women with newborn infants or children unable to bear sorrow, old people or young people, The Cruel Worker [Yama] goes about killing and heaping up corpses. Even though they see the cremation ground consuming pyres with its fiery mouth, some people are still intoxicated with immense wealth and pleasure. Of all the people who exist, are any more ignorant than those who live thus, without desiring to perform most excellent *aṟam*?

Like *Caṅkam* poets writing of the transience of life, Cāttaṉār, too, calls forth a tableau filled with sights from the cremation ground to encourage his readers to accept his moral instruction. In this case, he enjoins them to abandon the pursuit of wealth and pleasure in order to perform *aṟam*, "religious duty."[23]

The Desert Landscape in Classical Tamil Tradition

The *puṟam* elements that Cāttaṉār uses are immediately apparent, but the *akam* items are more subtly integrated into "The Story of the Cosmic Place." Those elements evoke the landscape of lovers' separation (*pālai*), allowing Cāttaṉār to exploit the associations this landscape calls to mind for his audience. Such associations create the proper mood for the discourse at the heart of his story.

Native elements, items conventionally associated with a particular *akam* landscape, convey the essence or flavor of the place. In Tamil literary tradition, grammarians label such elements *karupporuḷ*. Ramanujan appropriately translates the term as "native elements" because these items are considered indigenous to, or appropriate for, a given type of landscape.[24] *Karu* denotes "embryo" or "germ," while *poruḷ* means "thing" or "element," so the compound is used to describe elements that function as a kind of kernel or core of a particular landscape.[25] Such items also convey the essence of a given classical Tamil love poem. The presence of particular native elements easily allows a poem's reader to identify the specific landscape in which the poem is set.[26] Through Cāttaṉār's integration of particular native elements into "The Story of the Cosmic Place," he evokes a whole range of themes associated with the *pālai* landscape.

Pālai is translated variously as wasteland, desert, badlands, or arid tract. As we saw in chapter two of this book, each of the five landscapes of Tamil love poetry is conventionally associated with a particular phase of love: poets set lovers' union in *kuṟiñci* [mountain], patient waiting in *mullai* [forest], the husband's visit to the courtesan in *marutam* [countryside], anxious waiting in *neytal* [seashore], and long-term separation in *pālai* [desert]. While *kuṟiñci* deals with lovers' union, the other four act as settings for portrayal of various kinds of separation that lovers experience.[27] Poems set in the *pālai* landscape, however, portray a very specific type of separation.

Both Cāttaṉār and the classical Tamil poets who wrote *pālai* poems portray a type of separation that is long term and impersonal in source. In the *pālai* landscape, the hero undertakes a journey for reasons unrelated to his relationship with his beloved. Therefore, the long-term suffering of the *pālai* landscape does not resemble the short-term discomfort experienced in the forest (*mullai*), where the wife waits patiently for her husband, or at the seashore (*neytal*), where the heroine's waiting has an anxious quality. The separation in *pālai* also differs from that experienced by lovers in the cultivated lands (*marutam*), where the husband feels temporarily alienated from his wife, spends his time with courtesans, and arrives home to a sulking wife. While these other three situations deal with temporary separation arising out of lovers' intimacy, the extended separation caused by the hero's trek through the *pālai* tract has its source in outside demands beyond one's control — the desire for wealth, the need for education, or the call to act as an emissary for the king.[28] Cāttaṉār's creativity expresses itself in his ability to see the potential of *pālai* as a setting for his discussion of impermanence.

A brief look at a classical *pālai* poem will help acquaint the modern reader with the tradition of *pālai* literature, upon which Cāttaṉār draws for his description of the cremation ground in "The Story of the Cosmic Place." In the poem below, composed by Ōtalāntaiyār, the hero addresses his own heart (a common *Caṅkam* conceit), explaining to it that the memory of his beloved's virtues has accompanied him on his journey across the ghastly desert:[29]

They've come,
crossing even the hot forking desert paths

> where the sharp-toothed red dog of the jungle
> waits by the cactus clump
> to kill a wild pig
> for his mate
> now suffering pangs of labor,

all the way
they've come with you, O heart,

the gentle ways
of the woman you love.[30]

The elements and themes in this *pālai* poem are also found in Cāttaṉār's "The Story of the Cosmic Place."

The native elements Ōtalāntaiyār incorporates into this poem would immediately indicate to his audience that he has composed a *pālai* poem. The wild *cennāy,* translated as "the red dog" by Ramanujan, is a native of the desert tract. *Caṅkam* poets often portray him viciously preying on weaker animals, such as deer and pigs, using his sharp teeth to tear apart their flesh.[31] The *kaḷḷi* plant, which Ramanujan has translated as "cactus," also thrives in the wasteland. Variously translated as cactus, bramble, spurge, or prickly pear, the *kaḷḷi* is identified as *Euphorbia tiroucalli* by botanists. When its seeds ripen, they burst with an uncanny sound.[32] Tamil poets have described the way this eerie sound drives the pigeons away from the branches of the *kaḷḷi*. Such native elements evoke frightening associations appropriate to the desert.

The poem suggests the themes of separation, desolation, and death. The inset description of the wild dog and the pig acts as an image of the hero's situation. Just as the red dog seeks nourishment for its mate in pain, the hero seeks wealth for his wife. First and foremost then, Ōtalāntaiyār portrays the suffering of a man separated from his wife, with only the memory of her virtues to accompany him on his quest for wealth to sustain his family. The poet also emphasizes the desolation of the desert landscape: the wasteland burns with heat, its paths fork in confusing ways, and dangerous animals lurk behind its hostile vegetation. Finally, the wild dog's attack on the pig reminds the reader of the constant threat of death that one feels while passing through the *pālai*.

This classical *pālai* poem illustrates how *pālai* native elements have traditionally been associated with particular kinds of themes. Of all the five classical landscapes, the themes with which *pālai* has been associated are those most appropriate for the kind of message Cāttaṉār wants to convey in "The Story of the Cosmic Place." Cāttaṉār works with these traditional associations of *pālai* but uses them for his own purposes.

The Desert and Cāttaṉār's Cremation Ground

The description of the cremation ground that begins "The Story of the Cosmic Place" plays a crucial role in developing Cāttaṉār's argument about life's impermanence. That description is detailed and lengthy, comprising eighty-nine lines of description (lines 37-126), which make up more than half of the story proper. In addition to its unusual length, the description of the cremation ground appears to be carefully assembled. It contains some seemingly strange items: a goddess surrounded by severed heads hanging in trees, a shrieking vulture, and a clump of plants with branches that rattle in the wind. The modern reader might skim over such items. However, for the ancient Tamil reader familiar with the literary conventions governing the composition of *pālai* poems, these items, and ones like them, evoke graphic associations that create a mood appropriate for Cāttaṉār's discourse on the impermanence of existence.

In Cāttaṉār's description of the cremation ground, he includes many items traditionally associated with the *pālai* landscape (see Table 4). Cāttaṉār does not use these native elements in a mechanical way; their presence does far more than identify the landscape as *pālai*. Each element adds to the force and nuance of Cāttaṉār's argument. Attention to three representative native elements from three different categories[33] indicates some of the ways in which they add to Cāttaṉār's account: the goddess Kālī, the vulture, and the *uḷiñcil* plant.

Upon entering the cremation ground, one immediately moves into the large courtyard of the goddess Kālī:

> Within that unique cremation ground . . . are the huge grounds of the goddess who dwells in uninhabited land (*kāṭu*). In its courtyard rises a pedestal on which great offerings are placed. The grounds are surrounded by tall trees bent with the weight of the heads of warriors who bravely discharged their debts with the payment of their lives. (lines 50-53)

Cāttaṉār designates Kālī by the epithet "the goddess who dwells in the *kāṭu*." *Kāṭu* denotes wild, unsettled, untamed land. According to Tamil literary conventions, Kālī rules over the *pālai* landscape, a barren and uninhabited land.[34] Kālī's associations with death are suitable for poems of the *pālai* landscape, where vicious animals feed on their prey. Kālī also reigns appropriately over a cremation ground, where carrion-eating animals tear corpses to pieces.[35]

Table 4: Elements of the *Pālai* Landscape Found in "The Story of the Cosmic Place"

Element	Line number in chapter six
heads of warriors sacrificed	48-53
the goddess dwelling in uninhabited land (Kālī)	52
jackal	74, 100
hooting owl	75
horned owl	76
āṇṭalai [man's-head bird]	77
uḻiñcil	80
kaḷḷi	81
vākai	82
vulture	112
wild dog	114
kite	117

Both the presence of Kālī's female-ghoul attendants (line 118) and the human heads sacrificed to her accentuate the ghastly nature of the ultimate fate of human beings. In other Tamil texts, Kālī's ghouls (*pēy makaḷir*) act as ladies-in-waiting to the reigning queen Kālī. In Cayaṅkōṇṭar's twelfth-century poem *Kaliṅkattupparaṇi*, for example, two she-ghouls fan Kālī on each side as she sits in regal splendor.[36] In Cāttaṉār's story, the portrayal of just such a ghoul, consuming the life of the innocent young Cārṅkalaṉ, emphasizes the horrifying nature of death. The trunkless heads that Cāttaṉār describes result from warriors' vows to sacrifice their heads to the goddess should they be successful in battle.[37] These sacrifices to Kālī offer the reader a horrific image of death and dismemberment.

Cāttaṉār's use of another native element, the vulture (line 112), confronts the reader with the fact that death always lies in wait — it lurks ready to seize us at any moment. In the *pālai* landscape, Tamil poets portray vultures feeding on the corpses of men ambushed by dacoits (bandits) or killed by fierce desert-dwellers. For example, in a poem by Marutaṉ Iḷanākaṉār, vultures in the *pālai* landscape consume the intestines of men killed in battle with a marauding band:

> Red-eared vultures pick up the intestines of men
> who gave their lives for victory in battle
> and spread them out so one feels dread
> on rock-covered, forking roads.[38]

As the poet points out, the traveler who sees these vultures feeding on human flesh feels fear as he passes through the desert, aware that at any moment he could become the next victim. If vultures are appropriate in the *pālai* landscape, they seem even more appropriate in the cremation ground, where the stock of human bodies upon which they can feed is regularly replenished.

The *pālai* flora that Cāttaṉār mixes into his description serve to underline the final sterility of all human efforts. Plants such as *kaḷḷi, vākai,* and *uḻiñcil* possess a dried-up and foreboding appearance appropriate both to the *pālai* and to a cremation ground. Such plants can survive in the arid tract, while other trees and bushes wither away. Their cactus-like qualities, their sharp thorns and spikes, their ominously rattling pods, and their tiny leaves (which give little shade) reinforce the bleakness of the vista described in "The Story of the Cosmic Place."

The *uḻiñcil* plant, for example, evokes associations that advance Cāttaṉār's overall argument about the transience of human achievement and the inevitability of death. *Caṅkam* poets writing about the desert tract use the *uḻiñcil* plant in their poems because of its particular characteristics. According to the *Tamil Lexicon,* it is "a short tree with golden flowers and small leaves, the withering of which was considered a bad omen as it was believed to foreshadow trouble."[39] In addition, its dried-out seed pods make an eerie sound appropriate to the arid desert, as this poem demonstrates:

> They say the wasteland path he travels
> is full of hills, and
> difficult to cross,
> where the bitter, scorching wind
> beats the branches and rattles
> the dried-out pods of the *uḻiñcil* tree[40]

In such poems, poets sometimes use the barrenness of the desert plant as an image of the separation endured by lover and beloved. It can also stand for the lack of fruitfulness in their marriage during this period.[41] In Cāttaṉār's description of the cremation ground, the ominous empty rattle of the plant's pods becomes emblematic of the ultimately bleak and barren end of human endeavor.

Cāttaṉār succeeds in associating the cremation ground with *pālai* because the two settings are linked conceptually. Tamils use the term *kāṭu* to categorize cremation ground, desert, and a few similar types of geography. *Kāṭu* means unsettled land, a place that humans beings have not mastered. One, therefore, finds texts referring to wild lands (such as jungle, desert, or badlands) as *kāṭu*. *Kāṭu* contrasts sharply with *nāṭu,* the settled land that human beings know and can circumscribe. Thus, one finds authors referring to settlements, provinces, and countries as *nāṭu*. Of all the five classical landscapes, only *pālai* falls into the category of *kāṭu*. The cremation ground also fits the category of *kāṭu* since it lies outside human settlements.

In both *pālai* and cremation ground, human beings cannot control the events that occur. In each place, human beings face death without cultural comforts or illusions. The goddess Kālī, who dwells in the *kāṭu,* reigns appropriately over both desert and burning ground. The vulture feels equally at home among the corpses in the wasteland or the cremation ground. The rattling pods of the *uḻiñcil* signal the end of individual achievement in either setting.

These native elements of *pālai* provide Cāttaṉār with a special vocabulary to set the scene for his discourse on life's impermanence. Because Cāttaṉār can rely on his reader's knowledge of Tamil literary conventions, he can use native elements in evocative and efficient ways to phrase his new ideas in classical language. But ultimately Cāttaṉār does more than clothe Buddhist concepts in familiar language. He pushes his readers to recognize the limits of the worldview informing the five landscapes of love found in classical Tamil poetry. As part of a more radical agenda, he stretches the conventions to their utmost limits, using *pālai* elements to parody the assumptions of the classical love tradition. In this way, he urges the reader to accept a Buddhist interpretation of existence.

Moving Beyond the Classical Tamil View of Love

Cāttaṉār's description of the cremation ground culminates in an account of necrophagy (lines 105-17). The corpse upon which jackal, vulture, dog, and kite feed is not an ordinary corpse. Cāttaṉār's language in this passage indicates that these birds and animals devour the body of a once-lovely young girl, still adorned with pleasing makeup and comely jewelry. Despite her former beauty, the jackal gnaws relentlessly on her foot adorned with red paste, a cosmetic that Tamils think enhances a woman's attractiveness. Although brides wear this red paste as auspicious decoration, Cāttaṉār comments that this lady's foot is "a lump of wormy decaying flesh." Demonstrating the same lack of interest as the jackal in the woman's beauty, the vulture ferociously rips into the woman's mound-of-venus. Classical Tamil poets tenderly celebrate the shapely *mons veneris* in poem after poem of erotic love, but Cāttaṉār's jackal remains indifferent to its charms. In similar fashion, the wild dog tears apart her arm ornamented by bracelets, while the blood-thirsty kite bites into the woman's round breasts, whose erect nipples are decorated with fragrant sandalwood.

In this passage, Cāttaṉār takes descriptions that would be undeniably erotic in a love poem and turns them into repulsive accounts of necrophagy. Each item consumed — the breast, the mound-of-venus, the arm with bangles — is an element found in the accounts that *akam* poets present of a given heroine's beauty. But, as Cāttaṉār clearly proclaims in line 107, no matter how beautiful any human body may be, it is nothing more than "flesh, blood, and bones."

In the bizarre drama (lines 107-21) that follows the account of dismemberment, Cāttaṉār uses theatrical terms in order to make an argument about life's impermanence. In this passage, items necessary for a dramatic performance are easily identifiable. Cāttaṉār explains that the shrieks, cries, and howls of the vicious animals of prey sound like the beats of a *muḻavam* drum. Since drummers play this particular musical instrument as part of a marriage,[42] the reader envisions a wedding ceremony to be performed on stage. Instead, however, the drama turns out to be a grisly scene. The stage is a platform composed of accumulated ashes from cremated corpses. A female ghoul plays the actress, tearing apart her solitary prop, the charred head of a young woman. *Tolkāppiyam,* the first extant Tamil grammar, includes "dramatic usage" as one of the constituents of Tamil literary conventions.[43] In the passage just noted, Cāttaṉār distorts this dramatic element in order to show the workings of death.

Lest the reader remain unaware that the vocabulary of love has been transformed into a catalogue of cannibalism, lines 122-26 make that point explicit. Classical Tamil imagery conventionally used to praise the beauties of a heroine's appearance is called forth but then dismissed abruptly. In these lines, the ghoul does not ask whether the beautiful features before her are dark rain clouds or tresses as did, for example, the author of *Akanāṉūṟu* 126,[44] a poem containing most of the poetic images that Cāttaṉār parodies in this passage. Nor does that ghoul ask whether the corpse's eyes look like carp, another common *Caṅkam* conceit. Whether the lips before her bear a likeness to *kavir* flowers is of no interest. Despite the resemblance between the woman's teeth and lovely white pearls, that ghoul feels no compassion. Instead, she happily proceeds with her business of gorging herself on the corpse. In these lines, Cāttaṉār ruthlessly rejects the literary webs that poets spin, the dramatic conventions of love.

Cāttaṉār certainly did not originate ironic treatment of Tamil poetic conventions. Ramanujan comments that, within the corpus of classical poems, sometimes the whole generic frame brings a certain irony to the poem,[45] and elsewhere he translates *Kuṟuntokai* 226, a poem "dealing with the conventions themselves":

What She Said

Before I laughed with him
    nightly,

    the slow waves beating
    on his wide shores
    and the palmyra
    bringing forth heron-like flowers
    near the waters.

my eyes were like the lotus
my arms had the grace of the bamboo
my forehead was mistaken for the moon.

    But now.[46]

Ramanujan analyzes this poem in terms of the speaker's phase of love: "The speaker takes issue with the hackneyed phrases — 'eyes like the lotus,' 'forehead like the moon' — and says, in effect, that such phrases are fine only when one is happy in love."[47] In this poem, a *Caṅkam* poet comments on the conventions. Nonetheless, the poem's speaker does not reject the entire logic of *akam* poetry. She remains within the five phases of love, commenting ironically about her happiness in an earlier phase. Her world is still the world of lovers' union and separation depicted in the five landscapes.

Unlike the speaker in that poem, Cāttaṉār rejects the set of assumptions informing those five complementary landscapes. For him, *pālai* is the landscape that reveals the true nature of reality. The law of life's impermanence, summed up by the Buddhist doctrine of *anicca*, demonstrates itself most clearly in the *pālai* landscape. Cāttaṉār's story makes the case that the barren *pālai* is what really lies beneath outer appearance, even though our own ignorance leads us to view that appearance as real and permanent.[48] All the passions and desires experienced in the landscapes of love lead ultimately to suffering and separation, the subject matter portrayed in both *pālai* and the cremation ground.

In arguing that *pālai* is common to all experience, Cāttaṉār agrees with Tamil commentatorial tradition. Tamil grammarians recognize that other landscapes can easily become *pālai*. The "possibility of desert" lurks even for land filled with most luxuriant growth — if there is no rain. Thus, Tolkāppiyar labels the *pālai* the "*naṭuvunilattiṇai*," meaning the "middle" or "common landscape"[49] in the sense that it is implicit in all the others. Ramanujan explains,

> . . . it is thought that any mountain or forest may be parched to a wasteland in the heat of summer. . . . This fact adds further subtlety to the symbolism. *Pālai* (wasteland) associated with separation can happen even in the heart of union (*kuriñci* or mountain landscape).[50]

By exploiting the associations of the desert in his description of the cremation ground, Cāttaṉār argues that death stands waiting even while we experience life's sweetest pleasures.

In part, Cāttaṉār can use *pālai* to convey the Buddhist message of life's impermanence because it has traditionally differed in significant ways from the other *akam* landscapes. Compared to the other landscapes of love, *pālai* stands at the limits of both *Caṅkam* geography and *Caṅkam* concerns. Figure 1 demonstrates the sharp difference between *pālai* and the other landscapes. It indicates how different phases of love stand in relation to each other. Note that *pālai* stands over and against all four of the other landscapes. *Pālai*, the barren landscape, opposes the four fertile landscapes, which deal with love "*in situ*." Because *pālai* already lies at the edge of the *akam* world, Cāttaṉār uses it as the landscape in which to undermine the *akam* concern with sexual love.

Meditation on Life's Impermanence

At the same time that Cāttaṉār's language in the story calls to mind *kāñci* and *pālai*, he leads his readers through a narrative meditation on life's

Figure 1: *Pālai*'s Relationship to the Other Four Landscapes

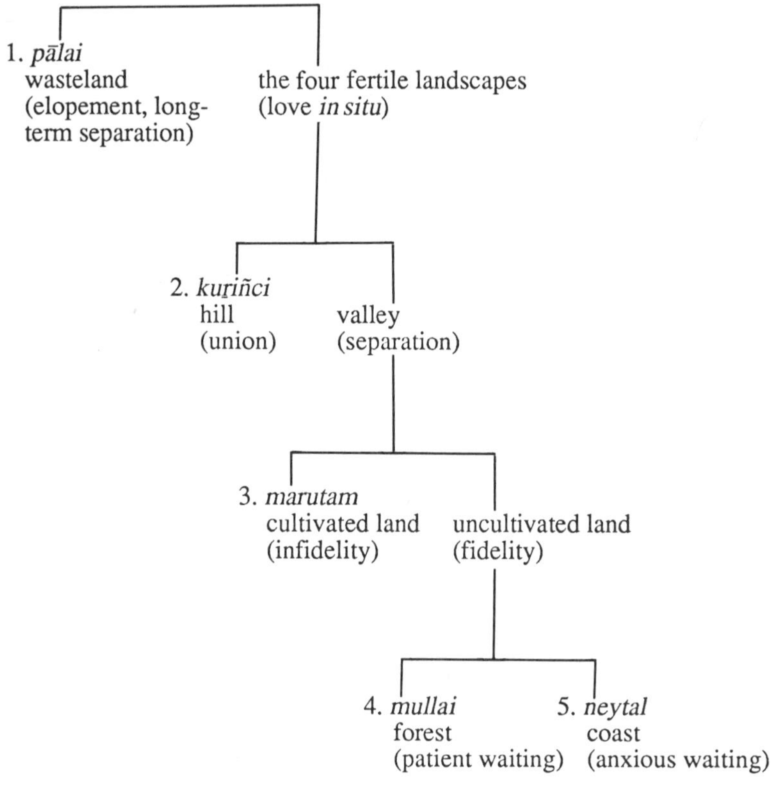

KEY:
words in italics = landscapes
words in parentheses = phases of love

Adaptation of figures 3 and 4 found in A. K. Ramanujan, "Form in Classical Tamil Poetry," in *Symposium on Dravidian Civilization,* ed. Andrée F. Sjoberg, Asian Series of the Center for Asian Studies of the University of Texas at Austin, no. 1 (Austin: Jenkins Publishing, 1971), pp. 80-81.

impermanence. Buddhist texts advise the serious monk to dwell in the charnel ground in order to realize the nature of life's impermanence by viewing the decay of human bodies. Through the description in Cāttaṉār's Tamil verses, he places his reader in a cremation ground, offering the opportunity to attain the insights of the meditating monk.

According to Buddhist tradition, the Buddha enjoined meditation in the cremation ground upon his monks. A well-known section of the *Satipaṭṭhānasutta* discusses the specific sights a monk should seek for the sake of contemplation: a decomposing body, a corpse being consumed by scavengers, a skeleton, and disintegrating bones. In each case the *sutta* ("verse" or "teaching") advises the monk to contemplate such sights in order to realize that his own body awaits the same fate. He should think, "this body, too, is of a similar nature, a similar constitution."[51]

The authors of later Buddhist meditation manuals wrote extensively upon the benefits of dwelling in the cremation ground. For example, in the *Visuddhimagga,* Buddhaghosa discusses the charnel-ground dweller in his section dealing with ascetic practices (*dhutaṅga*). That section ends with a list of the benefits of abiding in the burning ground:

> He (the adherent) acquires mindfulness of death; he lives diligently; the sign of foulness is available; greed for sense desires is removed; he constantly sees the body's true nature; he has a great sense of urgency.[52]

A responsive reader receives some of the same benefits by pondering Cāttaṉār's description of the cremation ground.[53]

The selection and arrangement of items in Cāttaṉār's lengthy description of the cremation ground increases our mindfulness of death. Table 5 demonstrates how Cāttaṉār's description brings thoughts of death to the fore. The smoke, the flames from corpse-burning, and crematory sheds stand out in his account of the sights of the ground. Among the sounds heard within the grounds, the calls of carrion-eating animals are prominent. Cāttaṉār's enumeration of the trees there focuses upon the grisly or macabre acts that take place beneath their branches. His list of funerary implements reminds us exactly what occurs during cremation. Cāttaṉār's account of the crematory panorama, spreading forth in the mind's eye, makes our contemplation of death unavoidable.

Buddhaghosa also credits the cremation ground with providing an opportunity for the monk to view the "sign of foulness." Chapter six of the

Table 5: Cāttaṉār's Description of the Cremation Ground

The Physical Layout and Inanimate Objects	
a gate	through which gods enter
a gate	depicting rice, sugarcane, water, and gardens
a gate	that has a tower covered with shining white lime
a gate	with an image holding a noose and trident
grounds	of the goddess who dwells in uninhabited land
death memorials	made of burnt clay, rising like high and low hills
offering posts	of powerful gods
stone platforms	that are raised
circles	where many paths intersect
huts	where guards eat, sleep, and dwell
flags of smoke	
festoons of flame	
sheds	sheltering the pyres

Sounds	
the tumult	of those who burn, abandon, dig graves, etc.
the noise	of the funeral drum, proclaiming there will be a pyre
the sound	of worship given to dead ascetics
the wails	of mourning for the other dead
the evil howl	of the long-faced jackal
the cry	of the horned owl summoning people to their death
the screech	of the hoot owl who eats flesh
the cry	of the man's-head bird who devours heads of corpses

(Table 5 cont.)

Trees and Shrubs	
Tāṉṟi Oṭuvai Uḻiñcil	grow tall
Kāṉṟai Cūrai Kaḷḷi	spreads evenly over dense ground
Vākai	where demons gather, on whose wide branches clouds settle
Veḷḷil	where birds rest and giddily consume pallid fat and flesh
Vaṉṉi	where those who vowed to live in the cremation ground cook
Iratti	where those who mortify their bodies make garlands of skulls
out in the open	where people who dine on corpses serve their guests

Funeral Implements	
fire pots	
funeral bowls	
unadorned biers	
cloth bundles	with ritual implements
discarded garlands	
earthenware pots	smashed
unhusked rice	
puffed rice	
riceball offerings	

Visuddhimagga describes this "sign of foulness" at length in the section on concentration (*samādhi*). Buddhaghosa enjoins the meditator to contemplate ten foul sights in the charnel ground: bloated things, livid (discolored) things, festering things, cut-up things, gnawed things, scattered (dismembered) things, hacked and scattered things, bleeding things, worm-infested things, and skeletons. Detailed instructions for fixing the mind upon these sights follow.[54] These sights enable the monk to concentrate his thoughts on the decay of the body.

Cāttaṉār includes three of these foul sights in his account of the sights and sounds that greeted Cāṅkalaṉ as he entered the cremation ground. Buddhist texts recommend dwelling in the cremation ground because it forces the meditator to see that what he perceives as "the self" is merely the sum of bodily parts. Cāttaṉār's account of the sight that met Cāṅkalaṉ proclaims that the body is merely the sum of its constituent elements — blood, flesh, and bones. He then goes on to describe the fate of various parts of a dismembered female corpse. They are strewn all about, being mangled by various carrion-eating birds and beasts. A worm-infested thing can also be contemplated, since the corpse's foot is swarming with maggots (line 109). The reader has plenty of opportunity to contemplate foul sights in Cāttaṉār's story.

Buddhaghosa also sees meditation in the cremation ground as a way to banish lust. He says, for example,

> But by rubbing out the stains on its [the body's] teeth with tooth sticks and mouth-washing and all that, by concealing its private parts under several cloths, by daubing it with nosegays and such things, it is worked up into a state that permits of its being taken as 'I' and 'mine.' So men delight in women and women in men without perceiving the true nature of its characteristic foulness, now masked by its adventitious adornment. But in the ultimate sense there is no place here even the size of an atom fit to lust after.[55]

Here Buddhaghosa describes how attractive bodily appearance wrongly gives the impression that there is an underlying, unchanging, personal entity called 'I.' Such appearances may lead men and women to lust after each other, but contemplation of the decay of the body's constituent parts reveals that such attraction is absurd.

Cāttaṉār uses the sights of the cremation ground to point out the absurdity of lusting after beautiful women. He does so in the passage that describes a ghoul eating the dismembered head of a young girl. We have already examined the way these lines parody certain assumptions of *Caṅkam* poets. This passage also functions to make the reader feel revulsion toward sexually attractive sights. In it, Cāttaṉār lists the physical features of a decaying corpse — tresses, eyes, a nose, lips, and teeth.

These features — once compared to clouds, carp, flowers, and pearls — have turned into mangled and wormy lumps of flesh. Poets conventionally praise them, but in this gruesome context one responds with repulsion rather than sexual desire.

A sense of urgency, which Buddhaghosa also considers to be a result of cremation ground meditation, comes through very strongly in lines 101-4 of Cāttaṉār's narrative, which culminates in Cāttaṉār's description of the cremation ground. In it, Cāttaṉār warns that Yama, the god of death, kills and heaps up the corpses of every kind of person. The sense of urgency derives from the image of "the cremation ground consuming pyres with its fiery mouth." Cāttaṉār makes it clear that such a sight should impel people to free themselves from their intoxication with wealth and pleasure, before it is too late.

Conclusions

In "The Story of the Cosmic Place," Cāttaṉār has provided us with a carefully crafted story. Though terse, the narrative displays several layers of meaning. Cāttaṉār has drawn upon traditional Tamil poetic conventions in the service of his Buddhist argument. From classical *puṟam* poetry Cāttaṉār borrows from the tradition of *kāñci* poetry, whose theme of life's transience permeates "The Story of the Cosmic Place." In a more subtle way, Cāttaṉār draws upon elements from the *akam* tradition of love in separation in order to develop his argument about life's impermanence. Cāttaṉār works with traditional situations and imagery, but he uses them in resourceful and unexpected ways.

Cāttaṉār also uses this imagery to mock the conventional worldview. In order to do so, Cāttaṉār chooses those traditional elements that are at the limits of the *Caṅkam* system. *Pālai* stands over and against the other four landscapes of love. Similarly, *kāñci* poems note the transience of the achievements that many other *puṟam* poems praise. In "The Story of the Cosmic Place," Cāttaṉār's parody of *pālai* elements shows the absurdity of sexual desire, and Campāpati's words affirm that even those who perform heroic deeds in the public sphere die like everyone else.[56]

The fact that Cāttaṉār can use *pālai* and *kāñci* as he does testifies to the richness of ancient Tamil literary conventions.[57] As Leonard Nathan notes in his comments about *Caṅkam* poetry,

> . . . this pervasive conventionality is itself exactly what frees poets to do startlingly unique things. . . . In that world, a slight discrepancy in convention, a small surprise of silence, could speak telling ironies or pathos.[58]

Cāttaṉār's slight transformation of these conventions enables him to say unique things — things that had never before been said in Tamil poetry.

Ultimately, Cāttaṉār's parody of *Caṅkam* elements serves to distance the reader from classical Tamil values and make him responsive to Buddhist ways of viewing the world. By structuring his story as a narrative contemplation of the cremation ground, Cāttaṉār allows his reader to vicariously experience the type of meditation enjoined on Buddhist monks. In this way Cāttaṉār prepares his reader for the story's description of the nature of the cosmos, an account analyzed in the next chapter of this monograph.

5

Cosmology as Rhetoric

Cāttaṉār uses conventions from classical Tamil tradition to help his audience gain access to his material, but it is the Buddhist tradition that supplies him with his philosophical arguments. In particular, Cāttaṉār draws from Buddhist cosmological tradition in the final section of "The Story of the Cosmic Place," which culminates with an account of how the universe is constituted. As Kenneth Burke comments in *The Rhetoric of Religion*, "Rhetoric is the art of persuasion, and religious cosmogonies are designed, in the last analysis, as exceptionally thoroughgoing modes of persuasion."[1] A comparison of Cāttaṉār's version of the story and other variants demonstrates how Cāttaṉār's cosmological materials in the story function as "exceptionally thoroughgoing modes of persuasion."

Cāttaṉār and "The Mustard Seed Story"

In "The Story of the Cosmic Place," Cāttaṉār has provided us with a variant of the well-known "Mustard Seed Story," which occurs in several places in Pali literature. In that story, a young woman named Gotamī, whose son has died, asks the Buddha to bring the boy back to life. The name of Cāttaṉār's protagonist, Kōtamai, is a Tamil transliteration of Gotamī. Kōtamai, too, seeks to bring her son back to life.

"The Mustard Seed Story" explains the circumstances under which Gotamī becomes a nun. When her only son dies, she becomes distraught with grief. Carrying her dead child with her, she wanders around in a daze, imploring those she meets to give her medicine that can bring her son back to life. Most of the villagers jeer at her, but one wise man suggests asking the Buddha for medicine. The Buddha promises to provide medicine if she will bring him a mustard seed from a house where no one has died. She goes from house to house, asking for a mustard seed. But she can accept none of them because in every village household someone has died. Gradually, she comes to see that everyone suffers the loss of loved ones; the impermanence of human life is one of the laws of the universe. With this realization, she accepts the death of her son, brings him to the cremation ground, and becomes a Buddhist nun.

Three Pali versions of "The Mustard Seed Story" are found in commentaries on particular books of the Pali Canon. One version of the story appears in *Manoratha Pūranī*, a commentary on the *Aṅguttara Nikāya*, and is attributed to Buddhaghosa.[2] In his commentary, Buddhaghosa tells the biographies of thirteen illustrious *bhikkhuṇīs*, "nuns," one of whom is Gotamī. The commentary on *Therīgāthā*, a collection of verses about the glories of detachment and arhatship experienced by Buddhist nuns, contains another version of "The Mustard Seed Story." The commentary on these verses, said to have been written by Dhammapāla, provides biographies of the women (including Gotamī) to whom the verses are attributed.[3] A third version of the story, also attributed to Buddhaghosa, exists in the commentary on the *Dhammapada*.[4] Although these three versions vary somewhat in their introductions and concluding sections (see the translations in Appendix B), the core of the story is the same in all three texts.

Despite minor differences in the three Pali variants, each one emphasizes the impermanence of all beings and things that exist in the world. Both the passage in the *Therīgāthā* commentary and the one in the *Manoratha Pūranī* contain a verse emphasizing the universality of death and the impermanence of existence. The verse, as translated by Caroline Rhys Davids, is as follows:

> No village law is this, no city law,
> No law for this clan, or for that alone;
> For the whole world — ay, and the gods in heav'n —
> This is the Law: ALL IS IMPERMANENT![5]

In the *Dhammapada* commentary, as well as the other two Pali texts, another verse notes that death destroys all things and pleasures:

> Whoso hath set his heart on sons or flocks and herds,
> To worldly pleasures given o'er whose thoughts, —
> Even as a torrent sweeps away a sleeping town,
> So Him the Prince of Death doth take and bear away.[6]

Both the events in this story and these verses focus upon the transience of all relationships and possessions.

Cāttaṉār's Tamil version resembles the Pali versions in both plot and characters. In each story an only son dies, and his distraught mother seeks to regain his life, learns that such a thing cannot be done, and — with that realization — puts her son on the funeral pyre. In each text the only child is young and the mother inconsolable when he dies. Most important, both the Tamil and Pali versions share the same messages, although they are developed in slightly different ways.

The Pali and Tamil versions reveal to listeners the inevitability of death for everyone. Both Gotamī and Kōtamai are ignorant precisely because each claims that her son's death is unique. The events in the Pali and Tamil versions of the story reveal to each mother that what she conceived of as a particular event — the death of her only son — turns out to be part of a universal pattern. All living beings are subject to death. In both the Pali and the Tamil versions, the protagonist learns to put her individual grief into a general context — the transient nature of life on this earth. In each case she then ceases to grieve.

Closely linked with the universality of death is the message that the dead cannot be brought back to life. Cāttaṉār develops this particular point at length in the Tamil version. In fact, Kōtamai's insistence that the goddess must bring her son back to life leads to the descent of inhabitants from different parts of the cosmos. The portrayal of Kōtamai's stubborn insistence, thus, provides Cāttaṉār with the opportunity to instruct his audience about the nature of Buddhist cosmology. It is here that Cāttaṉār's original treatment of the story lies.[7] Therefore, a close look at his cosmological account is warranted. The translation of the entire story can be found in the previous chapter of this monograph. In this selection from that translation, however, all the Tamil words for important cosmological terms have been placed in parentheses so that the reader can see how Cāttaṉār translates technical terms into his own language:

> . . . The goddess informed her [Kōtamai], "If the Primordial Lord were to give back your son's life, or those who wander inside the [burial] urn (*tāḻi*) of the sphere (*āḻi*) would give back his life, I would, too, ignorant woman! So let my powers show you that right now."
>
> Then out of the entire cosmos (*cakkaravāḷam*) — which contains the four traditional types of formless *brahmas* (*piramar*), the sixteen types of *brahmas* (*piramar*) with form, the two types of luminaries [sun and moon], the six types of gods (*teyvam*) who have attained great beauty, demons (*asuras*) of many kinds, the eight types of denizens of hell who suffer great misery, the assembly of stars that move through the vast

> sky, asterisms, and planets — the goddess Campāpati made those capable of giving boons come and stand before her.
>
> "This woman has suffered greatly," she said. "End her grief." But Kōtamai heard those gods from all parts of the cosmos answer in the very same way that Campāpati had. So she abandoned her desperate sorrow, put her son on a pyre in the cremation ground, and left.
>
> Then you see, the great Mayan̲ created this "Cosmic Place" in the place where the divine beings from all parts of the cosmos had gathered to demonstrate Campāpati's power. Following the prescriptive texts, he fashioned from beautiful terra cotta the creatures who live there and the places where they live. In order to inform people properly, this "Cosmic Place" shows each in its proper place: Mount Meru standing at the center of the Cakkara Mountains, surrounded by the seven types of mountain ranges that rise around it, the encircling oceans, the four islands described by tradition, two thousand small islands, and the other features.

The cosmological account reproduced above lies squarely within Buddhist tradition. Cāttan̲ār's account sets out (1) the different kinds of beings who inhabit the universe as well as the various places where they dwell, (2) the specific categories of gods in the cosmos, and (3) the distinct qualities of those deities. All three of these are central to the Buddhist understanding of the universe.

Standard Cosmological Features from Buddhist Tradition

In Cāttan̲ār's compact cosmological account, he enumerates the inhabitants of the cosmos in a formulaic way. Table 6 demonstrates the conventionalized nature of his account. Column two of the table lists the different kinds of cosmic residents that Cāttan̲ār mentions, while column three indicates the lines in chapter six of *Maṇimēkalai* where he mentions them. Column one reveals the way that those who live in the universe are categorized into subgroups or types (*vakai*). For example, one learns that there are only four types of formless *brahmas* but sixteen types of *brahmas* with form.

Table 6: Cosmic Inhabitants Listed by Cāttaṉār

Number of types	Type of being	Line in text
1. the four traditional (*maṟapiṉ*) types (*vakai*)	of formless *brahmas*	176
2. the sixteen types (*vakai*)	of *brahmas* with form	177
3. the two types (*vakai*)	of luminaries	178
4. the six types (*vakai*)	of groups of gods who attained great beauty	178-79
5. many types (*vakai*)	of demons	180
6. the eight types (*vakai*)	of hell-dwellers	180-81

The notion of "types of" assumes conventionally agreed-upon groups. Classification systems depend on consensus about categories; Cāttaṉār alludes to this consensus through his use of the term *vakai*, "type of," over and over again. The term occurs six times in the space of six lines. The use of such formulaic language points to an underlying system whose logic is shaped by religious assumptions.

Buddhist cosmological texts present particular aspects of Buddhist philosophy in a schematic and tangible form. In any culture, cosmology — the "geography of the universe" — is shaped by indigenous values and philosophical assumptions. In his classic work on Indian cosmology, Kirfel made the same point, in a roundabout way, when he wrote about Buddhist cosmography: "The division of the cosmos is not a natural one, as is discernible in the name (*cakravāla*), but rests on philosophical speculation."[8] What he says here, put in today's terms, is that cultural factors mold assumptions about the constituents of the cosmos. Concepts of salvation, as well as observations of the sky,[9] shape the way Buddhists have categorized the constituents of their cosmos.

At least three different influences shaped the Buddhist features central to Cāttaṉār's cosmological account.[10] The initial formulation concerning types of rebirth came from certain traditions about the second stage of the Buddha's enlightenment. An elaborate conception of the various levels of heavenly realms developed out of monastic interest in systematizing and analyzing the stages of meditation. Anti-Hindu polemic accounts for the placement of Hindu deities low on the celestial hierarchy found within the cosmos.

In order to understand the relationship between components of the cosmos while reading this chapter, the reader is encouraged to consult two visual aids. Figure 2 illustrates the different modes of rebirth available in the universe, the various geographical locations in which one can be reborn (known collectively as the *bhājana-loka*), and the three realms of the cosmos. Table 7 acts as a guide to the illustration, listing all of the specific rebirths available and the three realms in which they occur. Appendix C explains the methodological assumptions informing this figure and its accompanying table.

The Modes of Rebirth

Beginning with the first accounts of the Buddha's enlightenment, Buddhist traditions record a concern with the different modes of existence within the cosmos.[11] Reynolds analyzes the cosmological significance of the events that occurred during the second watch of the night on which the Buddha's enlightenment occurred in this way:

Figure 2: The Components of the Cosmos

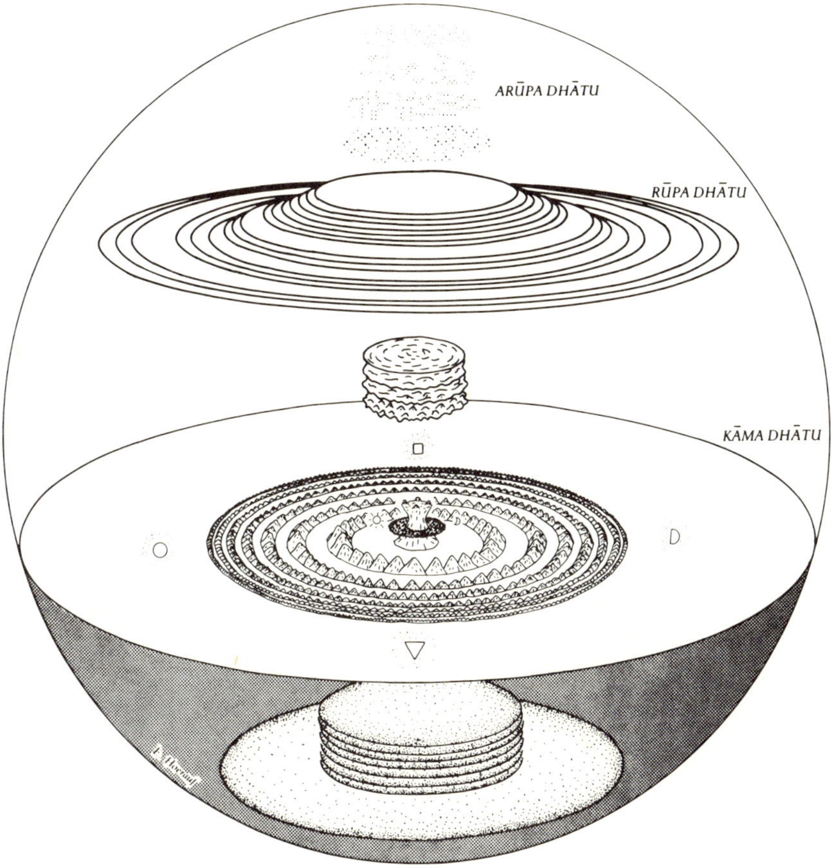

Table 7: The Beings Who Dwell in the Cosmos and the Realms in Which They Dwell

Mode of rebirth		Realm
	Heavens without form	
Gods	1. heaven of neither consciousness nor unconsciousness	*Arūpa Dhātu*
	2. heaven of absolute nonexistence	Realm of
	3. heaven of infinite consciousness	formlessness
	4. heaven of boundless space	
	Heavens with form	
	5. highest heaven	*Rūpa Dhātu*
	6. heaven of perfect vision	Realm of
	7. heaven of perfect form	form
	8. heaven without heat	
	9. heaven of immobile beings	
	10. heaven of unconscious beings	
	11. heaven of great results	
	12. heaven of universal purity	
	13. heaven of infinite purity	
	14. heaven of lesser purity	
	15. heaven of universal light	
	16. heaven of infinite light	
	17. heaven of lesser light	
	18. heaven of great Brahma	
	19. heaven of Brahma's ministers	
	20. heaven of Brahma's retainers	
	Heavens with passion	
	21. heaven of freedom of transformations	*Kāma Dhātu*
	22. heaven of transforming pleasures	Realm of
	23. heaven of satisfaction	desire
	24. heaven without night	
	25. heaven of the thirty-three [Hindu] gods	
	26. heaven of the four great kings	
Asuras		
Humans		
Ghosts		
Animals		
	Hot hells	
Denizens of hell	1. hell of reviving	
	2. hell of black ropes	
	3. hell of collected misery	
	4. hell of blazing lamentations	
	5. hell of smoky lamentations	
	6. hell of burning heat	
	7. hell of extreme heat	
	8. unceasing hell	

> . . . In the second watch of the night he [the Buddha] acquired the knowledge known as the divine eye, which enabled him to see the conditions and activities of all beings caught up in the existential cycle of suffering, death, and rebirth. . . . His acquisition of the divine eye established a starting point around which a whole range of tradition concerning the various levels of cosmic reality and the beings who populate them took form.[12]

Out of the traditions about the many creatures the Buddha saw with his divine eye during the second watch of the night, the various cosmological levels developed. The Buddha's vision of the many parts of the cosmos was phrased in terms of the manifold births and rebirths that creatures underwent according to the fruits of their past deeds:

> The visionary experience that was a part of the Buddha's own Enlightenment process . . . produced a series of vivid images of the heavenly realms in which the meritorious deeds of men were rewarded and of the hells in which men received retribution for their sins.[13]

This link between karma and levels of rebirth entailed a division of the cosmos into places of unfortunate rebirths and places of fortunate rebirths.

Out of this basic dichotomy developed the idea of a *gati*, a mode of rebirth for a sentient being.[14] There are six such modes, most of which are mentioned in Cāttaṉār's list of the types of beings that inhabit the cosmos. Buddhist texts usually list these six modes of rebirth (or destinies): the denizens of hell, animals, ghosts (Sanskrit *preta*; Pali *peta*), humans, demons (*asura*), and gods. According to one's karma, one will be reborn in one of these stations or levels of existence. The left-hand column on Table 7 reveals the spiritual level of each of these destinies: the residents of hell are at the bottom of the hierarchy, the gods are found in its upper section, and the rest exist in the middle.[15]

Cosmological texts also describe the particular locations where these groups of beings live; each one of these locations is mentioned by Cāttaṉār in lines 192-97 of chapter six. Individuals in the six modes of rebirth dwell in, on, above, or below one of the physical locations of the cosmos. As a unit, the entire set of locations is called the *bhājana-loka*, or "receptacle-world." Figure 2 shows Mount Meru standing at the center of the cosmos. Around it can be seen, rising in concentric circles, a series of seven mountain ranges separated by seven seas. Outside of the ranges, located in the last sea, stand four huge continents: Jambudvīpa is located in the south, Aparagodānīya in the west, Uttarakuru in the north, and Pūrvavideha in the east. Many small islands surround each of the four continents.

Within this "receptacle-world," beings of the various modes of rebirth dwell in various places. The denizens of hell dwell, for the most part, in the bowels of the earth, directly beneath the continent of Jambudvīpa.[16] Ghosts linger just under the continents or upon their surfaces. Animals roam over the earth, fly through the air, or swim in the rivers and seas. Human beings inhabit the four continents. According to most Buddhist sources, the demons dwell on Mount Meru's lower slopes or upon the seven mountain ranges. The gods live in heavens halfway up the slopes of Mount Meru, at the summit of Mount Meru, and high above Mount Meru.

A glance back at Cāttaṉār's cosmological account indicates that he has arranged it according to the Buddhist categories just described. His account contains a list of inhabitants, grouped according to their *gati*, and a description of the geographical features where they dwell, comprising the *bhājana-loka*. One feature in Cāttaṉār's list of the *gatis*, however, still needs explanation. In the discussion above, gods were listed as a single *gati*, and yet in Cāttaṉār's account he enumerates three types of gods: formless *brahmas*, *brahmas* with form, and groups of gods "who attained great beauty." In order to grasp the religiously crucial differences between these three types of deities, one must understand the category of *dhātu* [realm].

Stages of Meditation and the Proliferation of Heavens

Monastic involvement with the practice of meditation also influenced the development of Buddhist cosmology. The interest monks had in the various levels of meditation shaped the development of conceptions concerning specific heavenly realms into which one would be reborn if one had mastered particular stages of meditation. As a result, a great many heavens came to be included in cosmological accounts, grouped and associated with different stages (*dhyāna*) of meditation.

In addition to the proliferation of heavens, authors within the Buddhist tradition developed categories to classify those heavens. Buddhists came to perceive the cosmos as composed of three distinct types, each of which is known as a particular kind of *dhātu* [realm][17]: the *kāma*-[desire] *dhātu*, the *rūpa*-[possessing form] *dhātu*, and the *arūpa*-[formless] *dhātu*. Each of these three realms contains its own set of heavens.

Figure 2 shows the three realms marked on the right side of the diagram. On the accompanying Table 7, the realms are indicated in the right-hand column and correlated with their constituent parts in the middle column. The heavens numbered 21-26, and everything below them, comprise the *kāma* realm. The *rūpa* realm consists of heavens numbered 5-20, while those numbered 1-4 make up the *arūpa* realm.

Sentient beings who dwell in the lowest realm, that of *kāma*, are motivated by desire and passion; therein lies the source of their suffering. Craving binds them to the cycle of endless rebirth. As Table 7 indicates, the residents of the *kāma* realm include hell-dwellers, animals, ghosts, humans, demons, and the gods who dwell in the six lowest heavens. Those living in the lower depths of the *kāma* realm experience pain; those in the highest reaches experience pleasure. Cāttaṉār refers to the gods who dwell in this realm as "the six types of gods who have attained great beauty" because the deities in this world experience great aesthetic and sensual pleasures. Both the tortures of hell and the pleasures of the *kāma* heavens are integrally tied up with passion. Because the inhabitants of this realm have not yet committed themselves to renouncing passion, their realm is the lowest in the spiritual hierarchy.

People who have left behind their passions and now meditate to rid themselves of the remaining material factors,[18] which bind them to rebirth, are born into the next realm (the *rūpa-dhātu*) composed entirely of heavens. Although they lack desire, they still possess bodies. Buddhist tradition correlates the sixteen levels of birth within this world with specific *dhyānas*, stages of meditation copiously described in Buddhist meditation manuals.[19] According to tradition, when a meditating monk who has attained a particular meditational stage (*dhyāna*) dies, he is reborn in the heaven corresponding to his meditational achievement. Cāttaṉār refers to residents who dwell in the *rūpa* realm as the sixteen types of *brahmas* (Tamil *piramam*) with form.[20]

The inhabitants of the third and last realm possess neither desire nor corporeality. Rebirth in these four heavens is the result of concentrating on the topics called "the four immeasurables," meditations on the formless. Those in the heaven of boundless space (see Table 7, *arūpa-dhātu*) have been reborn "where meditative thought has transcended all limitations even of space." Those in the heaven of infinite consciousness perceive that "this unbounded space itself is seen only as the product of thought which is therefore infinite itself." In the heaven of absolute nonexistence, "unbounded space and infinite consciousness are seen as truly empty." In the heaven of neither consciousness nor unconsciousness, "the thought-process becomes so sublime and refined, that in deepest concentration the very object of thought is lost sight of."[21] Cāttaṉār refers to the inhabitants of these four heavens as "the four types of formless *brahmas*." Because the highest twenty (*rūpa* and *arūpa*) heavens are correlated with specific stages of meditation, they may be seen as a celestial blueprint for meditative progress.[22]

Cāttaṉār has incorporated into "The Story of the Cosmic Place" a set of categories for deities — dividing them progressively by the presence or absence of desire, corporeality, and consciousness. Those categories reflect the crucial role meditational achievement plays in Buddhism. As Kloetzli comments about cosmology and salvation in Buddhism, "All the various divisions of the vertical cosmology are interpreted in terms of the progress of the saint as he pursues the path of liberation."[23] By phrasing his account of the cosmos in terms of these categories, then, Cāttaṉār incorporates into his account an instructional chart indicating the steps toward liberation.

Anti-Hindu Polemic

Anti-Hindu sentiment also shaped Buddhist cosmology. Contempt for Hindu conceptions of salvation manifests itself most strikingly in the location of the six heavens in the *kāma* realm within the Buddhist cosmos. The four guardians of the quarters and other celestial functionaries, labeled "ever-intoxicated (with pride),"[24] dwell in the very lowest *kāma* heaven. Only one step above this group of supernatural beings with low status and passions expressed in prideful behavior, we find the thirty-three Hindu gods, located at the summit of Mount Meru and studded by the royal city of Indra, their king. This heaven (called the Trayastriṁśa heaven in Sanskrit; Tāvatiṃsa in Pali) abounds with pleasure gardens and jeweled mansions, in which all kinds of passions are pursued.

In Buddhist cosmology, the king of Hindu deities resides in a heaven inferior even to Māra, the evil tempter and god of death in Buddhist mythology. Gombrich's comment on the ranking of the heavens in the *kāma* realm explains this spatial relationship between Māra and Hindu gods:

> At the top of the sphere of desire [the *kāma* realm] are the six heavens inhabited by gods; and in the highest of them dwells Māra, or Death, the personification who tempted the Buddha not to preach but to die, and whose daughters are the forces of desire, especially sexual desire. To put Māra in the highest of the six heavens gives the game away; it is a mythological restatement of the fundamental message that just as Death and Desire are two sides of one coin, so the entire world of transmigration, the sphere of desire, is presided over by Death.[25]

Buddhist cosmology portrays life in the *kāma* heavens, characterized by pleasures, as hardly superior to rebirth in one of the lower modes of rebirth characterized by pain.[26] In either birth, the operative principle is desire, which necessarily leads to suffering.

By placing the Hindu gods so low in the heavenly hierarchy, authors who wrote cosmological texts reaffirmed the superiority of meditation and the inferiority of mere pleasures enjoyed in Hindu heavens. The schema insists that those passionate gods are prey to craving, the cause of suffering. By including this ranking of the heavens, Cāttaṉār incorporates a negative evaluation of Hindu deities into his didactic story.

Cosmos as Totality

The most comprehensive cosmological concept that Cāttaṉār incorporates into his story is *cakkaravāḷam* (Sanskrit *cakravāla*; Pali *cakkavāḷa*). Initially, *cakravāla* was the name for the ring of mountains that was thought to surround the world. Eventually the word came to be synonymous with *lokadhātu*, thus denoting the "Weltall," or entire universe.[27] The wider connotations of *cakravāla* stem from the meaning of its first member, *cakra*.[28] The primary meaning of the Sanskrit term *cakra* (Pali *cakka*) is "wheel," but in various Sanskrit texts, *cakra* denotes many different circular items including discus, circle, zodiac, and circular mystical diagram.

Cakra gains cosmic connotations when it comes to be used increasingly as a technical term in Buddhist texts. For example, its universal nuances are especially pronounced in the Sanskrit term *cakravarti* (Pali *cakkavatti*). Literally "he who sets rolling the wheel," the compound comes to stand for the "world-ruler." Reynolds comments upon the cosmic aspect of the wheel in early Buddhism in his discussion of the universal ruler in this way:

> In concert with the wheel which his charisma sets in motion, he [the *cakkavatti*] proceeds to conquer the four continents and thereby establish his universal authority. . . . The Cakkavatti is depicted as a cosmocrator whose conquest proceeded through the continents located at each of the four cardinal points, and whose rule radiated out from a central position either identified or closely associated with the central cosmic mountain of the Indian tradition, Mount Meru.[29]

Just as the *cakravarti* conquers the entire cosmos, the term *cakravāla* comes to mean entirety — the sum total of modes of existence for sentient beings. As Coomaraswamy puts it,

> Although, then the Wheel [*cakra*], as the "round of the world" and "earth plain," strictly speaking corresponds only to a given ensemble of conditions, it represents analogically the indefinite totality of all possible conditions, the entire *saṃsāra*.[30]

Because *cakra* comes to mean *saṃsāra* as a whole, Kloetzli also emphasizes that the *cakravāla* stands for structured reality in its totality:

> Because "cosmos" [*cakravāla*] refers to those structures of space and time which transform chaos into a "world," i.e., structures which support and sustain life, it must not be understood primarily as the physical universe, but rather as structured reality at every level, whether physical or spiritual.[31]

The Buddhist *cakravāla* is the totality within which all living creatures are constrained within a structured universe characterized by suffering.

Cāttaṉār titles chapter six of *Maṇimēkalai* "The Story of the Place of the *Cakkaravāḷam*" (which I have translated as "The Story of the Cosmic Place") because it concerns laws about the nature of reality that govern the cosmos — in its totality. Even the creatures from the heights and depths of the cosmos are unable to change those laws. They cannot circumvent the law of karma in order to bring Kōtamai's son back to life. Nor can other living beings escape Cāṅkalaṉ's fate. Cāttaṉār's cosmological account explains that beings — throughout the entire universe — come under the jurisdiction of the law of karmic retribution and life's impermanence.

Cāttaṉār's Way of Presenting Buddhist Cosmology

Despite the fact that Cāttaṉār presents an account of cosmology that strictly conforms to Buddhist tradition, his creativity in presenting that account must not be overlooked. That creativity lies, partially, in some of the rhetorical strategies he uses to make the material more intelligible to his Tamil readers.

Embedding Cosmological Instruction in a Story

By putting his cosmological account at the end of "The Story of the Cosmic Place," Cāttaṉār makes that description both comprehensible and memorable. Although the other Buddhist versions of "The Mustard Seed Story" do not conclude with cosmological descriptions, Cāttaṉār's ending is a logical culmination of the events that immediately precede it. In his version, the cosmological catalogue of the universe's inhabitants is presented in response to a series of demands that Kōtamai makes, all of which display her ignorance of the real nature of existence. Since Kōtamai stubbornly refuses to believe whatever the goddess tries to teach her, Campāpati eventually calls down the different cosmic beings to instruct the unbelieving mother.

The dialogue between goddess and mother begins when Kōtamai insists that the goddess Campāpati return her son to life. Campāpati patiently explains that such a deed is impossible; the body died as a result of her son's ignorance combined with the ripening of karma, which accrued from deeds done in the past. The workings of karma are unalterable, Campāpati argues, and so even the mother's mourning is inappropriate:

> Ripened deeds, buttressed by ignorance, ate the life of
> your son across whose chest lie the entwined threads.
> Stop your terrible grieving.

With this answer, the goddess attempts to educate Kōtamai about the nature of karma. Undeterred by the explanation, Kōtamai makes another demand, which indicates once again her ignorance about the real set of processes that cause events to occur; she now requests that Campāpati take her own life in exchange for the life of her dead son. Campāpati cannot grant this petition either. Instead, she points out that by now the boy has taken on a new body, in accordance with the character of the deeds that he had performed. The response of the goddess indicates that Kōtamai does not understand the process of rebirth.

Until now, Kōtamai and the goddess have been arguing about possible ways that Campāpati might remedy the situation; at this point, however, Kōtamai actually calls into question Campāpati's qualifications as a goddess. Because the deity claims she lacks the ability to grant Kōtamai's request, the disgruntled mother taunts her, "You are a very great deity and the Four Vedas, the good books of the brahmins, all say that divine beings give boons." Campāpati replies that her own limitations are not the issue at all — no deity can reverse the workings of karma:

> If the Primordial Lord were to give back your son's life,
> or those who wander inside the urn of the sphere would
> give back his life, I would, too, ignorant woman.

In order to demonstrate this point beyond any shadow of a doubt, Campāpati now calls down all the beings in the cosmos who are able to give boons. They also deny that they can bring the boy back to life, agreeing with Campāpati that such a task is impossible. Their affirmation of Campāpati's answer convinces the mother to abandon her request.

Intriguingly, in his description of the manner in which the goddess Campāpati calls down the boon-giving gods, Cāttaṉār lists more cosmic inhabitants than actually necessary:

> Then, out of the entire cosmos (*cakkaravāḷam*) — which contains the four traditional types of formless *brahmas*, the sixteen types of *brahmas* with form, the two types of luminaries [sun and moon], the six types of gods who have attained great beauty, demons (*asuras*) of many kinds, the eight types of denizens of hell who suffer great misery, the assembly of stars that move through the vast sky, asterisms, and planets — the goddess Campāpati made those capable of giving boons come and stand before her.

In the lines just quoted, Cāttaṉār refers to two different sets of beings: (1) the many different kinds of beings who live in the cosmos, all the way from deities to the denizens of hell, and (2) those beings capable of giving boons. Note that these two sets are not, by any means, identical. If

Cāttaṉār were simply interested in listing beings who grant boons, he need not have listed the highest *brahmas* since they are totally absorbed in meditation and uninvolved with human affairs. Nor need he have mentioned the denizens of hell. Besides being powerless to grant favors, they are in the process of being tortured with purgatorial punishments, so they would not be available to come to Kōtamai's aid.

Because Cāttaṉār has gone to some trouble to include extra cosmological material in his text, it seems likely that he sought to exploit this opportunity to instruct his reader about the nature of the beings in the upper reaches and lower depths of the cosmos rather than just to name the specific deities who grant boons. Otherwise, one wonders why he describes the former in detail while referring to the latter only in a summary manner as "those capable of giving boons." Similarly, the fact that he later lists the dwelling places of these beings provides even more evidence for this supposition since the style of the terrain where beings live (mountain ranges, oceans, or continents) is unrelated to their boon-giving capacity.

Cāttaṉār gains a great deal when he places his lesson on Buddhist cosmology at the end of "The Mustard Seed Story." By embedding his account of the constituents of the cosmos in a story, Cāttaṉār gives his readers a context within which to understand this material. The story makes them (1) realize that no being in the cosmos can alter the law of karma and (2) become aware of the many different categories of existence that are possible in the cosmos, according to Buddhist tradition. Cāttaṉār also makes his religious instruction easier to remember by situating it in a narrative, because information is more easily retained when associated with a story.

Use of Terminology

Anyone familiar with discussions found in Buddhist cosmological texts will immediately notice in Cāttaṉār's account the absence of the usual technical terminology. Except for his use of the term *cakkaravāḷam* (a Tamil transliteration of Sanskrit *cakravāla*), Cāttaṉār's description of the cosmos contains only terms that occur elsewhere in roughly contemporary or earlier Tamil literature. Cāttaṉār uses this Tamilized form of the term *cakravāla* for the first time in ancient Tamil literature. In fact, as far as scholars have been able to determine, the term itself appears nowhere else in ancient Tamil texts. And within *Maṇimēkalai* itself, the term first appears in the story with which we are currently concerned.[32]

Since his readers are unfamiliar with the term *cakkaravāḷam*, Cāttaṉār defines it by telling a story whose outcome illustrates its meaning. The story begins with a question about the term. The goddess tells "The Story of the Cosmic Place" when Cutamati, Maṇimēkalai's companion, asks the goddess why she uses the name "Cosmic Place" — *cakkaravāḷa-k-kōṭṭam* — in referring to the nearby cremation ground. The goddess responds by offering to explain, in detail, the meaning of the term. According to the text, the knowledge she will impart is extremely significant, since she tells the two young girls that they should listen to her tale — even if it takes until midnight to complete her rendition of it.[33] Then, in the course of "The Story of the Cosmic Place," Cāttaṉār makes the meaning of *cakkaravāḷam* clear through the events that transpire, as well as through a discussion of the various inhabitants of the cosmos and the places where they dwell.

In addition, Cāttaṉār provides a synonym for *cakkaravāḷam*, since it is unfamiliar to his sixth-century audience. At the point where Cāttaṉār first refers explicitly to the *cakkaravāḷam* in the story, he describes it as an *āḻi*.[34] The context is as follows: in line 173, Campāpati asks the deities who live in the upper half of the *cakkaravāḷam*, gods who are thought to grant boons, to attest to the irrevocability of events that occur as a result of karmic ripening. These deities are referred to as "those who wander in the urn of the sphere (*āḻi*)." The urn (*tāḻi*), shaped like a half-sphere, replicates the shape of the upper half of the cosmic sphere as seen by a viewer on earth.[35] The sphere (*āḻi*) of the cosmos is visualized here as consisting of two such jars placed mouth to mouth. By explaining the technical term *cakkaravāḷam* with the familiar Tamil *āḻi*, Cāttaṉār adequately conveys his point.

Except for *cakravāla*, Cāttaṉār uses only terms found in contemporary Tamil texts for his discussion of Buddhist cosmology. Even the Tamil transliteration *piramam*, which he uses to label the two highest groups of deities (described in Sanskrit as *brahmas*), can be found elsewhere in ancient Tamil texts. The same is true of the term Meru, the central world mountain.[36] Cāttaṉār uses the least technical language possible, thus ensuring maximum intelligibility when addressing an audience relatively unfamiliar with Buddhist cosmological tradition.

The Cosmic Model as Teaching Device

Cāttaṉār tells his reader twice in the space of four lines that he has presented his description of the cosmos in strict correspondence with established usage. Lines 197-98 say that Mayaṉ created each feature of his cosmic model so as to ensure it would be appropriately situated (literally, "in such a way that it receives the kind of place traditionally appropriate to it"). Second, in line 200, Mayaṉ is said to have fashioned the images *paṇpuṟa*. The term *paṇpu*, used in this type of context, occurs in Tamil literature where the author is making reference to various types of prescriptions. *Lifco*, a standard Tamil-English dictionary, glosses it as *vaḻakka muṟaimai*, "according to customary traditions," while commentators Vēṅkaṭacāmi Nāṭṭār and Turaicāmi Piḷḷai gloss it when it occurs here in *Maṇimēkalai* as *ilakkaṇappaṭi*, "according to the prescriptive texts."[37] Clearly, Cāttaṉār wanted his audience to know that the cosmological model described in the story was constructed in accordance with the authoritative works on the subject. In a culture where authoritative (*śāstraic*) texts are taken very seriously, such a statement demands respect.

Not only is his discussion explicitly traditional — it is self-consciously didactic as well. Cāttaṉār indicates that he conceives of this cosmic model as a teaching device. Line 198 explicitly says that the model was built to teach people; *aṟivu vara kāṭṭi* literally means "showing so knowledge comes." The cosmos functions as a teaching device at three levels. Those cosmic beings capable of giving boons descend to teach Kōtamai that karma cannot be altered. Mayaṉ builds a diorama preserving this cosmic demonstration as a visual aid to teach those who come to view it. And Cāttaṉār, in describing the cosmic model, reveals its lesson to his readers.

The model of the *cakravāla* in chapter six of *Maṇimēkalai* can be described as an *upāya*, a stratagem used to teach unenlightened beings about the nature of reality and salvation. Authors of Buddhist texts have written a great deal about the ways in which such stratagems can provide the means for the uninformed to enter onto the path leading to religious liberation. The term *upāya* implies a self-consciousness about technique and means. Cāttaṉār, like other Buddhist preachers, has used many rhetorical strategies in expounding Buddhism. However, here in his exposition of Buddhist cosmology he goes even further, actually labeling the model of the cosmos a teaching device.

In order to put Cāttaṉār's didacticism here in a wider perspective, it is fruitful to view it in light of Buddhist tradition. The cosmological strand of Buddhist thought, argues Reynolds, has always had an important teaching component at the popular level: ". . . the buddhological and cosmological strands have been in the foreground at the popular and royal levels of communal life."[38] In a discussion about a Thai cosmological text, Reynolds notes that its author "chose to use a kind of cosmological format in order to include material that could be effective in communicating the profundities of the doctrine to those who possessed only a minimum of religious sophistication and training."[39] In *Maṇimēkalai*, Cāttaṉār makes the most of the potential that Buddhist cosmological traditions possess for providing religious instruction to readers with little Buddhist training.

Cosmos as Cremation Ground

One of Cāttaṉār's most striking rhetorical strategies in "The Story of the Cosmic Place" is his identification of the cosmos with the cremation ground. Cāttaṉār carries out this identification through synecdoche, "a form of metaphor which in mentioning a part signifies the whole." One rule restricts the functioning of a synecdoche: ". . . the part selected to stand for the whole must be the part most directly associated with the subject under discussion."[40] For example, consider how one uses "foot soldiers" to refer to infantry and labels manual laborers "hands." Infantrymen are distinguished from other military units because they march rather than ride horses, pilot planes, etc. The resource that manual laborers can offer their employers is the work that they perform with their hands.

Cāttaṉār uses the cremation ground as a synecdoche for the cosmos. Since the cosmos encompasses everything, the cremation ground is only a tiny part of it. Yet Cāttaṉār uses the cremation ground as a synecdoche for the cosmos as a whole, implying that what we most associate with the cremation ground — the transience of sentient creatures — is a significant feature of the entire cosmos. Thus, synecdoche, as a rhetorical device, helps Cāttaṉār to expound upon the Buddhist idea of *anicca*, the impermanence of phenomenal existence. Cāttaṉār establishes the meaning of his metaphor in the introduction and conclusion to the story, in his description of the cremation ground's fortification, and in his discussion of the cosmos as composed of burial urns.

The lines that introduce Cāttaṉār's "The Story of the Cosmic Place" suggest that a special relationship exists between cremation ground and cosmos. At the beginning of the story the goddess tells Maṇimēkalai and Cutamati that, since it is now too late for them to go home, they should go to spend the night in the *cakkaravāḷa-k-kōṭṭam*, literally "the place of the cosmos." As we have seen, when Cutamati comments that everyone else in the city calls that place "the cremation ground," the goddess goes on to explain why the real name for the site is "the place of the cosmos." Cutamati says that the only people who call the site "the place of the cosmos" are the wise goddess Maṇimēkalā herself (labeled "rare," "superior," and "pre-eminent" in lines 26, 28, and 32) and the *viñcaiyaṉ* Marutavēkaṉ. The term *viñcaiyaṉ* means "he of knowledge" (derived from Sanskrit *vidya*). With the exception of these enlightened two, the ignorant townspeople see only a cremation ground when they come to the spot in question, and they call the site "the place of the cremation ground." Their awareness extends only to a recognition of what they see — not to its underlying cosmic significance.

The conclusion of Cāttaṉār's story demonstrates how an understanding of the cremation ground leads to knowledge about existence. At the end of the goddess's story, Cāttaṉār indicates that Maṇimēkalai has learned a great deal from it. Through her contemplation of the cremation ground as described by the goddess, Maṇimēkalai attains knowledge of the nature of existence for those living beings who continue to undergo rebirth: lines 206-8 report, "Maṇimēkalai, her heart sorrowful and drained [after hearing "The Story of the Cosmic Place"] commented on the nature of those who are born." The story revealed to her the fate of sentient beings who remain in the realm of *saṃsāra*.

If these framing passages (the introduction and conclusion) explain how to read the story,[41] particular features within the story indicate the true relationship between cosmos and cremation ground. One such revealing feature is the highly fortified wall enclosing the cremation ground. Cāttaṉār describes the cremation ground as "surrounded by a guarded fortress wall divided by these four clearly marked, towering gates." Wall is denoted by *iñci*, "walls of a fort" or "ramparts"; and the Tamil term *vāyil*, "gate" or "portal," denotes the wall's huge entranceways. These terms are part of an architectural context, particularly one that emphasizes the fortified and "battle-ready" nature of a city (expressed by Cāttaṉār as *ārum kaṭi*, "well-protected," in line 105). Significantly, Cāttaṉār describes these gates as clearly demarcated (*pāṛpaṭṭu*, "having undergone sectioning," "marked off") and towering above the surrounding countryside.

In purely pragmatic terms, why would a cremation ground need highly fortified walls and gates? In fact, it would not. Until modern times, cremation grounds — at least in Tamilnadu — did not have walls. Traditionally located at the very outskirts of human settlement, the burning ground was a marginal area whose link to society was relevant primarily when a death occurred. Neither the necessity to keep the intruders out nor the desire to enclose people within was felt. Hence, Cāttaṉār's highly fortified cremation ground is quite peculiar. The text itself attests to its exceptional nature in two places: in line 49, Cāttaṉār describes it as *ār*, "rare," "unusual," "unique." Still more striking, we learn in line 105 that Cāṅkalaṉ does not even recognize the place as a cremation ground — he thinks it is a fortified city.

When Cāttaṉār likens the cremation ground to a city, he calls up cosmic associations in the minds of his readers. Identifying the cremation ground with the cosmos is a two-part process. First, the cremation ground is likened to a city. Then, Cāttaṉār could build upon his readers' perception that the construction of a city oriented around the cardinal directions was patterned after the structure of the cosmos.

In mapping out the parallels between urban and cosmic geometry, Wheatley calls special attention to the city walls with prominent gates. In his *Pivot of the Four Quarters*, Wheatley emphasizes that cosmic symbolism in Asian city architecture manifests itself in cardinal orientation, axiality, and (most relevant to our discussion) massive walls with emphasis on the main gates. He says,

> Prominent among the morphological features which the ideal-type Chinese city shared with a majority of the great capitals of Asia were cardinal orientation, cardinal axiality, and a more or less square perimeter delimited by a massive wall.[42]

Elsewhere he notes that these walls included a "strong architectural emphasis on the main gates."[43] Coomaraswamy, as well, in setting out the main architectural features of an ancient Indian city, calls the presence of city gates one of "the most conspicuous and necessary parts of a city" and comments that "the plan [of a city] is rectangular, usually square with four gates, one in the middle of each wall, facing the four quarters."[44]

The immense proportions of such city walls testify to their symbolic significance and ultimate purpose. Wheatley's comment about city gates is instructive:

> The city gates, where power generated at the *axis mundi* flowed out from the confines of the ceremonial complex towards the cardinal points of the compass, possessed a heightened symbolic significance which, in virtually all Asian urban traditions, was expressed in massive constructions whose size far exceeded that necessary for the performance of their mundane function of granting access and according defense.[45]

Wheatley's point — that these massive constructions greatly surpass the dimensions required to fulfill their ordinary functions — is even truer in the case of Cāttaṉār's cremation ground, which requires no gates at all. Cāttaṉār has incorporated particular, cosmos-related allusions to the architecture of cities into his description of the cremation ground. These allusions suggest to his reader a sequence of identifications between cremation ground, city, and cosmos.

In his most explicit identification of cremation ground with cosmos, Cāttaṉār refers to the universe as composed of burial urns (*tāḻi*): in line 173, as we have seen above, Cāttaṉār describes the various deities in the upper half of the cosmos as wandering inside an [upside-down] burial urn. Since Buddhists conceive of the *cakravāla* as a sphere, Cāttaṉār's description indicates that the reader should visualize the cosmos as two burial urns, placed mouth to mouth. The implication, then, is that all creatures within the cosmic sphere move about in a vessel that inters their bodies. The burial urn image drives home the points that death lies at the end of one's life and that all existence is characterized by impermanence.

The rule restricting the composition of synecdoche prescribes that "the part selected to stand for the whole must be the part most directly associated with the subject under discussion." The ignorant person might think that a cremation ground has nothing to do with the cosmos. However, the person who truly grasps the meaning of "The Story of the Cosmic Place" sees that the transience of sentient existence, which the cremation ground represents, is one of the characteristics of existence most relevant to his or her understanding of the nature of reality. Thus, in literary terms, the cremation ground may be said to be the part selected to stand for the cosmos that is most directly associated with the subject of life's impermanence.

Conclusions

Cāttaṉār culminates his version of "The Mustard Seed Story" with a discourse on Buddhist cosmology. Into this discourse he incorporates a description of different inhabitants of the cosmos and the places they live. Although Cāttaṉār presents his account according to the standard (Single World) Buddhist cosmological tradition, he expresses cosmological concepts in a way that makes them especially accessible to his Tamil audience.

Cāttaṉār does more, however, than translate Pali and Sanskrit ideas into Tamil. He takes a story and reworks it, adding a new layer of meaning to the old one. Through his use of synecdoche he identifies the cosmos with the cremation ground. He uses that identification as a way of dramatizing the Buddhist message of *anicca*, the impermanence of life for all creatures within the cosmos.

"The Story of the Cosmic Place" demonstrates both Cāttaṉār's originality and the didactic power of Buddhist cosmology. As Strong points out, an understanding of the cosmos is a key component of Buddhist soteriology:

> Cosmology, to be sure, is an important part of all religions, but it is a crucial one in the case of Buddhism. Perhaps because of the absence in Buddhism of belief in any creator God, Buddhists have turned to cosmological knowledge for a sense of order in the world. Indeed an understanding of the world as it exists, that is, as it is said to exist, is a fundamental part of the whole process of enlightenment.[46]

Strong points out that the acquisition of cosmological knowledge is a crucial part of the process of enlightenment; Cāttaṉār seeks to impart such cosmological knowledge in his "The Story of the Cosmic Place."

6

Relationships between Laypeople and Renouncers

According to Buddhist texts, both renouncers and dedicated laypeople are necessary for the continuation of the religious tradition. Since not everyone can follow the path of renunciation, which usually culminates in the monastic life in Buddhism, Cāttaṉār does not argue that all his listeners should become nuns or monks. Instead, he includes examples of both laypeople and renouncers in *Maṇimēkalai*. Those desiring to participate in the Buddhist community can then choose the type and degree of participation appropriate to their dispositions and spiritual capabilities. In chapter twenty-two of *Maṇimēkalai*, Cāttaṉār explores the duties assigned to dedicated laypeople and indicates how laypeople should relate to renouncers. He does all of this through a "stories within a story" structure that comprises a great ascetic's speech to Prince Utayakumaraṉ's father, King Māvaṇ Kiḷḷi.

Chapter twenty-two, which records in its entirety the ascetic's speech, begins when the ascetic arrives in the royal court in order to inform the Cōḻa king that his son has died as a result of his lustful pursuit of the renouncer Maṇimēkalai. Rather than revealing this news to King Māvaṇ Kiḷḷi immediately, the holy man embarks on an elaborately structured address in which he informs the king of the evils of lust. During the course of his talk, the ascetic tells the stories of the chaste housewife Maruti and the renouncer Vicākai, each of whom had an encounter with a lustful male. In each case, that man died as a result of his inappropriate actions. The ascetic uses these stories in order to help the king put his own son's death in perspective. Since King Māvaṉ Kiḷḷi is born of the lineage of Cōḻa kings, who are known for their righteousness, the ascetic hopes to persuade the monarch to protect, rather than punish, Maṇimēkalai for indirectly causing the prince's death.

The ascetic's speech has an effect on the king because of the similarities in the events of the two illustrative stories the ascetic tells and the events that befall the king's son. Prince Utayakumaraṉ lusts after Maṇimēkalai, even though she is an ascetic, and follows her everywhere. Because no one can dissuade the prince from his obsessive attraction to her, the young nun finally attempts to elude him by taking the form of the demigoddess Kāyacaṇṭikai. He discovers this ruse and sets out to abduct her from the temple where she is staying. When Kāyacaṇṭikai's husband arrives, unaware of Maṇimēkalai's transformation, he thinks the prince is pursuing his wife and murders him in a fit of jealous rage.

The very same pattern — of lustful behavior leading to death — occurs in the two branch stories the ascetic tells. In the Maruti story, King Kakantaṉ's younger son lusts after a respectable brahmin wife and dies at the sword of his father as punishment. In the Vicākai story, King Kakantaṉ's elder son tries to abduct Vicākai. He, too, dies by the sword of his father because he wrongly approached a virtuous renouncer. A schematic representation reveals the relationships between the stories:

Location	Lustful prince	Wronged woman	Deliverer of justice
Main story	Prince Utayakumaraṉ	Maṇimēkalai	Kāyacaṇṭikai's husband
Branch story #1	Kakantaṉ's younger son	Maruti	Kakantaṉ
Branch story #2	Kakantaṉ's elder son	Vicākai	Kakantaṉ

The translation below indicates how the ascetic uses these parallels to demonstrate that Utayakumaraṉ's death was the appropriate retribution for his lustful deed.

Translation: "Maṇimēkalai Is Put under Protection"

Introduction to the branch story [Cāttaṉār sets the scene, describes how the ascetic blesses Māvaṉ Kiḷḷi, the Cōḻa king, and introduces the topic of the consequences of lustful behavior.]

After announcing themselves to the gate-keepers of the magnificent palace, one of the greatest among the distinguished ascetics approached the king there, saying, "May your white umbrella, towering above like the full moon at its zenith, give shade to the earth. May your spear and sceptre oversee all with compassion. May the discus you hold roll without evil. O king, may you live happily for all the years allotted to you.

"O king who rules the earth, just as it happened today, in ancient times, too, there were many men who lost their lives when their bad deeds took form. Some died because, full of intoxicating and ripened lust, they approached chaste women. Others died because in their hearts they desired women who took up great asceticism":

Story #1 [The ascetic tells King Māvaṇ Kiḷḷi how King Kakantaṉ's younger son approached Maruti with lust in his heart.]

Once, the Virgin Goddess[1] proclaimed to King Kantaṉ, "It is not appropriate for you to appear for battle before the tall one with the axe[2] who severed the branches of kingly families. Instead, leave the city."

In light of the Virgin's command, King Kantaṉ considered who should take over the rule of his city. He thought: Kakantaṉ is the son of a concubine. He is so brave that his enemies throughout the cool continent of Nāvalam Gardens[3] tremble before him. He never makes mistakes even when his foes rage against him. He is the proper one.

Calling him affectionately, the king said, "Since you are not of the kingly lineage, Paracurāmaṉ will not attack you. Kakantaṉ, protect this city, until the sweet words of the divine sage Akattiyaṉ [Agastya] end my distress by telling me to return." Then on the very day that he left in disguise, that resolute man appropriately renamed this city "Kākanti."[4]

One day, Kakantaṉ's son came to the mouth of the Kāviri River. There he saw a brahmin woman, Maruti, who had just bathed in its clear waters. Since she was unaccompanied, he thought that she was a loose woman. He said to her, "Come with me."

This woman, respectably adorned, became confused by his words. She thought to herself: "Women capable of bringing pouring rain to the hard-packed earth do not enter the hearts of other people. I entered the heart of another man. Thus, I am unfit to protect the three fires of my husband who wears the sacred thread." Because she felt terrible anxiety, she did not return to her house. Instead, in her confusion, she went to the roads' junction,[5] saying, "I am not guilty of failing my husband. Nonetheless, it was easy for the man who saw me to hide me in his heart. I have taken on the duties of a chaste wife who brings rain, and I don't know of any misdeed that I did, O god of the roads' junction. Has your justice failed?" After asking this, the woman with shining gold jewelry wept.

The very great *pūtam* appeared and addressed the respectably adorned woman: "Listen to me, [woman like a] young creeper. The ever-truthful poet [Tiruvaḷḷuvar] says, 'Great rain falls whenever summoned by a woman who worships her husband upon her awakening, not worshipping other gods.' You have not clearly understood the meaning of these words. Instead, you have listened to the false and frivolous words of others and enjoyed celebrating festivals where the strap-tied drum is played.

"Because you took to worshipping gods, woman, rain will not fall at your command. You cannot even burn the hearts of others as chaste women do.[6] But if you stop doing the things I have censured, O beautifully jeweled woman, rain will fall from the lofty, wide sky at your command. And my cruel noose will not bind you, as it does women who act as they please.

"As for the prince, only if the king fails to do justice within seven days, does my time to punish him come. O young creeper, seven days from now, King Kakantan̲ will hear of this incident. With his sword, he will punish that man who has an incorrigibly lustful heart," said the *pūtam*, who had contempt for miscreants.[7] Indeed, on the very day that the *pūtam* had predicted, the prince was cut down by King Kakantan̲'s sword.

Interlude [After completing Story #1, the ascetic blesses the king.]

"You who have the good fortune to rule the earth that is clothed in vast oceans, O bull among kings, listen further":

Story #2 [The ascetic tells the king how Kakantan̲'s elder son tried to abduct Vicākai.]

Once there lived a man named Tarumatattan̲ and his mother's brother's daughter, Vicākai. Her dark eyes were large and filled with joy. The handsomeness of these two cousins caught one's eye and surpassed the workmanship of a celestial painting, created and cherished by the gods. Gossip had spread throughout the town that Vicākai had agreed to a *gandharva* marriage with Tarumatattan̲ since he was her cross-cousin.[8]

In consequence, lustrous-browed Vicākai left home looking like an unfinished painting.[9] Entering the Place of Virtue, she addressed the brightly glittering image painted on the pillar: "Stop this terrible slander by the people all around me." Then, that

Speaking Image[10] praised her, saying to the people of that grand city, "This woman can call forth rain."

Vicākai knew that if the deity had not exonerated her, the obsessed townspeople would not have banished her supposed moral blemish from their minds. Therefore, she said, "I will not unite with my cross-cousin in this life. I will become his wife in my next birth." After explaining the nature of goodness to her mother, she joined a house of virgins.[11]

Afterwards, Tarumatattan̲ left the great city with his mother and father. As he left, he extolled the many virtues of the Speaking Image. He praised the image, saying, "You removed the distress into which we had sunk." Then he went to Southern Maturai, which abounds in many kinds of excellent wealth and illustrious people.

There Tarumatattan̲ vowed to himself, "I don't want any woman except Vicākai, the daughter of my mother's brother, whose hair is adorned with blossoming flowers. Let this birth pass away." Amassing great wealth by conducting trade in the proper way, he became a rich man with a treasury full of gold. Since he was an exalted person with ever-accumulating wealth, at the age of sixty he received the *eṭṭi* flower[12] from the king of the wide land.

On that day, a brahmin came to him and said, "Though you are wealthy and have much gold, what have you accomplished here? Even if men without chaste wives do many virtuous deeds, they still will not reach the celestial worlds. Have you not heard this? If you have, return to your own city without lingering here." So he left Southern Maturai, impoverishing it by his departure, and entered our city, O king of the wide land.

When virtuous, gold-bangled Vicākai heard that he had come to this city, she went out of her house without any shyness. There in the midst of many people stood Tarumatattan̲, who had always avoided evil. She said to him, "Now we no longer know each other. Where has beauty, which obsessed us in the past, hidden itself? You have reached the age of sixty. The five braids of my fragrant hair are mixed with grey. Youth and desire — where have they hidden themselves? Answer me now, you despondent man. In this birth I will not serve at your feet, but in the next birth I will serve you as wife.

"Youth does not remain. The body does not remain. Abundant and excellent kinds of wealth do not remain. Even sons will not enable you to reach celestial worlds. Only virtue, most excellent, helps you to reach those celestial worlds. So, give gifts," she said. In response to her advice, Tarumatattan̲ displayed his great wealth to the daughter of his maternal uncle. Then they did acts of goodness together that exceeded the number of stars in the lofty sky. That good woman with curved earrings grew old as a virgin.

[Earlier in her life,] soon after Vicākai, by the grace of the deity, had been exonerated from the slander spread throughout the wide city, she was coming down the banner-filled street one day in the company of many people. King Kakantaṉ's eldest son — whose younger brother had been killed on account of Maruti — was walking there. His heart darkened and hardened with lust. A garland of blooming flowers, from which light streamed, rested on top of his head, encircling his curly black hair. Full of desire, he reached for that garland, wishing to place it on Vicākai's hair. But as he said to her, "This is a wedding as described by the ancient ones,"[13] his fair hand, which was lifting off his garland, became stuck to his black hair.

When King Kakantaṉ heard that, on account of this woman, the fair hand that was raised to the garland had been unable to descend, he became twisted with bitter fury. Ignoring his suffering, the king cut his son down with his sword.

Ethical discourse on lust [The ascetic describes the evils of lust, first in general terms and then specifically, to condemn the deeds of Prince Utayakumaraṉ.]

"O king of kings, may you continue to protect the earth in every aeon," proclaimed one of the greatest among the distinguished ascetics as he concluded the story.

Then, the king of enduring excellence inquired, "Great ascetic on the path of goodness, you said, 'Just as it happened today,' and recounted many instructive things. Do such deeds occur even today?" asked the king with the victorious and far-reaching spear.

One of the greatest among the distinguished ascetics blessed him: "King, may your just sceptre refrain from evil. There are five practices forbidden by those who realize what should be accomplished in this world, whose seas are ancient.[14] Of these five, lust will induce the other four: intoxication, falsehood, theft, and murder. Those who eliminate lust eliminate evil practices. Is it not true that ascetics are the people who rid themselves of lust? Furthermore, is it not also true, O king of the wide land, that those who do not overcome lust will suffer in unbearable hells?

"Cittirāpati's daughter Mātavi, her long eyes highlighted with red lines, could not bear the harsh suffering of her lover [Kōvalaṉ], and so she joined a monastery of great ascetics. Maṇimēkalai, the daughter of Mātavi, still had unripened breasts and an immature voice, but she decided to take up asceticism, securing her food by begging alms from large and small houses and staying at the temple.

"Even though she had this ascetic nature, one man would not leave her alone. Lust hardened inside him because of his attraction to her. He followed her everywhere like a shadow. Even when Maṇimēkalai went to the temple and changed herself into the form of Kāyacaṇṭikai, he went fearlessly through the black darkness into that temple. Since Kāyacaṇṭikai had been there previously, her husband, a demigod with an unfailing sword, came there. Seeing a man, he thought that man had come here to see his wife.

"O king whose white umbrella resembles the moon, because your son Utayakumaraṉ's evil deed had come to fruition, it was he who did not stop pursuing Maṇimēkalai. Instead his evil deed compelled her to go to the temple and drove Utayakumaraṉ there in the deep dark of midnight. The deed summoned Kāyacaṇṭikai's demigod husband, with his unfailing sword. This same deed confused the mind of the vengeful demigod and made him think: 'That man came for my woman, who is a demigoddess.' It also caused the sword in the demigod's hand to cut down Utayakumaraṉ in the temple."

The king's response [King Māvaṇ Kiḷḷi considers the ascetic's words and then acts in accord with them.]

One of the greatest among the distinguished ascetics told the king all this, blessing him.

The Cōḻa king gazed at his commanding-general, saying, "The demigod's deed was inappropriate; he punished the prince when I should have done so. If the king does not protect, then there is neither chastity among women nor penance among ascetics. Our lineage is known for punishing even the injustice committed by its own sons.[15] The news that such a grievous sinner was born into our family must not reach the ears of other kings. Before word can spread, immediately put Utayakumaraṉ on the funeral pyre and place that daughter of the courtesan under our protection." Thus spoke the sovereign king whose broad crown glittered with ornaments.

The Duties of a Layperson

The Maruti Story

While the Maruti story shares with *Maṇimēkalai*'s main story the motif of the prince's lust, the preaching within the story focuses upon Maruti's need to become a truly chaste laywoman. The preacher within this story is a *pūtam*. Both *pūtam* and its Sanskrit equivalent, *bhūta*, have as their unmarked meaning a "being" (literally, a "has been," e.g., a divine being, a human being, or an animal being). However, in its more narrow sense, the term often connotes a being with associations of potential danger, and hence, it is often used to describe demons, goblins, and other nonhuman destructive beings. In Tamil literary contexts relevant to its usage here, a *pūtam* is portrayed as standing at the intersection of four roads in a city, guarding its citizens from evil-doers. This benevolent function, however, is carried out through destructive means; he protects the city by punishing miscreants with his hangman's noose.

Cilappatikāram (5:128) defines a city *pūtam*'s responsibilities in the course of describing the Kāvirippumpaṭṭiṉam *pūtam*, who dwells at the junction of four roads: he enforces proper behavior within the city. That passage systematically lists the types of people whose behavior is considered antisocial, detrimental to the overall welfare of the city, and thus worthy of punishment by the city guardian:

1. those who conceal themselves in asceticism without [truly] having that nature
2. adulterous wives who practice their vice in secret
3. treacherous royal ministers
4. men who desire other men's wives
5. witnesses who perjure themselves
6. slanderers[16]

Each of these types of people — false ascetics, adulterers, scheming ministers, perjurers, and calumniators — practices one type of behavior outwardly but thinks and behaves differently in secret. No such behavioral contradiction exists in virtuous people. To protect the latter from the former, the guardian of each city keeps watch.

The city guardian also chastises evil-doers as an aid to the king. According to tradition, the proper behavior of citizens is the responsibility of their monarch. Should he fail to do justice, however, the *pūtam* of the city will take upon himself the role of punishing wrongdoing (*Maṇimēkalai* 22:72-73). Both the king and the city guardian stand as agents who uphold societal values, and they are respected throughout the city. Thus, the guardian's reprimand of Maruti carries behind it the authority of the king and the consensus of the city's citizens.

What type of woman is Maruti, the audience for this city guardian's discourse? Maruti clearly perceives herself as a model brahmin housewife. Therefore, she thinks the source of the lustful prince's desire for her lies in the city guardian's neglect of his duty to protect citizens. As she says, "I took upon myself the duties of a chaste wife who brings rain, and I don't know of any misdeed that I did" (lines 53-54). As far as she is concerned, she has fulfilled all the obligations attendant upon her householding rule.

From the city guardian's point of view, however, Maruti has not fulfilled her true wifely role. Instead, while thinking she was a chaste and virtuous wife, she has frittered away her time by gossiping and attending Hindu religious festivals. By indulging in such frivolous pastimes, she has, according to the city guardian, neglected her real purpose in life — to serve her husband.

Cāttaṉār adds his own censure to that of the city guardian by referring to Maruti in ways that indicate that he views her as a superficially respectable woman whose inner state belies that respectability. Although Cāttaṉār uses standard descriptions of the jewelry that women wear throughout the text, use of the epithet, "respectably adorned woman," twice within a short discourse (lines 44 and 58) produces an ironic tone in this context. He labels her a woman *nēr iḻai*, literally "whose ornaments are straight." "Straight" here means appropriate, forthright, or of the type suitable to her role and position. A married woman's status is indicated by her jewelry,[17] which ideally symbolizes authentic chastity, purity of mind, and devotion. When it so indicates, it truly reflects a person's inner state. But when worn by a person lacking these inner qualities, such as Maruti, it makes an incorrect statement about the wearer. Since Maruti perceives only her superficially correct behavior, and the guardian comments upon her inner failings, the author's ironic use of the description of her jewelry juxtaposes these two perspectives; her actions are like superficial adornments of respectability, lacking resonance with her fundamental nature.

In order to rid her of her complacent and erroneous belief in her own virtue, the city guardian preaches to her about true virtue by quoting and interpreting couplet fifty-five of *Tirukkuṟaḷ*. Tiruvaḷḷuvar's *Tirukkuṟaḷ*, dated ca. A.D. 450-500, is a collection of aphorisms on *aṟam* [correct behavior and morality], *poruḷ* [wealth and politics], and *kāmam* [love]. A word-for-word gloss of couplet fifty-five is provided below because an understanding of the city guardian's discourse requires recognizing grammatical ambiguity in the verse:

teyvam	*toḻāḷ*	*koḻunaṉ toḻutu*	*eḻuvāḷ*
gods	not worshipping	her husband worshipping	she who awakes

pey	*eṉa*	*peyyum*	*peru*	*maḻai*
"rain!"	(when she) says	will fall	great	rain.

Literally, the couplet says, "She who arises worshipping her husband, not worshipping gods, will make great rain fall when she says, 'Rain!'"[18] The basic dynamic of the idea behind the *Tirukkuṟaḷ* verse is that chaste women gain so much power from their purity that they can miraculously influence events in the world around them. The couplet clearly attributes to chaste wives the ability to make rain fall. Because of the ambiguity of the verbal form *toḻāḷ*, however, the couplet can mean that rain will fall at the command of a woman who worships either (1) no other gods until she worships her husband or (2) no god except her husband.

The two interpretations of the couplet correspond respectively to the opinions of Maruti and the city guardian. Maruti interprets the line according to the first alternative, since she claims to have fulfilled all the duties of chaste wives who bring rain (line 53), even though she attends festivals where deities are worshipped. On the other hand, the city guardian interprets the verse according to the second alternative, since he reprimands Maruti for attending festivals that focus upon ritual worship of deities. According to him, only a woman who worships her husband exclusively can bring rain.[19] He explains to Maruti that only if she refrains from doing the things he has censured will she become truly chaste and command the rain clouds.

Although it might appear that there is nothing particularly Buddhist about the guardian's suggestion to Maruti, in fact his advice to this brahmin housewife is directed against a specific Hindu religious celebration, the Indra Festival. Cāttaṉār refers to the celebration (22:63) as "the festival during which the strap-tied drum is played" because the celebration begins when devotees mount the special drum stored in the temple dedicated to Indra onto an elephant and move in procession around the city, proclaiming that the holiday has commenced (*Maṇimēkalai* 1:27-30). We know from both chapter one of *Maṇimēkalai* and chapter five of *Cilappatikāram* that the residents of Pukār celebrate the twenty-eight day Indra Festival as their annual religious occasion. The Indra Festival is dedicated to the Vedic deity Indra and includes worship of the god Śiva as well (*Maṇimēkalai* 1:54). It is Maruti's participation in this festival to which the guardian objects.

Rather than idle away her time with acts of Hindu ritualism, the city guardian recommends that she concentrate upon wifely duties. He urges Maruti to abandon her attachment to attending carnival-like Hindu religious festivals and gossiping with other people who congregate at those festivals because such diversions distract her from real virtue. Instead, she should look to her home as the proper sphere for pursuing religious goals. In the process of quoting from the *Tirukkuraḷ*, the guardian here lays out an approved path of virtue for housewives.[20]

Because the *Tirukkuraḷ* has such a venerated position in Tamil culture,[21] the city guardian gains a great deal by structuring his discourse about the proper behavior for a housewife around it. First, he addresses his listener with words already familiar to her when he quotes the famous Tamil poet Tiruvaḷḷuvar. By doing so, he phrases his message of reprimand in terms of values to which he knows she already pays lip service. Second, when he structures his speech as a gloss upon a verse from a venerated text, he makes his argument in a traditional and accepted manner. That is, he formulates his moral instruction as if it were the logical outcome of a true understanding of a passage in a respected book.[22] Even if he has interpreted the text in a way that differs from the original intent of its author, this technique enlists the authoritative status of the older text to help validate his message. Third, the technique of quoting an older text is especially effective in this case because the city guardian bases his moral preaching upon a couplet from a text whose teachings are considered to be quintessentially true.[23] For these reasons, the city guardian's argument about what a good wife should avoid would be persuasive to Cāttaṉār's readers.

The Vicākai Story

In addition to eschewing Hindu festivals, a good layperson should practice "giving" (Sanskrit *dāna*; Tamil *tānam*),[24] according to Vicākai. In her discourse to Tarumatattaṉ, she stresses generosity as a key virtue for a layperson. Vicākai has her own sources of authority, despite the fact that her status is very different from that of the *pūtam*.

Vicākai can preach effectively because of her extraordinary personal purity. On two separate occasions, miraculous events bear witness to her virtuous nature. The earlier incident occurs in her youth, when the townspeople suspect her of having premarital sexual relations with her cross-cousin. According to Cāttaṉār's narrative, a deity dwelling in a pillar vindicates Vicākai by proclaiming she will give rain (another reference to Tiruvaḷḷuvar's definition of a chaste woman found in *Tirukkuṛaḷ*, line 55). Because of the deity's words, the townspeople must admit that she has remained above reproach. Another incident, whose denouement once again emphasizes Vicākai's purity, occurs after this earlier exoneration.[25] When King Kakantaṉ's elder son makes advances to Vicākai as she is walking down the street one day, Vicākai is protected from him by a miraculous manifestation of her chaste powers. Her chastity causes her would-be assailant's hand to stick to his head.

In addition to her morally pure inner state, both her resolution to join a house of virgins (line 100, *kaṉṉi māṭam*) and her long years of discipline spent there qualify her to preach. Her decision to join a community of virgins entails giving up of all hope of marital happiness in this life. Such commitment, in the face of her great love for Tarumatattaṉ, makes her all the more convincing as a preacher. Further, the long period of time she has spent in her community adds to her authority. Beyond the usual respect accorded to elders in ancient India, she has the venerability derived from her role as aged renouncer. Her experience, status, and age entitle her to provide a sermon on life's impermanence.

Tarumatattaṉ is a particularly appropriate audience for Vicākai's sermon. He is extremely wealthy, but he has acquired his riches through virtuous means. In addition, he has received the much coveted *eṭṭi* award, a sign of society's recognition that he plays an important role in the life of the city. In fact, he plays such a crucial role that when he leaves Maturai later on in the story, the city becomes impoverished. In terms of the ordinary standards of his merchant caste, he has reached the zenith of his career when the king honors him with the award. There could not be a more appropriate audience for a discourse that describes the transience of all material possessions than a man who owns so much. Thus, Vicākai urges him to give away money as a Buddhist act of devotion.

In his portrayal of Tarumatattaṉ listening to Vicākai's sermon, Cāttaṉār depicts the type of relationship between a layperson and a monk considered appropriate in Buddhist tradition. Ideally, the two have a reciprocal relationship — a member of a monastic order preaches the teachings of the Buddha, and the layperson gives generous donations to gain merit. Vicākai begins by telling Tarumatattaṉ that since all things are transient, one should behave generously by giving away one's wealth. Vicākai then points to the fading of their youthful beauty and desire as an example of life's impermanence. At the conclusion of her discourse, she urges Tarumatattaṉ to give gifts.

In response to Vicākai's sermon, Tarumatattaṉ undertakes appropriate action. As soon as Vicākai admonishes him to give (line 139, *tāṉam cey*, literally "perform/do giving"), he shows the nun his vast amounts of wealth, inviting her to join him in munificent acts. Then, we are told, Vicākai and Tarumatattaṉ perform more charitable deeds than there are stars in the sky.

In these two stories that the ascetic tells the king, Cāttaṉār sets out two complementary facets of proper lay behavior. As the Maruti story demonstrates, a devoted layperson should not become distracted from her real responsibilities through participation in Hindu rituals. Instead, as the Vicākai story explains, a Buddhist layperson's responsibility consists of performing *dāna*, "giving."

Royal Responsibility to Protect Female Renouncers

Because a king is an extremely powerful layperson, he can be especially effective in helping the Buddhist *saṅgha* to flourish. In his speech to King Māvaṇ Kiḷḷi, the great ascetic encourages the king to extend particular protection to female renouncers. Such protection entails punishment of men who seek to interfere with the religious discipline of nuns. In order to convince the king to accept such a role, the ascetic employs blessings or praise, story-telling, and "distancing" as rhetorical strategies.

The ascetic learned of Prince Utayakumaraṉ's murder soon after it occurred and has now come to inform Māvaṇ Kiḷḷi of his son's death. If the king thinks that Maṇimēkalai is responsible for the prince's death, instead of realizing that the prince brought his fate upon himself through sexual obsession, Maṇimēkalai's life is in danger. So, the ascetic must convince the Cōḻa king both that lustful behavior toward an ascetic woman deserves punishment and that a king must protect female renouncers.

In addition to his oratorial skills, the great ascetic who comes to confront Māvaṇ Kiḷḷi possesses impressive religious achievements, which lend special authority to his words. Cāttaṉār emphasizes repeatedly that the preacher in the story is one of the greatest ascetics in the land (*mātavar tammul ōr mātavaṉ*, literally "one great ascetic among great ascetics" — the way to phrase a superlative in Tamil). These ascetics dwell in the cremation ground and are renowned throughout the city.[26]

Although the ascetic directs his discourse primarily toward the Cōḻa king, he uses the social pressure created by the public occasion as a check upon any tendency the king might have to rule in an arbitrary manner. The king typically holds court surrounded by his courtiers, councilors, and military generals. (The text explicitly mentions the presence of the general of the Cōḻa army in line 205.) In addition to comprising an appreciative audience for the ascetic's oratorical sophistication, these men act as witnesses. Their presence encourages Māvaṇ Kiḷḷi not to act rashly.

The great ascetic punctuates his speech with formulaic language appropriate for the praise of great kings and chieftains as a way of eliciting the kind of response he seeks from the king. In composing the ascetic's speech, Cāttaṉār was able to draw material from a vast reservoir of traditional tributes because ancient Tamil poets had developed eulogy into a highly sophisticated art. In *Caṅkam* poetry, an entire *puṟam* subgenre contains poetry that extolls kings, chieftains, warriors, and gods. That subgenre is called *pāṭāṇ*, "praising." A section of *Tolkāppiyam*, the earliest extant Tamil grammar, sets out rules for praising and provides a list of types of praises.[27] The placement, context, and frequency of eulogistic interjections in the ascetic's narrative reveal that he has manipulated the vocabulary of traditional courtly praise as a way of encouraging the king to recognize the unique status of female renouncers.

The ascetic structures his discourse so as to avoid unpleasant topics for as long as possible, following the traditional strategy proposed in couplet 685 of *Tirukkuṟaḷ* and its accompanying traditional commentary. That couplet tells an emissary to a king's court that his speech will bear the best fruits if he avoids mentioning unpleasant things. The commentator Parimēlaḻakar goes one step further, suggesting, "When speaking about unpleasant matters, one should avoid harsh words and speak sweet words to please the king."[28] The great ascetic in *Maṇimēkalai* follows this advice by avoiding any direct accusation of Prince Utayakumaraṉ. Instead, he praises and blesses Māvaṇ Kiḷḷi with sweet words and, at the same time, uses those words to subtly remind him that he must rule fairly, even though his passions might encourage him in a different direction. These praises and blessings are first used to establish a general set of criteria for moral behavior, before telling the king of his son's death.

The ascetic begins by emphasizing the responsibilities and spheres of influence of a king as he pronounces an extended blessing (lines 13-18):

> May your white umbrella, towering above like the full moon at its zenith, give shade to the earth. May your spear and sceptre oversee all with compassion. May the discus you hold roll without evil. O king, may you live happily for all the years allotted to you.

The four emblems mentioned in these lines — the umbrella, the spear, the sceptre, and the discus — are associated with different aspects of kingship. An umbrella shelters those beneath it, symbolizing the manner in which the king protects his subjects.[29] The spear stands for his valor in war, while the sceptre symbolizes his vigilant administration of justice for his citizens. In battle he protects his country from outsiders, while through domestic administration he ensures that justice is carried out within the boundaries of his realm. The king's discus represents the vast extent of his rule and his kingdom as a whole. In the phrase, "May the discus you hold roll without evil," the speaker wishes Māvaṇ Kiḷḷi blameless rule throughout his kingdom. The ascetic concludes this section of his speech with a hope that the Cōḻa king might enjoy a long life.

Because Maṇimēkalai's fate is at stake, the ascetic dwells upon the nature of protection in the first two blessings. As the umbrella signifies, a king must protect his citizens from those who break the rules of society. The ascetic will go on to demonstrate that the renouncer, Maṇimēkalai, should have been protected from, rather than subjected to, the prince's advances. The spear and the sceptre ruling with grace stand for the compassion that the ascetic will soon argue Māvaṇ Kiḷḷi should show toward Maṇimēkalai. Thus the first part really contains a set of general instructions to the king that relate to the proper treatment of the young heroine.

The last two lines in this blessing comprise a warning to Māvaṇ Kiḷḷi — a warning whose import is fully understood only in reference to a pivotal scene in *Cilappatikāram*. In that text, when the hero, Kōvalaṉ, finally becomes disenchanted with his mistress and returns home impoverished, his faithful wife, Kaṇṇaki, offers him her jeweled anklet to sell. Therefore, Kōvalaṉ goes to Maturai, capital of the lineage of Pāṇṭiyaṉ kings, in order to sell his wife's jewelry. Unfortunately, a villainous goldsmith there has stolen the Pāṇṭiyaṉ queen's anklet, so when Kōvalaṉ arrives with his spouse's anklet, he is accused of the crime. For this supposed theft, King Neṭuñceliyaṉ commands that he be executed. This execution begins the erosion of that Pāṇṭiyaṉ monarch's righteous rule.

Kōvalaṉ's death leads the townspeople to evaluate King Neṭuñceliyaṉ's reign by referring to the same emblems of sovereignty that the great ascetic in *Maṇimēkalai* employs when he blesses King Māvaṇ Kiḷḷi. The disgruntled townspeople in *Cilappatikāram* say, for example, "the sheltering umbrella of the victorious king that had cooled the earth now generates heat." This comment condemns their Pāṇṭiyan̲ monarch; rather than sheltering his subjects from harm as a righteous king should, the ruler has himself become a source of burning affliction. Similarly they complain, "Since irremediable wrong has been done to this woman, the unbending and righteous sceptre of the king has been bent."[30] This statement refers to the classical tradition of describing the quality of a particular king's rule by a reference to the state of his sceptre: if the king rules justly, his sceptre remains straight (*ceṅkōl*), but if justice is neglected, his sceptre becomes curved or bent. The ascetic in *Maṇimēkalai* warns King Māvaṇ Kiḷḷi that he must continue to provide cooling shelter and rule with a just sceptre; the failure to do so brought about condemnation of King Neṭuñceliyan̲ in *Cilappatikāram.*

However, the Pāṇṭiyan̲ monarch earns far more than opprobrium; he loses his life as a result of his unrighteous judgment and Kōvalan̲'s subsequent execution. When Kaṇṇaki hears of the unjust death of her husband, she arrives at the Maturai court and, in a dramatic confrontation, accuses King Neṭuñceliyan̲ of wrongdoing. As soon as she conclusively proves to the king that he has allowed a terrible injustice to be perpetrated, he dies. In *Maṇimēkalai*, the ascetic's meeting with King Māvaṇ Kiḷḷi gains much of its heightened drama from its underlying similarity to the *Cilappatikāram* scene.[31] In each case, someone comes to court to confront a monarch with irrefutable evidence that injustice has prevailed. In the second half of the great ascetic's blessing in *Maṇimēkalai*, he says, "May the discus you hold roll without evil / O king, may you live happily for all the years allotted to you." The ascetic implies that only virtuous rule will earn him a long and prosperous life. In effect, he warns the Cōḻa monarch that his life is in danger if he departs from justice, as did the Pāṇṭiyan̲ king in *Cilappatikāram.*

The fact that the confrontation ends in exactly the way the ascetic intended indicates the effectiveness of the sermon. The king acknowledges that his son was rightly killed for wrongdoing, and then he commands that Maṇimēkalai be put under royal protection (*kāval*).[32] The ascetic's use of praise was effective in achieving his goal because it was based upon shared cultural perceptions of what a king, ideally, should be — a protector. By identifying the ideal of righteous kingship central in classical Tamil tradition with the protection of female renouncers, the ascetic convinces the king that he must also take care of Maṇimēkalai.

The ascetic also uses story-telling as a rhetorical device to convince both the king and members of his court of his claims. The ascetic tells two branch stories before giving the king news about his son's death, but he hints that these stories relate to matters at hand. After blessing Māvaṇ Kiḷḷi he prefaces his discourse with a summary of what he will soon relate in detail: "Just as it happened today, in ancient times, too, there were many men who lost their lives when their bad deeds took form" (lines 19-24). When the ascetic completes his rendition of these stories, the king anxiously asks the ascetic to clarify the relationship between the events he has just related and the present situation: ". . . you said, 'Just as it happened today,' and recounted many instructive things. Do such deeds occur even today?" (lines 163-65). Then, in answer to Māvaṇ Kiḷḷi's question, the ascetic relates the events leading up to Utayakumaraṉ's death.

By telling the illustrative stories first, the ascetic informs the monarch of precedents for the issues at hand. The two stories he tells occur during mythic times when Paraśurāma, an *avatāra* of Viṣṇu, stalked the earth.[33] The internal logic of each story leads the listener to conclude that there was only one appropriate course of action for the righteous king depicted in the story — to punish his lustful son. These stories function like modern legal precedents insofar as they establish the way a particular problem has been treated in the past. The stories make the monarch's duty clear.

The ascetic then moves from the branch stories to the formulation of a general moral principle. Basing the principle on the pattern established in the branch stories, he tells the king that lustful behavior is evil (lines 169-76), culminating his discourse with the question,". . . is it not also true, O king of the wide land, that those who do not overcome lust will suffer in unbearable hells?" Finally, he describes to the Cōḻa king the deeds of his own son, stressing similarities between the boy's actions and those of males in the branch stories. Because the ascetic follows this particular order in his address to Māvaṇ Kiḷḷi, he is able to influence the king's response. The king knows why Kakantaṉ's sons were executed, and if he is to be consistent, he must acknowledge that his son died for the same reasons.

As a final strategy, Cāttaṉār uses two rhetorical techniques to help King Māvaṇ Kiḷḷi maintain emotional detachment from events that affect him personally. One technique is postponement, deferring the discussion of Utayakumaraṉ's death as long as possible. In the first 176 lines of the ascetic's address, he praises the king, tells two branch stories, and expatiates upon the evils of lust in general terms. Not until line 177, in a speech comprised of 202 lines, does the ascetic begin to discuss the specific incident that prompted his journey to the court. Even when he commences this discussion, he does not reveal the name of the miscreant until the very end of his account. Note the order in which the ascetic describes the events leading up to the murder: the ascetic carefully establishes that Maṇimēkalai is a committed ascetic and almswoman (lines 179-83); he reports that a lustful male would not leave her alone (lines 184-86); he notes her trip to the temple and the arrival of the demigod (lines 187-93). Up to this point, the ascetic has referred to the man in question as "the one who did . . .," or "*ivaṉ*," which means "this male one." Not until line 195 does he state that the previously unidentified male pursuer is Prince Utayakumaraṉ. Until then, the king has not known that the villain being discussed is his own son.

As another way of encouraging the king to maintain emotional detachment from the situation, the ascetic identified a deed that the prince performed in a previous life as the agent of his lustful actions. As soon as the ascetic reveals the name of Maṇimēkalai's would-be assailant, he immediately shifts responsibility from the prince to the fruit of a past deed (his karma). According to line 193 of the narrative, because the fruit of an evil action Utayakumaraṉ had done in the past ripened, it caused Utayakumaraṉ to lust after Maṇimēkalai. The text identifies the evil deed (*tīviṉai*) specifically as the agent that drove Utayakumaraṉ to the temple and caused the demigod to kill him (lines 197-202):

> . . . because your son Utayakumaraṉ's evil deed had come to fruition, it was he who did not stop pursuing Maṇimēkalai. Instead his evil deed compelled her to go to the temple and drove Utayakumaraṉ there . . . It [the deed] confused the mind of the vengeful demigod and made him think "That man came for my woman" . . . It also caused the sword in the demigod's hand to cut down Utayakumaraṉ in the temple.[34]

In chapter twenty-one of *Maṇimēkalai*, Cāttaṉār reveals the identity of the deed that this passage credits with causing Utayakumaraṉ's death. In that chapter, Maṇimēkalai learns that Utayakumaraṉ, her husband in a previous life, had cut off the head of his cook in a pique of anger (21:36-114). The karma created by that deed causes his murder in this life. By emphasizing the prince's karma, the ascetic tries to shift the king's attention away from his son in order to make the king accept what has happened and also to preserve the king's ability to judge the situation dispassionately.

Likening Female Renouncers to Chaste Wives

Members of Cāttaṉār's sixth-century Tamil audience might have found certain aspects of female renunciation objectionable. Cāttaṉār depicts characters protesting female renunciation so that he can answer some of these objections later in the text. One of the most common criticisms voiced is that renunciation entails giving up one's *jāti-dharma*, the duties (*dharma*) one assumes by virtue of one's birth into a particular type of community (*jāti*). The reader finds the most sustained censure of abandoning one's *jāti-dharma* in chapter eighteen of *Maṇimēkalai.* There, Cittirāpati, Maṇimēkalai's grandmother, lectures to an assembly of dancing girls about the inappropriateness of Maṇimēkalai's decision to become a renouncer. Cittirāpati angrily informs her listeners that the code of conduct for a courtesan is to abandon men after taking all their money, rather than to take up religious discipline.

In her lecture, Cittirāpati voices some of the anti-renunciation sentiments that Cāttaṉār's sixth-century audience might have felt. She begins by comparing the courtesan to the lute that continues to play, though the particular minstrel who has owned it may die. In this image she indicates that a courtesan moves from client to client, without developing attachments to anyone in particular. She then notes that the courtesan uses up men's money like a bee who sucks the flower dry of honey and then abandons it. Because of her fickleness, the harlot is also like Lakṣmī, the goddess of prosperity, who leaves a person once the good karma he has earned is exhausted. Moving from imagery to explicit advice, Cittirāpati now urges her listeners to renounce impoverished customers rather than renounce one's *jāti-dharma*.[35] Later Cittirāpati tells the prince that, as part of his royal duty, he should *pāṉmaiyil piṇi*, "bind people to their nature," meaning that he should force citizens to practice the *dharma* of their *jāti*. She even implies that the prince should seduce Maṇimēkalai in order to ensure that she will fulfill her courtesan code for conduct (18:110-11) rather than continue to follow the path of religious asceticism, which Cittirāpati views with scorn.

Cāttaṉār cannot deny that Maṇimēkalai neglects the duties entailed by her birth into the courtesan *jāti* in order to become a renouncer. In fact, Cāttaṉār's claim that she can abandon the duties of the courtesan functions as the motivation for much of *Maṇimēkalai*'s plot. Believing that Maṇimēkalai is permanently bound to the *jāti-dharma* of a courtesan, Utayakumaraṉ never stops considering her to be the appropriate object of his sexual interest. Not only does she come from a lineage of courtesans, her own grandmother Cittirāpati presides as matriarch of the *jāti*. If a woman can never abandon her *jāti-dharma*, the prince's pursuit of Maṇimēkalai throughout the text makes complete sense. On the other hand, if (as Cāttaṉār claims) Maṇimēkalai can by an act of will reject her membership in the community (*jāti*) that nurtured her, she can embrace an entirely new status as a nun, which enables her to abandon her former duties and makes Utayakumaraṉ's attentions unsuitable.

Rather than denying that Maṇimēkalai forsakes the duties appropriate to her *jāti* by becoming a nun, Cāttaṉār denigrates those duties. His contempt for courtesan life informs Mātavi's speech to Maṇimēkalai in chapter two, where she tells her daughter of her conversion to Buddhism. There the mother decisively announces that her daughter must eschew the work of a prostitute, labeling it *tītoḻil*, an evil occupation (2:57). Later in *Maṇimēkalai*, the same message issues from the mouth of the queen, who defines the courtesan business as one entailing lying, lust, killing, and *uḷḷakkaḷavu*, stealing of hearts (24:78).[36]

In addition to discrediting the activities of the courtesan community, Cāttaṉār makes an even stronger case by claiming that a female renouncer is worthy of the respect and acclaim accorded to a chaste wife. He develops this argument through the structure of the ascetic's speech to King Māvaṇ Kiḷḷi. The ascetic carefully draws parallels between the chaste wife and the woman who gives up marriage in order to undertake ascetic discipline. In this way, Cāttaṉār likens the unfamiliar status of a

Buddhist nun to that of an ancient Tamil cultural ideal — the woman who practices absolute conjugal fidelity.

At the beginning of the ascetic's address (lines 19-24), we have seen that he identifies two types of women that one should not approach with lustful attentions. These two are chaste women and ascetic women (renouncers):

> . . . just as it happened today, in ancient times, too, there were many men who lost their lives when their bad deeds took form. Some died because, full of intoxicating and ripened lust, they approached *chaste women*. Others died because in their hearts they desired *women performing great asceticism* (emphasis added).

Shortly after these introductory comments, the ascetic gives an example of a chaste woman, Maruti, whose would-be assailant lost his life. Next, the ascetic gives a parallel example of a woman performing great asceticism, Vicākai. Her chastity protected her from the inappropriate attentions of a lustful man who later died as a result of his improper advances. When men with lust in their hearts sought after either type of woman, the result was identical.

In these two branch stories, the two types of women are most strikingly likened in terms of Tiruvaḷḷuvar's definition of a chaste woman, which Cāttaṉār applies to both Maruti and Vicākai. As we have seen, Maruti does everything a faithful wife should, except that she attends Hindu festivals. Once she refrains from participating in such celebrations, the city guardian tells her she will be able to make the rain fall, the power with which Tiruvaḷḷuvar credits chaste women. In Vicākai's case, the Speaking Image pronounces her capable of commanding the rain to fall, making reference to the same couplet by Tiruvaḷḷuvar.[37] Thus, both are presented as chaste women with the same miraculous powers, even though one has married and the other has chosen the life of a renouncer. Since the Vicākai story is the only one whose heroine is similar to Maṇimēkalai, it is significant that the ascetic includes the Maruti story at all. Not only is it included, it is presented, in specific ways, as a parallel story.

Conclusions

The great ascetic's discourse derives its complex structure from the techniques of nesting and juxtaposition. The frame of the narrative surfaces in the ascetic's introductory remarks, the blessings that recur periodically, the lecture on the evils of lust, and the disclosure of the prince's murder. The theme of this frame concerns the king's duty to protect female renouncers. Juxtaposed and nested within this frame are two stories about proper behavior for women — both renouncers and housewives. Through the ascetic's discourse, Cāttaṉār explores issues of both gender and religious role, examining the consequences of various types of behavior.

The nested stories of Vicākai and Maruti explore the consequences of female actions: they demonstrate that when women practice self-control, they gain extraordinary powers. Vicākai's decision to renounce fulfillment with Tarumatattaṉ and join a community of virgins, for example, gives her the ability to freeze her would-be abductor's hand in mid-air. It is her decision to control her sexuality that grants her this unusual power. Similarly, Maruti learns that rain will fall at her command if she abandons frivolous speech, curtails her attendance at Hindu festivals, and worships no gods other than her husband. By disciplining herself to live within these limits, she gains the miraculous power to command the skies and bring fertility to earth.

Many other South Asian texts also contain the formulation that deeds characterized by self-control yield special powers. The *purāṇas* abound with tales of those who performed penance to gain boons from the gods.[38] Parallel to Cāttaṉār's assumption that certain human beings can bring rain are Sanskrit tales such as that of Ṛśyaśṛnga, whose ascetic nature enables him to end drought throughout the kingdom.[39] Turning more specifically to Tamil materials about women, we find related evidence in texts and fieldwork data. Hart argues that *Caṅkam* poetry credits chaste wives with special powers.[40] In the same vein, *Cilappatikāram*'s Kaṇṇaki gains the ability to avenge her husband's death as a result of her great chastity and devotion to him — even though he abandoned her to live with a dancing girl. Autobiographical accounts collected by Egnor in present-day Tamilnadu also emphasize the *śakti* [power] that women gain from their sufferings. Reynolds, examining the various statuses possible among Tamil women, concludes that the austerities they perform enable them to gain a considerable amount of control over their lives as well as their husbands' lives. In her wide-ranging survey of these materials, Wadley emphasizes how crucial the element of self-control is to "the perceived powers of Tamil women."[41] It seems, then, that Cāttaṉār's emphasis on the fruits of female self-discipline is in consonance with many other South Asian materials.

Cāttaṉār, however, adds another variable to his discourse on the powers of women because he deals with both a female renouncer and a laywoman. Although the two deserve the same status and respect, they practice self-control and discipline in different ways. The female renouncer gives up sexual union, while the chaste housewife circumscribes her behavior and worships none but her husband. In each case, self-control yields rich consequences.

Complementary to the notion of female self-control is Cāttaṉār's idea that the king must support and protect such disciplined women, especially members of the monastic community. In arguing that point, Cāttaṉār encourages his audience to accept the Buddhist view of kingship rather than the Hindu one. Classical Hindu texts depict the righteous king as one who maintains the social order — by using his subjects' fear of his punishment, if necessary — and thus ensures that each citizen discharges the duties prescribed according to his or her own *jāti*.[42] For example, when Cittirāpati invites Prince Utayakumaraṉ to make Maṇimēkalai fulfill her courtesan duties by coercion if necessary, her argument assumes this concept of Hindu righteous rule. But the ascetic in *Maṇimēkalai* argues, in contrast, that a righteous king's real duty is to support and protect members of the monastic community. Aśoka, the first great patron-king of Buddhism in India, is credited with establishing the pattern of duties for such righteous kings.[43] In addition to his generous support for Buddhist institutions, Aśoka went out of his way to encourage their activities. As Reynolds comments,". . . there developed alongside the Buddhist Sangha, which was constituted by the order of monks and nuns and the laymen and women who supported them, the ideal of a Buddhist state governed by a pious monarch who modeled his rule after the example of Aśoka."[44] In chapter twenty-two of *Maṇimēkalai*, the great ascetic encourages the king to model himself after that type of ruler. If he does imitate Aśoka, the king's duty will be to protect the Buddhist nun, Maṇimēkalai, from further harm and encourage her activities.

It is the complex construction of the ascetic's speech that enables Cāttaṉār to explore all of these ideas. Through nesting and juxtaposition, he can make use of the branch story, classical Tamil blessings and praises, and precedents for correct action found in stories such as *Cilappatikāram*. What makes the ascetic's discourse compelling is his emphasis on the fruits of action: while certain deeds endow their actors with miraculous powers, others result in violent death. In edifying the king about right behavior, the ascetic simultaneously informs Cāttaṉār's readers about the proper attitudes toward chaste women, both ascetics and laywomen.

7

THE COMPARISON STORY

Texts that advocate the choice of one religious system over others necessarily provide a positive evaluation of that religious system and negative evaluations of competing religious systems. One of Cāttaṉār's major concerns is the evaluation of different religious traditions. This evaluative element appears throughout *Maṇimēkalai* but nowhere more explicitly than in chapter twenty-seven, the text's most polemical section. There Cāttaṉār portrays Maṇimēkalai systematically testing and finding flaws in the tenets of various religious schools of thought being espoused in Vañci at that time. In the process, the reader is offered a critique of current non-Buddhist viewpoints. Cāttaṉār's most entertaining critique, however, occurs in the comparison story of Āputtiraṉ's begging bowl, where he lambasts brahmanical Hinduism.

Criticism of Competing Religious Viewpoints

Evaluation and criticism of competing philosophical systems constitute the defining characteristics of an entire class of Indian texts. Basham sees *Maṇimēkalai* as a member of this class: "The text [*Maṇimēkalai*] is an example of a class of philosophic literature which, stripped of its fictional trappings, resulted in such works as *Civanānacittiyār*, and the *Sarva-darśana-saṁgraha*."[1] According to Basham, both *Maṇimēkalai* and the later Tamil Jain text, *Nīlakēci*, are designed to describe and refute philosophical systems other than the particular one that each espouses.

Basham sees *Nīlakēci* as providing a more extreme example of this class of text than *Maṇimēkalai* because the narrative — what Basham called the "fictional trappings" — is of less significance than in *Maṇimēkalai*. Basham says,

> The doctrines of the opposing sects are stated in *Maṇimēkalai* briefly, with an attempt at objectivity. . . . [*Nīlakēci*] seems to have been written by an author who had read the Buddhist *Maṇimēkalai*, and wished to provide a Jaina counterpart to that work. But the poem is a step nearer to the fully developed study of various philosophical systems than *Maṇimēkalai*, wherein the philosophy is subordinate to the story.[2]

Basham's viewpoint accounts for the polemical sections of *Maṇimēkalai* by placing them in the context of a whole set of texts whose authors intended to defend one philosophical position and reject others. However, in his evaluation of *Maṇimēkalai* as a polemical work, he ignores the polemical thrust of the text's stories and, most specifically, its comparison stories.

Comparison stories actually function implicitly in the same way that the polemical philosophical sections of *Maṇimēkalai* function explicitly. Both seek to establish the superiority of one given religious perspective and discredit one or several competing perspectives. An extremely straightforward comparison story in *Maṇimēkalai* (5:32-79), the account of Cutamati's conversion to Buddhism, demonstrates the way in which such a story can justify particular viewpoints and question other perspectives.

In this story, Cutamati describes how she came to reject Jainism and accept Buddhism. According to her account, one day when her father was walking along a street, he was viciously gored by a cow that had just given birth to a calf. Cutamati's father went to a nearby Jain monastery for aid, grasping his disemboweled organs in his hands. Cutamati's account emphasizes the inadequacy of the Jain response to the suffering of the old man: He [her father] cried,

> "O Jains, let me take refuge here!" But they angrily replied, "Such things are not appropriate here." So, those great ascetics of flawless appearance motioned to us to leave. Our eyes filled with tears, and we lamented in the street outside the monastery of the ascetics. "Are there any among you who actually practice virtue (*aṟam*)? We have no one to take care of us." (*Maṇimēkalai* 5:52-57)

When the Jain monks saw the old man heading toward them, his entrails in his hands, they recoiled in disgust and forbade him to enter into their compound. In Cutamati's description of the incident, the flawless outward appearance of the great ascetics contrasts starkly with their lack of inner moral commitment. Because of this incident, Cutamati, who had previously embraced the Jain religion, suddenly realized how hypocritical its practitioners were. Despite the injunctions against harming living creatures, which led the Jain monks to their well-known fastidious behavior,[3] these monks had refused to have mercy upon her suffering father. Bitterly, she came to the conclusion that the monks did not actually practice virtue (*aṟam*).

Immediately afterwards, they met a Buddhist monk who took one look at the situation and quickly came to the couple's aid. He picked up the elderly, suffering man and carried him to a Buddhist monastery. There the wounded father received nursing, and the two learned in great detail about the Buddha and his message of compassion. Thus, Cutamati explains the circumstances that led her to become a Buddhist.

The polemical design of this story stands out clearly. Cāttaṉār could have merely described the way a Buddhist monk helped Cutamati and her father, but instead he told the story in two stages. The story explicitly compares Jain and then Buddhist reactions when presented with the same situation of human suffering. The Jains threw the stricken man out of their monastic compound: they were tested and found wanting. In contrast, the Buddhists embraced Cutamati's helpless father, displaying true compassion. Not only does the story discredit the Jain monks, it also emphasizes the uniqueness of the Buddhist practice of compassionate acts.

The comparison story related above, a fairly straightforward one, performs some of the same rhetorical functions that the account of Maṇimēkalai's visit to Vañci (*Maṇimēkalai*, chapter 27) does. In each case, a competing religious perspective is tested and rejected. In the latter case the flaws are logical, and in the former they are moral. That is, Maṇimēkalai listens to various religious specialists in Vañci and then rejects their philosophical systems because they contain flawed reasoning. In the comparison story of Cutamati's father, the reader is urged to reject a particular religious perspective (in this case, the Jain one) because a representative of that religious worldview acted in an immoral and reprehensible manner. The comparison story differs in another way from the philosophical debate. Rather than discuss religious ideas in the abstract, comparison stories put them *in situ* and portray people acting upon the basis of such ideas. Such stories are not, therefore, mere "fictional trappings." They function as more graphic, immediate, and engaging ways to suggest the superiority of a particular religious system than an ordinary critique of that religion's philosophical assumptions.

In *Maṇimēkalai*, Cāttaṉār includes another comparison story, one more complex and symbolic than Cutamati's conversion story. This tale, the story of the miraculous begging bowl's origins, depicts and criticizes Hindu hypocrisy and greed. At the same time, it portrays its hero — later identified with the Buddhist religion — as a man of unlimited generosity and praises his behavior, implying its superiority to that exhibited by those representing Hinduism.

The story of the miraculous begging bowl deals with one man over the course of two sequential births. In the branch story translated and analyzed below, dealing with one of his lives and his eventual death (*Maṇimēkalai*, chapters 13-14), he is called Āputtiraṉ. Because of his commitment to the alleviation of human suffering, Āputtiraṉ performs many acts of great generosity. As a result of these generous deeds, in his next birth Āputtiraṉ becomes the just and effective King Puṇṇiyarācaṉ (see *Maṇimēkalai*, chapters 15 and 25), bringing rain to a land that had previously suffered from drought for twelve years.

Translation: "The Story of Āputtiraṉ's Begging Bowl"

There once was a man named Apañcikaṉ, a protector of the
Vedas [a brahmin] in Vāraṇāci. His brahmin wife, Cāli, passed
beyond the bounds of his protection[4] and then feared punishment 13:05
for failing her husband. In consequence, she decided to go on a
pilgrimage and bathe at Kumari in the south. While she was on the
road, her pregnancy came to term in the darkness, while others
slept. Since she did not feel any compassion for the child whom
she had borne, she abandoned him in a distant meadow and left. 10

A cow came there when she heard the distress of the starving,
motherless child. After licking the baby with her tongue, she
nursed it with sweet milk to comfort it. Then she stayed for seven
days, protecting and taking care of the baby.

One day Iḷampūti, a protector of the Vedas from Vayaṉaṅkōṭu, 15
was coming down the road. Hearing the cries of the weeping child,
Iḷampūti felt sorrow and shed tears. He thought, "This child is not
the son of a cow. He will be my son." So, he and his wife did
obeisance and took the child away, saying, "A distinguished male 20
has been born. May our lineage flourish." Then, they returned to
their town and rejoined their kinsmen.

Even before his chest had been adorned with the three strands,[5]
the boy, Āputtiraṉ,[6] was taught to recite the good texts fluently. 25
He learned well, without any errors of the tongue, all the things
appropriate for brahmins who possess the Vedas.

One day he entered the house of one of the town's brahmins. A
sacrifice was about to take place there, during the whole of which
the brahmins were intent only upon meat-eating.[7] The horns of a
cow had been covered with colorfully woven garlands. The cow
sighed and lowed piteously, frightened of its dreadful enemies, like 30
a deer caught in a net who fears the bow of the hunter adept at
killing. Seeing the grief of the lowing cow who stood there in fear,
Āputtiraṉ's heart trembled, and he wept profusely. Then he
thought to himself, "In the concealing darkness I will take the cow

and lead her away, ending her cruel suffering by this act of theft." Hiding these thoughts, he secreted himself in a corner. At night, taking the cow, he left that place.

Later, when he was going along the difficult, rocky path, the brahmins and other townspeople closed in on him. In the middle of the forest, they caught Āputtiraṉ and the cow. Then the leader of the brahmins, while beating him cruelly with a stick, said to Āputtiraṉ: "You who took the cow along this difficult path, you are not a human being.[8] Tell us what made you do this. We'll drive you out, you base, low-caste boy!"

In response, as the brahmin teacher stood there beating Āputtiraṉ, the cow gored him and tore out his intestines. Then the infuriated cow disappeared swiftly into the forest.

Āputtiraṉ said to those around him, "Don't do things that will bring you distress! Listen to what I have to say. The cow eats only the grass that grows on land set aside for grazing. With a virtuous heart, she graciously feeds excellent sweet milk to all the people in this wide land, beginning from the day they are born. So why are you angry with this cow? Tell me what you think, brahmins of the ancient Vedas."

The teacher said scornfully, "You mixed-up boy, you scorn the good books of the precious Vedas without understanding them. They were bestowed upon us by the son [Brahmā] of the creator of eternal souls [Viṣṇu] who holds the beautiful golden discus in his right hand. Ignorant one, you are only fit to be the son of a cow. You are not a human being."

Āputtiraṉ answered, "Ācalaṉ was the son of a cow. Ciruṅki was the son of a deer. Viriñci was the son of a tiger. Kēcakampaḷaṉ, whom eminent men praise, was the son of a fox, wasn't he? Now some of your lineages originated from these sages.[9] If it is true that you speak highly of these distinguished men in your good books, people of the four Vedas, can it be true that a lineage originating from a cow is degraded?"

Then one of the brahmins there said, "I know about the birth of this person. Once I met a Sanskrit lady traveling according to Vedic prescriptions. Her body was emaciated and sore from walking. This woman called Cāli, who had left her relatives, came to worship at the feet of Goddess Kumari according to traditional injunctions. When I asked her to tell me her village and why she came here, that lady of the great Vedas told me the story of her journey:

'I was once the precious wife of a Vedic teacher, foremost among Vāraṇāci brahmins. Behaving in a way not suitable for brahmins, I passed beyond the bounds of protection, scorning my husband. Due to fear of darkness, I traveled with wandering bands of people[10] in order to bathe at Kumari in the south. I passed ten furlongs beyond Great Korkai, city of the Pāṇṭiyaṉ king who has a golden chariot, to the area of cowherders' settlements. Since I did not have any compassion for the child I had borne, I abandoned him in a distant field and left. Is there any salvation for a sinner like me?'

"This is the son of that miserable woman. Since there was no use in telling this story before, I said nothing until now. Take care not to touch him. This boy is low caste."

Āputtiraṉ laughed a knowing laugh. He said, "Listen to the lineages from which the people of the great Vedas came. The two progenitors [Agastya and Vasiṣṭha] of the brahmins of the precious Vedas were the beloved sons of a divine courtesan who appeared before the lord of the ancient Vedas.[11] Surely, you cannot deny that? If that is the case, is Cāli to be blamed?" he said and stood laughing at those people of the four Vedas.

After this, thinking that the boy was not fit to live with brahmins who chant the Vedas, his father, Iḷampūti, and his mother drove him from the house. In all the villages where brahmins lived, people put rocks in Āputtiraṉ's begging bowl,[12] saying, "He is the thief who stole the cow."

So Āputtiraṉ went to Maturai in the south, where people resplendent with great wealth reside. There he lived on the courtyard porch in front of the Ceḻuṅkalai Temple[13] of Goddess Cintā Tēvi.[14] In that great southern city, he took up his almsbowl and visited all the excellent and faultless homes for alms. Then he called to the blind, deaf, lame, and unprotected people, and to those weak with disease. Telling them all to come, he fed them and ate what remained when they were all done. Then the protector,[15] Āputtiraṉ, used his begging bowl as a pillow and went to sleep.

One dark midnight filled with rain, some travelers who were exhausted by their difficult journey arrived at the porch where Āputtiraṉ was sleeping. After doing obeisance and praising him, they said, "Burning hunger afflicts us!" Āputtiraṉ, who begged for his own food, became distressed that he did not have any to satisfy their hunger.

Then the goddess Cintā Viḷakku[16] appeared in the famous Iruṅkalai Temple[17] and said,

> Hear me: May your sorrow perish! Do not be distressed! Instead arise and take this bowl. Even if this entire land becomes impoverished, this bowl will never be exhausted. The hands of those who receive food from it may ache from taking so much, but the bowl will never be empty.

As soon as the goddess put the bowl in Āputtiraṉ's hand, he worshipped that supreme goddess and praised her with these words:

> O Cintā Tēvi, eternal lamp of the Ceḻuṅkalai Temple, woman who dwells on the tongue,[18] you are the leader of the celestials, you are supreme among people on earth, and you end the suffering of other creatures.

From that very day, beginning with the travelers, he devoted himself to ending hunger, feeding living beings so much that the hands with which they ate ached. People, animals, and the birds of the trees constantly gathered around him. One heard the sweet noise of these living beings rising incessantly like the calling of birds gathered in a fruit tree.

Āputtiraṉ's deed, down on the earth surrounded by oceans, shook Intiraṉ's white carpet.[19] So Intiraṉ took the form of a brahmin with a bent-over body, walking feebly and supporting himself with a cane. Appearing on the vast earth before the leader and protector of precious living beings, he said, "I, Intiraṉ, have come. What do you think of that? Now, you can receive the fruits of your great giving."

Laughing like a simpleton, almost splitting his sides, Āputtiraṉ said, "I scorn you. Go away. Your dazzling gods up there may enjoy the fruits of the deeds they did down here. But, though you are an extremely victorious king and the god of the good heavenly land, there are no virtuous people, no protectors, none who take care of people, none who perform good *tapas*, and none who practice detachment up there. My divine begging bowl destroys the extreme hunger of miserable people who come to me, and their faces become happy. Compared to this, what can the king of the gods bestow on me? Food? Clothing? Women? Protectors?"

In response to Āputtiraṉ, the god with one thousand eyes gave wonderful things to those on earth, saying, "Let water spread throughout the wide land so that riches pour forth and poverty disappears. Then this protector, whose bowl overflows with food, will be disappointed when no one comes begging."

Previously, the good Pāṇṭiyaṉ country had lacked rain for twelve years, and many living beings died there. But now, the work of the rain helped the great land to flourish, so people no longer knew hunger. Because of that, the noise of eating on the temple porch of that nourisher of precious living beings stopped. Even wantons, ne'er-do-wells, runaways, and vagabonds lived merrily. People easily took up gambling, dicing, and wenching as ways of life.

Āputtiraṉ left his porch and went from town to town asking for hungry people. "Who is *he*, anyway?" everyone asked mockingly. The leader of precious living beings wanted to feed people, but since no one said, "You're here to feed me, aren't you?" he wandered by himself like an illustrious man who returns all alone after his wealth, comparable to Lakṣmī's, has been swallowed up by the vast ocean.

Then, some people who had traveled by ship across the sea approached him and did obeisance. They said, "Dedicated man, in the good country of Cāvaka,[20] since the cool rains refused to fall, people are perishing."

Āputtiraṉ thought to himself: "Because of the command of the king of the gods, no hungry people come to me. I hold a bowl that is like an old virgin spinster. I think I will go to that country." Then he embarked happily on the ship with the others.

Due to turbulent winds that stirred up the ocean, they dropped sail at Maṇipallavam Island. The boat stayed there for a day, and Āputtiraṉ went ashore. Since they thought he had re-embarked, the captain hoisted sail and set out through the moving waters in the darkness. After the boat left, Āputtiraṉ was very upset because no one lived there. He said, "I can't bear that this very great bowl[21] that nourishes living beings should only nourish me. I am suffering because the fruits of my *tapas* are exhausted. Since this unusual fate is mine, what is the good of carrying this bowl?"

Then he dropped the bowl into a pond with rich waters named Kōmuki[22] Tank and said, "Appear one day each year. If anyone practices the virtuous way (*aṟam*) of grace (*aruḷ*) and takes care of precious living beings, enter that person's hand."

I went to him at the time when he was giving up his life by a vow of fasting. When I asked what had happened, he spoke of the many things he had experienced. Intent on sustaining many living beings [in his next life], he abandoned his body on Maṇipallavam Island. He seemed like the sun that appears in the east after destroying the black darkness and then goes west.[23] He was reborn in the womb of a cow belonging to the industrious king who ruled Cāvaka.

Enlisting the Reader's Admiration for Āputtiraṉ

Throughout the story of Āputtiraṉ's birth and childhood, Cāttaṉār enlists the reader's sympathy for Āputtiraṉ. Cāttaṉār describes Āputtiraṉ's pitiful birth in detail — the darkness of night concealing Cāli's delivery of an illegitimate child, her uncaring abandonment of the infant, the empty field where the babe lay crying. But for the nursing of the compassionate cow, Āputtiraṉ would certainly have perished. Cāttaṉār's description of the baby's cries as "the distress of the starving, motherless child" conjures up a scene of great misery. Given the Indian cultural context, Cāttaṉār could have described Āputtiraṉ as tainted or polluted by his illegitimate birth (as other characters in the story do), but instead he describes the infant as an innocent and blameless baby.

Once Āputtiraṉ settles into Iḷampūti's family, Cāttaṉār depicts him as quickly mastering the traditional Vedic corpus. According to lines 23-24, Āputtiraṉ had learned to recite the ancient texts well, even before he underwent the *upanāyana* ceremony during which boys from the upper three *varṇas* are invested with their sacred threads. In portraying Āputtiraṉ as proficient in Vedic learning at a time when most brahmin boys are only beginning their studies, Cāttaṉār gives the reader a sense of the boy's extraordinary intelligence and eagerness to learn.

Cāttaṉār first describes Āputtiraṉ's unusual sensitivity toward the suffering of other living beings when the young boy decides to steal the cow held in captivity for the soon-to-be-held sacrifice.[24] From the beginning of the branch story, Cāttaṉār emphasizes the virtues of the cow. Only through her devotion does Āputtiraṉ survive his ignominious and wretched birth at all; she nurses him with sweet milk and protects him. As O'Flaherty has commented in relation to theriomorphic forms of Indian goddesses, the cow in Hindu myths is associated with fertility, nourishment, and selfless giving.[25] In fact, Āputtiraṉ himself makes the same point about the selflessness of cows when he says,

> The cow eats only the grass that grows on land set aside for grazing. With a virtuous (*aṟam*) heart, she graciously feeds excellent sweet milk to all the people in this wide land, beginning with the day they are born.

Āputtiraṉ feels it is wrong to hurt a cow because she takes so little and gives so much to all human beings.

Since Cāttaṉār has emphasized the cow's unselfish nature, her upcoming sacrificial slaughter seems like a travesty. Cāttaṉār's description of the captive cow emphasizes her helplessness and Āputtiraṉ's empathy with her suffering:

> The cow sighed and lowed piteously, frightened of its dreadful enemies, like a deer caught in a net who fears the bow of the hunter adept at killing. Seeing the grief of the lowing cow who stood there in fear, Āputtiraṉ's heart trembled, and he wept profusely.

Because of these two character portrayals, the audience tends to admire rather than condemn Āputtiraṉ's act of thievery when he rescues the cow and absconds to the forest.

As a result of Āputtiraṉ's plan to save the cow's life, he must endure extreme suffering. The path of their flight is harsh and stony. When pursuers catch up with the two fugitives, their brahmin leader gives Āputtiraṉ a sound beating with his frightful stick (*alaikkōḷ*, literally, "harassing stick") and insults him. First he tells him he is not a *makaṉ*. The speaker uses *makaṉ* in two senses: (1) son and (2) human being. He implies that Āputtiraṉ could not possibly be the real son of a brahmin because, by interrupting the Vedic sacrifice, he betrayed the brahmanical way of life. In addition, the guru mocks his name by saying he is not a human being because he is called Āputtiraṉ, "son of a cow." Finally, they call him *pulai*, "low caste"/"outcast"/"defiled." Such a label is the ultimate insult for a group that prides itself on its high rank and purity. Eventually, his parents drive him out of their home, and then the hostility he encounters in the rest of the brahmin community forces him to leave his village and seek refuge in Maturai at the Sarasvatī Temple.

Despite Āputtiraṉ's own unhappy life, however, he never forgets the needs of other unfortunate people living in Maturai. Every day, when he returns from his begging rounds, he shares his alms with the blind, deaf, lame, and sick people, and the "unprotected" people (orphans, widows, etc.). Even before Āputtiraṉ receives the inexhaustible begging bowl, the text explicitly refers to him as the protector (*kāvalaṉ*) of these people (*Maṇimēkalai* 13:115), an epithet often used to describe kings caring for helpless citizens. Once Āputtiraṉ receives the inexhaustible begging bowl from the goddess, his entire life revolves around ending the suffering of the land's people. The goddess Sarasvatī recognizes his compassionate nature, and when she gives him the inexhaustible begging bowl, she supplies him with the means to ameliorate suffering throughout the land. Cāttaṉār describes Āputtiraṉ's extraordinary generosity by comparing him to a fruit tree where many birds can flock to obtain food.

Āputtiraṉ's verbal exchange with Indra demonstrates that he cannot be tempted away from his self-appointed task by lures that Indra might offer. He compares the hedonistic lifestyle of the gods who live in Indra's celestial paradise to his own life and clearly implies that nothing Indra could grant him tempts him in the least. Āputtiraṉ's commitment to his task is clearly incorruptible.

Even the circumstances of Āputtiraṉ's death bear witness to his intelligence and compassion. When his generosity is no longer appreciated in Tamilnadu, he goes elsewhere to make his bowl useful, setting out for Cāvaka, where a terrible drought has occurred. There he hopes he can use his bowl to feed starving people. When it turns out that he is marooned on Maṇipallavam Island forever, he decides to end his life so he can take on a new birth, leaving his bowl for an appropriate successor. When he says, "I can't bear that this very great bowl that nourishes living beings should only nourish me," he shows once again his concern for all living beings, not just himself.

Disparaging Brahmanical Religiosity

At the same time that Cāttaṉār builds this positive image of Āputtiraṉ, he consistently casts aspersions upon brahmins, beginning with Āputtiraṉ's mother, Cāli. Although she is the wife of Apañcikaṉ, one of the most illustrious and learned brahmins in Benares, she secretly has sexual relations with another man and becomes pregnant as a result. Cāli seeks to rid herself of her sin by making a pilgrimage to the sacred site of Kanya Kumari, an act considered efficacious as penance for certain kinds of misdeeds. Since she is only concerned with restoring her lost ritual purity, she gives little thought to the fate of her illegitimate child. Carelessly leaving him to die, she goes on her way.

Cāttaṉār emphasizes that brahmins concern themselves with outward form rather than inner meaning in the epithets for, and descriptions of, brahmins he uses. He never describes brahmins as anything other than caretakers or chanters of the Vedas, as is indicated by the following list of literal translations of the terms used in chapter thirteen of *Maṇimēkalai* to denote brahmins:

Line	Description (English)	(Tamil)
15	protector of the secret (Vedas)	*maṟai ōmpāḷaṉ*
25	brahmins who possess chanting (Vedas)	*ōttu uṭai antaṇar*
55	brahmins of the ancient secret (Vedas)	*mutu maṟai antaṇir*
68	people of the four secret (Vedas)	*nāṉ maṟai mākkāḷ*
100	brahmins who chant (Vedas)	*otal antaṇar*

As this list demonstrates, Cāttaṉār labels "brahmins" as people who possess the Vedas and chant them. He uses the terms *maṟai* [secret] and *ōttu* [chanting, reciting] to denote Vedas. Although these terms have come to be synonyms for *vētam* (Sanskrit *Veda*), their etymological aspect would not be lost upon Cāttaṉār's audience. The Vedas are *maṟai*, secret, because they are limited to the twice-born *varṇas*. Cāttaṉār emphasizes *ōttu*, reciting, because the crucial point is to chant the verses rather than understand them.

Cāttaṉār most explicitly ridicules the hypocrisy of brahmanical ritual when he discusses how the priests feel about sacrifice. As a characterization of Vedic sacrifice, he uses the phrase *pulai cūḻ vēḷvi*, literally, "the sacrifice in which [eating] meat is considered." Cāttaṉār implies through this phrase that the real motives of brahmin priests are contemptible. Rather than consider the religious meaning of their role in Vedic sacrifice, the brahmins just think about the pleasures of eating meat after the sacrifice ends.

In the debate that occurs in the forest, Cāttaṉār reveals the gap between what brahmins claim and what is actually true. There Āputtiraṉ systematically discredits brahmanical assumptions in the most convincing way possible — by using incontestable brahmanical texts as evidence. By using proof that the brahmins must accept as authoritative, Cāttaṉār shows the brahmins "out-brahmanized" by the young upstart, Āputtiraṉ. Cāttaṉār demonstrates that Āputtiraṉ has read, thought about, and understood the true meaning of particular Vedic passages, whereas the brahmins merely possess the texts and mindlessly chant their verses. In addition, the evidence that Āputtiraṉ cites is shocking and embarrassing to the brahmin elders, thus adding insult to injury.

A brahmin begins by claiming that Āputtiraṉ had no right to steal the cow because, in doing so, he interfered with the sacrifice. Since the sacred Vedas enjoin sacrifice, the brahmin guru accuses Āputtiraṉ of showing scorn for the Vedas. The brahmin goes on to inform Āputtiraṉ that these books were given to their community by the god Brahmā. Thus, Āputtiraṉ's act indicates lack of respect for both these scriptures and their source. For this reason, he deserves the insulting name of "son of a cow"; his behavior demonstrates he is base and ignorant, like an animal.

Āputtiraṉ immediately turns this insult on its head by listing the names of Vedic sages who were also born from animals. The best-known of the sages he lists is Ṛśyaśṛnga (Tamil Ciruṅki), whose father was the great ascetic Vibhāṇḍaka. One day when that ascetic happened to see the celestial nymph Urvaśī, he had an involuntary emission of semen, which fell into a nearby stream. When a doe who came to drink out of its water swallowed the semen, she became pregnant and eventually gave birth to a human child. That boy, Ṛśyaśṛnga, was brought up by his father in their forest hermitage and grew up to be a great brahmanical sage. After listing sages such as Ṛśyaśṛnga, Āputtiraṉ goes on to taunt his opponent, saying, ". . . some of your lineage originated from these sages. If it is true that you speak highly of these distinguished men in your good books, people of the four Vedas, can it be true that a lineage originating from a cow is degraded?" Not only has Āputtiraṉ out-argued the brahmin by using evidence from the Vedic corpus to which his opponent can give no rejoinder, he has brought up the embarrassingly unorthodox births of several illustrious brahmanical sages.

Another brahmin reveals that Āputtiraṉ was the bastard son of a reprehensible brahmin woman, a fate far worse than being the son of a cow. This brahmin tells the story of Cāli's misdeeds and then warns his peers to shun the boy, saying, "This is the son of that miserable woman. . . . Take care not to touch him. This boy is low caste."

Āputtiraṉ responds in the same way as he did to the last charge against him, producing a story from the Vedas that portrays the illegitimate births of Agastya and Vasiṣṭha, two extremely venerated Vedic sages. Pointing out that the two *ṛṣis* were born of the seed spilt when a Vedic deity saw a celestial dancing girl, he challenges them to justify this ancient Vedic precedent of two illustrious brahmins born illegitimately. Then he taunts them about the story and concludes, "If that is the case, is Cāli to be blamed?" After these comments, Āputtiraṉ stands there, laughing at the way in which the brahmins have been thrown into confusion by his knowledge of the Vedic corpus and his ability to use examples of unorthodox practice portrayed there in order to taunt them. Cāttaṉār's denigration of brahmins culminates when Āputtiraṉ vanquishes them in debate.[26]

Discrediting Vedic Deities

In the second half of the story, Āputtiraṉ again opposes brahmanical religion, but this time his adversary is Indra (Tamil Intiraṉ), the king of the Vedic gods. Because Indra's white carpet in heaven shakes, warning him that an extremely virtuous human being has performed excessively good deeds, he descends to earth to offer Āputtiraṉ a boon. When Āputtiraṉ completely rejects Indra's offer, Indra flies into a rage. Determined to have revenge upon Āputtiraṉ, Indra then causes abundant rains to fall so that prosperity fills the land and no one is hungry. Suddenly, Āputtiraṉ's bowl is useless. It might, therefore, appear that Āputtiraṉ has indeed been bested by Indra.

Such an interpretation, however, ignores the ultimate outcome of the story and its underlying rhetoric. In the first place, Āputtiraṉ reaps the fruits of his good deeds in his next birth when he becomes a righteous king. In the second place, Cāttaṉār's depiction of Indra's revenge, creating such widespread prosperity that Āputtiraṉ's bowl becomes useless, enables *Maṇimēkalai*'s author to portray the king of the Vedic gods as vengeful, selfish, and hypocritical. By designating Indra to be Āputtiraṉ's opponent, Cāttaṉār's portrayal resonates with a huge set of incidents from Hindu mythology. Indra's actions in those myths make him an excellent target for Cāttaṉār's attack on brahmanical religion.

Indra as King of the Gods

In the Ṛg Veda, where the mythology of Indra begins, he performs brave deeds and acts as leader of the gods. In almost all of Indra's hymns, his ability to prevail in battle is stressed. As a virile warrior full of martial prowess, Indra epitomizes the heroic values of the Aryans. In addition to lauding Indra's military victories, Vedic hymns describe Indra as the king of the gods. In this role he protects his constituency, brings his worshippers prosperity, maintains hierarchy, and aids his ritual specialists. Vedic hymns such as this one praise Indra for aiding those who sacrifice to him:

> He who helps with his favour the one who presses and the one who cooks, the praiser and the preparer, he for whom prayer is nourishment, for whom Soma is the special gift, he, my people, is Indra.[27]

Particularly in the myth of Indra and the Paṇis, Indra plays the role of protector of the sacrifice. Srinivasan comments, ". . . this myth casts the demons as the supreme enemies of the sacrifice. They have posed a threat to the ritual by the nature of the wealth they have kept."[28] Here, Indra and the priests (kṣatriyas and brahmins) work together to vanquish the Paṇis, who are cow thieves. Indra cuts through Vala (RV X.67.6), rescues the cows, creates a path for them, and becomes their sole master.[29] In this myth, Indra acts as guardian of the sacrifice and protector of cows, in partnership with brahmin priests.

When Indra becomes associated with particular territories, his authority grows routinized. In classical Tamil texts, Indra rules as one of the five presiding deities of the five landscapes discussed in *Caṅkam* poetry. He reigns over *marutam*,[30] the agricultural tract, which seems appropriate given his long association with rain and fertility in general.[31] In the epics and *purāṇas*, Indra's role as king of the eastern direction is increasingly emphasized. As Bhattacharji comments,

> But in the epic Indra alone is guardian of the east, a position which was not exclusively his before. . . . This new position at once elevates and diminishes his rank for while the RV Indra was more a general than a king, more engaged in campaigns than in reigning, the epic Indra is a king *par excellence*; stationary, with a fixed capital where he reigns amidst glory and splendour.[32]

Sitting in state, surrounded by luxury, pleasure, and grandeur, Indra comes to be universally recognized as "a king *par excellence*."

As a widely acknowledged figure of Vedic authority, Indra fits well into Cāttaṉār's story of Āputtiraṉ. As king of all the gods and the epitome of martial Aryan values, Indra represents Vedic beliefs and values. When Cāttaṉār criticizes the chief of the Vedic pantheon, by implication he defames all the deities contained in it. By calling into question Indra's moral stance, Cāttaṉār indicates that true generosity surpasses the mechanical interaction between god and man found in Vedic religion.

In addition, when he casts Indra as Āputtiraṉ's opponent, Cāttaṉār can attack the manner in which brahmins and kṣatriya rulers collaborate to maintain their privileged place in society. As we have seen, Indra — representative of kṣatriya [warrior] values — defends priestly sacrifice and punishes cow theft in Vedic myths. This partnership between brahmins and kṣatriyas accounts for the telling symbolism of Indra's disguise when he comes to offer Āputtiraṉ a boon: "Intiraṉ took the form of a brahmin with a bent-over body, walking feebly and supporting himself with a cane" (*Maṇimēkalai* 14:30-31). The cane in the description is the *daṇḍa*, or staff of the king. The *daṇḍa* is a symbol of sovereignty and an agent of punishment, with which the king chastises any citizen who does not live according to his prescribed code of moral conduct (*dharma*).[33] In this image, Cāttaṉār captures the visual image of an old and rickety brahmanical tradition buttressed by kingly power (*daṇḍa*). Since Cāttaṉār seeks to undermine the justification for religiously validated social privilege, his choice of Indra as Āputtiraṉ's opponent is particularly appropriate.

Indra as Excessive Enjoyer of Pleasure

Other unsavory characteristics of Indra contribute to the inner logic of the Āputtiraṉ story. As brahmanical Hinduism grew to reject some aspects of Vedic religion and accept bhakti elements, Indra's portrayal in myths degenerated. In a good many incidents we find Indra using both unfair tactics and cheap tricks as substitutes for actual power. In one of his most notorious disguises, he takes on the form of the ascetic Gautama to mislead and seduce the ascetic's wife, Ahalyā.[34] As a result of this deception and other sexual misdeeds, he comes to be associated with lechery. Because of his seduction of Ahalyā, he is often described as covered with vaginas, which are transformed into red eyes in later, less explicit variants of the myth.

The theme of Indra as lecher is common in Tamil texts as well as Sanskrit ones. *Kamparāmāyaṇam* contains an elaborate account of the way in which Indra seduces and has intercourse with Ahalyā, by taking on her husband's form.[35] In reference to the same incident, in *Maṇimēkalai* Cittirāpati tells the prince that deities cannot be trusted because they have performed despicable deeds under the influence of lust; as one of her examples, she refers quite specifically to Indra's desire for Ahalyā and the one hundred red eyes he receives as a result of his sin (*Maṇimēkalai* 18:87-96). In the *Tirukkuṟaḷ*, Tiruvaḷḷuvar obliquely refers to Indra's punishment in an aphorism about how one must learn to control one's senses.[36] In a similar vein, in Tamil *intirapōkam* (Sanskrit *indra* plus *bhoga*, "enjoyment") comes to mean "indulgence" or "excessive pleasures of the senses."[37]

In addition to his over-indulgence in sexual pleasures, Indra is also known for the profligate life style enjoyed in his heavenly realm. Bhattacharji comments,

> . . . he does not fight formidable enemies in tough battles, nor does he destroy demons, or win cattle and wealth or light and water; but sitting on his throne he rules like an emperor who enjoys courtly pleasures after his expeditions are successfully carried through.[38]

Indra's courtly pleasures consist of splendiferous palaces, ornate adornments, and numerous deities to wait upon him. In the *Mahābhārata*, Nārada tells Yudhiṣṭhira about the splendor of Indra's palace:

> Śakra's (Indra's) celestial and splendid hall, which he won with his feats, was built by himself with the resplendence of fire. It is a hundred leagues wide and a hundred and fifty long, aerial, freely moving and five leagues high. Dispelling old age, grief, and fatigue, free from diseases, benign, beautiful, filled with chambers and seats, lovely and embellished with celestial trees is the hall where . . . the lord of the gods sits with Śacī.[39]

Indra enjoys life's pleasures — sexual, material, and aesthetic — to the utmost.

In the story of Āputtiraṉ, Indra's character as an "enjoyer" throws into relief Āputtiraṉ's unselfishness. Indra considers the self-centered enjoyment of pleasure paramount and assumes others feel the same way. For this reason, when Āputtiraṉ's excessive goodness makes Indra's white carpet shake, Indra assumes that if Āputtiraṉ, too, is provided with celestial pleasures, his commitment to virtuous giving will lessen. But instead Āputtiraṉ scorns the life led by deities such as Indra in those celestial spheres. He says,

> Your dazzling gods up there may enjoy the fruits of deeds they did down here . . . [but up there] there are no virtuous people (*aṟam cey mākkaḷ*), no protectors, none who take care of people, none who perform good *tapas*, and none who practice detachment.

Āputtiraṉ then compares the satisfaction of truly helping other people with the paltry pleasures of Indra's realm and rejects Indra's offer. Because the king of Vedic gods is a deity widely recognized as overly concerned with indulging his senses, the interaction between Āputtiraṉ and Indra is an excellent vehicle for Cāttaṉār's argument that generosity surpasses mere selfish pleasure.

Indra as Benchmark

Despite the fact that Indra's importance begins to decline in the epics and *purāṇas*, he remains a benchmark figure by which other heroes and deities are measured. One finds extraordinarily powerful kings and warriors commonly compared to Indra in the *Mahābhārata* and *Rāmāyaṇa*.[40] As time goes on, Indra's deeds become a standard by which other heroes measure themselves.[41] Indraship eventually becomes a rank or title: "It is by deeds that one attains the rank of a king or brahmin, or of some god, or of an Indra or a Brahmā."[42] "Indra" also enters the language of comparison in compounds like Narendra (*nara*, "man," plus Indra), meaning Indra of men, e.g., king of men, chief of men, best of men. Because Indra has become a benchmark figure, both human and divine usurpers challenge his authority quite often in these later texts.

The classic story of Indra's usurper, told in the *Viṣṇu Purāṇa* and the *Harivaṃśa*, concerns the conflict between Kṛṣṇa and the king of the gods. The story begins with the cowherders making preparations for an Indra Festival. Although they are content to worship Indra as they have always done, Kṛṣṇa persuades them to desist from this worship and thereby brings down upon them the wrath of Indra. In his anger, Indra sends so much rain that the cowherders think the end of the world is at hand. The cows weep out of fear. But Kṛṣṇa saves all beings from the flood by lifting up Mount Govardhana to form a giant umbrella, sheltering them from Indra's floods. Indra realizes that he has been beaten by Kṛṣṇa and arrives on the scene to perform an *abhiśeka*, "inauguration," ceremony and confer a title upon Kṛṣṇa by virtue of his authority as king of the gods.[43] This story glorifies Kṛṣṇa at Indra's expense, using Indra as a standard by which Kṛṣṇa's greatness can be demonstrated.

In early sections of the Tamil Śaivite *Tiruvilaiyāṭal Purāṇam*, challengers like Kṛṣṇa constantly threaten Indra's position so that his glory never seems completely secure.[44] In one myth, a king has performed ninety-nine sacrifices to bring about the birth of a son. If a human being ever performs one hundred sacrifices, he can usurp Indra's position. For this reason Indra, nervous about the steadily accumulating power generated by these ninety-nine sacrifices, tells the king to abandon them and perform a particular rite for a son. But when the king has that rite performed, a daughter he names Mīnākṣi is born instead. In this myth, a mortal threatens Indra's own power so much that Indra has to disuade him from continuing his course of action. In the same text, King Ukkirapāṇṭiyaṉ performs ninety-nine horse sacrifices (*aśvamedhas*), again making Indra so uneasy that he feels he must prevent Ukkirapāṇṭiyaṉ from continuing to sacrifice. Eventually, he decides to send Varuṇa down to destroy Maturai, the city where Ukkirapāṇṭiyaṉ reigns. Many other Tamil myths include this motif of someone performing nearly one hundred sacrifices, almost usurping Indra's power.

In numerous myths, Indra learns of threatening events taking place on earth by the heating of certain of his personal possessions — his throne, his blanket, or his carpet. These items become hot for a variety of reasons including the intent of others to dethrone him, the radiance generated by the good conduct (*śīla tejas*) of virtuous ascetics, or simply human beings performing virtuous acts. Generalizing about the formulaic motif of the heating up of Indra's possessions, O'Flaherty comments,

> Thus, the pattern that had been established in Vedic myths of gods and demons were now applied to gods and men: excessive power or virtue in an opponent was to be destroyed.[45]

These opponents constantly threaten Indra's authority (because it is theoretically secure), and in some cases they vanquish Indra, proving their own power in the process.

Indra as Āputtiraṉ's Opponent

In myths where excessive good deeds or penance brings a boon from Indra, he grants that boon to terminate the deeds of his opponents. Indra feels undermined when another being has acquired enough power through sacrifices or virtuous behavior to threaten his position. If the person performed ascetic acts to receive a boon, Indra grants that boon so that the person refrains from further asceticism. If the person was doing asceticism for other reasons, Indra attempts to prevent that person from continuing to perform threatening acts through trickery, misleading advice, or distraction — e.g., sending down beautiful celestial nymphs (*apsaras*) to tempt the *yogin* away from his asceticism. Thus the pattern is one of coercion on either or both sides — Indra coerced into granting a boon and/or the ascetic or virtuous human coerced into desisting from his threatening behavior.[46] In line with the pattern just described, Indra's interaction with Āputtiraṉ results in the termination of threatening action. By sending abundant rains to a land plagued by drought, Indra creates so much prosperity that no one goes hungry. As a result, Āputtiraṉ can no longer feed starving people.

Although Āputtiraṉ loses to Indra, the confrontation between them only serves to emphasize Indra's selfish, debauched, and hypocritical nature. Cāttaṉār clearly indicates that Indra brought rain not out of compassion for human suffering but to wreak vengeance upon Āputtiraṉ for refusing his boon. The prosperity created by Indra is improper because the evil people are rewarded as well as the good. While Cāttaṉār describes Āputtiraṉ as helping the needy (the blind, the deaf, etc.), he emphasizes, in contrast, that Indra helps even the wantons, ne'er-do-wells, runaways, vagabonds, gamblers, and prostitutes (*Maṇimēkalai* 14:61-64). Thus Indra's generosity, unlike Āputtiraṉ's, has no moral content or discrimination. Āputtiraṉ may have been defeated, but Cāttaṉār portrays the winner as reprehensible and morally bankrupt. Throughout the story, various rhetorical devices function to keep the reader on the side of Āputtiraṉ. In addition, Āputtiraṉ's good karma ripens, enabling him to return to the narrative in another birth as the heroic King Puṇṇiyarācaṉ, who banishes hunger in the land of Cāvaka.

Ultimately, the story emphasizes Āputtiraṉ's generosity rather than Indra's power. That generosity undermines Indra's authority, causing his white carpet to shake. In other purāṇic myths, ascetics are portrayed as doing penance to receive a boon from Indra, but Āputtiraṉ performs good deeds without even realizing that they might result in Indra's offer of a boon. Even before he obtains his miraculous bowl, he begs and gives away all his food, eating only the remains. After obtaining the bowl, his generosity is literally limitless. The story, therefore, can best be understood as part of a genre of Buddhist tales about the virtues of unlimited generosity. Āputtiraṉ belongs with Vessantara and King Aśoka by virtue of his tremendous commitment to giving (*dāna*).[47]

Lest the reader not realize that the unlimited generosity practiced by Āputtiraṉ is a Buddhist ideal, Cāttaṉār explicitly links Āputtiraṉ's actions with the Buddhist path through the inexhaustible begging bowl. Near the time of his death, Āputtiraṉ decides to leave his bowl behind so that another person who is motivated by the same concerns can continue his task. Therefore, he deposits the bowl in the Kōmuki Pond with the charge, "Appear one day each year. If anyone practices the virtuous way (*aṟam*) of grace (*aruḷ*) and takes care of precious lives, enter that person's hand." The identity of the one day on which the bowl appears is made clear in *Maṇimēkalai* (11:40-45): it appears each year on the birthday of the Buddha. When the Buddhist nun Maṇimēkalai comes to Maṇipallavam Island, she again takes up the task begun by Āputtiraṉ, beginning upon the birthday of the Buddha.

Conclusions

In the story of Āputtiraṉ's bowl, Cāttaṉār provides a narrative that encourages readers to critically evaluate Hinduism. Cāttaṉār consistently portrays brahmins as hypocritical, greedy, and narrow in outlook. Implicit comparison is made between the heartless brahmins who kill cows in sacrifices and heroic Āputtiraṉ who rescues helpless cows from slaughter. Brahmins who chant Vedic mantras by rote contrast vividly with Āputtiraṉ, the only person in the story who actually appears to have read and thought about the Vedas. After mocking those who offer sacrifices to the gods, Cāttaṉār goes on to attack the gods themselves. Cāttaṉār's choice of Indra as Āputtiraṉ's opponent was not arbitrary. As king of the gods, Indra comes to stand for the entire pantheon. As a well-known debauchee, he is already suspect. And, as a traditional benchmark figure in Indian mythology, he is an appropriate adversary for Āputtiraṉ. Cāttaṉār portrays Indra as selfish, coercive, and arrogant, showing that neither Hindu priests nor their deities are worthy of veneration.

On the other hand, Cāttaṉār encourages readers to admire Āputtiraṉ, the representative of Buddhist values. After sympathetically depicting Āputtiraṉ's birth, Cāttaṉār notes his outstanding intellectual abilities. Cāttaṉār's description of the pitiful sufferings of the cow builds up support for Āputtiraṉ's later rescue of the animal. After Āputtiraṉ moves to Maturai, Cāttaṉār portrays him as totally dedicated to feeding the needy, both before and after he receives the inexhaustible begging bowl. Then later in the text, Āputtiraṉ receives a fortunate rebirth as king of Cāvaka as a result of the good deeds performed in this life.

What Basham called "fictional trappings" can often be quite effective in advocating the acceptance of a particular religious perspective and attacking competing viewpoints. Rather than an abstract critique of mechanical brahmanical ritualism, Cāttaṉār provides us with flesh-and-blood brahmins who do not know the meaning of the words they chant and are stunned to find out the contents of certain Vedic texts. Similarly, the ideal of "unlimited generosity" is realized in the figure of Āputtiraṉ rather than merely included in lists of ethical prescriptions. Analysis of Āputtiraṉ's tale as a comparison story demonstrates that story literature can function as effective polemic while presenting an engaging narrative.[48]

Conclusions

In the sixteenth century, the Śaiva poet Civappirakācar called *Maṇimēkalai* an intricate text. In the twentieth century, Civappirakācar's statement deserves reaffirmation. Indeed, *Maṇimēkalai* is persuasive as well as intricate. This Tamil Buddhist text — the only one left of its kind — displays a rhetorical sophistication worthy of our attention.

Cāttaṉār often conveys his perspective by the sheer vividness of his scenes. As a powerful image of female renunciation, he shows us Maṇimēkalai locked inside the glass pavilion, the angry prince prowling at the door. To convey the adaptability of Buddhism, he gives us the shipwrecked merchant negotiating with the naked "savages" about the precise degree of virtue they can practice. He undermines the appeal of sexual love with a repulsively graphic tableau of a once-beautiful heroine's body dismembered in a cremation ground and eaten, limb by limb. He drives home the message of life's impermanence by identifying the entire cosmos with the cremation ground. He shows us the great ascetic carefully and brilliantly leading the king into a situation where he must protect the very woman, a Buddhist nun, whose actions led to the murder of his son. Almost perversely, Cāttaṉār even paints for us a scene of hypocritical brahmins waiting hungrily for the sacrifice of a cow. Cāttaṉār's ability to create such scenes and images accounts, in part, for his stories' memorability.

These individual scenes, however, gain their persuasive power from their rhetorical context. As we have observed, *Maṇimēkalai* comprises a set of stories that function to advance Cāttaṉār's overall goals, presenting the Buddhist worldview as reasonable, attractive, and satisfying. In chapter two, I showed how *Maṇimēkalai*'s main story defines, justifies, and advocates female renunciation through its portrayal of the heroine, using language from the *Caṅkam* landscape of clandestine lovers' union. In chapter three, I demonstrated how Cāttaṉār portrays the Buddhist code for conduct as adaptable and appropriate for all styles of life, by depicting the responses of a dramatized audience of cannibals who change their diet in order to practice *ahiṃsā*, noninjury to living beings. In chapter four, analysis indicated how the native elements of the desert landscape serve to set the scene for a discourse on life's impermanence in a story about a boy who ventures into a cremation ground. Chapter five examines the same story, placing it in the context of Buddhist cosmological tradition in order to show why the story so conclusively demonstrates the unalterability of karma. In chapter six, I discussed the relationship between renouncers and laypeople — especially kings — through an analysis of the many rhetorical strategies used in the ascetic's discourse to the father of the murdered prince. Finally, in chapter seven, I explored the use of a "comparison story" structure to cast aspersions on brahmanical tradition and praise the achievements of a great donor associated with Buddhism.

Much of the analysis just summarized focuses upon *Maṇimēkalai*'s branch stories. Scholars have long recognized that Indian traditional literature, both oral and written, makes use of stories for moral instruction.[1] And yet Cāttaṉār's didacticism has generally been the grounds for criticism, rather than the object of study. When we have, in fact, taken Cāttaṉār's pedagogical discourse seriously, the rhyme and reason of his stories have been revealed. Each story derives its inner logic from its illustration, justification, or advocacy of some particular religious ideal.

Maṇimēkalai's stories add up to far more than the sum of their parts. Each story contributes to Cāttaṉār's overall ideological goals, making the text as a whole more persuasive and religiously comprehensive than it would be if it contained only the story of Maṇimēkalai's renunciation. By following Ramanujan's suggestion that we investigate the "context sensitive designs" embedded in the text, we have discovered in *Maṇimēkalai* a coherence heretofore unrecognized.

In the final analysis, Cāttaṉār's rhetorical sophistication derives largely from his ability to make connections. In his handling of imagery, tale construction, character development, and story juxtaposition, Cāttaṉār consistently displays the ability to see the didactic potential in different bodies of literature. The popular features of Buddhist cosmological tradition, the range of subjects evoked by *Caṅkam* poetic convention, the fund of nefarious incidents from Indra mythology — all this Cāttaṉār pulls together to shape a series of stories surrounding the account of a courtesan's daughter who becomes a Buddhist nun.

A Community Envisioned

In addition to drawing upon Tamil, Buddhist, and Hindu materials, *Maṇimēkalai* bears the unmistakable flavor of pan-Indian *kathā* literature in its characters and plot. Compendia of tales such as the *Bṛhatkathā* and the *Kathāsarītsāgara* are excellent examples of such romantic, fairy-tale-like literature.[2] Motif analysis reveals a number of themes from pan-Indian *kathā* literature: the *viñcaiyaṉ* who can fly through the air, the sea voyage with its subsequent shipwreck and miraculous escape, the extraordinary glass pavilion that allows the prince observation but not entrance, the gift of the inexhaustible begging bowl, and the magnificent dharma seat that reveals events from past births. *Maṇimēkalai* is not by any means a historical snapshot, a realistically painted portrait, of Buddhism in sixth-century Tamilnadu. Instead, through his use of themes from *kathā* literature, Cāttaṉār constructs a world filled with miraculous events and marvelous encounters. The freedom granted to the author in such a world enables Cāttaṉār to envision an extraordinary community whose members — human, divine, and Nāka — become transformed by the Buddhist worldview.

Although *Maṇimēkalai* has come to be a text without a community of believers today (as I have argued in chapter one of this monograph), Cāttaṉār himself presents us with a Tamil Buddhist community through the stories in *Maṇimēkalai* — complete with flights through the air and an inexhaustible begging bowl. In the main story and his branch stories, Cāttaṉār explores what life would be like if living beings acted according to specific religious tenets. At the heart of this text is the connection between the spiritual growth of a single woman and the radical realignment of forces and values in the society around her. Through his skilful use of rhetorical strategies, he offers his readers a new way of revisioning their own beliefs, actions, and concepts of religious community.

In the middle of Cāttaṉār's dramatized community stands Maṇimēkalai, who willingly abandons the duties of her courtesan *jāti* in order to assume the status of a female renouncer. Her adoption of this role ultimately makes possible her pursuit of religious liberation. Thus, one can read *Maṇimēkalai* as an account of one woman's religious progress. But, in fact, Maṇimēkalai spends a great deal of time moving about in society. As soon as she receives her miraculous powers, she begins to distribute food and preach to those around her. With her words she encourages them to change the way they see themselves as discrete entities and the way they focus their lives around the pursuit of pleasure. Thus in her quest for her own salvation, she moves to transform society in ways consonant with Buddhist ideals.

In his portrayal of Maṇimēkalai, Cāttaṉār argues for a place for the female renouncer in Tamil society. In order to carve out that place, Cāttaṉār must make clear how this nun and the renunciatory values that she represents relate to other statuses with clearly recognized roles in Tamil culture: literary heroines, chaste wives, kings, people considered low on the social hierarchy, deities, and brahmins.

Most explicitly, Cāttaṉār defines the role of the female renouncer over and against the actions of the classical literary heroine. Cāttaṉār's description of Maṇimēkalai's relationship with the prince (as I have argued in chapter two of this monograph) is guided by the scenario of the lovers' tryst from *Caṅkam* poetry. Cāttaṉār defines a female renouncer by demonstrating how she differs from the lover uniting with her beloved. For the image of the young girl stealing out late at night to meet her man, Cāttaṉār substitutes Maṇimēkalai locking herself in the glass pavilion. In the branch story about the Cosmic Place (which I analyze in chapter four), Cāttaṉār goes even further. There he portrays a woman dressed for just such a clandestine tryst, dismembered and consumed in the cremation ground by ghouls and vultures. In these ways, Cāttaṉār begins to explain the unique qualities of a nun by showing how they differ from those of the classical heroine who figures in Tamil love poetry.

Cāttaṉār continues to develop his portrait of a female renouncer by likening her to a chaste wife, a woman to whom Tamil society already accords a great deal of respect. In the ascetic's discourse to the king (as I have argued in chapter six of this monograph), he uses two juxtaposed branch stories in order to argue that chaste wives as well as female renouncers have particular powers and particular privileges; both types of women can command the rain to fall, and both deserve protection from the advances of men with lust in their hearts. Cāttaṉār, thus, asserts the equivalence of the female renouncer and the chaste wife. In addition to sharing great self-discipline with the chaste wife, however, the female renouncer also has the ability to preach.

This ability to instruct others is crucial in Maṇimēkalai's relationship with the king. Most notably, Maṇimēkalai's earnest and persuasive words convince the monarch to transform his prison into an almshouse, where the needy can receive food and care. The prince's death also provides the nun with an occasion to preach to the queen. As a result of her words, the once-vengeful queen (who tried to kill her only hours before) now falls at her feet in gratitude for her instruction.

Although Cāttaṉār spends the majority of his time depicting the religious virtuoso at the center of society, he also has the vision to see his community extending to the very margins of that society. As my analysis of Cātuvaṉ's preaching to the Nākas indicates (in chapter three of this book), even those people who live practically like "savages" can be brought within the fold. By means of instruction geared to the capacities and disposition of his or her audience, a sensitive preacher can teach them a way to modify their behavior to live a more virtuous life.

Moving to the opposite end of the hierarchy of beings, we find that deities are also encompassed within Cāttaṉār's imagined Buddhist community. A variety of goddesses and gods — including Maṇimēkalā, Campāpati, and Indra — play a role in Cāttaṉār's text, but what matters most about that role is the limited and focused nature of their powers. The goddess Maṇimēkalā uses her miraculous abilities in the service of assisting her namesake in the quest for progress on the Buddhist path. Campāpati, although she possesses certain extraordinary capacities, is bound by the same laws as other living beings. She does not have the power to change the fate of individuals whose actions are the result of karma from past deeds. Campāpati demonstrates that neither she nor any other being in the cosmos can bring Kōtamai's son back to life because he died as a result of ignorance and the consequences of his past deeds (see chapter five). As for Indra, king of the Hindu gods, he comes off looking foolish and unworthy of admiration. In comparison to Āputtiraṉ, the archetypal Buddhist donor, Indra seems touchy, vengeful, and ultimately a figure of ridicule (as argued in chapter seven).

Although the omnipotence of Hindu goddesses is curtailed and Indra's deeds made ludicrous in Cāttaṉār's text, the abilities of the nun Maṇimēkalai are enhanced. Her extraordinary commitment to the Buddhist path wins her the inexhaustible begging bowl, the power to travel through the air, and the ability to change forms. These miraculous powers are harnessed for three purposes — to preserve her life when the queen attempts to kill her, to distribute food to the needy, and to preach effectively. That is, all of her supernatural powers are portrayed as protecting her from danger and enabling her to spread Buddhist ideas more effectively.

Cāttaṉār's envisioned community includes a range of members all the way from naked islanders to deities, but the arrogance and hypocrisy of brahmins will not be endured. In a typically Buddhist fashion, Cāttaṉār portrays the bastard Āputtiraṉ as heroic, but the brahmin priests as greedy and ignorant. The Buddhist community envisioned by Cāttaṉār is an open one where those born as courtesans, kings, former cannibals, and others can pursue a virtuous life without the mediation of brahmins or their sacrifices. Cāttaṉār's ability to write vivid and convincing stories, about a society where Buddhist ideas change the way people view the world, places him in a distinguished tradition of Buddhist writers who teach through the use of sophisticated rhetorical strategies.

Rhetoric in *Maṇimēkalai* and Other Buddhist Texts

In this book, I have used rhetorical analysis to show how — both in the main story and in the branch stories — Cāttaṉār has portrayed a community living according to Buddhist ideals and has argued for the acceptance of those ideals. My analysis suggests several parallels and family resemblances between the rhetorical strategies in *Maṇimēkalai* and certain other Indian Buddhist texts. The rhetorical perspective I have developed in this study of *Maṇimēkalai* may enable us to see these more familiar Buddhist texts in new ways.

In chapter two of this monograph, I explored at length the didactic potential of Cāttaṉār's story about a courtesan who embraces the life of a Buddhist nun. A survey of early Indian Buddhist texts indicates that his courtesan-turned-nun motif is not unique. Several scholars have suggested reasons for its appearance in Indian Buddhist texts. For example, in Horner's study of women in early Buddhism, she speculates about historical circumstances that might have made the monastic life an appropriate alternative for prostitutes, commenting,

> The Order of Almswomen yielded an accessible and honorable alternative to all those who wanted to relinquish the line of business they had hitherto been pursuing. To a large extent it was a prop and stay against any relapse into the conditions of their former way of living. For once admitted members found themselves expected to conform to a strict moral rule.[3]

In contrast, Winternitz focuses upon the aesthetic potential of the motif: "We hear repeatedly of former courtesans who became nuns, and the contrast between the life and conduct of the courtesan and the calm sanctity of the nun has a great artistic effect."[4] In addition to historical and aesthetic explanations, let us consider didactic reasons for the presence of the motif in Indian Buddhist texts.

As we saw in *Maṇimēkalai*, the courtesan is perceived as an object of sexual pleasure. She grows up in a *jāti* where she learns from her mother and grandmother how to make herself sexually attractive to men, use her beauty to entice clients, quickly extract their money, and then abandon them to penury. In chapter eighteen of *Maṇimēkalai*, Cittirāpati's pointed and angry speech to the assembly of dancing girls highlights the normative nature of such behavior for courtesans. Even after Maṇimēkalai decides to forsake that life, Utayakumaran̲ and Cittirāpati continue to demand that she make her lovely body available to the prince.

This emphasis on the courtesan's physical appearance is the key to interpreting a poem attributed to Ambapālī in the *Therīgāthā*, a Pali anthology of verses attributed to Buddhist nuns. Along with an anthology of verses composed by Buddhist monks (titled *Theragāthā*), the *Therīgāthā* has been described as a set of "religious poems which, in force and beauty, are fit to rank with the best productions of Indian lyric poetry."[5] Evidence suggests that the verses collected in the *Therīgāthā* were uttered between the end of the sixth century and the end of the third century B.C.[6] The *Therīgāthā* comprises nearly eighty poems containing a total of more than five hundred stanzas. Among the poems attributed to several former courtesans, Ambapālī's verses seem especially appropriate to our discussion here.[7]

As a rhetorical strategy, the poet of the poem uses the decay of Ambapālī's own body to comment on life's impermanence. Since Ambapālī is a courtesan, her "job description" is to be attractive. She supplements her natural beauty with cosmetics and jewelry. She indicates that from the ends of her glossy black hair, wreathed with fragrant flowers, to her soft feet, adorned with their golden anklets, she is a sight to behold. But then Ambapālī becomes a Buddhist nun, and eventually she grows old. Pondering the particulars of her body's decay, now she describes a very different sight. Her hair feels like coarse hemp, smells like dog fur, and has fallen out here and there. Her feet are cracked and wrinkled. From top to bottom, this once-beautiful courtesan's body displays the impermanence of existence. A few of the verses attributed to her indicate the language she uses to describe the transformation of her body:

> My hair adorned with flowers was fragrant
> Like a scented box.
> Now because of old age
> It has the stench of dog's fur.
> No teller of truth would say otherwise.
> . . .
> In the past my breasts were beautiful,
> Plump, round, firm, and high.
> Now they hang down like empty water bags.
> No teller of truth would say otherwise.
> . . .
> In the past my feet were lovely
> Like [slippers] padded with cotton.
> Now because of old age
> They are cracked and wrinkled.
> No teller of truth would say otherwise.[8]

For a courtesan, the appearance of the body is paramount. For the analysis of life's transience, the decay of the body is paramount. The speaker in this poem, who carefully noted the state of her greatest assets in the past, now systematically catalogues their decay.[9]

From a rhetorical perspective, the life of a courtesan provides excellent grist for the mill of Buddhist analysis. Buddhist preachers often have to work hard to persuade members of their audience who are content with their present lives that pleasurable experiences are transitory and ultimately dissatisfying. The courtesan's experience demonstrates the point clearly and quickly. Both for the woman and her client, the limited and ultimately unsatisfactory nature of their routine interactions are apparent.[10] In addition, the client rapidly expends his wealth and then finds himself abandoned, while the courtesan sees the mechanical nature of sexuality and watches her ripe young beauty quickly fade. The courtesan's experience can illustrate the flaws of a life based on sexual pleasure and, by extension, may recommend a life of celibacy. Since the Buddhist monastic life in ancient India entails the renunciation of sexuality, the courtesan-turned-nun motif has great didactic power. Earlier Indian writers like the poet who wrote the poem attributed to Ambapālī were well aware of this. It was Cāttaṉār, however, who structured an entire text around the transformation of a courtesan into a Buddhist nun.

Cāttaṉār also shares with other Buddhist writers the use of an entire set of cosmological categories for the sake of persuasion. A notable example occurs in *Aśokāvadāna*, a collection of stories from Northwest India dating ca. the second century A.D. Scholars do not know who composed the text or even whether it is the work of a single author, but they do agree that the text was influential throughout Asia.[11] Like *Maṇimēkalai*, this well-known Sanskrit Hinayana text also displays self-consciousness about religious didacticism. In it King Aśoka, who acts as a teacher and promoter of Buddhist doctrine, is called a "master of good means" (*upāya*). In chapter five of Strong's recent study of *Aśokāvadāna*, he provides a convincing reading of a series of stories about Aśoka's teaching techniques whose relationships with each other had previously remained obscure. Most relevant to our discussion here, he demonstrates how this set of stories uses the entire set of cosmological categories in his instruction about Buddhist doctrine.

Each story replicates the suffering of a different *gati* [mode of existence]. For example, in one tale Aśoka makes his brother king for a week, showering him with every luxury and pleasure, but tells him at the end of that time that he will be killed. The executioners constantly guard the door to the royal chamber and remind him of his forthcoming death. This situation replicates that of the gods, who foolishly mire themselves in pleasure while death awaits them at the conclusion of their heavenly sojourn. In another story, Aśoka builds a complete replica of hell itself, making the tortures and terrors of those who dwell in the infernal regions tangible. In yet another incident, Aśoka makes his brother beg for food. Whenever harem ladies fill his bowl with tasty viands, however, Aśoka reprimands them, forcing them to replace these foods with rotten beans. By doing so, Aśoka recreates the patterns of hungry ghosts. No matter what the ghost consumes, it turns to pus, excrement, and blood. A final story highlights the suffering of animals.[12]

This series of stories actually illustrates, in a methodical fashion, the suffering experienced by the five types of beings in the cosmos: gods, hell-dwellers, hungry ghosts, animals, and humans.[13] The key to interpreting the set of stories is found in a speech Aśoka makes to his brother:

> There are five sufferings, Vītaśoka, that characterize this Triple World: in hell, the suffering brought on by a blazing fire that causes great pain to the body; among the animals, the suffering coming from the fear of eating one another; among the pretas, the suffering of hunger and thirst; among humans, the suffering of the practice of striving; among the gods, the suffering that marks their fall from the divine state. Hard pressed by these sufferings of mind and body, the monks conceive of the constituents of existence as executioners, of the sense-organs as deserted villages, of the sense-objects as thieves, and of the whole Triple World as being consumed by the fire of impermanence.[14]

These stories portray how Aśoka's strategies teach others to experience and empathize with the suffering of beings from all of the different modes of existence.

Just as Aśoka teaches by dealing with an issue — suffering — in relation to each of the kinds of beings in the cosmos, Cāttaṉār teaches about the unalterability of karma by describing all the kinds of beings in the cosmos. In response to Kōtamai's demand that the goddess Campāpati bring her dead son back to life, the deity teaches the woman about the construction of the entire cosmos. She enumerates the different kinds of beings and calls down those capable of granting boons in order to demonstrate that no creature in the cosmos can bring her son back to life, since he died as a result of his karma's ripening. And on the spot where Campāpati teaches this lesson, the divine architect creates a model of the entire cosmos complete with beings from each mode of existence, located in the places where they dwell. Thus, Cāttaṉār notes, Kōtamai's cosmological lesson will continue to teach others as well.

Both Cāttaṉār and the author/compiler of *Aśokāvadāna* choose to frame their arguments about suffering and karma in cosmic terms. In doing so, they exploit the equation of the cosmos with totality. That is, Aśoka demonstrates that members of each mode of existence (*gati*) experience suffering. Campāpati shows that no one from any mode of existence (*gati*) can alter karma. In each case, the demonstration that a certain observable pattern exists throughout the entire cosmos elevates that pattern to a law governing existence: suffering is everywhere, and no one — anywhere — can alter karma. Such formulations force human beings to realize that their individual experience must be understood and accepted as an example of a universal law. The cosmological argument used in such cases enables the writer to nudge his readers beyond their limited personal experience to an understanding of the way things exist everywhere throughout the vast cosmos.

For another example of a rhetorical strategy in *Maṇimēkalai* with parallels in an earlier Buddhist text, consider Aśvaghoṣa's *kāvya* titled *Saundarananda.* Aśvaghoṣa, whom scholars believe to have written this text in the first or second century A.D., depicts the religious conversion of Nanda, the Buddha's brother, in this text. Aśvaghoṣa is widely recognized as an extraordinarily gifted poet. Just as relevant to our purpose here, in the final verses of *Saundarananda*, he proclaims his interest in using literature for the purpose of teaching Buddhist ideas. As he says in XVIII:63-64,

> Thus have I written this composition, which contains the secret of liberation, to promote tranquility, not enjoyment; I put it in the guise of a poem in order to attract those listeners whose minds are on other things. For whatever I have treated here other than liberation was done in accordance with the conventions of poetry,

> just as one might mix honey with a bitter medicine in order to make it palatable to take.[15]

Here Aśvaghoṣa reveals the intention behind his carefully-crafted verses — to promote religious liberation. It seems, therefore, particularly appropriate to compare how Aśvaghoṣa and Cāttaṉār exploit Indian conventions from love poetry in order to convey Buddhist teachings.[16]

Cāttaṉār manipulates Tamil literary conventions for his own purposes in his story about the Cosmic Place, as I have demonstrated in chapter four of this monograph. First, he incorporates native elements from the *pālai* landscape of separation, desolation, and death. The deity, birds, and plants familiar to his audience enable Cāttaṉār to create the proper mood for his discourse. But once Cāttaṉār has involved his reader in the cremation ground's activities, he proceeds to mock those poetic conventions as well as the values with which they are associated. His description of the cremation ground culminates with the dismemberment and consumption of a corpse of a woman. Ornamented with jewelry and adorned with cosmetics, she is described as if she were about to meet her lover for a clandestine tryst (of the type so often described in *akam* poetry). Cāttaṉār tells us that when a female ghoul gorges herself on this corpse's head, she does not bother to ask herself whether she is eating eyes or carp, teeth or pearls, tresses or clouds. These words cruelly mock the imagery used in the scenario of union conventionally described in Tamil love poetry.

Turning to *Saundarananda*, we find that Aśvaghoṣa uses poetic conventions to describe lovers' play in chapter four, and then in chapter six uses the same phrases in a slightly changed way to describe Sundarī's despair when her husband, Nanda, does not return home because he has become a Buddhist monk. Although some of the nuances of Aśvaghoṣa's artfulness are evident only in Sanskrit, a few examples in English translation can indicate his basic rhetorical strategy in these two chapters of his *kāvya*.

That strategy assumes that the Sanskrit literary connoisseur will read, remember, and contrast the language of chapter four with that found in chapter six. For example, in chapter six, Aśvaghoṣa describes Sundarī's necklaces hanging down as she anxiously wonders why Nanda has not come home. And later in the chapter, they lie scattered about and broken. The reader who appreciates and savors each verse of poetry will recall that in chapter four Aśvaghoṣa depicted those same necklaces as tossed up by her breasts in the midst of love play. In another set of parallel verses, Aśvaghoṣa uses the exact same construction to describe how she laughs out loud in love play (chapter four), then shrieks out loud in grief (chapter six). In chapter four, the author tells us that Sundarī and Nanda resemble *cakravāka* birds united in love, but when she learns that her husband entered the monastic order (in chapter six) Aśvaghoṣa likens her to a female *cakravāka* bird bewailing her fallen mate. Similarly, in love sport she frolicked like a playful female elephant; now she resembles an elephant wounded by a poisoned arrow. In Salomon's meticulous analysis of these two chapters, he has enumerated thirty-six examples of Aśvaghoṣa's self-conscious repetition, with slight changes, of the stereotyped language of love poetry, [17] agreeing with Johnston's comment that "every word in Aśvaghoṣa has its point."[18]

Salomon explains Aśvaghoṣa's goal in using such language by pointing to a key verse and turning point in *Saundarananda*'s chapter five, verse 44: "I see no kind of pleasure which does not turn into sorrow. Therefore, as one ought not to have an attachment to anything, so too one ought not to grieve at its loss."[19] For Salomon,

> . . . the entire complex of literary devices analyzed above serves no other purpose than to illustrate the fundamental Buddhist truth formulated in the first half of this verse. By presenting and contrasting the lovers' joys and the pangs of their separation in nearly identical words and images, the poet provides a series of poetic illustrations of the rule that pleasure and happiness invariably turn into suffering and sorrow.[20]

Cāttaṉār and Aśvaghoṣa use different conventions from love poetry and use them in different ways, but an analysis of the verses of each reveals the didactic power of those conventions.

Why can the manipulation of literary conventions be so effective as a mode of persuasion? Perhaps the answer lies in the very phrase "literary conventions." It refers to a system of phrases representing — in crystallized form — a consensus about particular activities, values, and language. Buddhist writers seek to provide a critique of accepted assumptions about the nature of existence. To do so, what better way than to play with conventional language used to discuss those assumptions? Both Aśvaghoṣa and Cāttaṉār use conventionalized language and then twist that language as a strategy to provide — from a Buddhist perspective — critiques of accepted societal viewpoints.

In this brief and impressionistic survey, we have seen ways in which a few of the most significant rhetorical strategies found in *Maṇimēkalai* play crucial roles in selected other Buddhist texts and explored the inner logic of these strategies. It is no accident that such texts as *Aśokāvadāna* and *Saundarananda* share certain modes of persuasion with *Maṇimēkalai*. Despite its undeniably Tamil origin and literary structure, from a rhetorical standpoint *Maṇimēkalai* shares a great deal with a particular set of Sanskrit and Pali texts whose major characteristics have been examined by Strong. He characterizes this group of texts as ones whose authors share an interest in story-telling and an ability to rework Buddhist tradition in ways that will enable them to propagate it more effectively. Strong argues that these writers share four major characteristics.

First, these authors are "reworkers of old legends and oral traditions." Strong notes that this reworking can be "poetic embellishment" (citing as an example Aśvaghoṣa's *Buddhacarita*) or "judicious selection of certain stories to be told" (giving Āryaśūra's *Jātakamālā* as illustration).[21] Although *Maṇimēkalai* differs from such texts because of the extent of the original material it contains, the impulse to select, rework, and embellish familiar tales is evident in, for example, Cāttaṉār's version of "The Mustard Seed Story."

Second, Strong emphasizes that these texts were written to preach and proselytize. He comments,

> . . . these writers used their literary skills actively to promote and reinforce the spread of Buddhism. It is important to remember that none of them operated in a context that was exclusively Buddhistic. Their works tended not to be heavily doctrinal but were designed to attract potential converts or maintain the faith of previous converts. They address the situation of the layman more than the monk or meditator.[22]

This statement, though referring to texts like those written by Aśvaghoṣa and Mātṛceṭa, applies well to *Maṇimēkalai*. For example, Cāttaṉār uses his literary skills in evoking *Caṅkam* landscapes to promote Buddhist ideals such as *ahiṃsā*. The structure and content of *Maṇimēkalai* indicate that part of his audience was not Buddhist. And, finally, the text's stories reveal that their intended audience was by no means limited to monks and meditators.

Third, Strong identifies certain common themes in these texts such as the doctrine of karma and devotion to the Buddha. Although devotion to the Buddha is not of primary importance in *Maṇimēkalai*, the doctrine of karma plays a large role. For example, the great ascetic even explains Utayakumaraṉ's death as a consequence of a murder he committed in his past birth. Similarly, Cātuvaṉ carefully explains to the Nāka guru the workings of karma and rebirth. Several other branch stories in *Maṇimēkalai* illustrate how past deeds lead to events in the present.

Finally Strong notes that these texts "stress the importance of material support for the Buddhist religion." Sometimes this simply entails "an advocacy of the merits of *dāna* (giving) to the Buddhist community." Other times it encompasses "an interest in the powers and potentials of the state — in particular the institution of kingship and its relationship to the Buddhist religion."[23] Both the story of Cātuvaṉ and the tale of Vicākai in *Maṇimēkalai* explicitly praise and encourage the virtue of giving (though not specifically giving to the Buddhist community). In addition to this general advocacy of giving, however, Cāttaṉār also demonstrates a more specific interest in the relationship between kingship and the monastic order. As the great ascetic's discourse in *Maṇimēkalai*'s chapter twenty-two demonstrates, Cāttaṉār envisions the just king as duty-bound to protect renouncers.

The comments in this section can only suggest certain rhetorical bonds between *Maṇimēkalai* and selected non-Tamil Buddhist texts that share some of its aims. Clearly, a comparative study of the use of rhetorical strategies in Indian Buddhist texts would be a fruitful endeavor, although it necessarily lies beyond the scope of this book. Even our analysis of the portrayal of Maṇimēkalai and Ambapālī, for example, reveals how Buddhist authors have used women's experiences as a way of preaching about the fleeting nature of sexual satisfaction. Our examination of stories in *Maṇimēkalai* and *Aśokāvadāna* suggests how writers can use the conventionalized Buddhist understanding of all the modes of rebirth (*gatis*) in order to explain the nature of the laws that govern existence within the cosmos. Our comparison of the use of literary conventions in *Maṇimēkalai* and *Saundarananda* demonstrates how effectively Buddhist writers can transform language from love poetry, in sophisticated ways, for the sake of religious instruction. Thus, this examination of the portrayal of women, the inclusion of branch stories, and the modes of religious rhetoric in *Maṇimēkalai* suggests the usefulness of rhetorical analysis in understanding other Buddhist texts as well.

APPENDIX A

AUTHORSHIP, GENRE, DATING, AND SECTARIAN AFFILIATION

Authorship

Little can be determined about the identity of Cīttalai Cāttaṉār, the poet to whom *Maṇimēkalai* is attributed. Other than the internal evidence provided in the prefaces (*patikam*) of the "twin" *kāppiyam*, we possess no biographical data about him. Line 89 from *Cilappatikāram*'s preface identifies him as a *kūla-vāṇikaṉ*,[1] a term scholars usually translate as "grain merchant."[2] Line 96 from *Maṇimēkalai*'s preface adds that he is a prosperous (*vaḷaṅkeḻu*) grain merchant.[3]

Traditional commentators preserved the story of the two poets, Ilaṅkō and Cāttaṉār, reading their works to each other, but many modern scholars dispute the authenticity of the incident. Aṭiyārkkunallār, the twelfth- or thirteenth-century commentator on *Cilappatikāram*, accepts the tradition of the two poets' interaction with each other. As a result, he follows tradition in claiming that *Maṇimēkalai* precedes *Cilappatikāram*, even though the former is a sequel to the latter in its story line.[4] Most later scholars claim that the tradition of how the two authors wrote their texts is not historically accurate.[5]

Even the exact identity of Cīttalai Cāttaṉār is a matter of dispute. Some scholars have claimed that the author of *Maṇimēkalai* is the same Cīttalai Cāttaṉār to whom a number of classical *akam* poems are attributed.[6] A traditional etymology is given for the *Caṅkam* poet's name: taking Cīttalai to be composed of *cīḻ*, "pus," and *talai*, "head," the story relates how the *Caṅkam* Cāttaṉār expressed his criticism of the poetry of other members of the literary assembly by poking his head with his writing stylus;[7] his aching head is referred to in a verse in praise of Tiruvaḷḷuvar.[8] Obeyesekere makes some intriguing hypotheses about the meaning of this story.[9] Other scholars take "Cīttalai" to be the name of Cāttaṉār's native place.[10] Scholars generally agree that "Cāttaṉār" refers to the poet's community. For example, Kandaswamy comes to the following conclusion, after considering other possible meanings for the term:

> The term 'Cāttaṉ' is formed by 'Cāttu' and 'aṉ' . . . The term 'Cāttu' stands for merchandise. Those poets, born in the family of merchants, got the name Cāttaṉār. Like the names Kappiyar and Valluvar, 'Cāttaṉār' is the name of a community.[11]

The "twin" *kāppiyam* tell us little else about Cāttaṉār, however, except that he composed his epic in excellent Tamil.[12]

Genre

Into what genre of literature does *Maṇimēkalai* fall? *Maṇimēkalai*'s true nature has been partially obscured by attempts to make it appear to conform to prescriptions for Sanskrit *mahā-kāvya.* Because such attempts are not entirely satisfactory, the modern reader may want to look into Tamil literary tradition as well, in order to gain a better understanding of the generic influences on Tamil texts like *Maṇimēkalai.*

According to Tamil tradition, *Maṇimēkalai* is more than just a *kāppiyam* — it is one of the five *peruṅ-kāppiyam.*[13] "*Peru*" means "great," and the term "*kāppiyam*" is a transliteration of the Sanskrit word *kāvya*, a form of poetry composed of classical, ornate, stanzaic verse.[14] It seems likely that, in designating five Tamil *peruṅ-kāppiyam*, Tamil commentators were self-consciously creating a Tamil parallel to the five great Sanskrit *mahā-kāvya* texts.[15]

Sanskrit writers like Dandin set out the standard features that a *mahā-kāvya* must contain,[16] and Tamil prescriptive texts followed suit. According to the Tamil text *Taṇṭiyalaṅkāram* (10th century A.D.?), a *peruṅ-kāppiyam* must begin with one of three types of invocations, concern a peerless hero, and encompass the four aims of man — wealth, love, duty, and religious liberation. In addition, it should contain descriptions of mountains, oceans, the countryside, fertile cities, the rise of the sun and moon, and other natural scenes. Further, it must depict weddings, coronations, sporting in a flower garden, water revels, drinking sweet liquor, begetting children, lovers' quarreling, lovers' union, kings consulting with ministers, the travels of ambassadors, making war, and winning in battle. Also, it must be composed in subdivisions labeled in specific ways. Finally, it should evoke *rasa* [relish] and *bhāva* [concrete emotion], creating in its audience a desire to hear more of the text.[17]

Maṇimēkalai does not contain all of these features. Jesudasan and Jesudasan comment upon the relevance of this list to it and its "twin" text in the following way:

> A glance at the above plan will show the vast difference of *Silappadihāram* and *Maṇimēhalai* from it. They have no heroes but only heroines. They are not concerned with coronations or embassies. The nature description is on conventional Sangam lines.[18]

Maṇimēkalai most notably departs from the prescriptions because it lacks a peerless hero; its protagonist is a woman, and the main male character is portrayed as the villain of the text. Since other Tamil *peruṅ-kāppiyam* also lack some of the prescribed features, perhaps such a rigid and detailed set of characteristics is unsuitable for the Tamil literary tradition.

Traditional discussions of the four goals of man (*purusārthas*) provide an example of how unilluminating Sanskrit prescriptions can be when used to analyze *Maṇimēkalai* and *Cilappatikāram*. According to prescription, a *mahā-kāvya* must deal with wealth (Sanskrit *artha*; Tamil *poruḷ*), love (Sanskrit *kāma*; Tamil *kāmam*), duty (Sanskrit *dharma*; Tamil *aṟam*), and religious liberation (Sanskrit *mokṣa*; Tamil *vīṭu*). Traditional Tamil commentators have claimed that *Cilappatikāram* deals with wealth, love, and duty, while *Maṇimēkalai* deals with religious liberation. In accordance with this assumption, they claim that neither text comprises a *peruṅ-kāppiyam* in and of itself, but as a composite, the two texts cover all four topics.[19] Hence, Tamil tradition has labeled the two "twin" *kāppiyam*.

A careful reading of the "twin" texts, however, shows the shortcomings of such an analysis. The claims of the commentators are partially accurate, since religious renunciation is not one of Iḷaṅkō's major concerns in *Cilappatikāram*.[20] To say, however, that Cāttaṉār deals only with religious renunciation is to ignore the comprehensiveness and complexity of the text. Cāttaṉār deals with both renunciation and duty (*dharma*, *aṟam*) throughout his epic. Since *Maṇimēkalai* attempts to explain Buddhism to those relatively unfamiliar with it, Cāttaṉār devotes a great deal of space to the explication of virtuous behavior (*aṟam*). We learn that the Nākas must not practice murder, Ātirai and Cātuvaṉ must become generous donors, and pious housewives must avoid frivolous activities. A great many of the branch stories explicitly define and extoll *aṟam*.[21] In addition, *Maṇimēkalai* does deal with topics included in works on *artha*.[22] Finally, Cāttaṉār does portray *kāma*, love, although he depicts it in an atypical way since the desires of the prince are thwarted for the sake of renunciation.[23]

One must conclude that generic analysis through such Sanskrit prescriptions does not really get at the heart of *Maṇimēkalai*. Without question the development of the Tamil *kāppiyam* was stimulated in certain ways by exposure to Sanskrit *mahā-kāvya*, but it did not develop entirely as a result of such exposure. Rather, the roots of Tamil sustained narrative lie in certain Tamil literary tendencies expressed toward the end of the *Caṅkam* period.

Both Zvelebil and Kandaswamy call attention to the fact that late *Caṅkam* works form a transition between the earlier anthologies of short poems and later narratives like *Cilappatikāram* and *Maṇimēkalai*.[24] Zvelebil directs our attention to the thirteenth-century commentator Aṭiyārkkunallār's discussion of the formal qualities of extended narrative.[25] In his commentary on *Cilappatikāram*, Aṭiyārkkunallār called poems of larger format that include both *akam* and *puṟam* material *toṭarnilaicceyyuḷ*, "connected" or "continuing poems," as opposed to isolated poems placed in anthologies (*taṉicceyyuḷ*). Aṭiyārkkunallār defined *Cilappatikāram* as "a poem whose stanzas are connected by their content," and this definition would apply to *Maṇimēkalai* as well.[26] From the perspective of Aṭiyārkkunallār, then, Tamil poets resourcefully developed the *Caṅkam* legacy into a comprehensive narrative genre, and *Maṇimēkalai* was part of this development.

Dating

As we have seen, the first dating of *Maṇimēkalai* is a relative one: Aṭiyārkkunallār claims that *Maṇimēkalai* predates *Cilappatikāram* because of the incidents portrayed in the *patikams* of each text. In addition to either agreeing or disagreeing with Aṭiyārkkunallār, scholars have chosen a wide range of evidence upon which to build their cases.

Scholarly dating of *Maṇimēkalai* varies from the *Caṅkam* period to the ninth century. Some Tamil scholars have dated *Maṇimēkalai* as early as the second century A.D. For example, Varatarāja Ayyar provides a second-century date,[27] and S. Krishnaswami Aiyangar claims that the "twin" texts were both written at the same time, both belonging to the *Caṅkam* period.[28] This very early dating of *Maṇimēkalai* seems to be popular among Tamil scholars of a more traditional bent. At the other extreme, Vaiyāpuri Piḷḷai has assigned *Maṇimēkalai* to the late eighth or early ninth century and considers the two "twin" texts to be roughly contemporary. He bases his case on the allusions made to *purānic* and epic literature. His orientation is more Sanskritic than that of writers mentioned earlier.[29]

Some scholars have also made claims about *Maṇimēkalai*'s date based upon philosophical materials contained in the chapters at the end of the text. Suryanarayana Sastri deals with the dating issue on the basis of the description of Sānkhyā philosophy contained in chapter twenty-seven of *Maṇimēkalai*,[30] while others try to date it on the basis of its chapter dealing with Buddhist logic. Some of these scholars claim that *Maṇimēkalai* is a seventh-century text. Therefore, it was written after Dignāga, the sixth-century Buddhist logician. Because they feel that the material on Buddhist logic in chapter twenty-nine is based on Dignāga's system, they assume *Maṇimēkalai* must be later.[31] Others dispute that dating, claiming that both Cāttaṉār and Dignāga shared a common source.[32] Suryanarayana Sastri claims that chapter twenty-nine is a later interpolation.[33] If one were to accept his view, it would not make sense to date the material in the rest of the text by evidence provided in that chapter. S. N. Kandaswamy treats *Maṇimēkalai*'s chapter on Buddhist logic extremely thoroughly, providing a concordance between chapter twenty-nine of *Maṇimēkalai* and the *Nyāyapraveśa*. Because he has examined the issue in great detail, his conclusions seem convincing. He argues that Cāttaṉār incorporated Dignāga's system into the text but made a few small changes in the process of translation.[34]

Both Kandaswamy and Zvelebil make convincing cases for dating *Maṇimēkalai* in the sixth century. Zvelebil uses internal evidence as the basis for his discussion and assigns approximate dates of A.D. 550 for *Maṇimēkalai* and A.D. 450 for *Cilappatikāram*.[35] Kandaswamy does a comprehensive survey of the issue, concluding that Cāttaṉār "lived in the latter half of the fifth century A.D. and the early part of the sixth century A.D."[36] Many of his conclusions about the dating issue seem reasonable because he places *Maṇimēkalai* in the context of events occurring outside of Tamilnadu. While the earliest dating of the text may be intended to vest *Maṇimēkalai* with a hoary *Caṅkam* venerability and the dating according to Buddhist logic attempts to date the entire work by a single chapter, the date agreed upon by Kandaswamy and Zvelebil seems most satisfactorily to account for the nature of *Maṇimēkalai* as a whole.

Sectarian Affiliation

Although *Maṇimēkalai* is a Buddhist text, the exact type of Buddhism it represents is not immediately apparent. One scholar claims that the text could not be a Mahayana text, while another seems to find evidence of the Mahayana perspective throughout the text. The sceptical reader, however, wonders whether such labels are appropriate for a work of story literature like *Maṇimēkalai*.

Many scholars have discussed Tamil Buddhism in a general way.[37] They have based their analysis on references to Buddhists and Buddhist practices found in Tamil texts, accounts of pilgrims, archaeological remains, and Tamil-Brahmi inscriptions. The conclusion one can draw from such studies is that Buddhism enjoyed a period of relative success and intellectual excitement in Tamilnadu after the compilation of the

Cankam anthologies (ca. first to third centuries A.D.) and before the consolidation of bhakti (ca. seventh to ninth centuries).

Where does *Maṇimēkalai* fit into this picture? Krishnaswami Aiyangar takes the text to be a Hinayana one. He says,

> There is here none [*sic*] of the features that the later schools of Buddhism indicate, so that we cannot exactly label the Buddhism contained in book XXX [of *Maṇimēkalai*] as of this school or that precisely. It may be said, however, to be of the Sthaviravāda and of the Sautrāntika school of Buddhism, which seems to be the form in vogue in this part of the country, and coming in for much criticism later.[38]

Later he says, "There is nothing that may be regarded as referring to any form of Mahāyāna Buddhism, particularly the Śūnyavāda as formulated by Nāgārjuna."[39] Both Balusamy and Alexander agree with Krishnaswami Aiyangar that the text is Hinayana. Balusamy says,

> The way in which the *nidhānās* [*sic*] are distributed under the three times (past, present, and future) in this epic is quite repugnant to the Mahayana school of thought. So the Maṇimēkalai treats only of the Hinayana.[40]

Alexander points out the lack of the text's reference to the Mahayana viewpoint: "It is very significant that the author of the *Maṇimēkalai* does not refer to Mahayanism anywhere in his book."[41] These authors argue, primarily because of the absence of certain features, that the text must be Hinayana. But such a conclusion is tentative because of the nature of the text. As Krishnaswami Aiyangar notes, *Maṇimēkalai* does not have as its main aim the exposition of Buddhist doctrine and therefore, "except in regard to the one occasion or two, . . . it would hardly be justifiable to expect anything like a full exposition of the character of Buddhism . . ."[42]

In contrast to Krishnaswami Aiyangar, Kandaswamy finds many examples of what he takes to be a Mahayana perspective in *Maṇimēkalai*. In his examination of the text, he calls attention to the following items:[43] the epithets used to refer to the Buddha (pp. 25, 101), evidence of the veneration of the Buddha — especially his footprint — in temples (p. 30), one reference to innumerable Buddhas (Tamil *eṇṇil puttarkaḷ*) (p. 33), the grouping of the twelve *nidānas* (p. 340), a mention of the term *pāramitā* (p. 30), and certain characters in the text who appear to demonstrate particular personal qualities found in lists of *pāramitās* and therefore are to be identified as *bodhisattvas* (pp. 120-139). Although the reference to uncountable Buddhas might indicate the presence of a Mahayana cosmological view,[44] the other items are problematical.

The epithets for the Buddha used in *Maṇimēkalai* stress his primacy, his knowledge, his gracious teaching, his lordliness, his accomplishment in destroying the illness of birth, and his heroism. Because several epithets describe him as foremost in knowledge (Tamil *pōti*), Kandaswamy automatically assumes they are translations of the technical term "*bodhisattva*" and, therefore, indicate a Mahayana perspective. It seems likely that his interpretation here is over-determined. Instead these epithets only refer to the Buddha as the master of knowledge; they are reasonable titles resulting from his experience of enlightenment.

Kandaswamy takes any mention of so-called "popular" Buddhist practices as indications of the Mahayana perspective. He appears to see the Mahayana school as a degeneration from an earlier and much purer form of Buddhism. His own ideas about the historical development of Buddhism are revealed in the following passage, which precedes his discussion of "The Temples of Buddha" as depicted in *Maṇimēkalai*:

> The doctrines of Hinayana failed to satisfy the needs of the people. The people needed a God to report their grievances and seek boons for redemption. At that time, due to the influence of Hinduism, the Mahayana Buddhism appeared. Mahayana Buddhism is theistic in character, where as [*sic*] the previous form is somewhat agnostic in character.[45]

By such reasoning, Kandaswamy then goes on to discuss all mention in *Maṇimēkalai* of veneration to the Buddha or deities linked with Buddhism as clearly indicative of Mahayana. Such an interpretation is challenged by recent scholarship on popular practices in early Buddhism, such as *stūpa*-building and veneration of relics.[46]

Kandaswamy makes similar claims elsewhere. For example, he assumes that mere mention of the *pāramitās* clearly indicates a Mahayana affiliation, even though they are often found in non-Mahayana texts. Even more dubious, Kandaswamy argues that certain wise and religiously committed, but otherwise unextraordinary, characters are *bodhisattvas*. About Caṅka Tarumaṉ (Sanskrit Sangha Dharma), he says,

> He admitted them in [*sic*] a Buddhist monastery. He relieved their suffering and saved Cutamati's father [who had been gored by a cow] from certain death. Later he preached Buddhism to them.
>
> Cattanar thus portrays Sangha Dharma, who must have had the qualities of a Bodhisattva. It has been said already that a Bodhisattva must have an abundance of pāramitas [*sic*]. Sangha Dharma should have practiced the pāramitas [*sic*]. Cattanar writes that Sangha Dharma, though he was standing in the burning sun at

> noon had his face emitting cool rays like the moon (V-60). In other words his patience and endurance were such that he could remain happy even under the scorching rays of the sun. This ability is called Cāntipāramita [*sic*] (perfection of endurance) . . .[47]

Kandaswamy makes similarly strained arguments about King Puṇṇiyarācaṉ and Aṟavaṇa Aṭikaḷ, important characters in *Maṇimēkalai.* But Cāttaṉār never labels these men *bodhisattvas.*

Since Kandaswamy's evidence for *Maṇimēkalai* as a Mahayana text does not consistently stand up to scrutiny, it is worth noting that even Kandaswamy is not convinced that it is appropriate to label the text "Mahayana." Rather, noting other elements, he says we must see the text as a combination of both perspectives. He sees Cāttaṉār as combining "the choicest [*sic*] principles of both Hinayana and Mahayana."[48] Later, in discussing why Cāttaṉār devotes so much space to an exposition of the theory of co-dependent origination (Sanskrit *patītya samutpāda*; Pali *paṭicca samuppāda*). Kandaswamy says,

> These two theories [co-dependent origination and the four noble truths] form the core or central principles of both Hinayana and Mahayana. Such common features are often chosen by the epic poet to be expounded, thereby exhibiting his search for harmony to synthesize the two sects of Buddhism.[49]

Both Kandaswamy's strained identifications of supposedly Mahayana elements and his argument that the text synthesizes ideas from both Buddhist schools indicate the difficulty of classifying *Maṇimēkalai* according to the traditionally accepted categories of Hinayana or Mahayana.

Scholars have used a number of methods to determine the sectarian affiliation of particular Buddhist materials. At times, one can determine the provenance of a text by determining whether it includes or refers to the major characteristics of Mahayana Buddhism, whether it contains formulaic Mahayana language, and/or whether its author explicitly labels the text a Mahayana one or refers to Mahayana *sūtras.* Buddhologists with greater experience in determining such matters might want to scrutinize *Maṇimēkalai.* I merely suggest below why such methods tend to produce meager results when applied to *Maṇimēkalai.*

According to Lamotte's classic article on the characteristics of Mahayana, it possesses three general characteristics: it substitutes the *bodhisattva* ideal for the *śravaka* one, it transforms Buddha as a teacher of men into Buddha as the god who is superior to other gods, and it calls not only the self but all aspects of existence "empty."[50] In *Maṇimēkalai*, as discussed above, there is no explicit mention of *bodhisattvas*, but *śravakas* do not play a large role in the narrative either. The Buddha is lauded primarily for his wisdom, but he does not find his way into the narrative often. Finally, there is no mention of the doctrine of *śūnyatā*, but the majority of the text is not concerned with doctrinal issues.

Schopen has recently argued that the Mahayana impulse can be discerned in certain formulaic language found in Buddhist inscriptions. In particular he mentions the frequent occurrence of a formulaic phrase about the transfer of merit and the use of the terms *śākyabhikṣus* and *paramopāsakas* to indicate Mahayana monks and laypeople respectively.[51] Neither the formula nor the terms appear in *Maṇimēkalai*. Their absence in itself, however, is inconclusive. Even the term *bhikkhuṇī* almost never appears in *Maṇimēkalai*,[52] whose author seems determined whenever possible to avoid technical religious terms. He refers to Maṇimēkalai's renunciation using the verb *tuṟa* [to renounce], a Tamil term rather than a transliteration of a Sanskrit or Pali term. Thus looking for specific Sanskrit formulaic language in this Tamil text is a fruitless enterprise.

Finally, Cāttaṉār does not ever identify his religious perspective as either a Mahayana or Hinayana one. He never explicitly mentions any Mahayana texts or proclaims himself to be part of any sectarian tradition. The closest he comes to any identification of the sources of his teaching is to describe the path that young Maṇimēkalai comes to follow as *piṭaka neṟi*,[53] the way of the *piṭakas*. Cāttaṉār never argues for a particular Buddhist sectarian perspective over and against any other Buddhist sectarian perspective.

Cāttaṉār appears to be addressing an audience that is not made up, for the most part, of Buddhist doctrinal specialists. A careful examination of *Maṇimēkalai*'s chapter twenty-seven reveals those to whom much of Cāttaṉār's rhetoric is addressed. In this chapter, Maṇimēkalai arrives in Vañci to hear the discourse of religious specialists from a variety of Hindu, Jain, and Ājīvika persuasions. She listens carefully to each of their viewpoints but rejects each one as unsatisfactory. Chapter thirty then portrays her as taking refuge in Buddhism because it is superior to the other *darśanas* [viewpoints] that she studied in Vañci. Her full commitment to Buddhism culminates the text. Why would Cāttaṉār devote one entire chapter to refuting non-Buddhist viewpoints and no chapters to Buddhist sectarian views if his goal were to debate or justify doctrinal issues within the Buddhist fold? Rather, it seems likely that he was concerned with persuading non-Buddhists that they should become Buddhists and assuring Buddhists that they should remain Buddhists.

This line of argument leads one to question the appropriateness of attempting to identify *Maṇimēkalai* with a particular Buddhist sect. *Maṇimēkalai* is, primarily, a popular text, intended to convey general Buddhist ideals through story-telling. Even the chapters of greatest doctrinal content, found at the end of the text, do not belie its popular nature. As we have seen, the chapter on non-Buddhist *darśanas* has a role in establishing the superiority of Buddhism in general. The account of

Buddhist logic in chapter twenty-nine, though detailed, is focused and limited to one chapter of the text.[54] It forms the prelude to Maṇimēkalai's understanding of key Buddhist teachings such as the twelve *nidānas.* The final chapter of *Maṇimēkalai* is a compact and formulaic collection of selected Buddhist teachings (co-dependent origination, the four noble truths, ways of asking questions, [55] and no-self). This chapter is a manual, rather than an elaborate treatise defending a Buddhist sectarian philosophical viewpoint.

Maṇimēkalai is not the only Buddhist text for whom the question of exact sectarian affiliation is somewhat irrelevant. Strong makes a similar claim about the *Aśokāvadāna.* After mentioning that it belongs to the Sanskritic Hinayanist milieu of Northwest India, whether or not it is a Sarvāstivādin text, Strong says,

> But perhaps it is wrong to worry about such categorizations. At the popular level, among the lay-oriented Buddhists whose interests the *Aśokāvadāna* addressed, these sectarian affiliations were of little concern. More important were the attraction of new converts, the reinforcement of the faith of established followers, and the encouragement of both devotion and donation. And all of this was best accomplished by the telling of popular, appealing stories about the religious exploits of others.[56]

A similar statement could accurately be made about *Maṇimēkalai* as well.

Appendix B

Translations of Three Pali Versions of "The Mustard Seed Story"

Version One: From the *Manoratha Pūranī,* a commentary on the *Aṅguttara Nikāya.*[1]

[Introductory Material]

In the twelfth Sutta by the words *lūkhacīvaradharānaṃ* ("those who wear a rough garment"), he points out Kisāgotamī as the chief among those who wear rags of the three kinds of roughness, taken from a dust heap.

Gotamī was the name of this woman, but as she was (apt to be) soon wearied, they called her Kisā Gotamī (the weakling). She, too, in the time of the Buddha Padumuttara was reborn in a noble family at Haṃsavatī, and when (while hearing the preaching of the Law) she had seen the Master exalt a certain Bhikkhunī to the chief place among those who wear rough garments, she, stoutly resolving, aspired to the same distinction.

["The Mustard Seed Story"]

And, after wandering in worlds of gods and men for a hundred thousand aeons, she [Gotamī] was reborn in the time of this Our Buddha, in a poor family at Sāvatthī. When she came of age she married. And she was treated with contempt, as being the daughter of poor folk.

Later on she bore a son, and thereupon she was treated with deference.

But when this child had come to an age to be able to run about hither and thither in play, it died.

And she grieved, thinking: "In this very household where I had been stripped of all advantage and honour, I rose to dignity from the moment of my child's birth! Surely these people will now try to cast out my son!"

So she took her child upon her side, and wandering from door to door, asked at one house after another, "Give me medicine for my child!" And, wherever they saw her the people jeered at her, clapping their hands, and saying, "Where did you ever yet see medicine for a dead child!" And yet, for all they spoke so, she could not understand.

Now a certain wise man saw her and thought to himself: "This woman is distraught through grief for her child. But though no other knows of any medicine for her, yet the Blessėd One will surely know." And he spoke thus to her: "Friend, there is no other who knows of any medicine for your child. (But) He who is greatest of all in the world of gods and men is dwelling in the Dhura Vihāra. Go then to him and ask him."

And she, thinking: "This man is telling me the truth," took her son and went and stood at the back of the assembly, as the Blessėd One was seated in the seat of the teacher. And she said to him: "Master, give me medicine for my child? [*sic*]"

The Master, seeing what destiny (was in store for her), said to her: "This is well done Gotamī, that you should come hither for medicine! Go now, enter the town, and starting from one end walk through the whole of it, and in whatsoever house death has never yet been, there get some white mustard-seed."

And she answered: "That will I, master!" and, joyful in heart, took her way townwards. And at the very first house she said, "The Blessėd One bids me get white mustard-seed as medicine for my child. Give me some mustard-seed."

"Here, then, Gotamī," said they, and brought mustard-seed and gave it to her. But she would not take it simply so, and she asked further, "But has anyone ever died in this house?"

"What are you saying, Gotamī? The number of those that have died here can no man count!"

"Then never mind, I must not accept the mustard-seed," she said, "The Blessėd One told me not to take it from any house where death has been."

But when she had gone in this same way to the second and to the third house, she thought to herself: "It will be the same throughout the whole city! This thing was surely (fore)seen by the Buddha in his mercy and love." And her heart was moved within her. And going forth out of the city, even to the open graveyard, she took her child by the hand, saying:

"Little one! I thought death had befallen thee (alone), but lo! it is the law common to thee and to all mankind!"

And she put him down in the graveyard, and uttered this verse:

"This is the Law not only for villages or towns —
Not for *one* family is this the Law,
For all the wide worlds both of men and gods,
This is the Law — that all must pass away!"

But when she had thus spoken, she went to the Master. And the Master said to her: "Did you get any mustard-seed, Gotamī?"

And she answered: "The work of the mustard-seed is done! (But) be you (now) a refuge unto me!"

Then the Master spoke this verse to her (which is in the Dhammapada): "To him who is wrapt in his children and his possessions, whose mind is distracted.

To him comes death, bearing (all) away, even as the flood bears away the sleeping village."

[Aftermath]

And at the end of the verse, even as she stood there, she reached the Fruit of the Paths, and she prayed that she might enter the Order. And the Master granted her wish. So, first paying solemn obeisance three times to the Master, she went to the home of the Bhikkhunīs and entered the Order.

And after rising to the higher grade in the Order, it was not long before, earnest in careful meditation, she perfected her Spiritual Insight.

Then the Master, even as in a vision, spoke this verse —

Let a man live a hundred years,
Beholding not the Deathless State,
'Twere better to have lived a single day
The life of him who knows the Deathless State.

And at the end of the stanza she attained Arahatship. And she became eminent in the greatest degree in the right observance of the Eight Requisites, and used to don robes rough in the three (prescribed) ways.

Afterwards, when the Master, seated at Jetavana, was assigning places to the Bhikkhunīs one after another, he gave to this Therī the chief place among those who wear the rough robe.

Version Two: From the commentary on the *Therīgāthā.*[2]

[Introductory Material]

Now she was born, when Padumuttara was Buddha, in the city of Haṃsavatī, in a clansman's family. And one day she heard the Master preach the Dhamma, and assign foremost rank to a Bhikkhunī with respect to the wearing of rough garments. She vowed that this rank should one day be hers.

["The Mustard Seed Story"]

In this Buddha-era she was reborn at Sāvatthī, in a poor family. Gotamī was her name, and from the leanness of her body she was called Lean Gotamī. And she was disdainfully treated when married, and was called a nobody's daughter. But when she bore a son, they paid her honour. Then, when he was old enough to run about and play, he died, and she was distraught with grief. And, mindful of the change in folk's treatment of her since his birth, she thought: 'They will even try to take my child and expose him.' So, taking the corpse upon her hip, she went, crazy with sorrow, from door to door, saying: 'Give me medicine for my child!' And people said with contempt: 'Medicine! What's the use?' She understood them not. But one sagacious person thought: 'Her mind is upset with grief for her child. He of the Tenfold Power will know of some medicine for her.' And he said: 'Dear woman, go to the Very Buddha, and ask him for medicine to give your child.' She went to the Vihāra at the time when the Master taught the Doctrine, and said: 'Exalted One, give me medicine for my child!' The Master, seeing the promise in her, said: 'Go, enter the town, and at any house where yet no man hath died, thence bring a little mustard-seed.' ''Tis well, lord!' she said, with mind relieved; and, going to the first house in the town, said: 'Let me take a little mustard, that I may give medicine to my child. If in this house no man hath yet died, give me a little mustard.' 'Who may say how many have not died here?' 'With such mustard, then, I have nought to do.' So she went on to a second and a third house, until, by the might of the

Buddha, her frenzy left her, her natural mind was restored, and she thought: 'Even this will be the order of things in the whole town. The Exalted One foresaw this out of his pity for my good.' And, thrilled at the thought, she left the town and laid her child in the charnel-field saying:

'No village law is this, no city law,
No law for this clan, or for that alone;
For the whole world — ay, and the gods in heav'n—
This is the Law: ALL IS IMPERMANENT!'

So saying, she went to the Master. And he said: 'Gotamī, hast thou gotten the little mustard?' And she said: 'Wrought is the work, lord, of the little mustard. Give thou me confirmation.' Then the Master spoke thus:

'To him whose heart on children and on goods
Is centered, cleaving to them in his thoughts,
Death cometh like a great flood in the night,
Bearing away the village in its sleep.'

[Aftermath]

When he had spoken, she was confirmed in the fruition of the First (the Stream-entry) Path, and asked for ordination. He consented, and she, thrice saluting by the right, went to the Bhikkhunīs, and was ordained. And not long afterwards, studying the causes of things, she caused her insight to grow. Then the Master said a Glory-verse:

'The man who, living for an hundred years,
Beholdeth never the Ambrosial Path,
Had better live no longer than one day,
So he behold within that day the Path.'

When he had finished, she attained Arahantship. And becoming pre-eminent in ascetic habits, she was wont to wear raiment of triple roughness. Then the Master, seated in the Jeta Grove in conclave, and assigning rank of merit to the Bhikkhunīs, proclaimed her first among the wearers of rough raiment.

Version Three: From the commentary on the *Dhammapada*.[3]

["The Mustard Seed Story"]

Now Kisā Gotamī had never seen death before. Therefore, when they came to remove the body [of her dead son] for burning, she forbade them to do so. Said she to herself, "I will seek medicine for my son." Placing the dead child on her hip, she went from house to house inquiring, "Know ye aught that will cure my son?" Everyone said to her, "Woman, thou art stark mad that thou goest from house to house seeking medicine for thy dead child." But she went her way, thinking, "Surely I shall find someone that knoweth medicine for my child."

Now a certain wise man saw her and thought to himself, "This my daughter hath no doubt borne and lost her first and only child, nor death hath seen before; I must help her." So he said to her, "Woman, as for me, I know not that wherewith to cure your child; but one there is that knoweth, and him I know." "Sir, who is it that doth know?" "Woman, the Teacher doth know; go ask him." "Good sir, I will go ask him."

So she went to the Teacher, paid obeisance to him, stood at his side, and asked him, "Venerable Sir, is it true, as men say, that thou dost know that wherewith to cure my child?" "Yea, that know I." "What shall I get?" "A pinch of white mustard seed." "That will I, Venerable Sir. But in whose house shall I get it?" "In whose house nor son nor daughter nor any other hath yet died." "Very well, Venerable Sir," she said, and paid obeisance to him. Then she placed the dead child on her hip, entered the village, stopped at the door of the very first house, and asked, "Have ye here any white mustard seed? They say it will cure my child." "Yea." "Well then, give it to me." They brought grains of white mustard seed and gave to her. She asked, "Friends, in the house wherein ye dwell hath son or daughter yet died?" "What sayest thou, woman? As for the living, they be few; only the dead be many." "Well then, take back your mustard seed; that is no medicine for my child." So saying, she gave back the mustard seed.

After this manner, going from house to house, she plied her quest. Never a house wherein she found the mustard seed she sought; and when the evening came, she thought, "Ah! 'tis a heavy task I took upon myself. I thought 'twas I alone had lost a child, but in every village the dead are more in number than the living." The while she thus reflected, hard became the heart the which erewhile was soft with mother's love. She took the child and in a forest laid him down, and going to the Teacher paid obeisance to him and beside him took her stand.

Said the Teacher, "Dids't thou get the single pinch of mustard seed?" "Nay, that did I not, Venerable Sir. In every village the dead are more in number than the living." Said the Teacher, "Vainly didst thou imagine that thou alone hadst lost a child. But all living beings are subject to an unchanging law, and it is this: The Prince of Death, like to a raging torrent, sweeps away into the sea of ruin all living beings; still are their longings unfulfilled." And instructing her in the Law, he pronounced the following Stanza,

Whoso hath set his heart on sons or flocks and herds,
To worldly pleasures given o'er whose thoughts, —
Even as a torrent sweeps away a sleeping town,
So him the Prince of Death doth take and bear away.

As the Teacher uttered the last word of the Stanza, Kisā Gotamī was established in the Fruit of Conversion. Likewise did many others also obtain the Fruit of Conversion, and the Fruits of the Second and Third Paths. Kisā Gotamī requested the Teacher to admit her to the Order; accordingly he sent her to the community of nuns and directed that she be admitted. Afterwards she made her full profession and came to be known as the nun Kisā Gotamī.

[Aftermath]

One day it was her turn to light the lamp in the Hall of Confession. Having lighted the lamp, she sat down and watched the tongues of flame. Some flared up and others flickered out. She took this for her Subject of Meditation and meditated as follows, "Even as it is with these flames, so also is it with living beings here in the world: some flare up, while others flicker out; they only that have reached Nibbāna are no more seen."

The Teacher, seated in his Perfumed Chamber, sent forth an apparition of himself, and standing as it were face to face with her, spoke and said, "Even as it is with these flames, so also is it with living beings here in the world: some flare up, while others flicker out; they only that have reached Nibbāna are no more seen. Therefore, better is the life of him that seeth Nibbāna, though he live but for an instant, than the lives of them that endure for a hundred years and yet see not Nibbāna." And joining the connection, he instructed her in the Law by pronouncing the following Stanza,

Though one should live a hundred years, the region of
the deathless never seeing,
'Twould be in vain; instead, 'twould better be
To live a single day, the region of the deathless seeing.

At the conclusion of the discourse Kisā Gotamī, even as she sat there, attained Arahatship and the Supernatural Faculties.

APPENDIX C

THE DESIGN OF FIGURE 2: BUDDHOLOGICAL AND CARTOGRAPHIC CONSIDERATIONS

The diagram of the Buddhist conception of the *cakravāla* is the result of a fruitful collaboration with Eugene Hoerauf, cartographer, Department of Geography, Western Washington University. Its product is an instructive visual representation of both the specific geographical details as well as the underlying principles that structure the Buddhist "version" of the cosmos. The Buddhological and cartographic decisions that inform this diagram are summarized below.

First and foremost, this drawing represents visually the model of the cosmos Cāttaṉār describes in *Maṇimēkalai* 6:176-81 and 192-97. Since in chapter five of this monograph I analyze Cāttaṉār's discussion of the cosmos, this diagram is provided as a visual aid to accompany my analysis. Therefore, all of the items listed by Cāttaṉār have been included in the illustration. The four formless *brahmas* are represented by the levels in which they dwell in the *arūpa* realm (heavens 1-4 on Table 7). The sixteen *brahmas* with form are similarly represented in the *rūpa* realm (heavens 5-20). The six gods who attained great beauty are found in the *kāma* realm, on Mount Meru or in layers drawn directly above Mount Meru. The demons (*asuras*) dwell on the seven mountain ranges, which encircle Mount Meru, or on the lower slopes of the mountains. The levels of hell are represented in the eight lowest levels of the drawing (hells 1-8). The two luminaries, the sun and the moon, are found on either side of Mount Meru. Unfortunately, it was impossible to include the stars, asterisms, and planets due to the small scale of the map.

Since, however, the information Cāttaṉār gives about the cosmos is a bit sparse for a map-maker, I have supplemented his account with information from other Buddhist texts cited in footnotes to chapter five. This strategy works because the aspects of Buddhist cosmography relevant here are, for the most part, highly conventionalized, as argued in chapter five. They differ only in small numerical details such as the exact number of *gatis*, *rūpa* heavens, hells, etc. Where the Buddhist variants disagree, I have chosen the one that seems, chronologically and geographically, closest to Cāttaṉār's text.[1] For example, since Southern Buddhist manuscripts include only the eight hot hells, I have taken Cāttaṉār's reference to the eight types of hell-dwellers to refer to these hot hells directly beneath Jambudvīpa. On the other hand, where no such factors present themselves, I have made decisions based upon cartographical considerations. For instance, the exact shape of the *kāma* heavens is not clear. Thus, I have taken the liberty of making them less wide than the higher heavens to represent visually their spiritual inferiority. Similarly, the shape of the *rūpa* heavens has been determined by the need to represent the *cakravāla* as a sphere as well as the desire to give a sense of spiritual ascent to their shape. Their actual shape is a matter of great controversy.[2]

This diagram also explicates certain underlying principles that structure Buddhist cosmography. Since the cosmos comprises a sphere, the diagram has been designed to portray that shape — insofar as a two-dimensional drawing can represent a three-dimensional shape. The diagram also emphasizes the value of upward spiritual progress, an informing principle of Buddhist cosmology. The suggestion of such spiritual progress has been visually emphasized by a strong central upward thrust from the lowest hells to the highest heavens. In addition, the shading in the infernal regions as well as the roughness or fineness of the lines is meant to convey the ranking among modes of existence. Hell is the darkest of all, and the *arūpa* heavens are so rarefied that they have been made to appear a mere haze. The lower *kāma* heavens are rough in texture, while the higher ones become progressively smoother. Thus the denigration of Hindu deities as well as the nature of hells is visually represented. Every attempt has been made to portray the highly schematized nature of Buddhist cosmography, especially in the depiction of the heavens.[3]

Cartographically, a few items also deserve mention. First the desire to emphasize the spherical shape of the *cakravāla* has guided the overall design and angle of the diagram. Second, although the *arūpa* realm does not really have any spatial correlation,[4] in order to make this diagram of the cosmos complete, that realm had to be represented. Mr. Hoerauf has admirably portrayed its rarefied quality in his hazy representation of the four highest heavens.

Notes

Introduction, pp. 1-6

1 See my concluding chapter for a discussion of this topic, as well as Isaline Blew Horner, *Women under Primitive Buddhism* (London: Routledge and Kegan Paul, 1930; reprint, Delhi: Motilal Banarsidass, 1975), pp. 88-94.

2 Each of the stories that I analyze in depth in this monograph takes up at least an entire chapter in *Maṇimēkalai:* "Cātuvan̠ and the Nākas" (chapter 16), "The Story of the Cosmic Place" (chapter 6), and the tale of Āputtiran̠ (chapters 13 and 14). The two stories of Maruti and Vicākai, as well as the speech in which they are nested, comprise chapter twenty-two of *Maṇimēkalai.* All the other branch stories are much shorter. For example, typical among this group of shorter stories is the tale of how Cutamati became a Buddhist, which comprises only forty-seven lines. The majority of these brief branch stories (not analyzed in this monograph) are of the following types: stories of the past lives of Maṇimēkalai, stories of events in the past of other characters, and stories of how particular spots came to be sacred places.

3 For a summary of the contents of chapter twenty-nine, see Paula Richman, s.v. "Indian Philosophy as Presented in *Maṇimēkalai*, a Tamil Buddhist Text," in *The Encyclopedia of Indian Philosophy* (Forthcoming). For a discussion of this chapter as an interpolation see Kamil Zvelebil, *Tamil Literature*, vol. 2, fasc. 1 of *Handbuch der Orientalistik*, gen. ed. Jan Gonda (Leiden: E. J. Brill, 1975), p. 116.

4 For example, the notion of an *ur*-text of the *Mahābhārata* greatly influenced the scholarship of nineteenth-century philologists. For a critical discussion of this school of scholarship, see Robert Goldman, "Structure, Substance, and Function in the Great Sanskrit Epics" (Paper presented at the Indian Literatures Conference, Chicago, April 1986).

5 Bryant, in dealing with a whole set of poems attributed to Sūrdās, wonders whether he should identify them as the result of "a Sūr tradition" or actually refer to Sūr himself:

> In an early draft, I attempted to make scrupulously explicit mention of this fact at every opportunity. "In the Sūr tradition," I would say; or, "we may then generalize that in poems from the tradition associated with the name Sūrdās. . ." It proved cumbersome, and worse: it rang false. It implied that Sūr was a fictive character, and he is not; he is a *mythic* character, bigger than life, not smaller. . . And so I give fair warning: while I shall mean "the Sūr tradition," I shall simply say, "Sūr."

See Kenneth Bryant, *Poems to the Child-God: Structures and Strategies in the Poetry of Sūrdās* (Berkeley: University of California Press, 1978), p. x. Although the case is somewhat different with Cāttaṉār, since we are dealing with a single text and not a huge set of poems, the principle remains the same. When I refer to Cāttaṉār, I refer to the author to whom Tamil tradition attributes *Maṇimēkalai*, whether he in fact wrote every word or not.

[6] For a discussion of stories used for religious instruction in Buddhist texts, see M. Winternitz, *A History of Indian Literature* (New York: Russell and Russell, 1933), vol. 2, pp. 100-156. In fact, Buddhists and Hindus share to some extent in the didactic use of tales and often use the same tale to emphasize values particular to their own tradition, as is seen in Roy C. Amore and Larry D. Shinn, *Lustful Maidens and Ascetic Kings: Buddhist and Hindu Stories of Life* (New York: Oxford University Press, 1986).

[7] The Tamil transliteration for *kāvya* is *kāppiyam*. Throughout this monograph, I follow the lead of David Shulman, who discusses *Maṇimēkalai* and *Cilappatikāram* in this way: "Contrary to common opinion, these [*Cilappatikāram* and *Maṇimēkalai*] are certainly not 'epics.' Tamil tradition appropriately classes them as *kāppiyam=kāvya*, ornate literary creations." See his *The King and the Clown in South Indian Myth and Poetry* (Princeton: Princeton University Press, 1985), p. 11.

Chap. 1: A Text without a Community, pp. 7-17

[1] Civappirakācar, *Civappirakāca Cuvāmikaḷ Pirapantattiraṭṭu* (Tinnevelly: South Indian Saiva Siddhanta Works Publishing Society [hereafter referred to as SISS], 1941), p. 69. This line comes from a type of poem in which the poet demonstrates his great literary skill by conveying two separate interpretations of each line simultaneously. In the

line quoted above, Civappirakācar plays on the double meanings of two words: "Maṇimēkalai" can refer either to the literary character with that name or to a jeweled belt. Thus the line can mean either, "How can one grasp the intricacy of the text about Maṇimēkalai?" or "How can one depict the thinness of the thread (-like waist) with a jeweled belt?" The second meaning uses the well-known Tamil conceit of a woman's waist so thin it is like a thread, in order to emphasize the beauty of the woman being described.

The Literary and Linguistic Community

[2] V. R. Ramachandra Dikshitar, trans., *The Cilappatikaram*, 2d ed. (Tinnevelly: SISS, 1978), p. 79.

[3] Despite the fact that most scholars reject as fictitious the belief that the two authors interacted in the ways portrayed in these prefaces, the tradition that they did indicates that ancient Tamil tradition perceived there to be strong links between the two works. For a full discussion of the dating and authorship debates, see Appendix A.

[4] K. Kailasapathy, *Tamil Heroic Poetry* (Oxford: Oxford University Press, 1968).

[5] Brenda E. F. Beck, "The Story of a Tamil Epic: Several Versions of *Silappadikaram* Compared," *The Journal of Tamil Studies* 1, no. 1 (1972): 23-38. Because the recitation issue remains unsettled, I usually refer to Cāttaṉār's "readers" rather than his "putative listeners," although the latter phrase might be technically more accurate.

[6] Stuart Blackburn and Joyce Flueckiger observe that ". . . even when an epic story is well-known to most audience members, the complete epic, from 'beginning to end,' is rarely found in performance or even in a series of performances. Complete epics are found only in written texts, the construct of scribes, publishers, and scholars." See their comments in the section titled "Epics Oral and Written" from the introduction to *The Oral Epic in India*, ed. Stuart Blackburn and Susan Wadley (Forthcoming).

Notes to p. 10

[7] Kamil Zvelebil, *Tamil Literature*, vol. 10, fasc. 1 of *A History of Indian Literature*, gen. ed. Jan Gonda (Wiesbaden: Otto Harrassowitz, 1974), p. 142 [hereafter cited as *History*]. *Nīlakēci*, a ninth-century Tamil text whose story line is slight, provides refutations for many of the competing philosophical systems of the time. Buddhism receives the most criticism since four chapters of the text criticize Buddhist ideas, while other philosophical systems receive only one chapter of criticism each. Naturally, in the course of commenting upon such a work, the commentator would quote from Tamil Buddhist works, thus providing us with valuable information about texts now lost. See A. Chakravarti, *Neelakesi: The Original Text and the Commentary of Samaya-Divakara-Vamana-Muni* (Kumbakonam: By the Author, 1936).

[8] Zvelebil, *History*, p. 142. Fragments of the text are contained in the anthology *Puṟattiraṭṭu*, as well as in the body of *Nīlakēci* and in its commentary. *Kuṇṭalakēci*, a late tenth-century text, relates the story of Kuṇṭalakēci, a girl from a merchant caste. When she falls in love with a young Buddhist man who has been condemned to death for gambling and robbery, her father arranges for his pardon and the two marry. Their happiness is short-lived, however, because one day Kuṇṭalakēci angers her husband in a quarrel, and he tries to murder her. In self-defense she kills him, but after his death she grows disgusted with the nature of existence and becomes a Buddhist nun. After debating with learned philosophers of different religious viewpoints, she finally attains release. The overall structure of *Kuṇṭalakēci* resembles *Maṇimēkalai* in several noteworthy ways. Both detail the religious progress of a young girl on the Buddhist path. In each case, the heroine causes (indirectly or directly) the death of the male protagonist. Both texts depict the heroine going to listen, sequentially, to experts expounding other religious viewpoints. Finally, each of the texts ends by portraying the Buddhist path as triumphant. For a translation of a Pali version of the Kuṇṭalakēci story, see Eugene Watson Burlingame, *Buddhist Legends Translated from the Original Pali Text of the Dhammapada Commentary*, Part 2, Harvard Oriental Series, vol. 29 (Cambridge: Harvard University Press, 1921), pp. 227-32.

[9] See the commentary on verse 387 in U. Vē. Cāminātaiyar, *Naṉṉūl Mūlamum Mayilai Nātaruraiyum* (Madras: Kabir Press, 1946), p. 212.

[10] In his autobiography, U. Vē. Cāminātaiyar plays on this traditional image of the jewelry of the Tamil mother when he describes the publication

of his edition of *Cilappatikāram* and his decision about what to publish next: "Now that the beloved Tamil muse had put on her Anklets again, and my readers were exhorting me to burnish the other jewels also for me to deck her with, I began to weigh in my mind what would be the most suitable to follow *Silappatikaaram.*" See U. V. Swaminathaiyer, *The Story of My Life* (Tiruvanmiyur: Mahamahopadhyaya Dr. U. V. Swaminathaiyer Library, 1980), p. 352 and p. 402 n. 2. This work is an abridged translation of Cāminātaiyar's *Eṉ Carittiram* (Madras: Kabir Press, 1950).

11 See Ti. Vē. Kōpālaiyar, ed., *Ilakkaṇakkottu: Mūlamum Uraiyum* (Tanjore: Sarasvati Mahal Library, 1973), p. 103.

12 For a discussion of the effects of such attitudes on Śaivite monastic education, see the discussion by Mayilai Cīni Vēṅkaṭacāmi in *Pattoṉpatām Nūṟṟaṇṭil Tamiḻ Ilakkiyam* (Madras: Cānti Nūlakam, 1962), pp. 76-80.

13 The rediscovery of *Maṇimēkalai* was part of the larger process of rediscovering ancient Tamil texts. Kamil Zvelebil, *Tamil Literature*, vol. 2, fasc. 1 of *Handbuch der Orientalistik*, gen. ed. Jan Gonda (Leiden: E. J. Brill, 1975) [hereafter cited as *Handbuch*], pp. 5-13, gives a good account of the way in which these forgotten texts were recovered. Also see A. K. Ramanujan, "Language and Social Change: The Tamil Example," in *Transition in South Asia: Problems of Modernization*, ed. Robert Crane, Program in Comparative Studies on Southern Asia, Monographs and Occasional Paper Series, no. 9 (Durham: Duke University, 1970), pp. 67-68.

14 For an account of the life of this great teacher and his most famous disciple's studies under his direction, see U. Vē. Cāminātaiyar, *Makāvittuvaṉ Śrī Mīṉāṭcicuntaram Piḷḷaiyavarkaḷ Carittiram* (Tiruvanmiyur: Mahamahopadhyaya Dr. U. V. Swaminathaiyer Library, 1965).

15 Swaminathaiyer, *Story of My Life*, p. 246.

16 Ibid., pp. 331, 367-71.

17 U. Vē. Cāminātaiyar's edition of *Maṇimēkalai* was not the first one to be published. The *Classified Catalogue of Books Registered from 1890-1900 at the Office of the Registrar of Books* (Madras: Government of Madras, 1932) notes an edition of *Maṇimēkalai* published by M. Shanmukam Pillai Aiyar in 1894 (Registration #235). According to Zvelebil, *Handbuch*, Vidvan Caṇmukam Piḷḷai published an (earlier?) edition in 1891. Julien Vinson mentions another edition of *Maṇimēkalai*

published in 1894 by Ka. Murugêçaçetti (Ka. Murukēca Ceṭṭi) in his *Légendes Bouddhistes et Djainas: Traduites du Tamoul*, tomes 5-6, Conteurs et Poetes du Tous Pays (Paris: G. P. Maisonneuve and Larose, 1900), vol. 1, p. 179.

These earlier editions, however, did not contain sufficient explanatory notes to make the text comprehensible to readers. It was Cāminātaiyar's editions that first made *Maṇimēkalai* accessible to Tamil readers in the nineteenth century. His first printed edition is U. Vē. Cāminātaiyar, ed., *Maṇimēkalai* (Madras: Jūpili Accukkūṭam, 1898). His later edition is U. Vē. Cāminātaiyar, ed., *Maṇimēkalai* (Madras: Commercial Press, 1921). It was reprinted in 1931, 1949, 1956, 1965, and 1981.

[18] See Na. Mu. Vēṅkaṭacāmi Nāṭṭār and Auvai Cu. Turaicāmi Piḷḷai, coms., *Maṇimēkalai* (Tinnevelly: SISS, 1946) and Po. Vē. Comacuntaraṉār, com., *Maṇimēkalai* (Tinnevelly: SISS, 1971). Both of these works have been reprinted several times. These commentators build upon and, in places, go beyond U. Vē. Cāminātaiyar's work. In particular Turaicāmi Piḷḷai makes an enormous contribution to our understanding of *Maṇimēkalai* because he provides extensive commentary on chapters twenty-seven, twenty-eight, and thirty that goes far beyond any of the notes provided by Cāminātaiyar.

[19] Among others, see T. N. C. Varataṉ, ed., *Maṇimēkalai Mūlam* (Madras: Lifco, 1964) and Puliyūr Kēcikaṉ, com., *Maṇimēkalai* (Madras: Pāri Nilaiyam, 1976).

[20] Abbreviated and popular translations may be found in A. Madhavaiah, *Manimekalai* (Madras: Indian Publishing House, 1923) and A. S. Panchapakesa Ayyar, *Manimekalai* (Madras: Alliance Co., 1947).

[21] The Tamil pandit Ilangumaran has written several children's tales published in extremely inexpensive pamphlets, based on stories contained in *Maṇimēkalai*.

[22] T. M. Pālacuntaram, *Maṇimēkalai Eṉṉum Maṅkaittuṟavu* (Tanjore: Lāli Elakṭirik Accukkūṭam, 1923) and Ē. Vēṅkaṭācalam Piḷḷai, *Maṇimēkalai* (*Oru Nāṭakam*) (Tinnevelly: SISS, 1946). A play based upon the story of Pīlivaḷai, a Nāga princess whose beauty causes the king to forget the Indra Festival celebration and thus brings complete destruction to his city, has also been dramatized: Ē. Eṉ. Perumāḷ, *Ilakkiya Nāṭakaṅkaḷ* (Nākarkoyil: Taṅkam Press, 1973), pp. 94-159. In addition, there is a play about Āputtiraṉ. See Cāmi. Citamparaṉār, *Āputtiraṉ Allatu Camūka Ūḻiyaṉ* (Madras: Ilakkiya Nilaiyam, 1974).

[23] Pāratitācan̲, *Maṇimēkalai Veṇpā* (Madras: An̲pu N̲ūlakam, 1962).

[24] Although he omits all the other branch stories from his version, he does retain the story of Āputtiran̲, notable for its mockery of brahmin hypocrisy. Ibid., vv. 121-22. Āputtiran̲ continues to be an attractive character to modern Tamil poets. See, for example, Mu. Mēttā's poem titled "Tēcappiṭāvukku Oru Teruppāṭakan̲in̲ Añcali," in his *Kaṇṇīr Pūkkaḷ* (Kōvai: Centamil̲ Press, 1974).

Religious Communities outside of Tamilnadu

[25] For example, Cātuvan̲ sails off with traders to recover the family fortune he has squandered (chapter 16). After his shipwreck, the merchant Cantiratattan̲ picks him up at the island where he has washed ashore. Āputtiran̲, as well, sails off to Java with a group of merchants (chapter 14).

[26] Richard Winstedt, *The Malays: A Cultural History* (London: Routledge and Kegan Paul, 1950), p. 139.

[27] The goddess's name Maṇimekhalā derives from the Sanskrit words *maṇi*, "jewel," and *mekhalā*, "girdle" or "belt." It usually denotes a piece of jewelry worn around a woman's waist. Although the goddess is referred to in *Cilappatikāram* as Maṇimēkalai, in the epic *Maṇimēkalai* she is consistently called Maṇimēkalāteyvam, "Maṇimēkalā-goddess." Since the final *ā* in her name is in the middle of a compound, it does not change to *ai*. Therefore, I will consistently refer to the young girl as Maṇimēkalai and the goddess as Maṇimēkalā to avoid confusion.

[28] Sylvain Lévi, "On Maṇimekhalā 'The Guardian of the Sea' (A Cambodian Document)," in *Mémorial Sylvain Lévi*, ed. Paul Hartmann (Paris: Rue Cujas, 1937), p. 382.

[29] E. B. Cowell, ed., *The Jātaka or Stories of the Buddha's Former Births* (London: Luzac and Co. for the Pali Text Society, 1907; reprint, Delhi: Cosmo Publications, 1978), vol. 4, pp. 10-13.

[30] Ibid., vol. 6, pp. 22-24.

[31] Lévi, "On Maṇimekhalā," pp. 383-86. Also see V. Raghavan, *The Ramayana in Greater India* (Surat: South Gujarat University, 1975), p. 58.

Notes to pp. 13-14

[32] Lévi, "More on Maṇimekhalā," in *Mémorial Sylvain Lévi*, pp. 386-89. Also see Raghavan, *Ramayana*, p. 69.

[33] We know, for example, that U. Vē. Cāminātaiyar based his 1898 printed edition of *Maṇimēkalai* on palm-leaf manuscripts he found both in Ceylon and Tamilnadu. In addition, a Theravadin pamphlet from the Śri Lankan Buddhist community does call attention to *Maṇimēkalai*: H. Dhammaratana Thera, "Buddhism in South India," *The Wheel Publication*, vols. 124-25 (1968). The fact that such a pamphlet had to be written indicates that *Maṇimēkalai* was not well-known in that community.

[34] Gananath Obeyesekere, *The Cult of the Goddess Pattini* (Chicago: University of Chicago Press, 1984), p. 528. Note that Obeyesekere finds strong Buddhist elements in *Cilappatikāram*. This opinion is not widely held among scholars of the text, who usually designate it Jain or "nonsectarian."

[35] Ibid., pp. 105, 149.

[36] Ibid., pp. 581, 589. This portrayal of Cāttaṉār, suggests Obeyesekere, implies that he is a mythic rather than a historical figure. For his evidence on this point, see pp. 588-90.

The Academic Community

[37] A detailed analysis of the secondary literature on *Maṇimēkalai* lies outside the scope of this chapter. For an examination of this material, see Paula Richman, "Religious Rhetoric in *Maṇimēkalai*" (Ph.D. diss., Department of South Asian Languages and Civilizations, University of Chicago, 1983), pp. 17-24.

[38] The earliest scholarly so-called translations are actually detailed chapter-by-chapter summaries that do translate some of the lines exactly but omit material freely. The first of this type is Julien Vinson, *Légendes Bouddhistes et Djainas: Traduites du Tamoul*, tomes 5-6, Conteurs et Poetes de Tous Pays (Paris: G. P. Maisonneuve and Larose, 1900). The second is G. U. Pope, *Mani-Mekhalai* (Madras: Meykandan Press, 1911). Krishnaswami Aiyangar, *Manimekhalai in its Historical Setting*, though a

more complete translation, omits sections of chapters freely. For example, his translation of chapter six does not include the description of the ghoul and the vultures consuming the dismembered female corpse, nor does he include Cāttaṉār's discussion of the sixfold forms (*aṟuvakai vaḻakku*) in chapter thirty. David Ludden also did a rough translation of the first twenty-five chapters in 1979 under the auspices of a National Endowment for the Humanities grant.

[39] T. P. Meenakshisundaram is one of the few who does not dismiss *Maṇimēkalai* because of Cāttaṉār's desire to preach Buddhism. In this statement, Meenakshisundaram lauds Cāttaṉār's pedagogic skills: ". . . the greatness of the poet is visible everywhere . . . He has in him the great teacher who can explain philosophy so as to appeal to the most illiterate." See *A History of Tamil Literature* (Annamalainagar: Annamalai University, 1965), p. 45

[40] C. Jesudasan and Hephzibah Jesudasan, *A History of Tamil Literature* (Calcutta: Y.M.C.A. Publishing House, 1961), p. 61. Also see p. 63, where they say, "All this propaganda, however, is less convincing for its being mixed up with the most astounding fiction of supernatural things that the human imagination is capable of . . . Art is sacrificed here to propaganda and there is jarring sectarianism, ill-concealed."

[41] K. V. Jakannātaṉ, *Tamiḻ Kāppiyaṅkaḷ: Ilakkaṇamum Ilakkiyamum,* Bulletin of the Tamil Department, no. 4 (Madras: University of Madras, 1940), p. 122 (my translation).

[42] See also M. R. Aṭaikkalacāmi, *Tamiḻ Ilakkiya Varalāṟu* (Madras: Pālnilā Patippakam, 1955), pp. 137-38.

[43] Pope, *Mani-Mekhalai,* p. 13.

[44] Pope's ten stages of conversion are (1) her moment of change, (2) her experiences in the crystal pavilion, (3) her experiences on Maṇipallavam Island, (4) her imprisonment, (5) her visit to Maṇipallavam Island with Āputtiraṉ, (6) her conversations in Vañci with Kaṇṇaki, etc., (7) her visits with diverse religious specialists, (8) her beneficent work in Kāñci, (9) studying under the guidance of Aṟavaṇa Aṭikaḷ, and (10) receiving the esoteric teaching of the Buddhist system. Pope's missionary interests encouraged him to see *Maṇimēkalai* in the light that he did. In places, Pope makes extremely insightful observations about the text; in some places, however, his perspective leads him astray. For a critique of Pope's work, see Richman, "Religious Rhetoric," pp. 31-32.

Notes to pp. 15-19

[45] See, for example, the articles cited in nn. 28 and 32.

[46] See, for example, S. Kuppuswami, "Problems of Identity in the Cultural History of Ancient India," *The Journal of Oriental Research, Madras* 1, no. 2 (April 1927): 191-201.

[47] S. N. Kandaswamy, *Buddhism as Expounded in Maṇimēkalai* (Annamalainagar: Annamalai University, 1978). Buddhologists may be interested in the following compilations found in Kandaswamy: a chart showing the distribution of Buddhist doctrine in the text (pp. 189-92), a concordance of logical fallacies as found in *Nyāyapraveśa* and *Maṇimēkalai* (pp. 291-305), and an extensive discussion of the Tamil terms Cāttaṉār uses to discuss the twelve *nidānas* (pp. 319-22). In places, Kandaswamy does more summarizing of the text than analyzing. Nonetheless, any future work on Buddhism in *Maṇimēkalai* will take Kandaswamy's spade work as its starting point. For a critique of Kandaswamy's research, see A. Velu Pillai, *Epigraphical Evidences for Tamil Studies* (Madras: International Institute of Tamil Studies, 1980), pp. 92-94.

Conclusions

[48] A. K. Ramanujan, "Is There an Indian Way of Thinking?" (Paper presented at the first workshop of the American Council of Learned Societies-Social Science Research Council Joint Committee on South Asia sponsored "Person in South Asia" project, Chicago, 16 September 1980 [revised 16 July 1981]), p. 16.

Chap. 2: Female Renunciation in the Main Story, pp. 19-35

The Structure of *Maṇimēkalai*'s Main Story

[1] The synopsis provided in this chapter is not intended to be a comprehensive summary of *Maṇimēkalai*'s main plot. Instead, I present an overview of the story, selectively focused on the conflict Maṇimēkalai feels between love and renunciation. The reader who desires a fuller summary of the text's plot can find one in Paula Richman, "Religious Rhetoric in *Maṇimēkalai*" (Ph.D. diss., Department of South Asian Languages and Civilizations, University of Chicago, 1983), pp. 39-56.

2 By now it has become dark. Because Maṇimēkalai and Cutamati fear that the prince may abduct Maṇimēkalai if she goes out into the street, they decide not to go home. The goddess Maṇimēkalā arrives and urges them to spend the night in the nearby cremation ground called "The Cosmic Place," where ascetics practice penance. She explains to the girls that their purity will remain unsullied if they stay there. When Cutamati asks the goddess to explain why she calls that location "The Cosmic Place," the deity reveals the story of how it came to receive such an unusual name. That branch story is analyzed in chapter four and five of this monograph.

3 This unusual seat is called the *taruma* (Tamil transliteration of Sanskrit dharma) *pīṭikai*, "seat" or "throne." In *Maṇimēkalai*, the seat reveals the events that transpired in one's past births. Scholars believe this throne is the same one described in the *Mahāvaṃśa*. According to the story recorded there, two kinsmen were fighting over the possession of the throne. The Buddha, out of compassion for them, took his almsbowl and went to the scene of the battle. Hovering above the battlefield, he caused darkness to descend and then allowed light to appear once more. This miracle convinced the two kinsmen to stop fighting. Then the Buddha sat on the throne, and hence, it is called the dharma throne. See Wilhelm Geiger and Mabel Haynes Bode, trans., *The Mahāvaṃśa; or, The Great Chronicle of Ceylon* (London: Henry Frowde for the Pali Text Society, Oxford University Press, 1912), pp. 5-7. An extremely condensed version of this story is found in *Maṇimēkalai* 8:44-63.

4 The branch story of the begging bowl's origin and career is analyzed in chapter seven of this monograph.

5 Ātirai became well-known for her chastity because of the many virtuous deeds she did during the time her husband was shipwrecked and the many generous gifts she bestowed after her husband's return. For an analysis of the story of Ātirai and her husband's shipwreck, see the next chapter.

6 The rhetorical strategies used by the ascetic when he talks to the king are analyzed in chapter six of this book.

7 The viewpoints represented in this section include several varieties of Hindu sectarian philosophy as well as Ājīvika, Sānkhya, and Vaiśeṣika systems of thought.

[8] Aṟavaṇa Aṭikaḷ fled to Kāñci because a flood destroyed Pukār. Pukār was deluged when its king forgot to celebrate the annual Indra Festival, bringing down upon it the divine curse. See chapter twenty-nine of *Maṇimēkalai* for an account of the causes of the flood. Kāñcīpuram was a center for the study of Buddhist logic. According to recently uncovered archaeological evidence, Kāviripaṭṭiṉam (another name for Pukār) contained an extensive monastic establishment with connections to Southeast Asia.

[9] The term "manual" is used by S. N. Kandaswamy, *Buddhism as Expounded in Maṇimēkalai* (Annamalainagar: Annamalai University, 1978), p. 313, in order to describe the contents of chapter thirty of the epic.

Monastic Procedures and Rules for Buddhist Nuns

[10] Two sets of rules apply to Buddhist nuns: rules for all members of the *saṅgha* and rules just for the female members of the *saṅgha.*

[11] Isaline Blew Horner, *Women under Primitive Buddhism: Laywomen and Almswomen* (London: Routledge and Kegan Paul, 1930; reprint, Delhi: Motilal Banarsidass, 1975), p. 104 n. 3. See also Horner, trans., *The Book of Discipline (Vinaya-Piṭaka)*, vol. 5 (London: Luzac and Co. for the Pali Text Society, 1963), p. 35 n. 3.

[12] Horner, *Women*, p. 249.

[13] For a translation and an extensive discussion of the logic behind the orientation ceremony format, see Horner, *Women*, pp. 138-54.

[14] For a discussion of this ceremony, see Sukumar Dutt, *Buddhist Monks and Monasteries of India: Their History and Their Contribution to Indian Culture* (London: George Allen and Unwin, 1962), p. 55, and Horner, *Women*, pp. 133-37.

[15] For a list of the Eight Chief Rules and an account of how they came into being, see Cullavagga X of the *Vinaya-Piṭaka* as translated in Horner, *Book of Discipline*, pp. 352-56. For a translation of the Eight Chief Rules from a different recension of the *Vinaya*, see the one by Frances Wilson in Diana Y. Paul, *Women in Buddhism: Images of the Feminine in Mahayana Tradition* (Berkeley: Asian Humanities Press, 1979), pp. 82-105. For a discussion of the historical significance of the Eight Chief Rules, see Nancy Auer Falk, "The Case of the Vanishing Nuns: The Fruits of Ambivalence in Ancient Indian Buddhism," in *Unspoken Worlds: Women's Religious Lives in Non-Western Cultures*, ed. Nancy A. Falk and Rita M. Gross (San Francisco: Harper and Row, 1980), pp. 213-16.

Portrayal of the Heroine's Renunciation

[16] A couple of poems describing an ascetic, as understood in classical Indian tradition, appear in the ancient Tamil corpus of poetry. See Auvai Cu. Turacāmi Piḷḷai, com., *Puṟanāṉūṟu*, vol. 2 (Tinnevelly: SISS, 1972), pp. 107-9, for *Puṟanāṉūṟu* 251 and 252.

[17] A. K. Ramanujan, trans., *Poems of Love and War from the Eight Anthologies and the Ten Long Poems of Classical Tamil* (New York: Columbia University Press, 1985), p. 251.

[18] Kenneth Bryant, *Poems to the Child-God: Structures and Strategies in the Poetry of Sūrdās* (Berkeley: University of California Press, 1978), p. 40.

[19] The reader who seeks an introduction to Tamil literary convention in general, rather than an introduction to the Tamil literary conventions used by Cāttaṉār, should consult the following works: A. K. Ramanujan, trans., *The Interior Landscape: Love Poems from a Classical Tamil Anthology* (Bloomington: Indiana University Press, 1967), pp. 97-115; Kamil Zvelebil, *The Smile of Murugan: On Tamil Literature of South India* (Leiden: E. J. Brill, 1973), pp. 45-118; M. Varadarajan, *The Treatment of Nature in Sangam Literature* (Tinnevelly: SISS, 1969); Rm. Periakaruppan, *Tradition and Talent in Cankam Poetry* (Madurai: Madurai Publishing House, 1976).

[20] The discussion of Cāttaṉār's use of landscape imagery is limited to the original five landscapes of Tamil poetic convention because the two later situations of love, *kaikkiḷai* and *peruntiṇai*, are not relevant to the discussion at hand.

[21] Sally Noble, "Landscape, Image, and Song in the *Cilappatikāram*" (Master's thesis, Department of South Asian Languages and Civilizations, University of Chicago, 1981), p. 24.

[22] For a discussion of this technique, called *uḷḷurai*, see Ramanujan, *Interior Landscape*, p. 109. The rutting elephant imagery recurs again in chapter eighteen and nineteen of *Maṇimēkalai*. With these references to the rutting elephant, Cāttaṉār may be alluding to the famous scene in Kālidāsa's fourth-century play *Śakuntalā*, where a rutting elephant enters the hermitage of Sage Kaṇva at the moment when the intruder King Duṣyanta, inflamed with passion for the beautiful Śakuntalā, contemplates her seduction (Act I). See P. Lal, trans., *Great Sanskrit Plays* (New York: New Directions, 1964), especially p. 21. Cf. the Buddha restraining the maddened elephant Nālāgiri with the calmness of his glance. This scene is found on a *stūpa* in Amaravati. See Jas. Burgess, *The Buddhist Stupas of Amaravati and Jaggayyapeta in the Krishna District, Madras Presidency, Surveyed in 1882* (1887; reprint, Varanasi: Indological Book House, 1970), pp. 73-74.

[23] It also serves as a starting point for a discussion on the decay of the human body over time. Whereas Utayakumaraṉ sees only Maṇimēkalai's present physical form, Cutamati urges him to realize how her body will decay as the years pass. She admonishes him to see the body as an object worthy of disgust, rather than an object of desire. Moving from the particular situation to general principles, Cutamati attempts to persuade the prince that all such desires are inappropriate.

[24] I have translated the phrase *paḷikkaṟai maṇṭapam*, as found in *Maṇimēkalai* 3:64 and elsewhere, as a glass pavilion — literally, glass-roomed pavilion or hall. *Paḷikku*, from the Pali word *palingu*, can indicate glass, crystal, or mirror. One is not dealing, I think, with some particular style of architecture but with a miraculous structure, whose symbolism is crucial to Cāttaṉār's message. His particular use of the symbolism of female enclosure becomes even clearer when contrasted with another example of female enclosure in a Tamil folktale called "The Four Daughters."

In this tale, when the four girls learn of their father's incestuous desire for them, they pray to the Goddess Pārvatī for aid, and she installs them in a sealed lacquer palace in the jungle. See S. M. Naṭēca Cāstiri, *Tirāviṭa Nāṭṭukkataikaḷ* (Madras: Pirēmā Piracuram, 1968), pp. 97-125. A. K. Ramanujan, in a study of Indian folktales concerning incest, comments on female enclosure in this tale as follows: "The palace has no doors or windows: a good image for virginity indeed." See Ramanujan's "The Indian Oedipus," in *Oedipus: A Folklore Casebook*, ed. Lowell Edmunds and Alan Dundes (New York: Garland Publishing, 1984), p. 250. The differences in the two images of female enclosure are significant. In "The Four Daughters," the girls are shut up so that no one can see them, in order to escape the improper advances of their father. But when a prince comes along, the sealed doors of the jungle palace fall open to him. In contrast, Maṇimēkalai runs into the glass pavilion in the grove in order to escape the attentions of the prince. Her location is known, she is visible to all, and yet she is unattainable by the prince — or any other man — because of her decision to renounce sexuality.

25 See, for example, chapter eight of *Maṇimēkalai*, which describes Maṇipallavam Island with imagery borrowed from the landscape of anxious waiting (*neytal*).

Combating Criticism of Female Renunciation

26 J. A. B. van Buitenen, trans., *The Mahābhārata* (Chicago: University of Chicago Press, 1978), vol. 3, p. 25.

27 Ibid., pp. 40-41.

28 V. R. Ramachandra Dikshitar, trans., *The Cilappatikaram*, 2d ed. (Tinnevelly: SISS, 1978), pp. 393-94. Another explanation for the fact that *Cilappatikāram* portrays Maṇimēkalai's tonsure while *Maṇimēkalai* does not could be that book three of *Cilappatikāram*, where that tonsure is depicted, is a later interpolation. Srinivas Iyengar, for example, is convinced that book three was not part of the original text. See his *History of the Tamils: From Earliest Times to 600 A.D.* (1929; reprint, Delhi: Asian Educational Services, 1982), pp. 597-606. Many scholars, however, have not accepted his hypothesis. For a refutation of this viewpoint, see Zvelebil, *Smile of Murugan*, p. 176.

[29] For an analysis of Indian symbolism of the cow as nurturing, see Wendy Doniger O'Flaherty, "Sacred Cows and Profane Mares in Indian Mythology," *History of Religions* 19, no. 1 (August 1979): 11.

Conclusions

[30] Kenneth Ch'en, *The Chinese Transformation of Buddhism* (Princeton: Princeton University Press, 1973), p. 45.

[31] For a discussion of this reciprocity see Horner, *Women*, p. 317.

[32] For one account of how Sujāta (also called Nandabalā) feeds the Buddha, see Edward B. Cowell, ed. and trans., *The Buddha-Karita or Life of Buddha by Asvaghosha* (1894; reprint, New Delhi: Cosmo Publications, 1977), p. 135.

[33] For the story of Visākhā, see Eugene Watson Burlingame, *Buddhist Legends Translated from the Original Pali Text of the Dhammapada Commentary*, Part 2, Harvard Oriental Series, vol. 29 (Cambridge: Harvard University Press, 1921), pp. 59-82. See also Horner, *Women*, pp. 329, 334. This theme of laywoman as nurturer is stressed in modern Theravadin Buddhism as well. See Charles F. Keyes, "Mother or Mistress but Never a Monk: Buddhist Notions of Female Gender in Rural Thailand," *American Ethnologist* 11, no. 2 (May 1984): 227-30, and his "Ambiguous Gender: Male Initiation in a Northern Thai Buddhist Society," in *Gender and Religion: On the Complexity of Symbols*, ed. Caroline Bynum et al. (Boston: Beacon Press, 1986), p. 80.

Chap. 3: The Portrayal of Persuasion, pp. 37-52

The Main Story and Branch Stories

[1] Arthur A. MacDonell, *A History of Sanskrit Literature* (1900; reprint, New York: Haskell House Publishers, 1968), pp. 281-83.

2 Edward Washburn Hopkins, *The Great Epic of India* (1901; reprint, Calcutta: Punthi Pustaka, 1978), p. 363.

3 Herbert H. Gowen, *A History of Indian Literature* (New York: Greenwood Press, 1968), p. 207. Robert Goldman has offered trenchant criticisms of such evaluations of the *Mahābhārata*'s structure. See his "Structure, Substance, and Function in the Great Sanskrit Epics" (Paper presented at the Indian Literatures Conference, Chicago, April 1986). In fact, both he and van Buitenen depart from earlier epic scholars in analyzing the contributions branch stories make in the epic narrative. See the introductory essays in Robert P. Goldman, trans., *The Rāmāyaṇa of Vālmīki: An Epic of Ancient India* (Princeton: Princeton University Press, 1984), vol. 1, p. 77, and J. A. B. van Buitenen's introduction to *The Mahābhārata* (Chicago: University of Chicago Press, 1975), vol. 2, pp. 182-215.

4 Mā. Ceṉpakam, *Kāppiyaṅkaḷ* (Madurai: Carpōji, 1977), p. 25.

5 My translation of Auvai Cu. Turaicāmi Piḷḷai, *Maṇimēkalai Ārāycci* (Tinnevelly: SISS, 1965), p. 43.

6 N. Balusamy, *Studies in Maṇimēkalai* (Madurai: Āthirai Pathippakam, 1965), p. 177.

7 Michael Pye, *Skilful Means: A Concept in Mahayana Buddhism* (London: Gerald Duckworth and Co., 1978), p. 1.

8 Leon Hurvitz, *Scripture of the Lotus Blossom of the Fine Dharma* (New York: Columbia University Press, 1976), p. 22.

9 Cf. the *Aśokāvadāna*. John Strong discusses the portrayal of King Aśoka as a "master of good means (*upāya*)" in his *The Legend of King Aśoka: A Study and Translation of the Aśokāvadāna* (Princeton: Princeton University Press, 1983), p. 134.

Translation: "Cātuvaṉ and the Nākas"

10 This image expresses the idea that her husband is as necessary to her as the pupil in her eye.

11 This verse refers to couplet number 55 from Tiruvaḷḷuvar's *Tirukkuṟaḷ*, which attributes the ability to make the rain fall to chaste women who worship their husbands. See Parimēlaḻakar, com., *Tirukkuṟaḷ* (Tinnevelly: SISS, 1979), p. 54.

Negotiations between the Preacher and the Cannibals

12 See the section on "Ahiṃsā and Animal Life" in Unto Tahtinen, *Ahiṃsā: Non-Violence in Indian Tradition* (London: Rider and Co., 1976), pp. 106-11, and Edward Conze, *Buddhist Thought in India* (London: George Allen and Unwin, 1962; reprint, Ann Arbor: University of Michigan Press, 1967), pp. 212-13.

Although the authors of Buddhist texts stress noninjury (*ahiṃsā*) as an important part of the Buddhist path, it is a form of behavior also commended in the writings of several other important Indian religious systems (notably, Hinduism and Jainism). By portraying religious behavior of this widely accepted nature, Cāttaṉār can win immediate approval for the Buddhist characters in his text from certain members of his presumably heterogenous audience and urge the others to consider alternatives to killing living beings.

13 In the analysis here, I am using the terms "savage" and "civilized" as they are implied in the text.

14 Eating this kind of meat is considered less sinful, according to Buddhist philosophy, than eating meat one has killed. In the former case, the eater does not intentionally kill the animal to provide food for himself. He simply takes advantage of the fact that the animal is already dead.

The Dramatized Audience as a Rhetorical Strategy

15 The point that a courtesan should never remain with one man long, especially if her client runs out of money, is assumed in this story as well as in tales such as that of Sānudāsa found in the *Bṛhatkathāślokasaṃgraha*. Sānudāsa learns this lesson painfully when he is unceremoniously thrown out of a courtesan establishment because he has lost his fortune, abandoned just as Cātuvaṉ has been abandoned in *Maṇimēkalai*. See J. A. B. van Buitenen, trans., *Tales of Ancient India* (New York: Bantam Books, 1961), p. 208.

16 Kamil Zvelebil, *The Smile of Murugan: On Tamil Literature of South India* (Leiden: E. J. Brill, 1973), p. 239.

17 A. K. Ramanujan, "On Women Saints," in *The Divine Consort: Rādhā and the Goddesses of India*, ed. John Stratton Hawley and Donna Marie Wulff (Berkeley: Berkeley Religious Studies Series, 1982), pp. 316-24.

18 J. A. B. van Buitenen, trans., *The Book of the Beginning*, vol. 1 of *The Mahābhārata* (Chicago: University of Chicago Press, 1973), pp. 68-123.

19 E. B. Cowell, ed., *The Jātaka or Stories of the Buddha's Former Births* (London: Luzac and Co. for the Pali Text Society, 1907; reprint, Delhi: Cosmo Publications, 1978), vol. 6, pp. 80-113.

20 For an ethnographic account of the modern-day Nāga tribe see Christoph von Furer-Haimendorf, *The Naked Nagas* (Calcutta: Thacker, Spink and Co., 1962).

21 Although *Maṇimēkalai's* audience might not necessarily have been familiar with the specific myths cited below, these myths suggest a general pattern of meaning for the term.

22 George Coedès, *The Indianized States of Southeast Asia* (Honolulu: University Press of Hawaii, 1968), p. 37, and George Coedès, "La Légende de la Nāgī," *Bulletin de l'École Française de l'Extrême-Orient* [hereafter referred to as *BEFEO*] 11 (1911): 391.

23 Coedès, *States*, p. 37, and Victor Goloubew, "Les Légendes de la Nāgī et de L'Apsaras," *BEFEO* 24 (1924): 501-10.

24 The theme of the great man who marries a Nāgī is explored in Jean Przyluski's "La princesse à l'odeur de poisson et la Nāgī dans les traditions de l'Asie orientale," in *Etudes Asiatiques* (Paris: Publications de l'École Française d'Extrême-Orient, 1925), vol. 2, pp. 265-84. For a good discussion of the relationship between all these legends see R. C. Majumdar, *Kambuja-Deśa or an Ancient Colony in Cambodia* (Philadelphia: Institute for the Study of Human Issues, 1980), pp. 17-20.

[25] Because there are many references to Nāgas in Indian and non-Indian Buddhist texts, the characterization given above does not necessarily fit all contexts that feature Nāgas. It is worth noting, however, that some of the more common Buddhist contexts do fit into the two categories discussed above. On the one hand, for example, the Nāgas described in the Thai myth associated with the Buddhist rocket festival clearly inhabit a society with kinship relations and social hierarchy like human society. See S. J. Tambiah, *Buddhism and the Spirit Cults in North-east Thailand* (London: Cambridge University Press, 1975), pp. 294-96. On the other hand, the Nāgas are said to consider themselves to be lacking in knowledge. As Telvatte Rahula comments, "Obsessed with the thought of their inferiority, they sometimes observe morality in order to obtain their release from this evil birth," in *A Critical Study of the Mahāvastu* (Delhi: Motilal Banarsidass, 1978), p. 172.

Particularly in Mahayana Buddhism, however, one finds a very different portrayal of Nāgas developing. In Bu-ston's history, for example, we find the myth that Nāgārjuna received the Perfection of Wisdom Literature from the Nāgas. See part two of E. Obermiller, trans., *History of Buddhism (Chos-ḥbyung) by Bu-ston*, Materialien zur Kunde des Buddhismus, no. 19 (Heidelberg: Otto Harrassowitz, 1932), p. 122.

[26] These examples of repetition, emphatic markers, demonstratives, parallel construction, and imperatives provided above would be considered *uttis,* "strategies for argument" of the subtype called *toṭarccol puṇarttal,* "joining words in a string." This technique involves devices used to make arguments cohesive and coherent syntactically. See *Naṉṉūl Kāṇṭikaiyurai* (Tinnevelly: SISS, 1979), sutra 14, p. 9. Similar kinds of devices, which guide the listener through the narrative and mark sections of special emphasis, can also be found in oral epic. For example, see Wadley's discussion of how prose sections can function in the North Indian epic called Dhola: "These prose sections facilitate the audience's comprehension of the story, whether they explain a song, inform the audience about who is speaking, or advance the story." See her chapter titled "Choosing a Path: Performative Strategies in the North Indian Epic Dhola," in *Oral Epics in India*, ed. Stuart Blackburn and Susan S. Wadley (Forthcoming).

Conclusions

27 Maria Leach, gen. ed., *Funk and Wagnalls Standard Dictionary of Folklore, Mythology, and Legend* (New York: Funk and Wagnalls, 1972), p. 415. Although many of Leach's definitions are not really standard, the term "frame story" has seldom been defined elsewhere. Most scholars using the term have not written explicitly about its definition. Recently, however, there has been new interest in framed stories among scholars of oral narrative. See, for example, Barbara Babcock's "The Story in the Story: Metanarration in Folk Narrative," in *Verbal Art as Performance,* ed. Richard Bauman (Prospect Heights, Ill.: Waveland Press, 1977), pp. 61-79. A concern with framing also motivates certain recent studies of texts in Indian regional languages. See, for example, Stuart Blackburn, "Domesticating the Cosmos: History and Structure in a Folktale from India," *Journal of Asian Studies* 45 (May 1986): 527-43, and Linda Hess, "Staring at Frames Till They Turn into Loops: An Excursion through Some Worlds of Tulsidas" (Paper presented at the Indian Literatures Conference, Chicago, April 1986).

28 See also a much older study of frame stories that focuses primarily upon European materials, from a comparative literature point of view: Otto Lohmann, *Die Rahmenerzahlung des Decameron* (Halle: Max Niemeyer Verlag, 1935).

29 John B. Humma, "The Narrative Framing Apparatus of Scott's *Old Morality,*" *Studies in the Novel* 12 (1980): 302. Humma's article elucidates the way in which Scott's attention to the roles of the framing narrative and framed narratives make the reader's literary experience richer.

30 R. F. Glancy, "Dickens and Christmas: His Framed-tale Themes," *Nineteenth Century Fiction* 35 (1980): 54.

31 Ibid., p. 72.

32 William Goetz, "The 'Frame' of *Turn of the Screw:* Framing the Reader In," *Studies in Short Fiction* 18 (1981): 71.

Chap. 4: Tamil Literary Conventions and Life's Impermanence, pp. 53-78

[1] Since Tamil literary critics have not provided any explanation of the logic informing the lengthy description of the cremation ground that occurs in the first section of the story, the effectiveness of Cāttaṉār's rhetoric there needs to be revealed. Although the modern reader might initially react with impatience or puzzlement when reading that long description, a knowledge of ancient Tamil literary conventions transforms this same description into a discourse evoking a rich set of associations. In this chapter, therefore, I set out the literary context that enables one to see how Cāttaṉār has incorporated particular classical Tamil poetic conventions into his narrative and attempt to understand what Cāttaṉār gained by doing so.

Translation: "The Story of the Cosmic Place"

[2] According to Cutamati's story, which she tells elsewhere in the epic (3:26-41), Marutavēkaṉ glimpsed her beauty while flying through the sky above a garden where she walked alone. He then abducted her. Mārutavēkaṉ is a member of a class of supernatural beings who can fly through the air. He is called a *viñcaiyaṉ*, a Tamil version of the Sanskrit *vidyādhara*, "he who possesses knowledge of the Science." These beings are the "Supermen" of pan-Indian *kathā* [tale] literature. "Mārutavēkaṉ" is typical of the names given to the wizards who figure in these tales. Cf. the *vidyādhara* named Mānasavega in C. H. Tawney, *The Kathā Sarīt Sāgara or Ocean of the Streams of Story Translated from the Original Sanskrit* (1880; reprint, Delhi: Munshiram Manoharlal, 1968), vol. 2, pp. 426-55.

[3] What I am translating as "The Cosmic Place" is the Tamil compound word *cakkaravāḷa-k-kōṭṭam*, literally "The Place of the Cosmos." Cāttaṉār's use of that particular construction suggests that he deliberately patterned that name after the term for cremation ground, *cuṭakāṭu-k-kōṭṭam*, literally "The Uninhabited Place of Burning." Since both constructions contain the term *kōṭṭam*, it would be best to translate them literally to indicate their parallel semantic construction, but for the sake of readability I have translated the latter to the more familiar "cremation ground."

[4] It is possible that the four gates here are associated with the four Hindu *lokapālas* [guardians of the directions]: Indra, Yama, Kubera, and Varuṇa. The first gate described by Cāttaṉār (6:39-41) could be the gate to Indra's heaven. Richly adorned with banners, it is said to be the portal through which divine beings enter. Cāttaṉār's description of the gate portraying "an angry terra-cotta image with clenched lips, holding a trident and a noose" (lines 45-47) brings to mind Yama, regent of the southern direction. Cāttaṉār mentions that the deity portrayed on this gate carries a trident and a noose. Yama's noose is his traditional possession, as iconographic texts testify. According to Hemādri, the thirteenth-century author of the encyclopedia titled *Caturvarga Cintāmaṇi,* Yama has, as another one of his symbols, a trident. See H. Krishna Sastri, *South Indian Images of Gods and Goddesses* (Delhi: Bhartiya Publishing House, 1974), p. 243. The relationship between the depictions on the last two gates is unclear. Possibly the gate that depicts rice, sugarcane, water, and gardens refers to Kubera, the god of riches who reigns in the north. The Tamil commentators are silent about the meaning of these four gates.

[5] Several of the items in this catalogue bear explanation. The offering posts are for performing ritual sacrifices, the stone platforms provide a place for those attending funeral ceremonies to rest, and the paths allow visitors to walk through the grounds. The guards keep their sticks near them — even while they are eating — in order to keep away roaming jackals.

[6] In this phrase the repetitious beat of the funeral drum is thought to say *uṇṭu, uṇṭu,* or "there is, there is." The message conveyed is that there is a pyre awaiting each of us.

[7] *Āṇṭalai,* literally, "man's-head bird," is a "fabulous bird of prey with a head like a man," according to the *Tamil Lexicon* (Madras: University of Madras, 1936), vol. 1, p. 221. According to the tradition, the bird feasts on human brains.

[8] The ascetics described as making garlands out of skulls are probably Kāpālikas, Śaiva ascetics. See David N. Lorenzen, *The Kāpālikas and Kālāmukhas: Two Lost Śaivite Sects* (Berkeley: University of California Press, 1972). The other group is probably the Mahāvratas. See Mā. Irācamāṇikkaṉār, *Caiva Camaya Vaḷarcci* (Madras: Auvai Ṉūlakam, 1958).

9 These items are the paraphernalia of a funeral ceremony. The fire pot carries the flames to be used in the funeral ritual, and the other bowl (*pularpey maṇṭai*) holds a snack offering for the dead. The unadorned bier is a funeral bier used by upper *jātis,* with highly decorated biers being used for lower *jāti* funerals. The cloth bundles listed hold ritual items for the ceremony, while the scattered garlands have been thrown away after the funeral procession carrying the body reached the pyre. The ceremonies utilized earthenware pots and various types of rice, which lie about on the ground afterwards.

10 *Aram* is used by Cāttaṉār to translate *dharma* (Sanskrit) or *dhamma* (Pali), meaning most generally "duty" or "righteousness," and more specifically, in the Buddhist context, "teaching" or "the words of the Buddha."

11 Apparently he used his dying breath to tell his mother about his fate, and then he expired.

12 The mother insists upon knowing exactly what type of being has caused the death of her son. She asks whether it was an *aṇaṅku* or a *pēy.* For a discussion of the various meanings of the term *aṇaṅku,* see George L. Hart, III, *The Poems of Ancient Tamil: Their Milieu and Their Sanskrit Counterparts* (Berkeley: University of California Press, 1975). For a contrasting analysis of *aṇaṅku* see V. S. Rajam, "AṆAṄKU: A Notion Semantically Reduced to Signify Female Sacred Power," *Journal of the American Oriental Society* 106 (1986): 257-72. I have translated *aṇaṅku* as demoness in this context because the term refers to a malevolent being. I have translated *pēy* as "ghoul" because, most characteristically, a Tamil *pēy* feeds upon corpses.

13 These threads indicate that the boy is a brahmin.

14 This comment seems to be a reference to, and a rejection of, the argument made in the *Bhagavad Gītā* that one can kill as an expression of one's caste duty. While Kṛṣṇa tells Arjuna that he must fight in the Mahābhārata war because it is his duty as a warrior, the goddess Campāpati maintains that all killing is wrong.

15 The upper half (and thus a half-sphere similar in shape to a burial urn) of the sphere-shaped *cakkaravāḷam* is being described.

16 An architect who makes palaces and cities for gods, demons, and certain humans.

17 Because of the extremely complex syntax of this section of the story, I have reversed its sequence in English in order to make it understandable. Hence, the line numbers in the margin are reversed.

Classical Tamil Poetry and the Transience of Life

18 The themes contained in this list are among those listed in Iḷampūraṇar, com., *Tolkāppiyam Poruḷatikāram* (Tinnevelly: SISS, 1977), sutra 77, pp. 127-28. I have slightly adapted the translation of S. Ilakkuvanār, *Tholkāppiyam (in English) with Critical Studies* (Madurai: Kuṟaḷ Neṟi Publishing House, 1963), pp. 170-71.

19 *Puṟanāṉūṟu* [henceforth abbreviated as *Puṟ*.] 356 as translated by A. K. Ramanujan, *Poems of Love and War from the Eight Anthologies and the Ten Long Poems of Classical Tamil* (New York: Columbia University Press, 1985), p. 191.

20 See Auvai Cu. Turaicāmi Piḷḷai, com., *Puṟanāṉūṟu* (Tinnevelly: SISS, 1972), vol. 2, *Puṟ*. 359, p. 317; *Puṟ*. 360, p. 320; *Puṟ*. 363, p. 329; and *Puṟ*. 238, p. 83.

21 Another excellent example of this pattern is *Puṟ*. 363, a poem that describes the cremation ground and then advocates renunciation. The second half of the poem, as translated by George L. Hart, III, trans., *Poets of the Tamil Anthologies* (Princeton: Princeton University Press, 1979), p. 208, reads,

> Before the ugly day
> when on the wide burning ground
> spread with milk-hedge [*kaḷḷi*] and thorns and marked
>   with rising biers
> a man of despised birth takes boiled, saltless rice
> and gives it to you turning away from your face
> so that you eat an unwanted sacrifice whose vessel
>   is the earth
> do what you have planned
> and give up the earth utterly, whose boundary is the sea.

22 This is my translation of *Pur̲.* 359 by Antuvaṅkīraṉai Kāviṭṭaṉār. For the original, see Turaicāmi Piḷḷai, *Pur̲.*, vol. 2, p. 317.

23 See the *Tamil Lexicon*, vol. 1, p. 174, for a list of the meanings of the term *ar̲am.* For a discussion of the Buddhist meanings of the term *dhamma,* see John Ross Carter, "Traditional Definitions of the Term *dhamma,*" *Philosophy East and West* 26 (July 1976): 329-37.

The Desert Landscape in Classical Tamil Tradition

24 A. K. Ramanujan, trans., *The Interior Landscape: Love Poems from a Classical Tamil Anthology* (Bloomington: Indiana University Press, 1967), p. 105. I have used Ramanujan's translation because it captures the nuances of the term.

25 Translating the term literally, Somasundaram Pillai defines *karupporuḷ* etymologically as "embryonic factors," noting that they are "the nucleus out of which developed the culture of each region [landscape]." See J. M. Somasundaram Pillai, *A History of Tamil Literature with Texts and Translations* (Annamalainagar: By the author, 1968), p. 55.

26 For this reason, Zvelebil calls them "diagnostic features." See Kamil Zvelebil, *The Smile of Murugan: On Tamil Literature of South India* (Leiden: E. J. Brill, 1973), p. 68.

27 *Mullai* sometimes deals with husband and wife together. Such poems, however, usually portray familial relationships rather than sexual union. For example, the happiness of the mother, father, and child together is featured. See the *mullai* poems translated in Ramanujan, *Poems of Love*, pp. 84-87.

28 See Nār̲kavirāca Nampi, *Akapporuḷ Viḷakkam* (Tinnevelly: SISS, 1979), sutra 62, p. 37.

29 The discussion of the *pālai* poem that follows does not provide an exhaustive analysis of *pālai* poems found in the classical anthologies. Instead, I have selected a poem for translation and analysis below because it uses *pālai* native elements and themes in ways that shed light on Cāttaṉār's description of the cremation ground in chapter six of *Maṇimēkalai.* In this section of my chapter, I seek not to demonstrate *Caṅkam* (classical Tamil) "influence" on Cāttaṉār but to give my reader — in a small way — some of the experience with *pālai* poems that Cāttaṉār assumed of his sixth-century audience. Once one is familiar with the elements and themes of classical *pālai* poems, they will stand out in Cāttaṉār's description of the burning ground. Also useful is "*Pālai* — An Introduction," in S. V. Subramanian, *Studies in Tamilology* (Madras: International Institute of Tamil Studies, 1982), pp. 139-49.

It is noteworthy that *pālai* tends to encompass themes from *puṟam* poetry, while other *akam* poems do not. On page 15 of *Tradition and Talent in Cankam Poetry* (Madurai: Madurai Publishing House, 1976), Rm. Periakaruppan comments that ". . . the mingling of Puṟam details in Akam is a minimum [sic] in Mullai and a maximum in Pālai." Later, he develops this point more specifically: "Pālaittinai [the *pālai* landscape] is the most flexible tiṇai [landscape], in the matter of mixing Puṟam details . . . Especially in the Pālai poems of Akanāṉūṟu, the Puṟam details are connected to a maximum extent." Ibid., p. 209.

30 *Aiṅkuṟuṉūṟu* 323 by Ōtalāntaiyār as translated by Ramanujan, *Poems of Love,* p. 60.

31 M. Varadarajan, *The Treatment of Nature in Sangam Literature* (Tinnevelly: SISS, 1969), p. 82.

32 Kârâvêlane, trans. and ed., *Kâreikkâlammeiyâr: Oeuvres Éditées et Traduites* (Pondichery: Institut Français d'Indologie, 1956), p. 48 n. 55; *Tamil Lexicon,* vol. 2, p. 158; and Varadarajan, *Treatment,* p. 158.

The Desert and Cāttaṉār's Cremation Ground

33 Commentators have categorized *karupporuḷ* into many different types. Those categories include season, time of day, birds, beasts, plants, water, pastimes, foods, instruments, deities, and melody types. The goddess Kālī falls into the deity category, the vulture into the bird

category, and the *uḷiñcil* into the plant category. For an extensive list of selected *karupporuḷ* for each landscape, see Ramanujan, *Landscape*, p. 106, and Zvelebil, *Smile*, p. 100.

34 The earliest available grammatical text concerning the *akam* landscape assigns deities to the other four regions but not to *pālai*. See Iḷampūraṇar, *Tolkāppiyam Poruḷatikāram,* sutra 5, p. 9. Later texts, however, allot the arid tract to Koṟṟavai, the goddess of victory on the battlefield. See Rm. Periakaruppan's discussion in *Tradition*, p. 81. As is the case with many Dravidian goddesses, she later becomes identified with the pan-Indian goddess Kālī or Durgā. See Nāṟkavirāca Nampi, *Akapporuḷ*, sutra 28, pp. 24 and 24A.

35 See C. G. Diehl, "The Goddess of Forests in Tamil Literature," *Tamil Culture* 9 (October-December 1964): 308-16.

36 Ā. Vī. Kaṉṉaiya Nāyuṭu, com., *Kaliṅkattupparaṇi* (Madras: Srī Pārati Accakam, 1955), chap. 7, v. 1. The elaboration of classical *pālai* descriptions becomes the basis for many of the standard features of this later *paraṇi* genre. In fact, as Shulman comments, *Kaliṅkattupparaṇi* portrays a battle from the perspective of Kālī's ghouls (whom he calls "demons"):

> [They. . .] complain to Kālī of their hunger, and she promises them a gruesome feast on the battlefield; the actual war is portrayed in lurid terms by the demons, who then satiate themselves on the corpses and praise the Chola king for having arranged this banquet. Much of the poem thus embodies a "demon's-eye view" of the world.

See David Dean Shulman, *The King and the Clown in South Indian Myth and Poetry* (Princeton: Princeton University Press, 1985), p. 278.

37 This *talai-pali,* or "sacrifice of the head," also appears in *Cilappatikāram.* The following description from *Maṇimēkalai's* "twin" text provides an elaborate description of the ritual beheading:

> Stone-slingers, and different classes of soldiers who held shields stained with blood and human flesh, as well as lances, patted themselves on their shoulders, shouting exultantly, and cut off their dark-haired heads . . . and willingly offered them upon the sacrificial altar with the prayer that the conquering king might ever be victorious, when those headless trunks seemed to speak through the drums of untanned leather these words of thunder: "We have given you our lives as sacrifice: Accept them."

V. R. Ramachandra Dikshitar, trans., *The Cilappatikaram,* 2d ed. (Tinnevelly: SISS, 1978), p. 124.

38 Hart, *Poets*, p. 116.

39 *Tamil Lexicon*, vol. 1, p. 468.

40 *Kuṟuntokai* 39 by Auvaiyār as translated by M. Shanmugam Pillai and David E. Ludden in *Kuṟuntokai: An Anthology of Classical Tamil Love Poetry* (Madurai: Koodal Publishers, 1976), p. 428. The translators mistakenly assumed that *vākai* and *uḻiñcil* were the same and translated *uḻiñcil* as *vākai.* I have changed it back to *uḻiñcil* in order to emphasize my point about *Caṅkam* poetic use of *uḻiñcil.*

41 In many South Asian poems, rain is linked with sexual union. This pattern is especially noticeable in certain *Caṅkam* poems. For example, see Ramanujan, *Landscape*, p. 59.

Moving Beyond the Classical Tamil View of Love

42 For mention of the *maṇamuḻavu* drum, see Nāṟkavirāca Nampi, *Akapporuḷ,* sutra 23, p. 24A, and Zvelebil, *Smile*, p. 101 n. 1.

43 Iḷampūraṇar, *Tolkāppiyam Poruḷatikāram,* sutra 56, p. 70.

44 Po. Vē. Cōmacuntaraṉār, com., *Akanāṉūṟu* (Tinnevelly: SISS, 1977), vol. 2, p. 20.

45 Ramanujan, *Poems of Love and War*, p. 278.

46 Ramanujan, *Landscape*, p. 111.

47 Ibid. In quoting this poem and Ramanujan's comments on it, I seek to emphasize that the *Caṅkam* poets themselves manipulated classical conventions for their own ends. In this sense, Cāttaṉār's mockery of these conventions has classical precedents. For a discussion of a similar rhetorical strategy in the anonymous twelfth-century *Caṅkararācentiracōlaṉ Ulā,* see Shulman, *King and Clown,* p. 318.

48 In relation to the idea of *pālai* as the landscape that reveals the true nature of reality, compare Shulman's analysis of the meaning of *pālai* in the later *paraṇi* genre:

> . . . the fantastic imagery is meant to . . . pry us loose from a conventional world in which the dimension of horror is muted or repressed.
>
> And yet this dimension is perceived by the poet as inherent in everyday experience . . . the horrifying presence of Kālī cannot be relegated to the liminal zone of the wilderness; in truth, she and her demons are always with us, even when we indulge in self-deluding phantasies of security.

See Shulman, *King and Clown*, p. 286.

49 Iḷampurāṇar, *Tolkāppiyam Poruḷatikāram,* sutra 11, p. 12. Also see Periakaruppan, *Tradition,* p. 168. There the term is translated as "common landscape."

50 Ramanujan, *Poems of Love and War,* pp. 237, 314. Also see Ramachandra Dikshitar, *Cilappatikaram,* p. 194, where the hot season is described as turning other landscapes into *pālai:* "You have come with your lady in the season when jungle [*mullai*] and mountain tracts [*kuriñci*] have given up their natural appearance and taken the form of a desert [*pālai*]." I have added the Tamil terms in brackets to this quote from *Cilappatikāram.*

Meditation on Life's Impermanence

51 Isaline B. Horner, *The Collection of the Middle Length Sayings (Majjhima-Nikāya)* (London: Luzac and Co. for the Pali Text Society, 1954), vol. 1, pp. 74-75. See also Nyanaponika Thera, *Satipaṭṭhāna: The Heart of Buddhist Meditation* (London: Rider and Co., 1962), pp. 67-68. Cf. K. R. Norman, trans., *The Elders' Verses I: Theragāthā* (London: Luzac and Co. for the Pali Text Society, 1969), pp. 36, 42.

52 Nyanamoli, trans., *The Path of Purification (Visuddhimagga) by Bhadantācariya Buddhaghoṣa* (Kandy: Buddhist Publication Society, 1979), p. 77. For a similar discussion of the benefits of dwelling in the cremation ground that emphasizes slightly different aspects see N. R. M. Ehara, Soma, and Kheminda, trans., *The Path of Freedom (Vimuttimagga)* (Kandy: Buddhist Publication Society, 1977), p. 34, where one reads,

> What are the merits of the observance of "(dwelling) among the graves"? One understands the feeling of the time of death. One perceives that all is impure. One acquires the homage of non-humans. One does not cause heedlessness to arise, overcomes passion and is much detached. One does not fear what common folk dread. One contemplates the emptiness of the body and is able to reject the thought of permanence.

53 I am not arguing that Cāttaṉār necessarily based his description of the cremation ground upon Buddhaghosa's text. Instead, it seems reasonable to assume that both Cāttaṉār and Buddhaghosa drew upon the cremation ground meditation tradition that has its origins in canonical sutras attributed to the Buddha.

54 Nyanamoli, *Path*, p. 185.

55 Ibid., p. 202.

Conclusions

56 "The Story of the Cosmic Place" points out (line 166) that even great kings who achieved famed victories are subject to death, just like the most ordinary of human beings.

57 Only recently have scholars begun to appreciate the versatility and power of Tamil literary conventions used after the time of the classical anthologies. See the papers from the panel titled "The Literary Legacy of Tamil Classicism" at the Eleventh Annual Conference on South Asia in Madison, Wisconsin, in November 1982: Sally Noble's "Narrative Structure in the *Cilappatikāram,*" Norman Cutler's "*Tirukkōvaiyār:* The Meeting of Tamil Classicism and Bhakti," Paula Richman's "Classical Tamil Poetic Convention in *Maṇimēkalai,* a Buddhist Epic," and David Buck's "*Caṅkam* Elements in Bharati's *Kuyil Pāṭṭu.*" Also valuable is the discussion of how *Caṅkam* material functioned in *ālvār* poetry in Friedhelm Hardy, *Viraha-Bhakti: The Early History of Kṛṣṇa Devotion in South India* (Delhi: Oxford University Press, 1983), pp. 316-19, 331-58, 377-85.

Recent research also indicates the versatility of imagery from the *pālai* landscape in particular. For a discussion of Kāraikkalammaiyār's adaptation of *pālai* literary conventions, see Norman Cutler, "The Poetry of the Tamil Saints" (Ph.D. diss., Department of South Asian Languages and Civilizations, University of Chicago, 1980), pp. 14-17. For an analysis of Kampaṉ's use of the *pālai* landscape, see David Dean Shulman, "The Crossing of the Wilderness: Landscape and Myth in the Tamil Story of Rāma," *Acta Orientalia* 42 (1981): 21-54.

58 Leonard Nathan, "A New Passage to India," review of *The Interior Landscape: Love Poems from a Classical Tamil Anthology,* trans. A. K. Ramanujan, *Mahfil: A Quarterly of South Asian Literature* 4 (Spring-Summer 1968): 113-15.

Chap. 5: Cosmology as Rhetoric, pp. 79-100

1 Kenneth Burke, *The Rhetoric of Religion: Studies in Logology* (Berkeley: University of California Press, 1970), p. v.

Cāttaṉār and "The Mustard Seed Story"

2 Mabel Bode, "Women Leaders of the Buddhist Reformation," *Journal of the Royal Asiatic Society of Great Britain and Ireland* 1893:791-96, contains the Pali text and translation.

[3] Both the commentary and the verses of the nuns are translated in Caroline Rhys Davids, trans., *Psalms of the Early Buddhists*, vol. 1 of *Psalms of the Sisters* (London: Luzac and Co. for the Pali Text Society, 1964), pp. 106-10. For the Pali version, see E. Muller, ed., *Paramatthadīpanī: Dhammapāla's Commentary on the Therīgathā* (London: Henry Frowde for the Pali Text Society, 1893), pp. 174-82.

[4] Eugene Watson Burlingame, *Buddhist Legends Translated from the Original Pali Text of the Dhammapada Commentary*, Part 2, Harvard Oriental Series, vol. 29 (Cambridge: Harvard University Press, 1921), pp. 257-60, contains the translation of the story. For the Pali version, see H. C. Norman, ed., *The Commentary on the Dhammapada* (London: Henry Frowde for the Pali Text Society, 1911; reprint, London: Luzac and Co. for the Pali Text Society, 1970), vol. 2, pp. 270-75. Note that even though the commentary on the *Dhammapada* and the *Manoratha Pūranī* are attributed to Buddhaghosa, the two versions of the Gotamī story contained in these two commentaries differ a great deal.

[5] Rhys Davids, *Psalms*, p. 107.

[6] Burlingame, *Buddhist Legends*, p. 259.

[7] I am assuming that Cāttaṉār knew the Pali story and incorporated it into his story of the "Cosmic Place." Since in a sense Cāttaṉār's larger task included making Pali texts meaningful to Tamil audiences, his re-creation of this particular story in *Maṇimēkalai* makes perfect sense. On the other hand, it is also possible, though I think much less likely, that both Cāttaṉār's story and the Pali version were based on a general story that was a common source for both. In either case, a comparison of Cāttaṉār's story with the Pali one will highlight his originality.

There are, of course, other differences between the Tamil and Pali versions of the story besides the ones I have analyzed in this chapter and the previous chapter. Most obviously, the Pali story includes the Buddha and ends with Gotamī joining the order of nuns. In addition, Cāttaṉār's version of the story is extremely brief, almost perfunctory. The dialogue between the mother and the goddess is fairly lengthy and more drawn-out than the interchange between Gotamī and the Buddha in the Pali texts. Also, in the Tamil version, the "law of impermanence" is not specifically mentioned by name although the events in the story all demonstrate that law. Finally, the Tamil version highlights an explication of the workings of karma.

Notes to p. 84

The reader who wants to analyze the meaning of "The Mustard Seed Story" in greater detail or compare it to other Indian and Greek stories with similar themes is encouraged to consult Jakob H. Thiessen, *Die Legende von Kisâgotamî: Eine Literarhistorische Untersuchung* (Breslau: Verlag von Wilhelm Kobner, 1880).

A story with a heroine by the name of Kisāgotamī is found in a Burmese text, but that version of the tale does not contain the mustard seed incident at all. Rather, it turns out to be a story about Paṭācārā. See Captain T. Rogers, *Buddhaghosha's Parables Translated from the Burmese* (London: Trubner and Co., 1870), pp. 98-102.

Standard Cosmological Features from Buddhist Tradition

8 Willibald Kirfel, *Die Kosmographie der Inder nach den Quellen Dargestellt* (Bonn: Kurt Schroeder, 1920), p. 207.

9 Frank E. Reynolds and Mani B. Reynolds, *Three Worlds According to King Ruang: A Thai Buddhist Cosmology*, Berkeley Buddhist Studies Series, no. 4 (Berkeley: Center for South and Southeast Asian Studies, University of California, 1982), pp. 277-89.

10 In the section of the body of the text that follows, I synthesize primary and secondary material on Buddhist cosmological thinking within the Single World system (*cakravāla*) school, the earliest cosmological system in Buddhism. A comprehensive account of the development of Buddhist cosmology lies beyond the scope of this monograph. Instead, I will discuss the major patterns in Buddhist cosmology that shaped the traditions upon which Cāttaṉār drew. For this reason, my discussion will emphasize only the aspects of Buddhist cosmological thought relevant to an explication of Cāttaṉār's cosmological account at the end of the "The Story of the Cosmic Place."

For those interested in exploring the *cakravāla* cosmology in greater detail, the following primary sources will be helpful. Louis de La Vallée Poussin, ed. and trans., *L'Abhidharmakośa de Vasubandhu,* Melanges Chinois et Bouddhiques, vol. 16 (Brussels: Institut Belge des Hautes Etudes Chinoises, 1971), tome 2 (chap. 3) and tome 5 (chap. 8); Pathamakyan Ashin Thittila, trans., *The Book of Analysis (Vibhaṅga)* (London: Pali Text Society, 1969). Pages 516-39 concern the three *dhātus.* Especially interesting are pages 540-43, which enumerate the gods of the three realms; Shwe Zan Aung and Caroline Rhys Davids, trans., *Compendium of Philosophy* (London: Luzac and Co. for the Pali Text Society, 1910; reprint, 1972); Nyanamoli, trans., *The Path of Purification* (Colombo: R. Semage, 1964); and Reynolds, *Three Worlds.*

The following secondary works are also recommended: William Montgomery McGovern, *A Manual of Buddhist Philosophy* (London, 1923; reprint, Lucknow: Oriental Reprinters, 1976); Paul Mus, *La Lumière sur les Six Voies: Tableau de la Transmigration Bouddhique D'après des Sources Sankrites, Pāli, Tibétaines, et Chinoises En Majeure Parties Inédites,* Travaux et Mémoires de L'Institut D'Ethnologie, vol. 35 (Paris: Institut D'Ethnologie, 1939); Richard F. Gombrich, "Ancient Indian Cosmology," in *Ancient Cosmologies,* ed. Carmen Blacker and Michael Loewe (London: George Allen and Unwin, 1975); H. G. A. van Zeyst, "*Arūpa-Loka,*" in *Encyclopedia of Buddhism,* ed. G. P. Malasekera (Colombo: Government of Ceylon, 1966); Kirfel, *Die Kosmographie der Inder,* J. R. Haldar, *Early Buddhist Mythology* (New Delhi: Manohar, 1977); H. Kern, *Manual of Indian Buddhism* (1898; reprint, Delhi: Motilal Banarsidass, 1974), pp. 57-60; Louis de La Vallée Poussin, "Cosmogony and Cosmology (Buddhist)," in *Encyclopedia of Religion and Ethics,* ed. James Hastings (New York: Charles Scribner's Sons, 1912), vol. 4, pp. 129-38.

For those interested in an overview of other Buddhist cosmological systems in addition to the Single World system, Randy Kloetzli, *Buddhist Cosmology (From Single World System to Pure Land: Science and Theology in the Images of Motion and Light)* (Delhi: Motilal Banarsidass, 1983) is recommended, especially his chapter titled "Bibliographical Resources." Pages 145-50 of his bibliography deal with the single *cakravāla* cosmological system, and pages 150-60 deal with multiple *cakravāla* as well as Pure Land cosmological traditions.

11 E. H. Johnston, ed. and trans., *The Buddhacarita or, Acts of the Buddha* (Lahore: University of the Punjab, 1936; reprint, New Delhi: Oriental Books Reprint Corp., 1972), vol. 2, p. 203, gives this account of the sights (in various *gatis*) that the Buddha saw during the second watch of the night.

12 Reynolds, *Three Worlds,* p. 12.

13 Ibid., p. 15.

Notes to pp. 87-89

[14] *Gati*, from the root *gam*, "to go," possesses a wide set of literal and figurative meanings. It denotes "gait," "course," "motion," "flight," and "departure," as well as "state," "condition," "transmigration," and "human lot." In Buddhist texts, the term *gati* is used as a technical term for the six (or five) modes of existence for sentient beings. Some scholars translate the term as "destiny," since the various *gatis* represent the range of fates available to living creatures. McGovern notes that the *gati* classification is "the most important of all Buddhist classifications of sentient beings." See McGovern, *Manual*, p. 73.

Pali and Sanskrit terminology are used in this chapter to explain the characteristics of Buddhist cosmology. In many cases, the term is the same in both Sanskrit and Pali. *Gati* and *dhātu* fit in this category. Where the terms are different, I provide both. For example, I indicate the Sanskrit form of *preta* and the Pali form of *peta*.

[15] Some texts only list five *gatis*, omitting the *asuras*, or demons. See McGovern, *Manual*, p. 73, and especially Mus, *La Lumière*, pp. 168-71. A certain amount of ambiguity exists in the classifications of these so-called "demons" in Buddhist texts. Sometimes they are classified among the ghosts or among the animals. See Mus, *La Lumière*, pp. 155-83.

[16] Cāttaṉār refers only to the eight hot hells, but in other texts different types of hells are mentioned, including the eight cold hells, the eight dark hells, and the 84,000 frontier hells. See McGovern, *Manual*, p. 61, and Daigan Matsunaga and Alicia Matsunaga, *The Buddhist Concept of Hell* (New York: Philosophical Library, 1972).

[17] The three realms are called *bhūmis*, rather than *dhātus*, in some texts. See Reynolds, *Three Worlds*, p. 16.

[18] The material that binds them to rebirth. Ibid.

[19] For discussions of the correlations between *dhyānas* (Pali *jhānas*) and rebirth, see Kloetzli, *Buddhist Cosmology*, pp. 29-30; Reynolds, *Three Worlds*, pp. 358-59; McGovern, *Manual*, pp. 68-69; Gombrich, "Ancient Indian Cosmology," p. 134; and van Zeyst, "*Arūpa-Loka*," pp. 103-4.

[20] Cāttaṉār calls the deities in the *kāma* realm "*teyvam*" (from Sanskrit *deva*) but calls the deities in the *rūpa* and *arūpa* realms "*piramam*" (from Sanskrit *brahma*).

[21] These are van Zeyst's descriptions of the four highest heavens. See "*Arūpa-Loka*," pp. 103-4.

[22] There are certain inconsistencies in this cosmological system, despite the manner in which it is an "elaborate spatial metaphor for spiritual progress," as Gombrich notes in "Ancient Indian Cosmology," p. 134. One of the logical contradictions is pointed out by McGovern, *Manual*, p. 69: "Yet, notwithstanding their many merits, rebirth in one of these abodes was deprecated, as the duration of life is so inconceivably long that progress to the supreme goal of Nirvāṇa is seriously delayed."

[23] Kloetzli, *Buddhist Cosmology*, p. 30.

[24] McGovern, *Manual*, p. 64.

[25] Gombrich, "Ancient Indian Cosmology," p. 134.

[26] Even though lower heavens are technically inferior, many Buddhist laypeople aspire to rebirth in them, rather than in the *arūpa* heavens. Thus, when *nirvāṇa* is too distant a goal, a certain amount of ambivalence toward the lower heavens exists.

[27] Kirfel, *Die Kosmographie*, pp. 180-81.

[28] The meaning of *vāla* remains obscure.

[29] Frank Reynolds, "The Two Wheels of Dhamma: A Study of Early Buddhism," in *The Two Wheels of Dhamma: Essays on the Theravada Tradition in India and Ceylon*, ed. Bardwell L. Smith (Chambersburg, Penn.: American Academy of Religion, 1972), p. 20.

[30] Ananda K. Coomaraswamy, *Elements of Buddhist Iconography* (Cambridge: Harvard University Press, 1935; reprint, Delhi: Munshiram Manoharlal Publishers, 1979), p. 26.

[31] Kloetzli, *Buddhist Cosmology*, p. 19.

Cāttanār's Way of Presenting Buddhist Cosmology

[32] *Index des Mots de la Litterature Tamoule Ancienne* (Pondichery: Institut Français D'Indologie, 1967), vol. 2, p. 608.

[33] Two young unmarried women would not normally be out alone at that time of night. If a woman were out, conventionally she would be going to a clandestine tryst with her lover, according to grammatical texts dealing with *Caṅkam* poetry.

[34] *Index des Mots*, vol. 1, p. 148. Since the Sanskrit term *cakra*, the basis of *cakravāla*, also means "wheel" or "sphere," Cāttaṉār's choice of synonym is appropriate. Iḷaṅkō, author of *Maṇimēkalai*'s "twin" text *Cilappatikāram*, uses *āḻi* in this same sense in the last line of chapter seven. There Mātavi praises the king, saying that he will bring the whole world under his dominion. The text uses "all that lies within the circle (*āḻi*) of mountains (*māl*) in a series (*varai*)" to refer to the whole world. Later commentators gloss this phrase as referring to the *cakkaravāḷa* mountains, which surround the sphere of the world and its various inhabitants. These mountains are said to form the outer boundary of the cosmos. See Na. Mu. Vēṅkaṭacāmi Nāṭṭār, com., *Cilappatikāram* (Tinnevelly: SISS, 1968), p. 191.

[35] The significance of the term *tāḻi* as (burial) urn is discussed later in this chapter.

[36] *Index des Mots*, vol. 3, p. 1018, for *piramam*; vol. 3, p. 1295, for Meru.

[37] Na. Mu. Vēṅkaṭacāmi Nāṭṭār and Auvai Cu. Turaicāmi Piḷḷai, coms., *Maṇimēkalai* (Tinnevelly: SISS, 1946), commentary on 6:200, p. 102.

[38] Reynolds, *Three Worlds*, p. 13.

[39] Ibid., p. 7.

Cosmos as Cremation Ground

40 The definition and examples come from William Flint Thrall, Addison Hibbard, and C. Hugh Holman, *A Handbook to Literature* (New York: Odyssey Press, 1960), p. 481.

41 Babcock's comments are particularly appropriate here. She stresses the importance of beginnings and endings of narrative: ". . . they are one of the ways in which a narrator sets up an interpretive frame which tells us . . . this is such and such a type of story and should be understood and judged accordingly." See Barbara A. Babcock, "The Story in the Story: Metanarration in Folk Narrative," in *Verbal Art as Performance*, ed. Richard Bauman (Prospect Heights, Ill.: Waveland Press, 1977), p. 71.

42 Paul Wheatley, *The Pivot of the Four Quarters* (Chicago: Aldine Publishing, 1971), p. 460.

43 Ibid., p. 450.

44 Ananda K. Coomaraswamy, "Early Indian Architecture: I. Cities and City-Gates, Etc.," *Eastern Art (An Annual)* 2 (1930): 218. For other discussions of the four gates in an ideally laid-out Indian city, see Manmatha Nāth Dutt Shastrī, *Agni Purāṇam: A Prose English Translation*, Chowkhamba Sanskrit Series, no. 54 (Varanasi: The Chowkhamba Sanskrit Series Office, 1967), vol. 1, p. 429; B. D. Basu, *The Sukranīti*, vol. 13 of *Sacred Books of the Hindus* (Allahabad: Sudhindranātha Vasu, 1923), p. 29; Amita Ray, *Villages, Towns, and Secular Buildings in Ancient India* (Calcutta: Firma K. L. Mukhopadhyay, 1964), pp. 50-51; Binode Behari Dutt, *Town Planning in India* (Calcutta: Thacker, Spink and Co., 1925), pp. 95-99, 340-51.

45 Wheatley, *Pivot*, p. 468.

Conclusions

46 John Strong, *The Legend of King Aśoka: A Study and Translation of the Aśokāvadāna* (Princeton: Princeton University Press, 1983), p. 104.

Chap. 6: Relationships between Laypeople and Renouncers, pp. 101-21

Translation: "Maṇimēkalai Is Put under Protection"

1 Tamil *kaṉṉi* (Sanskrit *kanyā*).

2 "The tall one with the axe" refers to the Vaiṣṇavite *avatāra*, Paraśurāma (Tamil Paracurāmaṉ). He was born into the lineage of the Bhārgavas, who were for many years the family gurus of the Haihaya kings. When many members of his clan were murdered by the kṣatriyas for refusing to lend them money, Paraśurāma vowed to exterminate their killers. According to tradition, he circled the world eighteen times to annihilate the kṣatriya race.

3 Tamil equivalent of the Sanskrit term for the southern continent, Jambudvīpa. *Nāvalam* is the Tamil term for the tree named *Jambu* in Sanskrit.

4 He renamed it after its regent in his absence.

5 A major intersection in the city (literally "four ways' crossing"), where an image of a guardian stands, protecting the city by punishing those who transgress its laws.

6 This line indicates that the power of chaste women was believed to be so great that they would burn the hearts of men who lusted after them.

7 Commentators have taken the phrase *ikanta pūtam* to mean "the *pūtam* who transcends evil." See Na. Mu. Vēṅkaṭacāmi Nāṭṭār and Auvai Cu. Turaicāmi Piḷḷai, coms., *Maṇimēkalai* (1946; reprint, Tinnevelly: SISS, 1964), p. 317, and U. Vē. Cāminātaiyar, *Maṇimēkalai* (Madras: Kabir Press, 1965), p. 245, for their gloss of chapter 22, line 77. This gloss seems overinterpretive. The verb *ika* can have the sense "to have contempt for" or "to deride," and context suggests that meaning here.

8 A *gandharva* marriage is one not sanctified by any formal religious rites. Here the term is being used as a euphemism for premarital intercourse. Since one's cross-cousin is the preferred mate in the Tamil kinship system, people began to gossip that the two cousins were lovers.

[9] This simile means that she departed from her home without her jewelry.

[10] *Nāvuṭaippāvai* literally means "the image possessing a tongue." This epithet describes the image painted onto a pillar in a local shrine and believed to reveal the truth.

[11] Most likely a nunnery.

[12] An emblem of honor given to merchants by kings.

[13] The term is used here again as a euphemism for sexual intercourse without the sanction of an orthodox marriage ceremony.

[14] The ascetic here refers to the traditional Buddhist *pañca śīla*, the five moral precepts that Buddhist laypeople should observe: no improper sexual behavior, no drinking, no lying, no thievery, and no killing.

[15] A reference to the Cōḻa king, Manunītikaṇṭacōḻan, who carried out justice by killing his own son, who had accidentally run over a young calf with his chariot. See Na. Mu. Vēṅkaṭacāmi Nāṭṭār, com., *Cilappatikāram* (Tinnevelly: SISS, 1968), p. 434. For a discussion of this legend and a photograph of temple sculpture portraying it, see David Shulman, *Tamil Temple Myths* (Princeton: Princeton University Press, 1980), pp. 101-2.

The Duties of a Layperson

[16] Vēṅkaṭacāmi Nāṭṭār, *Cilappatikāram*, p. 120.

[17] Holly Baker Reynolds, "The Auspicious Married Woman," in *The Powers of Tamil Women*, ed. Susan S. Wadley, Foreign and Comparative Studies South Asian Series, no. 6 (Syracuse: Maxwell School of Citizenship and Public Affairs, 1980), p. 38.

[18] Parimēlaḻakar, com., *Tirukkuṟaḷ* (Tinnevelly: SISS, 1979), p. 54.

[19] Tamil commentators have interpreted the couplet as the city guardian did. A glance at the major commentators' glosses of the couplet reveals their unanimity on this point. See *Tirukkuṟaḷ Uraikkottu* (Tiruppaṉantāḷ, Tamilnadu: Śrī Kāsimaṭam, 1960), vol. 1: Aṟattuppāl, pp. 56-57.

[20] For a discussion of the Buddha's discourses to householders, as recorded in the Pali Canon, see Dipak Kumar Barua's second chapter, titled "Discourses to the Laity," in *An Analytical Study of Four Nikāyas* (Calcutta: Rabindra Bharati University, 1971), pp. 64-120. Particularly interesting, in the context of my analysis of the Maruti story, is Barua's discussion of the prohibition against pious laypeople's attendance at fairs. Some of the objectionable activities that take place on such occasions also occur at the Indra Festival, which the city guardian forbids Maruti to attend. Such events include the performances of dancing girls, which were thought to encourage idleness. (See Barua, pp. 77-78.) For a discussion of the Buddha's preaching on the duties of wives, see Barua, pp. 109-10 and 112-14.

[21] Evidence in *Maṇimēkalai* and elsewhere suggests that ancient Tamilians held the *Tirukkuṟaḷ* in high esteem. For example, Cāttaṉār makes indirect and direct reference to the *Tirukkuṟaḷ* five times just in this chapter. In addition, several other verses in the text resemble or allude to *Tirukkuṟaḷ* verses. In the context of Tamil literature, such borrowing constitutes a form of tribute rather than plagiary.

Tamil literature contains many other indications of veneration for the *Tirukkuṟaḷ*. Many commentators — including one of the greatest in Tamil literary history, Parimēlaḷakar — wrote glosses on the *Tirukkuṟaḷ*. The existence of *Tiruvaḷḷuvamālai*, consisting exclusively of praises about the *Tirukkuṟaḷ*, indicates the remarkable respect Tiruvaḷḷuvar's text had earned.

[22] This use of older texts is explicitly designated as an *utti*, a rhetorical device titled *āṇai kuṟal*, "quoting a previous authority," to be used when arguing a point. See Iḷampūraṇar, com., *Tolkāppiyam: Poruḷatikāram* (Tinnevelly: SISS, 1977), sutra 656, p. 582.

[23] In *Maṇimēkalai* itself, Tiruvaḷḷuvar is called the *ap poyyil pulavaṉ*, "that poet without falsehood" (22:61). In addition, two of the *Tirukkuṟaḷ*'s traditional epithets highlight the fact that it is considered to contain the truth: "Words without Falsehood" and "Truthful Praise." See Zvelebil, *The Smile of Murugan: On Tamil Literature of South India* (Leiden: E. J. Brill, 1973), p. 156.

24 Discourses on *dāna* are standard forms of popular Buddhist instruction. In fact, they form one part of the three-fold "graduated discourse": a discussion of the benefits of giving (*dāna kathā*) followed by a discourse on moral precepts (*śīla kathā*) and then finally an account of the way laypeople will be born into a heaven if they practice giving and moral precepts (*svarga kathā*). See, for example, the discourse to householders in the *Anguttara Nikāya*, Book of Eights, chapter 3, as translated by E. M. Hare in *The Book of Gradual Sayings*, Pali Text Society Translation Series, no. 26 (London: Luzac and Co. for the Pali Text Society, 1965), vol. 4, p. 143. Cf. the Buddha's sermon to the brahmin Pokkharasādi, which is described in this way: ". . . the Blessed One discoursed in due order; that is to say, he spake to him of generosity [*dāna*], of right conduct [*śīla*], of heaven [*svarga*], of the danger, the vanity, and the defilements of lusts, of the advantage of renunciation." See *Dīgha Nikāya* I, 109-10, as translated by T. W. Rhys Davids in *Dialogues of the Buddha*, part 1, *Sacred Books of the Buddhists* (London: Humphrey Milford for Oxford University Press, 1923), vol. 2, p. 135.

Also valuable are the comments on this graduated discourse by Daigan and Alicia Matsunaga, *The Buddhist Concept of Hell* (New York: Philosophical Library, 1972), p. 24. For the centrality of gift-giving in Buddhist ideology, see Ronald Inden, "The Ceremony of the Great Gift (*Mahādāna*): Structure and Historical Context in Indian Ritual and Society," in *Asie du Sud: Traditions et Changements* (Paris: Colloques Internationeau Du Centre National De La Recherche Scientifique, 1980), pp. 131-36.

25 Curiously enough, the story of this incident follows the description of Vicākai and Tarumatattaṉ's reunion in their old age, and yet it concerns Vicākai as a young girl. Clearly outside of the story's chronological order, this incident functions as an additional witness to the power of Vicākai's chastity. In this "flashback," the power of Vicākai's chastity physically protects her from male lust.

Royal Responsibility to Protect Female Renouncers

26 This motif of the ascetic narrator who tells a cautionary or enlightening tale to a king is central to the rhetoric of tale-telling in such works as the *Mahābhārata*. See, for example, its Book of the Forest, where

the ascetic Mārkaṇḍeya (among others) tells diverse stories about proper action to King Yudhiṣṭhira. For a particularly close parallel to the topic addressed in the story of Maruti in *Maṇimēkalai*, see the story of Sāvitrī, where the renown Mārkaṇḍeya tells Yudhiṣṭhira, the archetypal king, the story of Sāvitrī, the archetypal chaste wife: J. A. B. van Buitenen, trans., *The Mahābhārata* (Chicago: University of Chicago Press, 1975), vol. 2, pp. 760-78.

27 Iḷampūraṇar, com., *Tolkāppiyam: Poruḷatikāram*, pp. 135-42. *Cilappatikāram*, a text much closer to *Maṇimēkalai* in date, has as one of its major themes the general praise of a king and his kingdom. See Sally Noble, "Landscape, Image, and Song in the *Cilappatikāram*" (Master's thesis, Department of South Asian Languages and Civilizations, University of Chicago, 1981), pp. 39, 59.

28 Parimēlaḻakar, *Tirukkuraḷ*, p. 60.

29 Tolkāppiyar's explicit mention of the royal umbrella as one of the subjects of kingly praise indicates its central role in formulations of ancient Tamil kingship: traditional topics of praise for the king include the theme of *kuṭai nilai*, where the umbrella is praised as a symbol of good government. See Iḷampūraṇar, *Tolkāppiyam: Poruḷatikāram*, sutra 87, p. 142. Cf. Kampaṉ's description in *Irāmāvatāram* of the ideal king, who possesses a cooling umbrella (or parasol) and a straight sceptre. David Shulman translates and analyzes these passages in *The King and the Clown in South Indian Myth and Poetry* (Princeton: Princeton University Press, 1985), pp. 48-50.

30 Verses 17-18 of chapter 19 of *Cilappatikāram* as translated in Ramachandra Dikshitar, *The Cilappatikaram*, p. 282.

31 See Shulman's excellent analysis of this key *Cilappatikāram* scene in *King and Clown*, pp. 58-63. I am indebted to K. Paramasivam for calling my attention to the fact that the *Cilappatikāram* scene is the subtext for the confrontation between the ascetic and the king in *Maṇimēkalai*. My analysis of the confrontation developed as a result of his comment.

32 For a different interpretation of the term *kāval*, see the commentary on lines 205-15 in Vēṅkaṭacāmi Nāṭṭār and Turaicāmi Piḷḷai, *Maṇimēkalai*, p. 326. These commentators have interpreted *kāval*, "protection," in a negative way as "imprisonment," indicating a very different outcome for this scene. If their interpretation were correct, what would have been the point of the ascetic's carefully constructed discourse?

[33] For an account of the Paraśurāma story, see Cornelia Dimmitt and J. A. B. van Buitenen, trans., *Classical Hindu Mythology* (Philadelphia: Temple University Press, 1978), pp. 82-85. An analysis of the development of the Paraśurāma story can be found in Adalbert J. Gail, "Paraśurāma: Brahmin and Warrior," *Indologica Taurinensia* 6 (1978): 151-54.

[34] *Tīviṉai* is the subject of the following verbal forms in lines 193-203: *uruttu* [took form, came to fruition], *oḻiyāṉāka* [would not leave off (pursuing)], *ēṟṟi* [caused to go], *uyttu* [drove], *kūy* [called], *kalakki* [confused], and *eṟintatu* [cut down, felled].

Likening Female Renouncers to Chaste Wives

[35] In 18:20, when Cittirāpati discusses how the courtesan should be like the bee who abandons flowers that have been sucked dry, she uses the verb *tuṟa*, to renounce, in describing the bee's actions as a mockery of religious renunciation. I was first made aware of the irony of this usage by David Ludden, "*Maṇimēkalai*" (partial translation) (Philadelphia, 1979, photocopy), p. 104 n. 1.

[36] See Paula Richman, "The Portrayal of a Female Renouncer in a Tamil Buddhist Text," in *Gender and Religion: On the Complexity of Symbols*, ed. Caroline Bynum et al. (Boston: Beacon Press, 1986), pp. 143-65, for a discussion of the courtesan profession in relation to Buddhist philosophy.

[37] In fact, Vicākai is — if anything — more pure than Maruti: Maruti is almost abducted by Kakantaṉ's younger son. When Kakantaṉ's elder son simply begins to make advances to Vicākai, his hand immediately becomes stuck to his head, a miraculous indication of Vicākai's powers.

Conclusions

[38] For an analysis of the dynamics in various versions of the Ṛśyaśṛnga story, see Wendy Doniger O'Flaherty, *Asceticism and*

Eroticism in the Mythology of Śiva (London: Oxford University Press, 1973), pp. 40-42. Frédérique Apffel Marglin links the story of the courtesan seducing Ṛśyaśṛnga with the auspiciousness of *devadāsīs* and their association with water in rituals and temple sculpture. See *Wives of the God-King: The Rituals of the Devadasis of Puri* (Delhi: Oxford University Press, 1986), pp. 98-101.

39 Ibid., pp. 42-52.

40 George L. Hart, III, *The Poems of Ancient Tamil: Their Milieu and Their Sanskrit Counterparts* (Berkeley: University of California Press, 1975).

41 See Margaret Egnor, "On the Meaning of Śakti to Women in Tamil Nadu"; Holly Baker Reynolds, "The Auspicious Married Woman"; and Susan S. Wadley, "The Paradoxical Powers of Tamil Women," pp. 1-34, 35-60, and 153-67 respectively in Wadley, *Tamil Women.*

42 See, for example, Georg Bühler, trans., *The Laws of Manu* (New York: Dover Publications, 1969), pp. 218-21, especially vv. 14, 17, and 25.

43 John Strong, *The Legend of King Aśoka: A Study and Translation of the Aśokāvadāna* (Princeton: Princeton University Press, 1983), especially pp. 49-56.

44 Frank Reynolds, "The Two Wheels of Dhamma: A Study of Early Buddhism," in *The Two Wheels of Dhamma: Essays on the Theravada Tradition in India and Ceylon*, ed. Bardwell L. Smith (Chambersburg, Penn.: American Academy of Religion, 1972), pp. 29-30.

Chap. 7: The Comparison Story, pp. 123-42

Criticism of Competing Religious Viewpoints

1 A. L. Basham, *History and Doctrines of the Ājīvikas: A Vanished Indian Religion* (London: Luzac and Co., 1951; reprint, Delhi: Motilal Banarsidass, 1981), p. 198. The two texts that Basham mentions are systematic expositions and refutations of philosophical schools in competition with the ones held by their authors. For a discussion of the *Civañāṉacittiyār*, see Mariasusai Dhavamony, *Love of God According to*

Śaiva Siddhānta (Oxford: Clarendon Press, 1971), p. 224. For a translation of the other text, see E. B. Cowell and A. E. Gough, trans., *The Sarva-Darśana-Saṃgraha or Review of the Different Systems of Hindu Philosophy by Madhava Āchārya*, Chowkhamba Sanskrit Studies, vol. 10 (Varanasi: Chowkhamba Sanskrit Series Office, 1978).

2 Basham, *History*, pp. 198-99.

3 Because Jain monks adhere rigidly to the proscription against harming living creatures, they became well-known in India for the extreme measures they would take to ensure that they did not inadvertently injure any living being. Such measures include straining their drinking water to avoid consuming tiny creatures and sweeping the path in front of them as they walk to avoid stepping upon insects. As Tahtinen comments, "The Jainas have taken vegetarianism to its logical conclusions. No other religious community in India has gone so far to avoid the killing of any kind of organic life for the purpose of nourishment." See Unto Tahtinen, *Ahiṃsā: Non-Violence in Indian Tradition* (London: Rider and Co., 1976).

Translation: "The Story of Āputtiraṉ's Begging Bowl"

4 This phrase has two meanings, both of which imply that Cāli became unchaste. It means either (1) she passed beyond the boundaries of protection, which would mean she crossed over the limits of her husband's rule, or (2) she passed beyond the doorstep, which is protection, i.e., outside of her house and thus beyond the limits of propriety. Subsequent events imply that she became pregnant by a man other than her husband.

5 The three strands refer to the sacred thread worn by brahmins and put on during the *upanāyana* ceremony, which ritually indicates the beginning of the boy's period of studenthood, under the guidance of his guru.

6 Āputtiraṉ literally means "son [*puttiraṉ*] of a cow [*ā*]."

7 This is a disparaging comment since it describes the rite not in terms of its religious significance but in terms of the benefits accruing to the participants at the conclusion of the rite.

8 There is a pun in the Tamil here with both meanings of the term *makaṉ*, "son" and "human being," intended.

[9] Except for Ciruṅki — which refers to (Ṛśya)śṛnga, the son of a deer — none of these so-called "eminent" *ṛṣis* is well-known in the classical Sanskrit or Tamil corpus. For a Sanskrit version of the story of Ṛśyaśṛnga, see J. A. B. van Buitenen, trans., *The Mahābhārata* (Chicago: University of Chicago Press, 1975), vol. 2, pp. 432-41. For a Pali version, see E. B. Cowell, ed., *The Jātaka or Stories of the Buddha's Former Births* (London: Luzac and Co. for the Pali Text Society, 1907; reprint, Delhi: Cosmo Publications, 1978), vol. 5, pp. 79-84. For a discussion of other versions of the story, see Heinrich Lüders, "Die Saga von Ṛṣyaśṛṅga," *Nachrichte Göttingen Akademie*, Philologisch-Historische Klasse, 1897, pp. 87-135.

[10] The term used here indicates a vaguely disreputable group of people, not pilgrims.

[11] Āputtiraṉ's jibe here refers to the fact that the semen that conceived the great brahmanical sages Agastya and Vasiṣṭha was spilled at the sight of a heavenly dancing girl.

[12] Putting rocks in a mendicant's begging bowl is a gesture of the highest contempt. For example, verse 375 of *Paḻamoḻi Nāṉūṟu* says that one should give alms to a mendicant without his even having to ask. The verse notes that the extreme opposite of this good behavior is putting rocks in a begging bowl, which one should never do. Symbolically, such an action constitutes the inversion of Maṇimēkalai's begging bowl. See Ma. Irācamāṇikkam Piḷḷai, com., *Paḻamoḻi Nāṉūṟu* (Tinnevelly: SISS, 1974), p. 263.

[13] Temple of the "fertile" or "rich arts," i.e., a temple to Sarasvatī, the goddess of learning and art.

[14] Epithet for the goddess Sarasvatī, meaning "Goddess of Thought."

[15] "Protector of all" and "protector of living beings" are epithets Cāttaṉār consistently uses to refer to Āputtiraṉ after he goes to Maturai and begins to feed people, first by begging for alms and later with his inexhaustible begging bowl. Throughout *Maṇimēkalai*, it is assumed that the person who gives food to sustain the body also protects the *uyir*, "the life-breath," "soul," or "life" of a human being.

[16] Epithet for the goddess Sarasvatī, meaning "Lamp of Thought."

17 Another name for the temple, with the same meaning as *Celuṅkalai*, "fertile" or "rich arts."

18 Sarasvatī is called the goddess on the tongue for two reasons. First, she is said to live on the tongue of Brahmā, the creator god and her consort. Second, she is thought to be the inspiration of poets, and thus she lives on their tongues when they sing their verses.

19 When ascetics do too much *tapas*, kings perform too many horse sacrifices, or a donor gives too much away, Indra learns of the fact. In Pali and Sanskrit texts, Indra learns of such deeds in a variety of ways. Sometimes his seat is said to heat up. Other times his white blanket, his white carpet, or his mansion are said to shake or tremble. For a discussion of the way various personal possessions of Indra are affected by such extraordinary deeds, see Minoru Hara, "Indra and Tapas," *The Adyar Library Bulletin* 39 (1975): 139-42 n.2.

20 Most likely Java.

21 His suffering is unique. Whereas many people suffer because they do not have enough food, his problem is that his bowl is overflowing with food but there is no one to consume the food.

22 Literally, "Cow's mouth" Tank. In this story, cows are portrayed as extremely generous, so it is appropriate that the inexhaustible begging bowl, which enables Maṇimēkalai to practice extreme generosity, comes out of a pond bearing the name of "cow."

23 Āputtiraṉ is like the sun that disappears after chasing away darkness and reappears again in the east because he ends this birth after having chased away the darkness of hunger and will reappear in another birth.

Enlisting the Reader's Admiration for Āputtiraṉ

24 From a modern perspective, one of the most startling things about the story of Āputtiraṉ is the portrayal of brahmins looking forward to eating the meat of a cow.

[25] Wendy Doniger O'Flaherty, "Sacred Cows and Profane Mares in Indian Mythology," *History of Religions* 19, no. 1 (August 1979): 1-25.

Disparaging Brahmanical Religiosity

[26] It is appropriate that the goddess Sarasvatī bestows the miraculous bowl upon Āputtiraṉ, since she is the goddess of wisdom and Cāttaṉār has taken pains to emphasize that Āputtiraṉ is frightfully intelligent — so much so that he can out-debate the venerated brahmins and they find him threatening. Even the *Laws of Manu* rank Āputtiraṉ's type of intelligence higher than the type of knowledge exhibited by the brahmins of Vayaṉaṅkōṭu: "(Even forgetful) students of the (sacred) books are more distinguished than the ignorant, those who remember them surpass the (forgetful) students, those who possess a knowledge (of the meaning) are more distinguished than those who (only) remember the words . . ." See chap. 12, v. 103 in Georg Bühler, trans., *The Laws of Manu* (New York: Dover Publications, 1969), pp. 507-8.

Discrediting Vedic Deities

[27] Wendy Doniger O'Flaherty, trans., *The Rig Veda: An Anthology* (Harmondsworth: Penguin Books, 1981), p. 162.

[28] Doris Srinivasan, "The Myth of the Paṇis in the Ṛg Veda," *Journal of the American Oriental Society* 93, no. 1 (January-March 1973): 51.

[29] Ibid., pp. 49-50.

[30] Nāṟkavirāca Nampi, *Akapporuḷ Viḷakkam* (Tinnevelly: SISS, 1979), sutra 23, p. 21.

[31] Edward Washburn Hopkins, "Indra as a God of Fertility," *Journal of the American Oriental Society* 36 (1916): 242-68.

[32] Sukumari Bhattacharji, *The Indian Theogony* (Cambridge: Cambridge University Press, 1965), p. 264.

[33] For an example of a classical discussion of the importance of *daṇḍa* to a kṣatriya, see the *rājadharma* debate in the *Mahābhārata*: Pratap Chandra Roy, trans., *The Mahabharata of Krishna-Dwaipayana Vyasa* (Calcutta: Oriental Publishing Co., 1927-32), vol. 7, pp. 27-29.

[34] Manmatha Nath Dutt, ed., *Bāla Kānda*, vol. 1 of *The Ramayana Translated into English Prose from the Original Sanskrit of Valmiki* (Calcutta: Girish Chandra Chackravati, 1891), pp. 115-17.

[35] Vai. Mu. Kōpālakirushṇamācāriyar, com., *Pāla Kāṇṭam*, vol. 1 of *Kamparāmāyaṇam* (Madras: Vai. Mu. Kōpālakirushṇamācāriyar Co., 1965), pp. 388-89, vv. 546-47.

[36] Parimēlaḻakar, com., *Tirukkuraḷ* (Tinnevelly: SISS, 1979), sutra 25, p. 12.

[37] Many of the terms for the senses are derived from Indra's name, cf. *intiriyam*, "organ of sense" or "semen," and *intiriyañānam*, "sensation."

[38] Bhattacharji, *Theogony*, p. 264.

[39] van Buitenen, *Mahābhārata*, vol. 2, p. 46.

[40] Ibid., vol. 2, p. 63, where King Bṛhadratha is compared to Indra, and vol. 2, p. 78, where Arjuna's martial prowess is said to be appropriate because he is the son of Indra, for example. See also, J. L. Brockington's analysis of Indra in the *Rāmāyaṇa* in *Righteous Rāma: The Evolution of an Epic* (Delhi: Oxford University Press, 1985), pp. 195-96.

[41] van Buitenen, *Mahābhārata*, vol. 2, p. 132.

[42] Heinrich Zimmer, *Myths and Symbols in Indian Art and Civilization* (Princeton: Princeton University Press, 1974), p. 8.

[43] Manmatha Nath Dutt, trans., *A Prose English Translation of the Harivamsha* (Calcutta: Elysium Press, 1897), pp. 282-315. The story is also found in Horace Hayman Wilson, trans., *The Vishṇu Purāṇa: A System of Hindu Mythology and Tradition* (London: Trubner and Co., 1868), pp. 416-23.

[44] The two stories explicated below are found in Na. Mu. Vēṅkaṭacāmi Nāṭṭār, com., *Maturai Kaṇṭam*, vol. 1 of *Tiruvilaiyāṭal Purāṇam* (Tinnevelly: SISS, 1965), pp. 305, 521.

45 Wendy Doniger O'Flaherty, *The Origins of Evil in Hindu Mythology* (Berkeley: University of California Press, 1976), p. 80.

Indra as Āputtiraṉ's Opponent

46 In this chapter's analysis of Indra mythology, I have not discussed Indra in Buddhist texts because Cāttaṉār is clearly treating Indra's portrayal in Hindu texts as his point of reference. In Buddhist materials, Indra's change of name to Śakra (Pali Sakka) — formerly just one of Indra's epithets — signals a change in his personality as well. In the *Jātakas*, Sakka often acts as a helpmeet, enabling the *bodhisattva* to perfect the *pāramitās* so that eventually he can attain Buddhahood. For example in the *Vessantara Jātaka*, Sakka comes in disguise to request that Vessantara give him his wife. In this way, Sakka enables Vessantara to perfect the *pāramitā* of *dāna*, "giving." In some Buddhist *suttas*, Indra is portrayed as the worldly person *par excellence*. In such passages he is depicted as benefiting from Buddhist sermons about the ways in which he can cut off craving. In other Buddhist *suttas*, Indra is very Buddhist, often portrayed as praising and venerating the Buddha, admiring *arhats*, or giving gifts to the *saṅgha*. For an examination of these passages, see J. R. Haldar, *Early Buddhist Mythology* (New Delhi: Manohar, 1977), pp. 82-89, and M. Winternitz, *A History of Indian Literature* (New York: Russell and Russell, 1933), vol. 2, pp. 43, 86.

47 Vessantara gives away with pleasure not only his material possessions but his wife and children as well. See Cowell, ed., *The Jātaka*, vol. 6, pp. 247-305, as well as Margaret Cone and Richard F. Gombrich, *The Perfect Generosity of Prince Vessantara: A Buddhist Epic* (Oxford: Oxford University Press, 1977). King Aśoka also gives away his riches with abandon. After he no longer has access to the state treasury, he gives away the very plates upon which he has been eating and finally, upon his deathbed, the half a myrobalan fruit that he possesses. See John Strong, *The Legend of King Aśoka: A Study and Translation of the Aśokāvadāna* (Princeton: Princeton University Press, 1983), pp. 286-92.

Conclusions

[48] In this chapter I have used Hindu myths about Indra to show why the Āputtiraṉ story functions as a critique of brahmanical Hinduism. But, like any complex piece of literature, the story of Āputtiraṉ has more than one point. Indeed, David Dean Shulman provides another reading of the Āputtiraṉ story as a tale concerned with kingship and renunciation. Shulman's interpretation considers Āputtiraṉ over the course of two lifetimes, emphasizing his desire in the latter life to renounce the kingship of Cāvaka. My interpretation, in contrast, focuses primarily upon the branch story of Āputtiraṉ's previous life, emphasizing his confrontation with Indra. For Shulman's interpretation, see *The King and the Clown in South Indian Myth and Poetry* (Princeton: Princeton University Press, 1985), pp. 64-75.

Conclusions, pp. 143-55

[1] Those who attend oral narrative performances in India are familiar with the many branch stories told along with the main story. Indian story-telling has traditionally been a lengthy affair, often extending over one or many nights. The addition of stories within stories is a logical form of enlarging the narrative in ways both interesting and varied. For an analysis of the social and narrative context of a present day oral epic, see Gene H. Roghair, *The Epic of Palnāḍu* (Oxford: Oxford University Press, 1982). Roghair's comments about the singing of this epic (p. 64) deserve to be cited here since they echo statements made in this monograph about coherence in South Asian texts:

> The stories and episodes are not randomly told, nor are they told in an order that is dependent upon the singer's whim. The epic as a whole possesses a unity that must be respected. Given that unity, the singer is at liberty to present his material as he sees fit. It may be as straightforward narrative, story within a story, or repetition with different or additional details.

A Community Envisioned

[2] See, for example, the stories in C. H. Tawney, *The Kathā Sarīt Sāgara or Ocean of the Streams of Story Translated from the Original Sanskrit* (1880; reprint, Delhi: Munshiram Manoharlal, 1968) and J. A. B. van Buitenen, trans., *Tales of Ancient India* (New York: Bantam Books, 1961). In fact, from the perspective of *kathā* tradition, one need not be surprised that Cāttaṉār describes Maṇimēkalai, though a nun, as an attractive woman. (See the discussion of this description in chapter two of this monograph.) She is — after all — not only a former courtesan but a manifestation of the multiform goddess of romance who flies through the air and bestows great gifts.

Rhetoric in *Maṇimēkalai* and Other Buddhist Texts

[3] Isaline Blew Horner, *Women under Primitive Buddhism* (London: Routledge and Kegan Paul, 1930; reprint, Delhi: Motilal Banarsidass, 1975), p. 185.

[4] M. Winternitz, *A History of Indian Literature* (New York: Russell and Russell, 1933), vol. 2, p. 105.

[5] Ibid., p. 100.

[6] K. R. Norman, trans., *The Elders' Verses II: Therīgāthās* (London: Luzac and Co. for the Pali Text Society, 1971), pp. 28-29, and A. K. Warder, *Pali Metre: A Contribution to the History of Indian Literature* (London: Luzac and Co. for the Pali Text Society, 1967), pp. 98, 135-56, 226.

[7] Not all of the nuns to whom poems are attributed in this collection necessarily composed those particular poems. On page 101 of Winternitz's *History*, he says,

> . . . neither is the tradition of the names of the Theras and Therīs as authors of the verses on the whole, trustworthy. However, the tradition is right in assuming for these poems, not one author, but many authors, and certainly in ascribing the authorship of the songs partly

> to monks and partly to nuns. Some of the songs which are ascribed to various authors may, of course, in reality be the work of only one poet, and conversely, some stanzas ascribed to one and the same poet, might have been composed by various authors.

Norman, too, argues that "it is clear that many of the verses were not uttered by the therīs in the first place at all." He notes that some of them may have been spoken to specific nuns, who then became associated with their later recitation. See his discussion in *Elders' Verses II*, pp. xix-xx.

[8] For the Pali version of this poem (stanzas 252-70), see Hermann Oldenberg and Richard Pischel, eds., *The Thera- and Therî-Gâthâ: Stanzas Ascribed to Elders of the Buddhist Order of Recluses* (London: Luzac and Co. for the Pali Text Society, 1966), pp. 147-50. The translation above is that of Karen Lang, as found in her article "Lord Death's Snare: Gender-Related Imagery in the Theragāthā and the Therīgāthā," *Journal of Feminist Studies in Religion* 1 (Fall 1986): 74-75. For other translations, see Norman, *Elders' Verses II*, pp. 28-29, and Caroline Rhys Davids, trans., *Psalms of the Early Buddhists*, vol. 1 of *Psalms of the Sisters* (London: Luzac and Co. for the Pali Text Society, 1964), pp. 121-24.

[9] For an analysis of the poetic skill in this song attributed to Ambapālī, see Siegfried Lienhard, "Sur La Structure Poétique des Theratherīgāthā," *Journal Asiatique* 263 (1975): 379-80. Also, for a passage in *Maṇimēkalai* that uses precisely the same structure, see lines 40-70 of chapter twenty. There Maṇimēkalai seeks to explain to Utayakumaraṉ the impermanence of the body. To do so she points to an old woman once known for her beauty and catalogues the decay of her body from head to toe. Although the specific features and images are somewhat different from the Ambapālī poems, the format and point of her speech are the same.

[10] For a more extensive treatment of this issue, see Paula Richman, "The Portrayal of a Female Renouncer in a Tamil Buddhist Text," in *Gender and Religion: On the Complexity of Symbols*, ed. Caroline Bynum et al. (Boston: Beacon Press, 1986), pp. 156-58.

[11] The same basic version of the Aśoka legend was popular in Northwest India, but it is known throughout Asia (Central Asia, China, Korea, Japan, and Tibet) through the many translations of it made in the Buddhist world. See John S. Strong, *The Legend of King Aśoka: A Study*

and Translation of the Aśokāvadāna (Princeton: Princeton University Press, 1983), pp. 18-26 and 26-37, for a discussion of the text's religious and literary milieu.

12 The four stories summarized here will be found in the Sanskrit as follows: Sujitkumar Mukhopadhyaya, ed., *The Aśokāvadāna* (New Delhi: Sahitya Akademi, 1963), pp. 56-61 (suffering of a god), 44-46 (suffering of hell-dwellers), 62-67 (suffering of a hungry ghost), 71-74 (suffering of animals). In Strong, *Aśokāvadāna,* they are translated on pp. 221-26 (gods), 211-13 (hell-dwellers), 227-31 (hungry ghost), 234-38 (animals).

13 In this system only five modes of existence (*gati*) are mentioned. For a discussion of the *gati* system, see chapter five of this monograph.

14 Mukhopadhyaya, *Aśokāvadāna*, p. 60, and Strong, *Aśokāvadāna*, p. 225.

15 E. H. Johnston, ed. and trans., *The Saundarananda of Aśvaghoṣa* (Lahore, 1928-32: reprint, Delhi: Motilal Banarsidass, 1975), p. 141. The translation here is that of Richard Salomon, "The Structure of a Buddhist Poem: Aśvaghoṣa's *Saundarananda*" (Paper presented at the South Asia Colloquium of the Pacific Northwest, Seattle, December 1981), p. 83. The intention to propagate Buddhism also informs another work of Aśvaghoṣa, the *Buddhacarita.* For an analysis of its rhetoric and structure, see Indira Peterson, "Recurrence and Structure in Sanskrit Literary Epic: A Study of Bhāravi's *Kirātārjunīya*" (Ph.D. diss., Department of Sanskrit and Indian Studies, Harvard University, 1976), pp. 351-90. I am grateful to Peterson for helpful suggestions for the writing of this section of my concluding chapter.

16 Also noteworthy is the fact that Aśvaghoṣa's poems were known not only to his native North India but in South India as well. For evidence of familiarity with Aśvaghoṣa's poetry throughout South India (and Southeast Asia), see J. Takakusu, trans., *A Record of the Buddhist Religion as Practised in India and the Malay Archipelago (A.D. 671-695) by I-Tsing* (Oxford: Clarendon Press, 1896), pp. 165-66.

17 Salomon, "Structure of a Buddhist Poem," pp. 73-82.

18 Johnston, *The Saundarananda*, p. 162.

19 Ibid., p. 34. The translation here is that of Salomon, "Structure of a Buddhist Poem," p. 84.

[20] Ibid., pp. 84-85.

[21] Strong, *Aśokāvadāna*, pp. 32-33.

[22] Ibid., p. 33.

[23] Ibid., p. 35.

Appendix A: Authorship, Genre, Dating, and Sectarian Affiliation, pp. 157-66

Authorship

[1] Na. Mu. Vēṅkaṭacāmi Nāṭṭār, com., *Cilappatikāram* (Tinnevelly: SISS, 1968), p. 4.

[2] See, for example, J. M. Somasundaram Pillai, *A History of Tamil Literature with Texts and Translations* (Annamalainagar: By the author, 1968), p. 361; N. Balusamy, *Studies in Maṇimēkalai* (Madurai: Āthirai Pathippakam, 1965), p. 226; S. Krishnaswami Aiyangar, *Manimekhalai in its Historical Setting* (London: Luzac and Co., 1928), p. 8. Ramachandra Dikshitar takes the term as indicating that Cāttaṉār belonged to a community of corn-chandlers. See V. R. Ramachandra Dikshitar, trans., *The Cilappatikaram*, 2d ed. (Tinnevelly: SISS, 1978), p. 88 n. 1.

[3] Na. Mu. Vēṅkaṭacāmi Nāṭṭār and Auvai Cu. Turaicāmi Piḷḷai, coms., *Maṇimēkalai* (Tinnevelly: SISS, 1946), p. 4.

[4] Kamil Zvelebil, *Tamil Literature*, vol. 2, fasc. 1 of *Handbuch der Orientalistik*, gen. ed. Jan Gonda (Leiden: E. J. Brill, 1975), p. 115. [Hereafter cited as *Handbuch.*]

[5] For example, Meenakshisundaram says, "Though it is sometimes claimed to be earlier than *Cilappatikāram*, a careful reading shows that this epic would have meant nothing to an audience which was not familiar with *Cilappatikāram*." See T. P. Meenakshisundaram, *A History of Tamil Literature* (Annamalainagar: Annamalai University, 1965), p. 43. Since the material in the *patikams* [prefaces] concerns the process by which the

two texts came to be written, it must be later than the actual text. Some scholars feel that its lateness makes it unreliable, and they ignore it in dating the text. For example, Zvelebil rejects Aṭiyārkkunallār's claims, dating *Cilappatikāram* ca. A. D. 450 and *Maṇimēkalai* ca. A.D. 550. See *Handbuch*, p. 114.

6 A Cīttalai Cāttaṉār composed the following *Caṅkam* poems: *Akanāṉūṟu* 53, 134, 320; and *Naṟṟiṇai* 36, 127, 339. *Kuṟuntokai* 154 is the work of a Maturai Cīttalai Cāttaṉār, while Maturai Kūlavāṇikaṉ Cīttalai Cāttaṉār composed *Akanāṉūṟu* 229 and 306 as well as *Puṟanāṉūṟu* 59. Are all of these Cāttaṉārs the same person? Balusamy concludes that they were three separate *Caṅkam* poets. See his *Studies*, pp. 229-32. For a similar conclusion, see S. Vaiyapuri Pillai, *History of Tamil Language and Literature* (Madras: New Century Book House, 1956), p. 149. For another consideration of Cāttaṉār's identity, see S. S. Bharati, "Maṇimēkalaiyiṉ Kālamum Itai Iyaṟṟiyavarum," *Centamiḻ* 43 (July-August 1943): 301-12. Krishnaswami Aiyangar identifies the author of *Maṇimēkalai* with a single *Caṅkam* poet who composed the classical poems listed above. In doing so, he pushes the dating of the Tamil Buddhist text back to the second century. See his *Manimekhalai*, p. 10.

7 A. Mu. Paramacivāṉantam, *Cāttaṉār* (Aṇṇāmalainagar: Aṇṇāmalai Palkalai Kaḻakam, 1974), p. 16, and Krishnaswami Aiyangar, *Manimekhalai*, p. 10.

8 See the *Tiruvaḷḷuvarmālai* verse by Maruttuvaṉ Tāmōtaraṉār in Parimēlaḻakar, com., *Tirukkuṟaḷ* (Tinnevelly: SISS, 1979), p. 511.

9 Obeyesekere, an anthropologist whose research focuses on Pattiṉi rituals in Sri Lanka, uses the story of Cāttaṉār's great head pain to come to his own understanding of the meaning of Cāttaṉār's name, a meaning that seems in consonance with Sri Lankan ritual context. After discussing the story, he says,

> . . . I shall tentatively gloss *cāttaṉ* as arhat or, better, "a Buddhist religious specialist." . . . But what kind of specialist? The author's first name, "Cīttalai," gives us the clue. It is more plausible to derive *cīttalai* from the Sanskrit *sītala*, "cool." Thus according to my line of thought, Cāttaṉ is not an arhat-type religious specialist but a Buddhist healer. In the east coast text he appears

in the context of the *cooling* of the goddess; he intercedes on behalf of the folk and asks her to be gracious (forgiving).

See Gananath Obeyesekere, *The Cult of the Goddess Pattini* (Chicago: University of Chicago Press, 1984), p. 589.

[10] See Balusamy, *Studies*, p. 228, and S. N. Kandaswamy, *Buddhism as Expounded in Maṇimēkalai* (Annamalainagar: Annamalai University, 1978), pp. 28-29.

[11] Kandaswamy, *Buddhism*, p. 29.

[12] Na. Mu. Vēṅkaṭacāmi Nāṭṭār, *Maṇimēkalai*, p. 4 (*patikam*, line 97).

Genre

[13] In some ways, the title "the five *peruṅ-kāppiyam*" is misleading. These five do not comprise the greatest ancient and medieval extended narrative written in Tamil. The two Tamil *kāppiyam* universally recognized as the greatest in Tamil literature, *Kamparāmāyaṇam* and *Periya Purāṇam*, are absent from the list. In addition, two of the five noted above no longer exist and do not appear to have had a great effect on later Tamil literature. Common sense suggests that the title "the five *peruṅ-kāppiyam*," as used in histories of Tamil literature, may be a title for five early extended narratives rather than an evaluation of the quality of all Tamil texts of that type.

[14] Although it is generally accepted that *kāppiyam* derives from *kāvya*, Balusamy claims the word is from the Tamil verb *kāppu*, "to protect" or "to contain." See Balusamy, *Studies*, p. 163.

[15] The following are conventionally designated "the five *mahā-kāvyas*" in Sanskrit: *Raghuvaṃśa, Kumārasaṃbhava, Kirātārjuniya, Śiśupālavadha,* and *Naishadhacarita.*

[16] See Arthur A. MacDonell, *A History of Sanskrit Literature* (New York: D. Appleton and Co., 1900; reprint, New York: Haskell House Publishers, 1968), pp. 326-30; A. Berriedale Keith, *A History of Sanskrit Literature* (Oxford: Oxford University Press, 1956), p. 92.

Notes to pp. 159-60

[17] V. C. Āṟumukam Cērvai, ed., *Taṇṭiyalaṅkāram Śrī Cuppiramaniyatēcikar Uraiyuṭan* (Madras: Madras Ripon Press, 1920), pp. 5-6, sutra 6. *Taṇṭiyalaṅkāram* is a Tamil translation of Dandin's *Kāvyādarśa*, according to C. Jesudasan and Hephzibah Jesudasan, *A History of Tamil Literature* (Calcutta: Y.M.C.A. Publishing House, 1961), p. 143. For another discussion of *peruṅ-kāppiyam*, see K. V. Jakannātaṉ, *Tamiḻ Kāppiyaṅkaḷ: Ilakkaṇamum Ilakkiyamum*, Bulletin of the Tamil Department, no. 4 (Madras: University of Madras, 1940), especially pp. 74-78.

[18] Jesudasan and Jesudasan, *Tamil Literature*, p. 144. Later on the same page, the Jesudasans note that in the "twin" texts "only the sub-divisions seem to be from Sanskrit." That is, according to convention, *peruṅ-kāppiyam* must be divided according to particular Sanskrit subdivisions. The subdivisions they refer to are *kāṇḍam* and *kātai.*

[19] This argument begins with Aṭiyārkkunāllar's commentary on *Cilappatikāram* and is repeated in most standard histories of Tamil literature.

[20] The last chapter of *Cilappatikāram*, however, does contain a description of Maṇimēkalai's tonsure in preparation for entering a Buddhist monastic order.

[21] Note, for example, the key didactic passage in "The Story of the Cosmic Place." The long and ghastly description of the cremation ground culminates with this question: "Even though they see the cremation ground consuming pyres with its fiery mouth, some people are still intoxicated with immense wealth and pleasure. Of all the people who exist, are any more ignorant than those who live thus, without desiring to perform the most excellent *aṟam*?" (*Maṇimēkalai* 6:101-4).

[22] Chapter twenty-five of *Maṇimēkalai*, for example, deals with the duties of a king.

[23] Indeed, a good deal of *Maṇimēkalai*'s main story concerns Utayakumaraṉ's love for Maṇimēkalai.

[24] See Kamil Zvelebil, *Tamil Literature*, vol. 10, fasc. 1 of *A History of Indian Literature*, gen. ed. Jan Gonda (Weisbaden: Otto Harrassowitz, 1974), p. 131, where he makes this comment about the literary potential of late *Caṅkam* works:

> On the other hand, it should be noted that, while considering Kalittokai and Paripāṭal as later classical collections forming a kind of transition between the bardic age and later early feudal periods, we may venture the guess that elements of narration and dialogue developing into dramatic scenes could further develop into a dramatic epic [*peruṅ-kāppiyam*].

Kandaswamy also sees *Maṇimēkalai*'s form in a similar way, commenting that it and texts like it are "the natural outgrowth" of later *Caṅkam* texts. See his *Buddhism*, p. 20.

25 Zvelebil, *History*, p. 130.

26 U. Vē. Cāminātaiyar, ed., *Cilappatikāra Mūlamum Arumpatavuraiyum Aṭiyarkkunallāruraiyum* (Madras: Kabir Press, 1968), p. 24.

Dating

27 E. S. Varatarāja Ayyar, *Tamiḻ Ilakkiya Varalāṟu* (Madras: Aṇṇāmalai Palkalai Kaḻakam, 1957), p. 148.

28 Krishnaswami Aiyangar, *Manimekhalai*, pp. 11-12. Balusamy, *Studies*, p. 238, gives an early third-century date.

29 S. Vaiyāpuri Piḷḷai, *Kāviyakālam* (Madras: Tamiḻ Puttakālayam, 1962), pp. 33, 141, and his *History of Tamil Language and Literature* (Madras: New Century Book House, 1956), p. 153.

30 S. S. Suryanarayana Sastri, "The Maṇimēkalai Account of the Sāṁkhya," *Journal of Indian History* 8, no. 3 (December 1929): 322-27.

31 S. Kuppuswami, "Problems of Identity in the Cultural History of Ancient India," *The Journal of Oriental Research, Madras* 1, no. 2 (April 1927): 192, and K. A. Nilakanta Sastri, *The Cōḻas* (Madras: University of Madras, 1955), pp. 55-56, 62 n. 117. The issue is discussed further in K. G. Sesha Aiyar, "The Date of Maṇimēkalai," *The Journal of Oriental Research, Madras* 1, no. 4 (October 1927): 321-29.

32 Krishnaswami Aiyangar, *Manimekhalai*, pp. 34-107.

33 S. S. Suryanarayana Sastri, "Buddhist Logic in the Maṇimēkalai," *Journal of Indian History* 9, no. 3 (December 1930): 336.

34 Kandaswamy says, "It is more reasonable to suggest that the poet [Cāttaṉār] ingeniously incorporated his translation of Buddhist logic in his epic as an addition to the advancement of Tamil knowledge, than to imagine that Dignāga plucked out the 29th Chapter of Maṇimēkalai and elaborated [*sic*] in his various treatises . . . Cāttaṉār collected and selected key points of their logical texts, combined with his own treatise (XXIX Chapter) to suit the genius of the Tamil language." See his *Buddhism*, p. 256.

35 See Zvelebil, *Handbuch*, pp. 114-16. Zvelebil assigns A.D. 550 and A.D. 450 as dates for *Maṇimēkalai* and its "twin" text, respectively. It is not clear why one hundred years need have elapsed between the writing of the two works. The striking similarities in language, imagery, style, and word-use point to a similar literary climate for both. Thus, it seems reasonable to assume that Cāttaṉār composed *Maṇimēkalai* during the sixth century and that *Cilappatikāram* preceded it, but not necessarily by a long period of time.

36 See Kandaswamy, *Buddhism*, pp. 5-74. Other scholars from other areas of specialty concur with the period suggested by Kandaswamy. See A. L. Basham, *History and Doctrines of the Ājīvikas: A Vanished Indian Religion* (London: Luzac and Co., 1951; reprint, Delhi: Motitlal Banarsidass, 1981), p. 197. This date also seems appropriate according to the system of dating Tamil texts established in Friedhelm Hardy, *Viraha-Bhakti: The Early History of Kṛṣṇa Devotion in South India* (Delhi: Oxford University Press, 1983), especially pp. 125, 202.

Sectarian Affiliation

37 In parts of South India, it seems possible that Buddhism did not disappear until as late as the fourteenth century. In Tamilnadu, two of the most important Buddhist areas appear to have been the coastal town of Kāviripaṭṭiṉam and the city of Kāñcīpuram. See K. A. Nilakanta Sastri, "Mahāyāna Buddhism in South India," *Bulletin of Tibetology* 2

(November 1965): 11-21. See also K. Indrapala, "Buddhism among the Tamils A.D. 1000-1500," in *Proceedings of the Fifth International Conference-Seminar on Tamil Studies* (Madras: International Association of Tamil Studies, 1981), vol. 2, pp. 12/27-12/39.

The pioneering study of Buddhism in Tamilnadu is Mayilai Cīni Vēṅkaṭacāmi, *Pauttamum Tamiḻum* (Tinnevelly: SISS, 1940; reprint, 1972). Another general survey of relevant materials is K. A. Nilakanta Sastri, "Buddhism in the Tamil Country," *March of India* 8, no. 12A (November 1956): 51-54. For a discussion of Buddhism in Tamilnadu based primarily on literary references, see V. R. Ramachandra Dikshitar, "Buddhism in Tamil Literature," in *Buddhistic Studies*, ed. Bimala Churn Law (Calcutta: Thacker, Spink and Co., 1931; reprint, Delhi: Indological Book House, 1983), pp. 673-98; Glenn E. Yocum, "Buddhism Through Hindu Eyes: Śaivas and Buddhists in Medieval Tamilnadu," in *Traditions in Contact and Change*, ed. Peter Slater and Donald Wiebe (Waterloo, Ontario: Wilfrid Laurier University Press, 1983), pp. 143-62, 690-93; and Xavier S. Thani Nayagam, "Earliest Jain and Buddhist Teaching," *Tamil Culture* 8 (October-December 1959): 337-49.

C. Minakshi's "Buddhism in South India," in *South Indian Studies II*, ed. R. Nagaswamy (Madras: Society for Archaeological, Historical, and Epigraphical Research, 1978), pp. 83-131, deals with literary and epigraphical sources on Buddhism in South India. See also T. N. Vasudeva Rao, *Buddhism in the Tamil Country* (Annamalainagar: Annamalai University, 1979) and Iravatham Mahadevan, "Corpus of Tamil-Brahmi Inscriptions," in *Seminar on Inscriptions* (Madras: State Department of Archaeology, Government of Tamilnadu, 1966), pp. 57-73. Of particular interest is inscription 33 at Aḻakarmalai, which mentions a great nun (*tavirai*, from the Sanskrit *sthavirā*). A. Velu Pillai's recent survey provides a critical review of secondary literature relevant to Buddhism in Tamilnadu, so the interested reader is invited to consult his footnotes for more extensive bibliographical guidance. See his *Epigraphical Evidences for Tamil Studies* (Madras: International Institute of Tamil Studies, 1980), pp. 86-116. See also Indrapala, "Buddhism among the Tamils," p. 12/37 n. 1.

[38] Krishnaswami Aiyangar, *Manimekhalai*, p. xxvii. He makes the same point in "The Buddhism of Manimekhalai," in *Buddhistic Studies*, p. 11.

39 Krishnaswami Aiyangar, *Manimekhalai*, p. xxvii. For an overview of the doctrines of these schools of Buddhism, see Edward Conze, *Buddhist Thought in India* (London: George Allen and Unwin, 1962; reprint, Ann Arbor: University of Michigan Press, 1967), pp. 119-58.

40 Balusamy, *Studies*, p. 122.

41 P. C. Alexander, *Buddhism in Kerala*, Annamalai University Historical Series, no. 8 (Annamalainagar: The Registrar, Annamalai University, 1949), pp. 141-42.

42 Krishnaswami Aiyangar, "Buddhism," p. 11.

43 All the page numbers in parentheses in this paragraph refer to Kandaswamy, *Buddhism*.

44 See Randy Kloetzli, *Buddhist Cosmology (From Single World System to Pure Land: Science and Technology in the Images of Motion and Light)* (Delhi: Motilal Banarsidass, 1983), chap. 5. Note, however, that other cosmological details point to a Hinayana provenance. For example, see the discussion of the eight hot hells in Appendix C.

45 Kandaswamy, *Buddhism*, p. 108.

46 See, for example, André Bareau, "La Construction et le Culte du Stūpa d'après le Vinaya Piṭaka," *BEFEO* 50 (1962): 229-74, as well as his "Le Parinirvāṇa du Bouddha et la Naissance de la Religion Bouddhique," *BEFEO* 61 (1974): 275-99. Also see John Strong, "Buddhism and Filial Piety: The Indian Antecedents to a 'Chinese' Problem," in *Traditions in Contact and Change*, pp. 171-86, 699-701.

47 Kandaswamy, *Buddhism*, p. 125.

48 Ibid., p. 98.

49 Ibid., p. 314.

50 Étienne Lamotte, "Sur la Formation du Mahāyāna," in *Asiatica: Festschrift Friedrich Weller* (Leipzig: Otto Harrassowitz, 1954), pp. 377-81.

51 Gregory Schopen, "Mahāyāna in Indian Inscriptions," *Indo-Iranian Journal* 21 (January 1979): 1-19.

[52] The term *pikkuṇi* (Tamil translation of *bhikkhuṇī*) appears only twice in the entire text: 15:69 and 23:25. See *Index des Mots de la Litterature Tamoule Ancienne* (Pondichery: Institut Français D'Indologie, 1967), vol. 3, p. 1013.

[53] *Maṇimēkalai*, 26:66.

[54] The presence of a chapter on Buddhist logic (chapter twenty-nine) remains another element whose significance is debatable. Since Buddhist logic developed primarily in the Mahayana tradition, does its presence in the text immediately identify it as a Mahayana text? Or is its presence in the text an indication that chapter thirty is a later interpolation? An insistence on categorizing the text as either Hinayana or Mahayana might lead one toward one of these two positions just mentioned, but neither one is fully satisfactory.

[55] This section of chapter thirty is extremely similar to a passage from *The Questions of King Milinda.* See Kandaswamy's comparison of the two in *Buddhism*, pp. 363-67.

[56] John Strong, *The Legend of King Aśoka: A Study and Translation of the Aśokāvadāna* (Princeton: Princeton University Press, 1983), p. 165.

Appendix B: Translations of Three Pali Versions of "The Mustard Seed Story," pp. 167-74

[1] Mabel Bode, "Women Leaders of the Buddhist Reformation," *Journal of the Royal Asiatic Society of Great Britain and Ireland*, 1893: 793-96.

[2] Caroline Rhys Davids, trans., *Psalms of the Early Buddhists*, vol. 1 of *Psalms of the Sisters* (London: Luzac and Co. for the Pali Text Society, 1964), pp. 106-8.

[3] Eugene Watson Burlingame, *Buddhist Legends Translated from the Original Pali Text of the Dhammapada Commentary*, Part 2, Harvard Oriental Series, vol. 29 (Cambridge: Harvard University Press, 1921), pp. 258-60.

Appendix C: The Design of Figure 2, pp. 175-76

1 These variations in detail usually correlate with schools of Buddhism. For example, in the Southern school of Buddhism (the school from which the Pali names of the eight hot hells have been translated in Table 7), the hells are called Sañjīva, Kāḷasutta, Saṅghāta, Jālaroruva, Dhūmaroruva, Tapana, Patāpana, and Avīci. In texts of the Northern school, the Sanskrit names of the hells are basically the same except for a small variation in hells 4 and 5, which are called Raurava and Mahāraurava. See H. Kern, *Manual of Indian Buddhism* (Strassburg, 1898; reprint, Delhi: Motilal Banarsidass, 1974), p. 58. The Northern texts usually, however, also include a set of cold hells and frontier hells. See William Montgomery McGovern, *A Manual of Buddhist Philosophy* (London, 1923; reprint, Lucknow: Oriental Reprinters, 1976), p. 61. While both schools postulate the same number of *kāma* and *arūpa* heavens, they do disagree about the number of *rūpa* heavens. Some Northern texts give seventeen *rūpa* heavens: Brahmakāyika, Brahmapurohita, Mahābrahma, Parīttābha, Apramāṇābha, Abhāsvara, Parīttaśubha, Apramāṇaśubha, Śubhakṛtsna, Anabhraka, Puṇyaprasava, Bṛhatphala, Abṛha, Atapa, Sudrśa, Sudarśana, and Akaniṣṭha. See McGovern, *Buddhist Philosophy*, p. 67. Others give eighteen heavens, adding Brahmapāriṣadya. See Kern, *Indian Buddhism*, p. 58. Cāttaṉār only mentions sixteen *rūpa* heavens, the standard number in the Southern school. The sixteen he refers to must, therefore, be Brahmapārisajja, Brahmapurohita, Mahābrahma, Parittābha, Appamāṇābha, Ābhassara, Parittasubha, Appamāṇasubha, Subhakiṇha, Vehapphala, Asaññasatta, Avihā, Atappā, Sudassā, Sudassī, Akaniṭṭha. See J. R. Haldar, *Early Buddhist Mythology* (New Delhi: Manohar, 1977), pp. 31-36, and Kern, *Indian Buddhism*, p. 58.

2 Louis de La Vallée Poussin, ed. and trans., *L'Abhidharmakośa de Vasubandhu*, Mélanges Chinois et Bouddhiques, vol. 6 (Brussels: Institut Belge des Hautes Études Chinoises, 1971), tome 2 (chap. 3), p. 169.

3 Willibald Kirfel, *Die Kosmographie der Inder nach den Quellen Dargestellt* (Bonn: Kurt Schroeder, 1920), p. 13*, where Kirfel notes "In Buddhism, the description of heavenly pleasures is even more schematized and sharply detailed than in other [Indian] sources."

4 La Vallée Poussin, *L'Abhidharmakośa*, pp. 4-5.

BIBLIOGRAPHY

WORKS IN SOUTH ASIAN LANGUAGES

Āṟumukam Cērvai, V. C., ed. *Taṇṭiyalaṅkāram Śrī Cuppiramaniyatēcikar Uraiyuṭaṉ*. Madras: Madras Ripon Press, 1920.

Aṭaikkalacāmi, M. R. *Tamiḻ Ilakkiya Varalāṟu*. Madras: Pālnilā Patippakam, 1955.

Bharati, S. S. "Maṇimēkalaiyiṉ Kālamum Itai Iyaṟṟiyavarum." *Centamiḻ* 43 (July-August 1943): 301-312.

Cāminātaiyar, U. Vē. *Eṉ Carittiram*. Madras: Kapīr Accukkūṭam, 1950.

________. *Makāvittuvaṉ Śrī Mīṉāṭcicuntaram Piḷḷaiyavarkaḷ Carittiram*. Tiruvanmiyur: Mahamahopadhyaya Dr. U. V. Swaminathaiyer Library, 1965.

________. *Niṉaivu Mañcari, Mutal Pākam*. Madras: Kēcari Accukkūṭam, 1940.

________, ed. *Cilappatikāra Mūlamum Arumpatavuraiyum Aṭiyarkkunallāruraiyum*. Madras: Kabir Press, 1968.

________, ed. *Cīvakacintāmaṇi Mūlamum Nacciṉārkkiṉiyaruraiyum*. Madras: Kabir Press, 1969.

________, ed. *Maṇimēkalai*. Madras: Jūpili Accukkūṭam, 1898.

________, ed. *Maṇimēkalai*. Madras: Commercial Press, 1921.

________, ed. *Maṇimēkalai*. Madras: Kabir Press, 1965.

________, ed. *Nannūl Mūlamum Mayilai Nātaruraiyum.* Madras: Kabir Press, 1946.

Ceṇpakam, Mā. *Kāppiyaṅkaḷ.* Madurai: Carpōji, 1977.

Citamparaṉār, Cāmi. *Āputtiraṉ Allatu Camūka Ūḷiyaṉ.* Madras: Ilakkiya Nilaiyam, 1974.

Civappirakācar. *Civappirakāca Cuvāmikaḷ Pirapantattiraṭṭu.* Tinnevelly: South India Saiva Siddhanta Works Publishing Society [SISS], 1941.

Cōmacuntaraṉār, Po. Vē., com. *Aiṅkuṟunūṟu.* Tinnevelly: SISS, 1979.

________. *Akanāṉūṟu.* 2 vols. Tinnevelly: SISS, 1977.

________. *Kuṟuntokai.* Tinnevelly: SISS, 1978.

________. *Maṇimēkalai.* Tinnevelly: SISS, 1971.

Iḷampūraṇar, com. *Tolkāppiyam Poruḷatikāram.* Tinnevelly: SISS, 1977.

Irācamāṇikkaṉār, Mā. *Caiva Camaya Vaḷarcci.* Madras: Auvai Ṉūlakam, 1958.

Irācamāṇikkam Piḷḷai, Ma., com. *Paṟamoḻi Nāṉūṟu.* Tinnevelly: SISS, 1974.

Irāmacāmippulavar, Cu. A., comp. *Mēṟkōḷ Viḷakkakkatai Akaravaricai.* 2 vols. Tinnevelly: SISS, 1963.

Jakannātaṉ, K. V. *Tamiḻ Kāppiyaṅkaḷ: Ilakkaṇamum Ilakkiyamum.* Bulletin of the Tamil Department, no. 4. Madras: University of Madras, 1940.

Kāciṟācaṉ, Ira. *Kāppiyattamiḻ.* Madurai: Aruḷ Nātar Patippakam, 1976.

Kaṉṉaiya Nāyuṭu, Ā. Vī., com. *Kaliṅkattupparaṇi.* Madras: Śrī Pārati Accakam, 1955.

Kēcikaṉ, Puliyūr, com. *Maṇimēkalai.* Madras: Pāri Nilaiyam, 1976.

Kōpālaiyar, Ti. Vē., ed. *Ilakkaṇakkottu: Mūlamum Uraiyum.* Tanjore: Sarasvati Mahal Library, 1973.

Kōpālakirushṇamācāriyar, Vai. Mu., com. *Kamparāmāyaṇam.* 6 vols. in 7. Madras: Vai. Mu. Kōpālakirushṇamācāriyar Co., 1962-67.

Mēttā, Mu. *Kaṇṇīr Pūkkaḷ.* Kōvai: Centamiḻ Press, 1974.

Mukhopadhyaya, Sujitkumar. *The Aśokāvadāna.* New Delhi: Sahitya Akademi, 1963.

Muller, E., ed. *Paramatthadīpanī: Dhammapāla's Commentary on the Therīgathā.* London: Henry Frowde for the Pali Text Society, 1983.

Naṉṉūl Kāṇṭikaiyurai. Tinnevelly: SISS, 1979.

Nāṟkavirāca Nampi. *Akapporuḷ Viḷakkam.* Tinnevelly: SISS, 1979.

Naṭēca Cāstiri, S. M. *Tirāviṭa Nāṭṭukkataikaḷ.* Madras: Pirēmā Piracuram, 1968.

Norman, H. C., ed. *The Commentary on the Dhammapada.* 5 vols. in 4. London: Luzac and Co. for the Pali Text Society, 1970.

Pālacuntaram, T. M. *Maṇimēkalai Eṉṉum Maṅkaitturavu.* Tanjore: Lāli Elakṭirik Accukkūṭam, 1923.

Paramacivāṉantam, A. Mu. *Cāttaṉār.* Aṇṇāmalainagar: Aṇṇāmalai Palkalai Kaḻakam, 1974.

Paratitācaṉ. *Maṇimēkalai Veṇpā.* Madras: Aṉpu Ṉūlakam, 1962.

Parimēlaḻakar, com. *Tirukkuṟaḷ.* Tinnevelly: SISS, 1979.

Perumāḷ, Ē. Eṉ. *Ilakkiya Nāṭakaṅkaḷ.* Nākarkoyil: Taṅkam Press, 1973.

Tirukkuṟaḷ Uraikkottu. 3 vols. Tiruppaṉantāḷ, Tamilnadu: Śrī Kāsimaṭam, 1960-61.

Turaicāmi Piḷḷai, Auvai Cu. *Maṇimēkalai Ārāycci.* Tinnevelly: SISS, 1965.

________, com. *Puṟanāṉūṟu.* 2 vols. Tinnevelly: SISS, 1972-77.

Vaiyāpuri Piḷḷai, S. *Kāviyakālam.* Madras: Tamiḻ Puttakālayam, 1962.

Varataṉ, T. N. C., ed. *Maṇimēkalai Mūlam.* Madras: Lifco, 1964.

Varatarāja Ayyar, E. S. *Tamiḻ Ilakkiya Varalāṟu.* Madras: Aṇṇāmalai Palkalai Kaḻakam, 1957.

Vēṅkaṭācalam Piḷḷai, Ē. *Maṇimēkalai (Oru Nāṭakam).* Tinnevelly: SISS, 1946.

Vēṅkaṭacāmi, Mayilai Cini. *Pattoṉpatām Nūṟṟaṇṭil Tamiḻ Ilakkiyam.* Madras: Cānti Nūlakam, 1962.

________. *Pauttamum Tamiḻum.* Tinnevelly: SISS, 1972.

Vēṅkaṭacāmi Nāṭṭār, Na. Mu., com. *Cilappatikāram.* Tinnevelly: SISS, 1968.

________. *Tiruvilaiyāṭal Purāṇam.* 3 vols. Tinnevelly: SISS, 1965.

Vēṅkaṭacāmi Nāṭṭār, Na. Mu., and Turaicāmi Piḷḷai, Auvai Cu., coms. *Maṇimēkalai.* 1946. Reprint. Tinnevelly: SISS, 1964.

WORKS IN EUROPEAN LANGUAGES

Alexander, P. C. *Buddhism in Kerala.* Annamalai University Historical Series, no. 8. Annamalainagar: The Registrar, Annamalai University, 1949.

Amore, Roy C., and Shinn, Larry D. *Lustful Maidens and Ascetic Kings: Buddhist and Hindu Stories of Life.* New York: Oxford University Press, 1981.

Aung, Shwe Zan, and Rhys Davids, Caroline, trans. *Compendium of Philosophy.* London: Luzac and Co. for the Pali Text Society, 1910. Reprint, 1972.

Babcock, Barbara A. "The Story in the Story: Metanarration in Folk Narrative." In *Verbal Art as Performance*, edited by Richard Bauman, pp. 61-79. Prospect Heights, Ill.: Waveland Press, 1977.

Balusamy, N. *Studies in Maṇimēkalai.* Madurai: Āthirai Pathippakam, 1965.

Bareau, André. "La Construction et le Culte du Stūpa d'après le Vinaya Piṭaka." *Bulletin de l'École Française d'Extrême-Orient* [*BEFEO*] 50 (1962): 229-74.

________. "Le Parinirvāṇa du Bouddha et la Naissance de la Religion Bouddhique." *BEFEO* 61 (1974): 275-99.

Barua, Dipak Kumar. *An Analytical Study of Four Nikāyas.* Calcutta: Rabindra Bharati University, 1971.

Basham, A. L. *History and Doctrines of the Ājīvikas: A Vanished Indian Religion.* London: Luzac and Co., 1951. Reprint. Delhi: Motilal Banarsidass, 1981.

Basu, B. D. *The Sukranīti.* Vol. 13 of *Sacred Books of the Hindus.* Allahabad: Sudhindranātha Vasu, 1923.

Beck, Brenda E. F. "The Study of a Tamil Epic: Several Versions of *Silappadikaram* Compared." *Journal of Tamil Studies* 1, no. 1 (1972): 23-38.

Bhattacharji, Sukumari. *The Indian Theogony*. Cambridge: Cambridge University Press, 1965.

Blackburn, Stuart. "Domesticating the Cosmos: History and Structure in a Folktale from India." *Journal of Asian Studies* 45 (May 1986): 527-43.

Bode, Mabel. "Women Leaders of the Buddhist Reformation." *Journal of the Royal Asiatic Society of Great Britain and Ireland*, 1893: 517-66, 763-98.

Brockington, J. L. *Righteous Rāma: The Evolution of an Epic*. Delhi: Oxford University Press, 1985.

Bryant, Kenneth E. *Poems to the Child-God: Structures and Strategies in the Poetry of Sūrdās*. Berkeley: University of California Press, 1978.

Buck, David. "Caṅkam Elements in Bharati's *Kuyil Pāṭṭu*." Paper presented at the Eleventh Annual Conference on South Asia in Madison, Wisconsin, November 1982.

Bühler, Georg, trans. *The Laws of Manu*. New York: Dover Publications, 1969.

Burgess, Jas. *The Buddhist Stupas of Amaravati and Jaggayyapeta in the Krishna District, Madras Presidency, Surveyed in 1882*. 1887. Reprint. Varanasi: Indological Book House, 1970.

Burke, Kenneth. *The Rhetoric of Religion: Studies in Logology*. Berkeley: University of California Press, 1970.

Burlingame, Eugene Watson. *Buddhist Legends Translated from the Original Pali Text of the Dhammapada Commentary*. Part 2. Harvard Oriental Series, vol. 29. Cambridge: Harvard University Press, 1921.

Carter, John Ross. "Traditional Definitions of the Term *dhamma*." *Philosophy East and West* 26 (July 1976): 329-37.

Chakravarti, A., trans. *Neelakesi: The Original Text and the Commentary of Samaya-Divakara-Vamana-Muni*. Kumbakonam: By the author, 1936.

Chelliah, J. V., trans. *Pattupattu: Ten Tamil Idylls.* 2d ed. Tinnevelly: SISS, 1962.

Ch'en, Kenneth. *The Chinese Transformation of Buddhism.* Princeton: Princeton University Press, 1973.

Classified Catalogue of Books Registered from 1890-1900 at the Office of the Registrar of Books. Madras: Government of Madras, 1932.

Coedès, George. *The Indianized States of Southeast Asia.* Honolulu: University Press of Hawaii, 1968.

________. "La Légende de la Nāgī." *BEFEO* 11 (1911): 391-93.

Cone, Margaret, and Gombrich, Richard F. *The Perfect Generosity of Prince Vessantara: A Buddhist Epic.* Oxford: Oxford University Press, 1977.

Conze, Edward. *Buddhist Thought in India.* London: George Allen and Unwin, 1962. Reprint. Ann Arbor: University of Michigan Press, 1967.

Coomaraswamy, Ananda K. "Early Indian Architecture: I. Cities and City-Gates, Etc." *Eastern Art: (An Annual)* 2 (1930): 208-23.

________. *Elements of Buddhist Iconography.* Cambridge: Harvard University Press, 1935. Reprint. Delhi: Munshiram Manoharlal Publishers, 1979.

Cowell, E. B., ed. and trans. *The Buddha-Karita or Life of the Buddha by Asvaghosha.* 1894. Reprint. New Delhi: Cosmo Publications, 1977.

________, ed. and trans. *The Jātaka or Stories of the Buddha's Former Births.* 6 vols. London: Luzac and Co. for the Pali Text Society, 1907. Reprint. Delhi: Cosmo Publications, 1978.

Cowell, E. B., and Gough, A. E., trans. *The Sarva-Darśana-Saṃgraha or Review of the Different Systems of Hindu Philosophy by Madhava Āchārya.* Chowkhamba Sanskrit Studies, vol. 10. Varanasi: Chowkhamba Sanskrit Series Office, 1978.

Cutler, Norman. "The Poetry of the Tamil Saints." Ph.D. diss., Department of South Asian Languages and Civilizations, University of Chicago, 1980.

________. "*Tirukkōvaiyār:* The Meeting of Tamil Classicism and Bhakti." Paper presented at the Eleventh Annual Conference on South Asia in Madison, Wisconsin, November 1982.

Dhammaratana Thera, H. "Buddhism in South India." *The Wheel Publication*, vols. 124-25 (1968).

Dhavamony, Mariasusai. *Love of God According to Śaiva Siddhānta.* Oxford: Clarendon Press, 1971.

Diehl, C. G. "The Goddess of Forests in Tamil Literature." *Tamil Culture* 9 (October-December 1964): 308-16.

Dimmitt, Cornelia, and van Buitenen, J. A. B., trans. *Classical Hindu Mythology.* Philadelphia: Temple University Press, 1978.

Dimock, Edward C.; Gerow, Edwin; Naim, C. M.; Ramanujan, A. K.; Roadarmel, Gordon; and van Buitenen, J. A. B. *The Literatures of India: An Introduction.* Chicago: University of Chicago Press, 1974; Phoenix Books, 1978.

Dutt, Binode Behari. *Town Planning in Ancient India.* Calcutta: Thacker, Spink and Co., 1925.

Dutt, Manmatha Nath, ed. *The Ramayana Translated into English Prose from the Original Sanskrit of Valmiki.* 7 vols. in 4. Calcutta: Girish Chandra Chackravati, 1891-94.

________, trans. *A Prose English Translation of the Harivamsha.* Calcutta: Elysium Press, 1897.

Dutt, Sukumar. *Buddhist Monks and Monasteries of India: Their History and Their Contribution to Indian Culture.* London: George Allen and Unwin, 1962.

Egnor, Margaret. "On the Meaning of Śakti to Women in Tamil Nadu." In *The Powers of Tamil Women*, edited by Susan S. Wadley, pp. 1-34. Foreign and Comparative Studies South Asian Series, no. 6. Syracuse: Maxwell School of Citizenship and Public Affairs, 1980.

Ehara, N. R. M.; Soma; and Kheminda, trans. *The Path of Freedom (Vimuttimagga).* Kandy: Buddhist Publication Society, 1977.

Falk, Nancy Auer. "The Case of the Vanishing Nuns: The Fruits of Ambivalence in Ancient Indian Buddhism." In *Unspoken Worlds: Women's Religious Lives in Non-Western Cultures*, edited by Nancy A. Falk and Rita M. Gross, pp. 207-24. San Francisco: Harper and Row, 1980.

Fitzgerald, James. "The *Mokṣa* Anthology of the Great *Bhārata*: An Initial Survey of Structural Issues, Themes, and Rhetorical Strategies." Ph.D. diss., Department of South Asian Languages and Civilizations, University of Chicago, 1980.

Furer-Haimendorf, Christoph von. *The Naked Nagas.* Calcutta: Thacker, Spink and Co., 1962.

Gail, Adalbert J. "Paraśurāma: Brahmin and Warrior." *Indologica Taurinensia* 6 (1978): 151-54.

Geertz, Clifford. "Religion as a Cultural System." In *Anthropological Approaches to the Study of Religion*, edited by Michael Banton, pp. 1-46. London: Tavistock Publications, 1968.

Geiger, Wilhelm, and Bode, Mabel, trans. *The Mahāvaṃśa; or, The Great Chronicle of Ceylon.* London: Henry Frowde for the Pali Text Society, Oxford University Press, 1912.

Glancy, R. F. "Dickens and Christmas: His Framed-tale Themes." *Nineteenth Century Fiction* 35 (1980): 52-72.

Gnanamurthy, T. E. *A Critical Study of Cīvakacintāmaṇi.* Coimbatore: Kalaikathir, 1966.

Goetz, William. "The 'Frame' of *Turn of the Screw:* Framing the Reader In." *Studies in Short Fiction* 18 (1981): 71-74.

Goldman, Robert. "Structure, Substance, and Function in the Great Sanskrit Epics." Paper presented at the Indian Literatures Conference, Chicago, April 1986.

________, trans. *The Rāmāyaṇa of Vālmīki: An Epic of Ancient India.* Vol. 1. Princeton: Princeton University Press, 1984.

Goloubew, Victor. "Les Légendes de la Nāgī et de l'Apsaras." *BEFEO* 24 (1924): 501-10.

Gombrich, Richard F. "Ancient Indian Cosmology." In *Ancient Cosmologies*, edited by Carmen Blacker and Michael Loewe, pp. 110-42. London: George Allen and Unwin, 1975.

———. *Precept and Practice: Traditional Buddhism in the Rural Highlands of Ceylon.* Oxford: Clarendon Press, 1971.

Gowen, Herbert H. *A History of Indian Literature.* New York: Greenwood Press, 1968.

Gunasegaram, S. J. "Manimekalai." *Tamil Culture* 10 (April-June 1963): 42-52.

Haldar, J. R. *Early Buddhist Mythology.* New Delhi: Manohar, 1977.

Hara, Minoru. "Indra and Tapas." *The Adyar Library Bulletin* 39 (1975): 129-60.

Hardy, Friedhelm. *Viraha-Bhakti: The Early History of Kṛṣṇa Devotion in South India.* Delhi: Oxford University Press, 1983.

Hare, E. M., trans. *The Book of the Gradual Sayings (Anguttara-Nikāya).* Vol. 4. London: Luzac and Co. for the Pali Text Society, 1965.

Hart, George L., III. *The Poems of Ancient Tamil: Their Milieu and Their Sanskrit Counterparts.* Berkeley: University of California Press, 1975.

———, trans. *Poets of the Tamil Anthologies.* Princeton: Princeton University Press, 1979.

Hess, Linda. "Staring at Frames Till They Turn into Loops: An Excursion through Some Worlds of Tulsidas." Paper presented at the Indian Literatures Conference, Chicago, April 1986.

Hopkins, Edward Washburn. *The Great Epic of India.* 1901. Reprint. Calcutta: Punthi Pustaka, 1978.

———. "Indra as a God of Fertility." *Journal of the American Oriental Society* 36 (1916): 242-68.

Horner, Isaline Blew. *The Collection of the Middle Length Sayings (Majjhima-Nikāya).* 3 vols. London: Luzac and Co. for the Pali Text Society, 1954-59.

———. *Women under Primitive Buddhism: Laywomen and Almswomen.* London: Routledge and Kegan Paul, 1930. Reprint. Delhi: Motilal Banarsidass, 1975.

———, trans. *The Book of Discipline (Vinaya-Piṭaka).* 6 vols. London: Luzac and Co. for the Pali Text Society, 1949-66.

Humma, John B. "The Narrative Framing Apparatus of Scott's *Old Morality*." *Studies in the Novel* 12 (1980): 301-15.

Hurvitz, Leon. *Scripture of the Lotus Blossom of the Fine Dharma*. New York: Columbia University Press, 1976.

Ilakkuvanār, S. *Tholkāppiyam (in English) with Critical Studies*. Madurai: Kuṛaḷ Neṛi Publishing House, 1963.

Inden, Ronald. "The Ceremony of the Great Gift (*Mahādāna*): Structure and Historical Context in Indian Ritual and Society." In *Asie du Sud: Traditions et Changements*, pp. 131-36. Paris: Colloques Internationeau Du Centre National De La Recherche Scientifique, 1980.

Index des Mots de la Litterature Tamoule Ancienne. 3 vols. Pondichery: Institut Français D'Indologie, 1967.

Indrapala, K. "Buddhism among the Tamils A.D. 1000-1500." In *Proceedings of the Fifth International Conference-Seminar on Tamil Studies*, edited by M. Arunachalam, vol. 2, pp. 12/27-12/39. Madras: International Association of Tamil Studies, 1981.

Jesudasan, C., and Jesudasan, Hephzibah. *A History of Tamil Literature*. Calcutta: Y.M.C.A. Publishing House, 1961.

Johnston, E. H., ed. and trans. *The Buddhacarita or Acts of the Buddha*. Lahore: University of the Punjab, 1935-36. Reprint. New Delhi: Oriental Books Reprint Corp., 1972.

________, ed. and trans. *The Saundarananda of Aśvaghoṣa*. Lahore, 1928-32. Reprint. Delhi: Motilal Banarsidass, 1975.

Kailasapathy, K. *Tamil Heroic Poetry*. Oxford: Oxford University Press, 1968.

Kandaswamy, S. N. *Buddhism as Expounded in Maṇimēkalai*. Annamalainagar: Annamalai University, 1978.

Kârâvêlane, ed. and trans. *Kâreikkâlammeiyâr: Oeuvres Éditées et Traduites*. Pondichery: Institut Français D'Indologie, 1956.

Keith, A. Berriedale. *A History of Sanskrit Literature*. Oxford: Oxford University Press, 1956.

Kern, H. *Manual of Indian Buddhism*. Strassburg, 1898. Reprint. Delhi: Motilal Banarsidass, 1974.

Keyes, Charles F. "Ambiguous Gender: Male Initiation in a Northern Thai Buddhist Society." In *Gender and Religion: On the Complexity of Symbols*, edited by Caroline Bynum, et al., pp. 66-96. Boston: Beacon Press, 1986.

________. "Mother or Mistress but Never a Monk: Buddhist Notions of Female Gender in Rural Thailand." *American Ethnologist* 11, no. 2 (May 1984): 223-41.

Kirfel, Willibald. *Die Kosmographie der Inder nach den Quellen Dargestellt.* Bonn: Kurt Schroeder, 1920.

Kloetzli, Randy. *Buddhist Cosmology (From Single World System to Pure Land: Science and Theology in the Images of Motion and Light).* Delhi: Motilal Banarsidass, 1983.

Krishna Sastri, H. *South Indian Images of Gods and Goddesses.* Delhi: Bhartiya Publishing House, 1974.

Krishnaswami Aiyangar, S. "The Buddhism of Maṇimēkalai. In *Buddhistic Studies*, edited by Bimala Churn Law, pp. 1-25. Calcutta: Thacker, Spink and Co., 1931. Reprint. Delhi: Indological Book House, 1983.

________. *Manimekhalai in Its Historical Setting.* London: Luzac and Co., 1928.

Kuppuswami, S. "Problems of Identity in the Cultural History of Ancient India." *The Journal of Oriental Research, Madras* 1, no. 2 (April 1927): 191-201.

Lal, P., trans. *Great Sanskrit Plays.* New York: New Directions, 1964.

Lamotte, Étienne. "Sur La Formation du Mahāyāna." In *Asiatica: Festschrift Friedrich Weller*, pp. 377-96. Leipzig: Otto Harrassowitz, 1954.

Lang, Karen. "Lord Death's Snare: Gender-Related Imagery in the Theragāthā and the Therīgāthā." *Journal of Feminist Studies in Religion* 1 (Fall 1986): 63-79.

La Vallée Poussin, Louis de. "Cosmogony and Cosmology: Buddhist." In *Encyclopedia of Religions and Ethics*, edited by James Hastings, vol. 4, pp. 129-38. New York: Charles Scribner's Sons, 1912.

________, ed. and trans. *L'Abhidharmakośa de Vasubandhu.* Mélanges Chinois et Bouddhiques, vol. 16, tomes 2, 5. Brussels: Institut Belge des Hautes Études Chinoises, 1971.

Leach, Maria, gen. ed. *Funk and Wagnalls Standard Dictionary of Folklore, Mythology, and Legend.* New York: Funk and Wagnalls, 1972.

Lévi, Sylvain. "Maṇimekhalā, Divinité de la Mer," "On Maṇimekhalā, 'The Guardian of the Sea' (A Cambodian Document)," and "More on Maṇimekhalā." In *Mémorial Sylvain Lévi*, edited by Paul Hartmann, pp. 371-89. Paris: Rue Cujas, 1937.

Lienhard, Siegfried. "Sur La Structure Poétique des Theratherīgāthā." *Journal Asiatique* 263 (1975): 375-96.

Lohmann, Otto. *Die Rahmenerzahlung des Decameron.* Halle: Max Niemeyer Verlag, 1935.

Lorenzen, David N. *The Kāpālikas and Kālāmukhas: Two Lost Śaivite Sects.* Berkeley: University of California Press, 1972.

Ludden, David. "*Maṇimēkalai*" (Partial translation). Philadelphia, 1979. Photocopy.

Lüders, Heinrich. "Die Saga von Ṛṣyaśṛṅga." *Nachrichte Göttingen Akademie.* Philologisch-Historische Klasse, 1897:87-135.

MacDonell, Arthur A. *A History of Sanskrit Literature.* New York: D. Appleton and Co., 1900. Reprint. New York: Haskell House Publishers, 1968.

Madhavaiah, A. *Manimekalai.* Madras: Indian Publishing House, 1923.

Mahadevan, Iravatham. "Corpus of Tamil-Brahmi Inscriptions." In *Seminar on Inscriptions*, pp. 57-73. Madras: State Department of Archaeology, Government of Tamilnadu, 1966.

Majumdar, R. C. *Kambuja-Deśa or an Ancient Colony in Cambodia.* Philadelphia: Institute for the Study of Human Issues, 1980.

Mani, Vettam. *Purāṇic Encyclopedia.* Delhi: Motilal Banarsidass, 1979.

Marglin, Frédérique Apffel. *Wives of the God-King: The Rituals of the Devadasis of Puri.* Delhi: Oxford University Press, 1986.

Matsunaga, Daigan, and Matsunaga, Alicia. *The Buddhist Concept of Hell.* New York: Philosophical Library, 1972.

McGovern, William M. *A Manual of Buddhist Philosophy.* London, 1923. Reprint. Lucknow: Oriental Reprinters, 1976.

Meenakshisundaram, T. P. *A History of Tamil Literature.* Annamalainagar: Annamalai University, 1965.

Minakshi, C. "Buddhism in South India." In *South Indian Studies II*, edited by R. Nagaswamy, pp. 83-131. Madras: Society for Archaeological, Historical, and Epigraphical Research, 1978.

Mus, Paul. *La Lumière sur les Six Voies: Tableau de las Transmigration Bouddhique D'après des Sources Sanskrites, Pāli, Tibétaines, et Chinoises En Majeure Partie Inédites.* Travaux et Memoires de L'Institut D'Ethnologie, vol. 35. Paris: Institut D'Ethnologie, 1939.

Nathan, Leonard. "A New Passage to India." Review of *The Interior Landscape: Love Poems from a Classical Tamil Anthology*, translated by A. K. Ramanujan. *Mahfil: A Quarterly of South Asian Literature* 4 (Spring-Summer 1968): 113-18.

Nilakanta Sastri, K. A. "Buddhism in the Tamil Country." *March of India* 8, no. 12A (November 1956): 51-54.

________. *The Cōḻas.* Madras: University of Madras, 1955.

________. "Mahāyāna Buddhism in South India." *Bulletin of Tibetology* 2 (November 1965): 11-21.

Noble, Sally. "Landscape, Image, and Song in the *Cilappatikāram.*" Master's thesis, Department of South Asian Languages and Civilizations, University of Chicago, 1981.

________. "Narrative Structure in the *Cilappatikāram.*" Paper presented at the Eleventh Annual Conference on South Asia in Madison, Wisconsin, November 1982.

Norman, K. R., trans. *The Elders' Verses I: Theragāthā.* London: Luzac and Co. for the Pali Text Society, 1969.

________, trans. *The Elders' Verses II: Therīgāthās.* London: Luzac and Co. for the Pali Text Society, 1971.

Nyanamoli, trans. *The Path of Purification (Visuddhimagga) by Bhadantācariya Buddhaghoṣa.* Kandy: Buddhist Publication Society, 1979.

Nyanaponika Thera. *Satipaṭṭhāna: The Heart of Buddhist Meditation.* London: Rider and Co., 1962.

Obermiller, E., trans. *History of Buddhism (Chos-ḥbyung) by Bu-ston.* Materialien zur Kunde des Buddhismus, issue 19. Heidelberg: Otto Harrassowitz, 1932.

Obeyesekere, Gananath. *The Cult of the Goddess Pattini.* Chicago: University of Chicago Press, 1984.

O'Flaherty, Wendy Doniger. *Asceticism and Eroticism in the Mythology of Śiva.* London: Oxford University Press, 1973.

________. *The Origins of Evil in Hindu Mythology.* Berkeley: University of California Press, 1976.

________. "Sacred Cows and Profane Mares in Indian Mythology." *History of Religions* 19, no. 1 (August 1979): 1-25.

________, trans. *Hindu Myths.* Harmondsworth: Penguin Books, 1975.

________, trans. *The Rig Veda: An Anthology.* Harmondsworth: Penguin Books, 1981.

Oldenberg, Hermann, and Pischel, Richard, eds. *The Thera- and Therî-Gâthâ: Stanzas Ascribed to Elders of the Buddhist Order of Recluses.* London: Luzac and Co. for the Pali Text Society, 1966.

Panchapakesa Ayyar, A. S. *Manimekalai.* Madras: Alliance Co., 1947.

Paul, Diana Y. *Women in Buddhism: Images of the Feminine in Mahāyāna Tradition.* Berkeley: Asian Humanities Press, 1979.

Periakaruppan, Rm. *Tradition and Talent in Cankam Poetry.* Madurai: Madurai Publishing House, 1976.

Peterson, Indira. "Recurrence and Structure in Sanskrit Literary Epic: A Study of Bhāravi's Kirātārjunīya." Ph.D. diss., Department of Sanskrit and Indian Studies, Harvard University, 1976.

Pope, G. U. *Mani-Mekhalai.* Madras: Meykandan Press, 1911.

Przyluski, Jean. "La princesse à l'odeur de poisson et la Nāgī dans les traditions de l'Asie orientale." In *Etudes Asiatiques*, vol. 2, pp. 265-84. Paris: Publications de l'Ecole Française d'Extrême-Orient, 1925.

Pye, Michael. *Skilful Means: A Concept in Mahayana Buddhism.* London: Gerald Duckworth and Co., 1978.

Raghavan, V. *The Ramayana in Greater India.* Surat: South Gujarat University, 1975.

Rahula, Telvatte. *A Critical Study of the Mahāvastu.* Delhi: Motilal Banarsidass, 1978.

Rajam, V. S. "AṆAṄKU: A Notion Semantically Reduced to Signify Female Sacred Power." *Journal of the American Oriental Society* 106 (1986): 257-72.

Ramachandra Dikshitar, V. R. "Buddhism in Tamil Literature." In *Buddhistic Studies*, edited by Bimala Churn Law, pp. 673-98. Calcutta: Thacker, Spink and Co., 1931. Reprint. Delhi: Indological Book House, 1983.

________, trans. *The Cilappatikaram.* 2d ed. Tinnevelly: SISS, 1978.

Ramanujan, A. K. "Form in Classical Tamil Poetry." In *Symposium on Dravidian Civilization*, edited by Andrée Sjoberg, pp. 73-103. Asian Series of the Center for Asian Studies at the University of Texas at Austin, no. 1. Austin: Jenkins Publishing, 1971.

________. "The Indian Oedipus." In *Oedipus: A Folklore Casebook*, edited by Lowell Edmunds and Alan Dundes, pp. 235-61. New York: Garland Publishing, 1984.

________. "Is There an Indian Way of Thinking?" Paper presented at the first workshop of the American Council of Learned Societies-Social Science Research Council Joint Committee on South Asia sponsored "Person in South Asia" project, Chicago, 16 September 1980 [revised 16 July 1981].

________. "Language and Social Change: The Tamil Example." In *Transition in South Asia: Problems of Modernization*, edited by Robert Crane, pp. 61-84. Program in Comparative Studies on Southern Asia, Monographs and Occasional Paper Series, no. 9. Durham: Duke University, 1970.

________. "On Women Saints." In *The Divine Consort: Rādhā and the Goddesses of India*, edited by John Stratton Hawley and Donna Marie Wulff, pp. 316-24. Berkeley: Berkeley Religious Studies Series, 1982.

________, trans. *The Interior Landscape: Love Poems from a Classical Tamil Anthology.* Bloomington: Indiana University Press, 1967.

________, trans. *Poems of Love and War from the Eight Anthologies and the Ten Long Poems of Classical Tamil.* New York: Columbia University Press, 1985.

Ray, Amita. *Villages, Towns, and Secular Buildings in Ancient India.* Calcutta: Firma K. L. Mukhopadhyay, 1964.

Reynolds, Frank E. "The Two Wheels of Dhamma: A Study of Early Buddhism." In *The Two Wheels of Dhamma: Essays on the Theravada Tradition in India and Ceylon*, edited by Bardwell L. Smith, pp. 6-30. Chambersburg, Penn.: American Academy of Religion, 1972.

Reynolds, Frank E., and Reynolds, Mani B. *Three Worlds According to King Ruang: A Thai Buddhist Cosmology.* Berkeley Buddhist Studies Series, no. 4. Berkeley: Center for South and Southeast Asian Studies, University of California, 1982.

Reynolds, Holly Baker. "The Auspicious Married Woman." In *The Powers of Tamil Women*, edited by Susan S. Wadley, pp. 35-60. Foreign and Comparative Studies South Asian Series, no. 6. Syracuse: Maxwell School of Citizenship and Public Affairs, 1980.

Rhys Davids, Caroline, trans. *Psalms of the Early Buddhists.* Vol. 1 of *Psalms of the Sisters.* London: Luzac and Co. for the Pali Text Society, 1964.

Rhys Davids, T. W., trans. *Dialogues of the Buddha, Part I.* Vol. 2 of *Sacred Books of the Buddhists.* London: Humphrey Milford for Oxford University Press, 1923.

Rhys Davids, T. W., and Stede, William. *The Pali Text Society's Pali-English Dictionary.* London: Pali Text Society, 1979.

Richman, Paula. "Classical Tamil Poetic Convention in *Maṇimēkalai*, a Buddhist Epic." Paper presented at the Eleventh Annual Conference on South Asia in Madison, Wisconsin, November 1982.

________. s.v. "Indian Philosophy as Presented in *Maṇimēkalai*, a Tamil Buddhist Text." In *Encyclopedia of Indian Philosophy.* Forthcoming.

________. "The Portrayal of a Female Renouncer in a Tamil Buddhist Text." In *Gender and Religion: On the Complexity of Symbols*, edited by Caroline Bynum et al., pp. 143-65. Boston: Beacon Press, 1986.

________. "Religious Rhetoric in *Maṇimēkalai*." Ph.D. diss., Department of South Asian Languages and Civilizations, University of Chicago, 1983.

Rogers, Captain T. *Buddhaghosha's Parables Translated from the Burmese.* London: Trubner and Co., 1870.

Roghair, Gene H. *The Epic of Palnāḍu.* Oxford: Oxford University Press, 1982.

Roy, Pratap Chandra, trans. *The Mahabharata of Krishna-Dwaipayana Vyasa.* 12 vols. Calcutta: Oriental Publishing, 1927-32.

Salomon, Richard. "The Structure of a Buddhist Poem: Aśvaghoṣa's *Saundarananda.*" Paper presented at the South Asia Colloquium of the Pacific Northwest, Seattle, December 1981.

Schopen, Gregory. "Mahāyāna in Indian Inscriptions." *Indo-Iranian Journal* 21 (January 1979): 1-19.

Sesha Aiyar, K. G. "The Date of Maṇimēkalai." *The Journal of Oriental Research, Madras* 1, no. 4 (October 1927): 321-29.

Shanmugam Pillai, M., and Ludden, David E., trans. *Kuṟuntokai: An Anthology of Classical Tamil Love Poetry.* Madurai: Koodal Publishers, 1976.

Shastrī, Manmatha Nāth Dutt. *Agni Purāṇam: A Prose English Translation.* 2 vols. Chowkhamba Sanskrit Studies, no. 54. Varanasi: Chowkhamba Sanskrit Series Office, 1967.

Shulman, David Dean. "The Crossing of the Wilderness: Landscape and Myth in the Tamil Story of Rāma." *Acta Orientalia* 42 (1981): 21-54.

________. *The King and the Clown in South Indian Myth and Poetry.* Princeton: Princeton University Press, 1985.

________. *Tamil Temple Myths.* Princeton: Princeton University Press, 1980.

Somasundaram Pillai, J. M. *A History of Tamil Literature with Texts and Translations.* Annamalainagar: By the author, 1968.

Srinivasan, Doris. "The Myth of the Paṇis in the Ṛg Veda." *Journal of the American Oriental Society* 93, no. 1 (January-March 1973): 44-57.

Stein, Burton. *Peasant State and Society in Medieval South India.* Delhi: Oxford University Press, 1980.

Strong, John. "Buddhism and Filial Piety: The Indian Antecedents to a 'Chinese' Problem." In *Traditions in Contact and Change*, edited by Peter Slater and Donald Wiebe, pp. 171-86 and 699-701. Waterloo, Ontario: Wilfrid Laurier University Press, 1983.

________. *The Legend of King Aśoka: A Study and Translation of the Aśokāvadāna.* Princeton: Princeton University Press, 1983.

Subramanian, Nellai K. "Sankhya Philosophy in Manimekalai and Neelakesi." In *Proceedings of the Fifth International Conference-Seminar on Tamil Studies*, edited by M. Arunachalam, vol. 2, pp. 12/2-12/26. Madras: International Association of Tamil Research, 1981.

Subramanian, S. V. "*Palai — An Introduction.*" In *Studies in Tamilology*, pp. 139-49. Madras: International Institute of Tamil Studies, 1982.

Suleiman, Susan R., and Crosman, Inge, eds. *The Reader in the Text: Essays in Audience and Interpretation.* Princeton: Princeton University Press, 1980.

Suryanarayana Sastri, S. S. "Buddhist Logic in the Maṇimēkalai." *Journal of Indian History* 9, no. 3 (December 1930): 330-36.

________. "The Maṇimēkalai Account of the Sāṁkhya." *Journal of Indian History* 8, no. 3 (December 1929): 322-27.

Swaminathaiyer, U. V. *The Story of My Life.* (English translation of his autobiography abridged by K. V. Jagannathan.) Tiruvanmiyur: Mahamahopadhyaya Dr. U. V. Swaminathaiyer Library, 1980.

Tahtinen, Unto. *Ahiṃsā: Non-Violence in Indian Tradition.* London: Rider and Co., 1976.

Takakusu, J., trans. *A Record of the Buddhist Religion as Practised in India and the Malay Archipelago (A.D. 671-695) by I-Tsing.* Oxford: Clarendon Press, 1896.

Tambiah, S. J. *Buddhism and the Spirit Cults in North-east Thailand.* London: Cambridge University Press, 1975.

Tamil Lexicon. 6 vols. Madras: University of Madras, 1936.

Tawney, C. H. *The Kathā Sarīt Sāgara or Oceans of the Streams of Story Translated from the Original Sanskrit.* 2 vols. 1880. Reprint. Delhi: Munshiram Manoharlal, 1968.

Thani Nayagam, Xavier S. "Earliest Jain and Buddhist Teaching." *Tamil Culture* 8 (October-December 1959): 337-49.

Thiessen, Jakob H. *Die Legende von Kisâgotamî: Eine Literarhistorische Untersuchung.* Breslau: Verlag von Wilhelm Kobner, 1880.

Thittila, Pathamakyan Ashin, trans. *The Book of Analysis (Vibhaṅga).* London: Pali Text Society, 1969.

Thrall, William Flint; Hibbard, Addison; and Holman, C. Hugh. *A Handbook to Literature.* New York: Odyssey Press, 1960.

Tompkins, Jane P. *Reader-Response Criticism: From Formalism to Post-Structuralism.* Baltimore: Johns Hopkins University Press, 1980.

Vaiyapuri Pillai, S. *History of Tamil Language and Literature.* Madras: New Century Book House, 1956.

van Buitenen, J. A. B., trans. *The Mahābhārata.* 3 vols. Chicago: University of Chicago Press, 1973-78.

________, trans. *Tales of Ancient India.* New York: Bantam Books, 1961.

van Zeyst, H. G. A. "*Arūpa-Loka.*" In *Encyclopedia of Buddhism*, edited by G. P. Malasekera. Colombo: Government of Ceylon, 1966.

Varadarajan, M. *The Treatment of Nature in Sangam Literature.* Tinnevelly: SISS, 1969.

Vasudeva Rao, T. N. *Buddhism in the Tamil Country.* Annamalainagar: Annamalai University, 1979.

Velu Pillai, A. *Epigraphical Evidences for Tamil Studies.* Madras: International Institute of Tamil Studies, 1980.

Vijayalakshmy, R. *A Study of Cīvakacintāmaṇi: Particularly from the Point of View of Interaction of Sanskrit Language and Literature with Tamil.* L. D. Series, no. 82. Ahmedabad: L. D. Institute of Indology, 1981.

Vijayavenugopal, G. "Some Buddhist Poems in Tamil." *Journal of the International Association of Buddhist Studies* 2 (1979): 93-97.

Vinson, Julien. *Légendes Bouddhistes et Djainas: Traduites du Tamoul.* Conteurs et Poetes du Tous Pays, tomes 5-6. Paris: G. P. Maisonneuve and Larose, 1900.

Wadley, Susan S. "Choosing a Path: Performative Strategies in the North Indian Epic Dhola." In *Oral Epics in India*, edited by Stuart Blackburn and Susan S. Wadley. Forthcoming.

________. "The Paradoxical Powers of Tamil Women." In *The Powers of Tamil Women*, edited by Susan S. Wadley, pp. 153-67. Foreign and Comparative Studies South Asian Series, no. 6. Syracuse: Maxwell School of Citizenship and Public Affairs, 1980.

Warder, A. K. *Indian Kāvya Literature.* 2 vols. Delhi: Motilal Banarsidass, 1974.

Wheatley, Paul. *The Pivot of the Four Quarters.* Chicago: Aldine Publishing, 1971.

Wilson, Horace Hayman, trans. *The Vishṇu Purāṇa: A System of Hindu Mythology and Tradition.* London: Trubner and Co., 1868.

Winstedt, Richard. *The Malays: A Cultural History.* London: Routledge and Kegan Paul, 1950.

Winternitz, M. *A History of Indian Literature.* 2 vols. New York: Russell and Russell, 1933.

Yocum, Glenn E. "Buddhism through Hindu Eyes: Śaivas and Buddhists in Medieval Tamilnadu." In *Traditions in Contact and Change*, edited by Peter Slater and Donald Wiebe, pp. 143-62 and 690-93. Waterloo, Ontario: Wilfrid Laurier University Press, 1983.

Zimmer, Heinrich. *Myths and Symbols in Indian Art and Civilization.* Princeton: Princeton University Press, 1974.

Zvelebil, Kamil V. *The Smile of Murugan: On Tamil Literature of South India.* Leiden: E. J. Brill, 1973.

________. *Tamil Literature.* Vol. 2, fasc. 1 of *Handbuch Der Orientalistik.* Edited by Jan Gonda. Leiden: E. J. Brill, 1975.

________. *Tamil Literature.* Vol. 10, fasc. 1 of *A History of Indian Literature.* Edited by Jan Gonda. Weisbaden: Otto Harrassowitz, 1974.

Index

A

Abhiśeka, 139
Agastya, 134
Ahalyā, 137
Ahiṃsā, 4, 39, 48, 143, 154, 194 n.12
  Nākas, 42-43, 46, 51
Aimperuṅkāppiyam, 10, 235 n.13
Ājīvika philosophy, 187 n.7
Akam poetry, 26, 69, 70, 71, 77, 152, 160, 203 n.29
  "The Story of the Cosmic Place," 58, 62
Akanāṉūṟu, 70
Alexander, P. C. (cited), 162
Āḻi, 95, 214 n.34
Āḻvār poetry, 208 n.57
Ambapālī, 148, 149, 155, 231 n.9
Aṇaṅku, 200 n.12
Aṅguttara Nikāya, 80, 167
Anicca, 4, 58, 71, 97, 100. *See also* Impermanence of life
Āṇṭalai, 199 n.7
  table, 66
Antuvaṅkīraṉai Kāviṭṭaṉār, 60
Apañcikaṉ, 133
Aparagodānīya, 87
Āputtiraṉ, 126, 130-42, 147, 177 n.2, 183 n.24, 183 n.25, 224 n.15, 225 n.23, 226 n.26, 229 n.48. *See also* "The Story of Āputtiraṉ's Begging Bowl"
  begging bowl, 123
  Maṇimēkalai and, 185 n.44
  meaning of name, 223 n.6
  play about, 182 n.22
Arabian Nights, 50, 51
Aṟam, 49, 62, 109, 125, 131, 159, 200 n.10, 202 n.23, 236 n.21
Aṟavaṇa Aṭikaḷ, 2, 21-25, 164, 185 n.44, 188 n.8
Architecture, 98-99
Arjuna, 13, 31, 32, 227 n.40
Artha, 159
Arūpa dhātu, 88-89, 175-76, 212 n.20, 213 n.26, 242 n.1
  ill., 85
  table, 86
Āryaśūra, 154
Ascetics, 113, 140, 189 n.16, 225 n.19
  false, 108
  female, 38, 119
  male, 26
  narrators, 219 n.26
Aśoka, King, 121, 141, 150-51, 193 n.9, 228 n.47, 231 n.11
Aśokāvadāna, 150, 151, 153, 155, 166
Asuras, 87, 175, 212 n.15
  table, 86
Aśvaghoṣa, 151-54, 232 n.16
Ātirai, 21, 39, 159, 187 n.5
Aṭiyārkkunallār, 157, 160

B

Balusamy, N. (cited), 38, 162
Basham, A. L. (cited), 123-24, 142
Begging bowl, 125-26, 145, 224 n.12. *See also* "The Story of Āputtiraṉ's Begging Bowl"
  Āputtiraṉ's, 123-30
  Maṇimēkalai's, 21, 24, 33, 35, 39, 147
Bhagavad Gītā, 200 n.14
Bhājana-loka, 84, 87, 88
Bhakti, 137, 162
Bharatidasan, 12
Bhārgavas, 216 n.2
Bhikkhuṇī, 24, 80, 165, 241 n.52. *See also Bhikṣuṇī*
Bhikkhuṇī-saṅgha, 24, 25
Bhikṣuṇī, 24. *See also Bhikkhuṇī*
Bhūmis, 212 n.17
Bhūridatta Jātaka, 47
Bhūta, 107
Bodhisattvas, 162-64
Brahmā, 134, 225 n.18
Brahmanism, 4, 183 n.24

Brahmas, 82, 88, 89, 94, 95, 175, 212 n.20
table, 83
Brahmins, 133-36, 141, 143, 147, 223 n.5, 225 n.24, 226 n.26
Branch stories, 2-4, 37-39, 46, 50, 102, 115-16, 121, 144, 154, 193 n.3
aṟam in, 159
Indian story-telling and, 229 n.1
table, 3
Bṛhatkathā, 144
Bṛhatkathāślokasaṃgraha, 194 n.15
Buddha, 73, 154, 187 n.3, 190 n.22, 192 n.32, 211 n.11
begging bowl and, 21
enlightenment, 84, 87
Mahayana, 39, 162-65
"The Mustard Seed Story," 80
Buddhacarita (Aśvaghoṣa), 154
Buddhaghosa, 73, 76, 77, 80
Buddhism, 4, 34, 38-39, 46, 58, 78, 143, 147-55, 159, 180 n.7. *See also* Cosmology
Chinese, 34
Cutamati's conversion, 124
Hinayana, 162-66, 240 n.44
Indra, 228 n.46
logic, 161, 241 n.54
Mahayana, 161-66, 196 n.25
Maṇimēkalai and, 5, 9-10, 15, 21-26, 161-66, 186 n.47
monastic procedures, 23-26, 73, 88-89
nuns, 23-25, 119, 147, 149, 188 n.10
religious instruction, 5, 22, 94, 96, 178 n.6
renunciation, 101
Tamilnadu and, 7, 10, 14, 161, 238 n.37
Theravadin, 192 n.33
wheel, 91
women in, 147-48
Buddhism as Expounded in Maṇimēkalai (Kandaswamy), 15
Buddhist literature, 5, 10

C

Cakka, 91. *See also Cakra*
Cakkaravāḷakkōṭṭam, 53, 94, 97
Cakkaravāḷam, 90, 94-95. *See also Cakkavāḷa, Cakravāla*
Cakkaravāḷa mountains, 214 n.34
Cakkavāḷa, 90. *See also Cakkaravāḷam, Cakravāla*
Cakkavatti, 91. *See also Cakravarti*
Cakra, 91, 214 n.34. *See also Cakka*
Cakravāla, 84, 90-91, 94-96, 99, 175-76, 210 n.10, 214 n.34. *See also Cakkaravāḷam, Cakkavāḷa*
Cakravarti, 91. *See also Cakkavatti*
Cāli, 130, 133, 134
Camaya Tivākara Vāmaṉa Muṉivar, 10
Cambodian literature, 13, 48
Cāminātaiyar, U. Vē., 7, 11-12, 181 n.17, 184 n.33
Campāpati, 92-93, 146, 151
Caṅkam literature, 26-27, 58, 160, 162, 236 n.24, 214 n.33
poetry, 58, 62-68, 70-71, 76-78, 113, 120, 145, 205 n.41, 206 n.47
Cannibalism, 43, 46, 69
Cantiratattaṉ, 183 n.25
Cārṅkalaṉ, 67, 76, 92, 98
Cāttaṉār, Cīttalai, 5, 8, 14, 157-58, 161, 178 n.5, 184 n.36, 233 n.2, 234 n.6
Cātuvaṉ, 42-52, 154, 159, 183 n.25
table, 45
"Cātuvaṉ and the Nākas," 37, 43-52, 146, 177 n.2
table, 3, 45
translation, 39-42
Cāvaka, 132, 140, 142, 229 n.48
Cayaṅkōṇṭar, 67
Celibacy, 25-26, 35
Ceṉpakam, Mā. (cited), 38
Ceylon, 184 n.33
China, 34
Cilampu, 10
Cilappatikāram, 8-10, 12-14, 121, 159-60, 178 n.7, 204 n.37, 214 n.34, 236 n.19
Cāttaṉār, 157
courtesans, 47
dating of, 160-61, 233 n.5, 238 n.35, 238 n.35
Indra Festival, 110
kingship in, 114-15, 220 n.31
landscape imagery, 206 n.50
Maṇimēkalai, 32-33, 183 n.27, 191 n.28, 236 n.20
praise of a king, 220 n.27
pūtam, 108
religion in, 9, 184 n.34
Ciruṅki, 134. *See also* Ṛśyaśṛnga
Cittirāpati, 22, 117-18, 121, 137, 148, 221 n.35
Civanānacittiyār, 123
Civappirakācar, 7, 16, 143, 178 n.1

Cōla kings, 102
Comparison stories, 124-25, 142
Confucianism, 34
Coomaraswamy, Ananda K. (cited), 98-99
"The Cosmic Place," 187 n.2. *See also* "The Story of the Cosmic Place"
Cosmology, 4, 79-100, 144, 149-51, 175-76, 210 n.10, 213 n.22
  ill., 85
  tables, 83, 86
Courtesans, 20, 46-47, 63, 117-18, 147-49, 194 n.15, 221 n.35
Cows, 131-32, 134, 141, 225 n.22, 225 n.24
  imagery, 33, 192 n.29
Cremation grounds, 53, 59-62, 65-78, 143, 152, 198 n.1, 198 n.3, 207 n.52, 236 n.21
  architecture, 98-99
  ascetics, 113
  cosmos and, 96-100
  meditation in, 73, 76-77, 207 n.53
  table, 74-75
Cross-cousins, 104-5, 216 n.8
Cutamati, 20, 28, 94, 97, 124-25, 177 n.2, 187 n.2, 190 n.23
Cuvāmināta Tēcikar, 10

D
Dāna, 4, 21, 111-12, 141, 154, 219 n.24. *See also Tānam*
Daṇḍa, 136-37, 227 n.33
Darśanas, 9, 23, 165
Death, 59-60, 64, 67, 68, 71, 73, 80-81, 99, 150. *See also* Impermanence of life
Decay: of human body, 93, 190 n.23
Desert landscape, 62-78, 143-44. *See also Pālai*
  tables, 66, 72
Deva, 212 n.20. *See also Teyvam*
Dhamma, 200 n.10, 202 n.23
Dhammapada, 80, 172
Dhammapāla, 80
Dharma, 117-18, 136, 159, 200 n.10
Dharma seat, 20, 21, 145, 187 n.3
Dhātu, 88, 212 n.14, 212 n.17
Dhyānas, 88, 89, 212 n.19
Dickens, Charles, 51
Dignāga, 15, 161
Discus, 114
Dramatized audience, 46-52, 143
Durgā, 204 n.34

E
Egnor, Margaret (cited), 120
Eight Chief Rules, 25, 189 n.15
Elephants: imagery, 28, 190 n.22
Eṭṭi award, 111
Etukai, 9

F
Female enclosure, 30, 190-91 n.24
Female renouncers, 4, 112-19, 145-46. *See also* Renouncers
Female renunciation, 2, 19-35, 58, 143
"The Four Daughters," 190-91 n.24
Framed stories, 50-52, 197 n.27, 197 n.28, 197 n.29
Funan, 48
Funeral ceremonies, 62, 199 n.5, 200 n.9. *See also* Cremation grounds

G
Gandharva marriage, 216 n.8
Gates, 98-99, 215 n.44
  table, 74
Gatis, 87, 88, 150-51, 176, 212 n.14, 212 n.15, 232 n.13
Gautama (husband of Ahalyā), 137
Ghouls, 60, 61, 67, 69-70, 76, 204 n.36
Giving, 111-12, 141, 154, 219 n.24. *See also Dāna*
Glancy, R. F. (cited), 51
Glass pavilion, 20, 30, 190 n. 24
Gods, 87, 88
  tables, 83, 86
Goetz, William (cited), 52
Gotamī, 79-82, 209 n.7. *See also* Kōtamai, Kisāgotamī

H
Haihaya kings, 216 n.2
Harivaṃśa, 139
Heavens, 84, 88-89, 90, 176, 213 n.26, 242 n.1
  table, 86
Hells, 88, 176, 212 n.16, 242 n.1
  table, 86
Hiṃsā, 46
Hinayana Buddhism, 162-66, 240 n.44
Hinduism, 10, 84, 90, 110, 112, 125, 178 n.6, 187 n.7, 194 n.12, 199 n.4
  brahmanical, 123, 133, 137, 229 n.48
  festivals, 119, 120
  kingship, 121

Hindu literature, 5
Hoerauf, Eugene, 175-76
Horner, Isaline Blew (cited), 147-48
Humma, John B. (cited), 51

I

Ilakkaṇakottu, 10
Iḷaṅkō, Prince, 8, 157, 159, 214 n.34
Impermanence of life, 53-78, 80, 81, 92, 97, 99, 111, 143, 148-49, 231 n.9. *See also* Death
Indian texts, 16
Indra, 132, 135-42, 146-47, 199 n.4, 225 n.19, 227 n.37. *See also* Intiraṉ
  Buddhist texts, 228 n.46
  Hinduism, 90, 229 n.48
Indra Festival, 110, 139, 182 n.22, 188 n.8, 218 n.20
Intiraṉ, 135. *See also* Indra
Intirapōkam, 137

J

Jainism, 124-25, 194 n.12, 223 n.3
Jambu, 216 n.3
Jambudvīpa, 87, 88, 176, 216 n.3
Janamejaya, 47
Jātakamālā (Āryaśūra), 154
Jātaka stories, 13, 228 n.46
Jāti, 117-18, 121, 145, 148
Jāti-dharma, 117-18
Jewelry, 10, 33, 109, 180 n.10
Jhānas, 212 n.19

K

Kakantaṉ, King, 102, 111, 116, 221 n.37
Kālī, 65, 67, 68, 203 n.33, 204 n.34, 204 n.36
Kālidāsa, 190 n.22
Kaliṅkattupparaṇi (Cayaṅkōṇṭar), 67, 204 n.36
Kaḷḷi, 60, 64, 67
  tables, 66, 75
Kāma (god of love), 33
Kāma (lust), 159. *See also Kāmam*
Kāma dhātu, 88-89, 90, 175-76, 212 n.20, 242 n.1
  ill., 85
  table, 86
Kāmam, 109, 159. *See also Kāma*
Kamparāmāyaṇam, 137, 235 n.13. *See also Rāmāyaṇa*
Kāñci (city), 13, 22, 23, 185 n.44, 188 n.8. *See also* Kāñcīpuram
Kāñci (poetry), 58-62, 71, 77
Kāñcīpuram, 188 n.8, 238 n.37
Kāṇḍam, 236 n.18
Kandaswamy, S. N. (cited), 15, 16, 158, 160, 162, 163-64, 186 n.47
Kaṇṇaki, 8, 13-14, 114-15, 120, 185 n.44
Kanya Kumari, 133
Kāpālikas, 199 n.8
Kāppiyam, 7-8, 10, 158-60, 178 n.7, 235 n.13, 235 n.14
Kāppu, 235 n.14
Karma, 4, 87, 117, 144, 154
  "The Mustard Seed Story," 92-94, 96, 146-47, 151, 209 n.7
Karuṇā, 21
Karupporuḷ, 27, 62, 202 n.25, 203 n.33
  table, 29
Kātai, 236 n. 18
Kataiyaṅkaṇṇaṉār, 59-60
Kathā literature, 144-45, 230 n.2
Kathāsarītsāgara, 144
Kāṭu, 65, 68
Kauṇḍinya, 48
Kāval, 115
Kāviripaṭṭiṉam, 13, 188 n.8, 238 n.37
Kāvya, 5, 7, 151, 152, 158, 178 n.7, 235 n.14
Kāyacaṇṭikai, 22, 102
Kiḷaikkatai, 2
Kingship, 114-17, 120-21, 146, 154, 220 n.29
  royal duties, 112-17
Kirātārjuniya, 235 n.15
Kirfel, Willibald (cited), 84
Kisāgotamī, 210 n.7. *See also* Gotamī, Kōtamai
Kōmuki Pond, 141
Koṟṟavai, 204 n.34
Kōtamai, 79-82, 92-94, 96, 147, 151. *See also* Gotamī, Kisāgotamī, "The Mustard Seed Story"
Kōvalaṉ, 8, 12-13, 19-20, 32, 47, 114-15
Krishnaswami Aiyangar, S. (cited), 160, 162, 184 n.38
Kṛṣṇa, 139
Kṣatriyas, 136, 227 n.33
Kubera, 199 n.4
Kumārasaṃbhava, 235 n.15
Kuṇṭalakēci, 10, 180 n.8
Kuṇṭalam, 10

Kuriñci, 27, 28, 63, 71, 206 n.50
tables, 29, 72
Kuruntokai, 70
Kuṭai nilai, 220 n.29

L

Lakṣmī, 118
Lamotte, Étienne (cited), 164
Landscape imagery, 27-30, 136, 143, 154, 191 n.25, 203 n.29, 203 n.33, 206 n.50
desert, 62-78
native elements, 62-68, 152
tables, 29, 66, 72
Laypeople, 24, 101-21, 144, 218 n.20
women, 4, 35, 192 n.33
Lévi, Sylvain (cited), 13, 15
Lokadhātu, 91
Lokapālas, 199 n.4
Ludden, David (cited), 185 n.38
Lust, 102-7, 108, 116-17, 119

M

Mahābhārata, 31, 37-38, 47, 137-38, 177 n.4, 193 n.3, 219 n.26
Mahājanaka-Jātaka, 13
Mahākāvya, 158-60, 235 n.15
Mahāvaṃśa, 187 n.3
Mahāvratas, 199 n.8
Mahayana Buddhism, 161-66, 196 n.25
Mānasavega, 198 n.2
Maṇi, 10, 183 n.27
Māṇikkavācakar, 10
Maṇimēkalā, 20, 53, 97, 146, 183 n.27. *See also* Maṇimekhalā
Maṇimēkalai: begging bowl, 21, 24, 33, 35, 39, 147
Buddhism, 21-26
female roles, 35
miraculous powers, 21, 24, 147
spiritual journey, 2, 20
tonsure, 32-33, 191 n.28, 236 n.20
Maṇimēkalai: audience, 9-10
authorship, 8, 157-58, 234 n.6
Buddhism, 5, 9-10, 15, 21-26, 161-66, 186 n.47
dating of, 160-61, 238 n.35, 238 n.36
editions, 12, 181 n.17, 182 n.18-20, 184 n.33
rediscovery, 11-12
religious unity, 5
table, 3
translations, 6, 14, 184 n.38
"Maṇimēkalai Is Put under Protection": translation, 102-7
Maṇimēkalāteyvam, 183 n.27
Maṇimekhalā, 12-15, 183 n.27. *See also* Maṇimēkalā
Maṇipallavam Island, 20, 21, 24, 39, 132, 141, 185 n.44, 191 n.25
Manoratha Pūranī, 80, 167
Manunītikaṇṭacōlan, 217 n.15
Māra, 90
Mārkaṇḍeya, 220 n.26
Marutam, 27, 63, 136
tables, 29, 72
Marutan̲ Iḷanākan̲ār, 67
Marutavēkan̲, 97, 198 n.2
Maruti, 101, 102, 107-11, 112, 119, 120, 177 n.2, 220 n.26, 221 n.37
Mātavi, 8, 19, 32, 118, 214 n.34
Māṭrceṭa, 154
Maturai, 8, 14, 111, 114, 132, 139, 224 n.15
Māvaṇ Kiḷḷi, 101-2, 112-16, 118
Mayan̲, 95, 96
Mayilainātar, 10
Meditation, 73, 76-77, 84, 88-89, 90
Mēkalai, 10. *See also Mekhalā*
Mekhalā, 10, 183 n.27. *See also* *Mēkalai*
Merchants, 12, 37, 111-12, 183 n.25
Mīnākṣi, 139
Mīn̲āṭci Cuntaram Piḷḷai, 11
Mokṣa, 159
Monastic procedures, 23-26, 73, 88-89
Mount Govardhana, 139
Mount Meru, 87, 88, 90, 91, 95, 175
Mullai, 27, 63, 202 n.27, 206 n.50
tables, 29, 72
Murukan̲, 27, 28
"The Mustard Seed Story," 79-82, 92, 94, 100, 154, 210 n.7
translations, 167-74
Mutaliyār, Rāmacūvami, 11

N

Nāgārjuna, 196 n.25
Nāgas, 47-50, 195 n.20, 196 n.25. *See also* Nākas
Naishadhacarita, 235 n.15
Nākas, 43-52, 154, 159. *See also* "Cātuvan̲ and the Nākas," Nāgas
table, 45
Nanda, 151-52
Nandabalā, 192 n.32
Nan̲n̲ūl, 10

Nārada, 137
Nāṭu, 68
Naṭuvunilattiṇai, 71
Nāvalam, 216 n.3
Neṭuñceliyaṉ, King, 114-15
Neytal, 27, 63, 191 n.25
  tables, 29, 72
Nidānas, 9, 23, 162, 166, 186 n.47
Nīlakēci, 10, 11, 123-24, 180 n.7, 180 n.8
Nirvāṇa, 213 n.22, 213 n.26
Nuns, 23-25, 119, 147, 149, 188 n.10
Nyāyapraveśa, 161, 186 n.47

O

Obeyesekere, Gananath (cited), 14, 158, 184 n.34, 184 n.36
Old Morality (Scott), 51
Ōtalāntaiyār, 63-64

P

Pālai, 27, 62-78, 152, 203 n.29, 204 n.34, 204 n.36, 206 n.48, 206 n.50, 208 n.57
  plants, 67
  tables, 29, 66, 72
Paḷikkaṟai maṇṭapam, 190 n.24
Paḷikku, 190 n.24. *See also Palingu*
Palingu, 190 n.24. *See also Paḷikku*
Pañca śīla, 217 n.14
Pāṇḍavas, 31
Paṇis, 136
Pāṇṭiyaṉ kings, 114
Paracurāmaṉ, 216 n.2
Pāramitās, 162-63
Paramopāsakas, 165
Paraṇi, 204 n.36, 206 n.48
Paraśurāma, 13, 116, 216 n.2
Parimēlaḷakar, 113, 218 n.21
Pārvatī, 191 n.24
Paṭācārā, 210 n.7
Pāṭāṇ, 113. *See also* Praising
Pattiṉi, 13-14, 234 n.9
Pavāraṇā, 25. *See also Pravāraṇā*
Periya Purāṇam, 235 n.13
Peruṅkāppiyam, 158-59, 235 n.13, 236 n.18
Peta, 87
Pēy, 200 n.12
Pēy makaḷir, 67
Pikkuṇi, 241 n.52. *See also Bhikkhuṇī, Bhikṣuṇī*
Pīlivaḷai, 182 n.22
Pimpicārakatai, 10
Piramam, 89, 95. *See also Brahmas*
Pivot of the Four Quarters (Wheatley), 98
Pope, G. U. (cited), 15, 16, 184 n.38, 185 n.44
Poruḷ, 62, 109, 159
Poṣadha, 25. *See also Uposatha*
Praising, 113-15, 220 n.27
Pravāraṇā, 25. *See also Pavāraṇā*
Preta, 87
Pukār, 20, 21, 25, 31, 110, 188 n.8
Puṇṇiyarācaṉ, King, 126, 140, 164
Puṟam poetry, 26, 58, 62, 77, 113,160, 203 n.29
Puṟanāṉūṟu, 60
Purāṇas, 120, 136, 138
Purattiraṭṭu, 180 n.8
Puruṣārtha, 8, 159
Pūrvavideha, 87
Pūtam, 107-8, 111, 216 n.7
Pye, Michael (cited), 39

R

Raghuvaṃśa, 235 n.15
Rama I, King, 13
Ramanujan, A. K. (cited), 16, 26, 47, 51, 62, 70, 144, 191 n.24
Rāmaparusa, 13
Rāmāyaṇa, 13, 138. *See also Kamparāmāyaṇam*
Rebirth, 23, 34, 42, 84-90, 93, 97, 154, 212 n.19, 213 n.22
  Āputtiraṉ's, 142
  table, 86
Recitation, 8, 9, 179 n.5, 179 n.6
Religious tradition, 5, 123-25
Renouncers, 101-21, 144
  female, 4, 31, 112-19, 145-46
Reynolds, Frank (cited), 84, 96, 121
Reynolds, Holly Baker (cited), 120
Rhetorical strategies, 4, 34, 48-50, 112, 115, 116, 125, 144, 145, 147-55, 196 n.26, 206 n.47, 218 n.22
  "The Mustard Seed Story," 92
  "The Story of the Cosmic Place," 60, 96-99
Roghair, Gene H. (cited), 229 n.1
Ṛśyaśṛnga, 120, 134, 221 n.38, 224 n.9. *See also* Ciruṅki
Rūpa dhātu, 88-89, 175-76, 212 n.20, 242 n.1
  ill., 85
  table, 86

S
Sacrifices, 131, 139-40, 225 n.19
Saints, 47
Śaivite, 10-11
Sakka, 228 n.46. *See also* Śakra
Śakra, 228 n.46. *See also* Sakka
Śakti, 120
Śakuntalā (Kālidāsa), 190 n.22
Śākyabhikṣus, 165
Salomon, Richard (cited), 153
Saṃkha-Jātaka, 13
Saṃsāra, 42, 91, 97
Saṅgha, 24, 112, 188 n.10
Sānkhya philosophy, 187 n.7
Sānudāsa, 194 n.15
Sarasvatī, 132, 224 n.13, 224 n.16, 225 n.18, 226 n.26
Sarvadarśanasaṁgraha, 123
Satipaṭṭhānasutta, 73
Saundarananda, 151-55
Sāvitrī, 220 n.26
Sceptre, 114-15, 220 n.29
Scheherazade, 50
Schopen, Gregory (cited), 165
Sexuality, 31, 120, 148, 149, 155
Sexual love, 53, 71, 77, 120, 143, 205 n.41
Shulman, David Dean (cited), 178 n.7, 204 n.36, 229 n.48
Sinhalese texts, 14
Śiśupālavadha, 235 n.15
Śiva, 10, 110
Skilful Means (Pye), 39
Spear, 114
Śravaka, 164
Sri Lanka, 11, 12, 13-14, 184 n.33, 234 n.9
"The Story of Āputtiraṉ's Begging Bowl," 130-42. *See also* Āputtiraṉ
  translation, 126-30
"The Story of the Cosmic Place," 53-100, 146, 152, 207 n.56, 236 n.21
  translation, 54-58
"The Story of the Place of the Cakkaravāḷam," 92
Story-telling, 5, 112, 115-16, 153, 165-66, 219 n.26, 229 n.1
Strong, John (cited), 100, 150, 153-54, 166
Suffering, 150-51
Sujāta, 35
Sumatra, 12
Sundarī, 152
Śūnyatā, 165
Sūrdās, 177 n.5
Suryanarayana Sastri, S. S. (cited), 160, 161

T
Talai-pali, 204 n.37
Tāli, 95, 99
Tamil literary conventions, 2, 26, 34, 53-78, 152, 153, 155, 198 n.1, 208 n.57. *See also* Landscape imagery
  love, 27-30
  table, 29
Tamil literature, 5, 6, 10, 11, 14-15, 26, 181 n.13, 218 n.21
  poetry, 26-32, 58-68, 146, 152-55, 160, 190 n.20
Tamilnadu (South India), 7, 10, 11, 12, 14, 98, 120, 132, 161, 184 n.33
  Buddhism in, 101, 161, 238 n.37
Tānam, 111. *See also Dāna*
Taṉicceyyuḷ, 160
Taṇṭiyalaṅkāram, 158
Tarumatattaṉ, 111-12, 120, 219 n.25
Tāvatiṃsa, 90. *See also* Trayastriṃśa
Teyvam, 212 n.20. *See also Deva*
Theragāthā, 148
Theravadin Buddhism, 192 n.33
Therīgāthā, 80, 148, 170
Tiṇai: table, 29. *See also* Landscape imagery
Tirukkuṟaḷ (Tiruvaḷḷuvar), 109-11, 113, 137, 194 n.11, 218 n.21, 218 n.23
Tiruvaḷḷuvamālai, 218 n.21
Tiruvaḷḷuvar, 110, 111, 119, 137, 158, 194 n.11, 218 n.23
Tiruvāvaṭuturai, 11
Tiruvilaiyāṭal Purāṇam, 139
Tolkāppiyam, 113
Tolkāppiyar, 71
Toṭarnilaicceyyuḷ, 160
Transience of life. *See* Impermanence of life
Trayastriṃśa, 90. *See also* Tāvatiṃsa
Turaicāmi Piḷḷai, Auvai Cu. (cited), 38
The Turn of the Screw (James), 52

U
Ukkirapāṇṭiyaṉ, King, 139
Uliñcil, 65, 67-68, 204 n.33, 205 n.40
  tables, 66, 75
Uḷḷurai, 190 n.22
Umbrella (royal), 114, 220 n.29

Upanāyana ceremony, 131, 223 n.5
Upasampadā, 24
Upāya, 39, 96, 150, 193 n.9
Uposatha, 25. *See also Poṣadha*
Uri: table, 29. *See also* Landscape imagery
Ur-text, 4, 177 n.4
Urvaśī, 134
Utayakumaraṉ, Prince, 1-2, 19-22, 28, 30, 113, 118, 121, 148, 190 n.23, 231 n.9, 236 n.23
  death of, 22, 102, 112, 116-17, 154
Uttarakuru, 87
Uvavaṉam Garden, 20, 28, 30, 31

V

Vaiśampāyana, 31
Vaiśeṣika philosophy, 187 n.7
Vaiyāpuri Piḷḷai, S. (cited), 160
Vakai (type), 84
  table, 83
Vākai (plant), 67, 205 n.40
  tables, 66, 75
Vāla, 213 n.28
Vaḷaiyam, 10
Vaḷaiyāpati, 10
Vañci, 14, 22, 23, 123, 125, 165, 185 n.44
Varatarāja Ayyar, E. S. (cited), 160
Varjun, 13
Varṣa, 25. *See also Vassa*
Varuṇa, 139, 199 n.4
Vasiṣṭha, 134
Vassa, 25. *See also Varṣa*
Vedas, 93, 133-35. *See also Vētam*
Vēṅkai, 27
Vessantara, 141, 228 n.47
Vētam, 133. *See also* Vedas
Vibhāṇḍaka, 134
Vicākai, 101, 102, 111-12, 119, 120, 154, 177 n.2, 219 n.25, 221 n.37
Vidya, 97
Vidyādhara, 198 n.2
Vinaya, 23, 25, 189 n.15
Viñcaiyaṉ, 97, 144, 198 n.2
Vinson, Julien, 11
  cited, 184 n.38
Vīracōḻiyam, 11
Virāṭa, 31
Visākhā, 35
Viṣṇu Purāṇa, 139
Visuddhimagga (Buddhaghosa), 73, 76
Vīṭu, 159
Vulture, 65, 67, 68, 203 n.33

W

Wadley, Susan S. (cited), 120
Wheatley, Paul (cited), 98, 99
Winternitz, M. (cited), 148, 230 n.7
Women, 147-48
  chaste, 109, 111, 117-21, 146, 216 n.6, 219 n.25, 220 n.26
  ghouls, 60, 61, 67, 69
  laywomen, 4, 24, 35, 192 n.33
  married, 109
  unmarried, 214 n.33
  wifely duties, 110, 111, 218 n.20

Y

Yama, 59, 62, 77, 199 n.4
Yudhiṣṭhira, King, 31, 137, 220 n.26

Z

Zvelebil, Kamil (cited), 160, 161

NOTE ON THE AUTHOR

PAULA RICHMAN, assistant professor of religion at Oberlin College, received her Ph.D. in South Asian languages and civilizations at the University of Chicago. Her research on *Maṇimēkalai* was funded by a Fulbright-Hays Doctoral Dissertation Abroad Fellowship and by a National Endowment for the Humanities Summer Stipend. Her recent publications include "Framed Narrative and the Dramatized Audience in a Tamil Buddhist Epic," in *Asian Folklore Studies* (April 1985) and "The Portrayal of a Female Renouncer in a Tamil Buddhist Text," in *Gender and Religion: On the Complexity of Symbols*, which she co-edited with Caroline Bynum and Stevan Harrell (Boston: Beacon Press, 1986). Richman's current research focuses on *piḷḷaittamiḻ*, a genre of Tamil devotional literature in which the poet lauds a deity, envisioning and addressing the god or goddess as an infant.

FOR MORE THAN TWO DECADES, teaching and research within the Maxwell School of Syracuse University have reflected a strong concern with the world outside our national borders. The contemporary crises in world population, food, and energy have served to dramatize anew the interdependence of nations and regions, and the importance of external events and forces. The Foreign and Comparative Studies Program — created in 1975 by the unification of existing programs in East African, Latin American, South Asian, and Soviet and East European studies — reflects the Maxwell School's continuing awareness of the imperative for attention to developments and circumstances outside of the United States. The Program maintains the resources and activities associated with each of the earlier program areas. It also encompasses foreign area interests of a broadly comparative nature, without focus on a specific geographic region, and those interests not formerly represented in earlier, regional programs.

THE FOREIGN AND COMPARATIVE STUDIES PUBLICATIONS are a central part of the Program's activities. Currently published are an African Series, a Latin American Series, and a South Asian Series. The series are a medium for publishing manuscripts of a length greater than that of a journal article, but less than usual book length. Other materials, such as symposia papers, are occasionally published. Manuscripts are accepted on many aspects of the historical, social, cultural, economic, and political institutions relevant to the peoples of the area within the Program's scope. Scholars are invited to submit relevant manuscripts for consideration in these series.

FOREIGN AND COMPARATIVE STUDIES PROGRAM:

Marwyn S. Samuels, *Director*
Joanna C. Giansanti, *Managing Editor*
Mary Beth Ritter

SOUTH ASIAN SERIES EDITORIAL COMMITTEE:

Susan S. Wadley, *Chair*
Tej K. Bhatia
James S. Duncan

FOREIGN AND COMPARATIVE STUDIES PROGRAM
Syracuse University
724 Comstock Avenue
Syracuse, New York 13244-4230
315-443-2552

THE MAXWELL SCHOOL of Citizenship and Public Affairs, founded in 1924, is the social sciences division of Syracuse University. From its inception, Maxwell has been a center for teaching and research in public policy as well as for training in public service and academic careers. In addition to the traditional departments (anthropology, economics, geography, history, political science, and sociology) there are degree-granting programs in public administration, social science, and international relations. Research-oriented, nondegree programs include metropolitan studies, health and society studies, foreign and comparative studies, technology and information policy, center for the study of citizenship, social and political psychology, women's studies, and program for the analysis and resolution of conflicts.

This volume was edited and composed on a Macintosh Plus using Microsoft Word. The final pages were produced on the Apple LaserWriter Plus.

The text is in Times, and the South Asian characters used in this volume are based on Times and were created by FACS with the Fontographer Professional Font Editor.